Lecture Notes in Computer S

Edited by G. Goos, J. Hartmanis and J. var

Springer
Berlin
Heidelberg
New York
Barcelona
Budapest
Hong Kong
London
Milan
Paris
Singapore
Tokyo

Witold Litwin   Tadeusz Morzy
Gottfried Vossen (Eds.)

Advances
in Databases and
Information Systems

Second East European Symposium, ADBIS'98
Poznań, Poland, September 7-10, 1998
Proceedings

 Springer

Series Editors

Gerhard Goos, Karlsruhe University, Germany
Juris Hartmanis, Cornell University, NY, USA
Jan van Leeuwen, Utrecht University, The Netherlands

Volume Editors

Witold Litwin
Université Paris 9 Dauphine
Pl. du Maréchal Lattre de Tassigny, F-75016 Paris, France
E-mail: Witold.Litwin@dauphine.fr

Tadeusz Morzy
Institute of Computing Science, Poznań University of Technology
ul. Piotrowo, 60-965 Poznań, Poland
E-mail: morzy@put.poznan.pl

Gottfried Vossen
Institut für Wirtschaftsinformatik, Universität Münster
Steinfurter Str. 107, D-48149 Münster, Germany
E-mail: vossen@wi-inf.uni-muenster.de

Cataloging-in-Publication data applied for

Die Deutsche Bibliothek - CIP-Einheitsaufnahme

Advances in databases and information systems : second east
European symposium ; proceedings / ADBIS '98, Poznań, Poland,
September 7 - 10, 1998. Witold Litwin ... (ed.). - Berlin ; Heidelberg
; New York ; Barcelona ; Budapest ; Hong Kong ; London ; Milan ;
Paris ; Singapore ; Tokyo : Springer, 1998
  (Lecture notes in computer science ; Vol. 1475)
  ISBN 3-540-64924-7

CR Subject Classification (1991): H.2, H.5.1, H.4.3, H.3, I.2.4

ISSN 0302-9743
ISBN 3-540-64924-7 Springer-Verlag Berlin Heidelberg New York

Typesetting: Camera-ready by author
SPIN 10638693   06/3142 – 5 4 3 2 1 0   Printed on acid-free paper

Foreword

The 2nd East European Symposium on Advances in Databases and Information Systems (ADBIS), organized in cooperation with the Association of Computing Machinery (ACM) and its Special Interest Group on Management of Data (SIGMOD), was held September 7–10, 1998, in Poznań, Poland. It continues and consolidates the series of ADBIS workshops, organized by the Moscow ACM SIGMOD Chapter, transformed into an annual, international Symposium, organized every year in different countries of Eastern Europe. The 1st East European Symposium on Advances in Databases and Information Systems was held in 1997 in St. Petersburg, Russia.

Database technology is at the heart of many mission–critical applications such as on–line transaction processing (banking, inventory systems, financial systems), on–line analytical processing (data warehousing, data mining), business workflow management, interoperable systems, or information systems on global networks. The aim of the symposium is to provide a forum for the presentation, discussion, and dissemination of new results, new concepts, tools, and techniques for database management and their use in information system management and development. We hope the 2nd East European Symposium on Advances in Databases and Information Systems also provides a forum that increases interaction and collaboration between research communities of Eastern Europe and the rest of the world in the area of databases and information systems.

These proceedings contain 25 contributed papers selected out of 90 submissions. These papers cover a wide spectrum of topics ranging from Web–related issues and data mining to core database technologies such as schema integration, database and information system design, optimization, storage, and version management. In addition to the research papers, the conference also includes two invited talks on data mining and on workflow management, and three industrial contributions. Moreover, the proceedings include six poster presentations given during a special session called "East meets West" whose aim is to bring together researchers from both East and West Europe to communicate their achievements and to promote cooperation between both communities. The conference is preceded by two tutorials on data integration and on managing multimedia information in a database environment.

We would like to express our sincere thanks to the people who have contributed to the success of ADBIS'98: the authors who submitted papers to the symposium, the program committee members for ensuring the quality of the scientific program, the industrial track chair, Witek Staniszkis, for organizing the industrial session, Tomasz Imieliński and C. Mohan, for giving the invited talks, Juliusz Jezierski, Krzysztof Jankiewicz, and Maciej Zakrzewicz for their software and help in organizing the program committee work. On the behalf of the chairs of ADBIS'98 we would like to express our special thanks to Piotr Krzyżagórski whose continuous and coordinative activity ensured the success of ADBIS'98. Heartfelt thanks also go to Robert Wrembel for his setting up and maintaining the homepage of ADBIS'98, Czarek Sobaniec and Darek Wawrzyniak for assembling the proceedings, Alfred Hofmann of Springer-Verlag for accepting these proceedings for the LNCS series, Iza Tkocz for financial arrangements, the Steering Committee and, particularly, Leonid Kalinichenko for guidance and helpful advice.

June 1998

Witold Litwin
Tadeusz Morzy
Gottfried Vossen

Conference Organization

General Chair

Tadeusz Morzy (Poznań University of Technology, Poland)

Program Committee Co–Chairs

Witold Litwin (University Paris 9 Dauphine, France)
Gottfried Vossen (University of Münster, Germany)

Industrial Track Chair

Witold Staniszkis (Rodan–System, Poland)

ACM SIGMOD Advisor

Marek Rusinkiewicz (MCC, USA)

European Coordinator

Johann Eder (University of Klagenfurt, Austria)

Program Committee

Divyakant Agrawal (UC Santa Barbara, USA)
Suad Alagić (Wichita State University, USA)
Yuri Breitbart (Lucent Technologies — Bell Laboratories, USA)
Jerzy Brzeziński (Poznań University of Technology, Poland)
Omran Bukhres (Purdue University, USA)
Wojciech Cellary (University of Economics at Poznań, Poland)
Jan Chomicki (Monmouth University, USA)
Bogdan Czejdo (Loyola University, USA)
Janis Grundspenkis (Riga Technical University, Latvija)
Remigijus Gustas (University of Karlstad, Sweden)
Abdelsalam Helal (MCC, USA)
Leonid Kalinichenko (Institute for Problems of Informatics,
Russian Academy of Sciences, Russia)
Wolfgang Klas (University of Ulm, Germany)

Mikhail Kogalovsky (Market Economy Institute, Russian Academy of Sciences, Russia)
Ralf Kramer (Forschungszentrum Informatik (FZI), Germany)
Sergey Kuznetsov (Institute for System Programming, Russian Academy of Sciences, Russia)
Pericles Loucopoulos (UMIST, United Kingdom)
Florian Matthes (TU Hamburg–Harburg, Germany)
Yannis Manolopoulos (Aristotle University, Greece)
Rainer Manthey (University of Bonn, Germany)
Guido Moerkotte (University of Mannheim, Germany)
Pavol Navrat (Slovak University of Technology in Bratislava, Slovakia)
Nikolaj Nikitchenko (Kiev Taras Shevchenko University, Ukraine)
Boris Novikov (University of St. Petersburg, Russia)
Priit Parmakson (Concordia International University, Estonia)
Alain Pirotte (University of Louvain, Belgium)
Erhard Rahm (University of Leipzig, Germany)
Tore Risch (Linkoping University, Sweden)
Colette Rolland (University Paris 1 Panthéon Sorbonne, France)
Silvio Salza (Università di Roma "La Sapienza", Italy)
Michel Scholl (CNAM and INRIA, France)
Július Štuller (Institute of Computer Science, Academy of Sciences, Czech Republic)
Kazimierz Subieta (Institute of Computer Science, Polish Academy of Sciences, Poland)
Bernhard Thalheim (TU Cottbus, Germany)
Benkt Wangler (Stockholm University/KTH, Sweden)
Tatjana Welzer (University of Maribor, Slovenia)
Viacheslav Wolfengagen (JurInfoR–MSU Institute for Contemporary Education, Russia)
Alexandre Zamulin (Institute of Informatics Systems, Russia)

Steering Committee Members

Radu Bercaru (Romania)
Albertas Caplinskas (Lithuania)
Janis Eiduks (Latvia)
Hele–Mai Haav (Estonia)
Leonid Kalinichenko (Russia, Chair of Steering Committee)
Mikhail Kogalovsky (Russia)

Tadeusz Morzy (Poland)
Pavol Navrat (Slovakia)
Boris Novikov (Russia)
Jaroslav Pokorny (Czech Republic)
Anatoly Stogny (Ukraine)
Tatjana Welzer (Slovenia)
Viacheslav Wolfengagen (Russia)

Local Organizing Committee Chairs

Piotr Krzyżagórski, Robert Wrembel (Poznań University of Technology, Poland)

Additional Referees

Eric Bruckner
Wolfram Clauss
Michael Dobrovnik
Francesco Donini
Martin Durand
Vladimir Evstigneev
Thomas Feyer
Cristian Ghezzi
Georgios Giannopoulos
Paul Johannesson
Panos Kardasis
Wassili Kazakos
Tomasz Koszlajda

Sergey Kotov
Svetlana Kouznetsova
Ling Lin
Nikos Lorentzos
Panos Louridas
Holger Maertens
Maciej Matysiak
Robert Mueller
Alex Nanopoulos
Nikolaos Prekas
Francesco Quaglia
Kim Reed
Joerg Rieckmann

Jérôme Siméon
Cezary Sobaniec
Jose Solorzano
Thomas Stoehr
Michal Szychowiak
Athena Vakali
Radek Vingralek
Dariusz Wawrzyniak
Nur Yilmazturk
Maciej Zakrzewicz
Esteban Zimanyi

Sponsoring Institution

State Committee for Scientific Research (KBN), Poland

Table of Contents

Invited Papers

Regular Papers

Query Languages

Optimization

Collaborative Systems

East Meets West

Schema Integration

Storage and Version Management

Object Systems

Knowledge Discovery and the Web

System Design

Industrial Track

Recent Progress in Data Integration — A Tutorial

Daniela Florescu[1] and Alon Levy[2]

[1] INRIA, projet Rodin, Le Chesnay Cedex, 78153, France
Daniela.Florescu@inria.fr
[2] University of Washington, Dept. of Computer Science and Engineering
Seattle, WA 98195-2350
alon@cs.washington.edu

1 Description

In the last few years there has been considerable interest in the problem of providing access to large collections of distributed heterogeneous information sources (e.g., sources on the World-Wide Web, company-wide databases). This interest has spawned a significant amount of research in Database Systems and related fields (e.g., Artificial Intelligence, Operating Systems, Human Computer Interaction). This has led to the development of several research prototypes for information integration and recently, we are seeing the beginnings of an industry addressing this problem.

The goal of this tutorial is to survey the work on information integration, to illustrate the common principles underlying this body of work, to assess the state of the art, and identify the open research problems in this area. The tutorial will illustrate the issues involved in information integration through several implemented systems.

2 Outline

The tutorial is covering the following topics.

- Problem definition
  - What is information integration?
  - Characteristics of information sources that make the problem hard
  - The goal of information integration systems
- Related technologies
  - Information retrieval
  - Web search engines
  - Multidatabase and distributed database systems
- Issues in building an information integration system
  - System architecture
  - Describing information sources
  - Query processing and optimization

- Semi-structured data
- Wrapper generation
- System architecture
  - Mediated schema
  - Mappings between source schemas and mediated schema
  - Query translator and planner
  - Wrappers
- Describing information sources
  - Semantic content: constraints on the contents of the source; methods for specifying mapping between the source and the mediated schema:
    * Using datalog rules
    * Using logical views
    * Using description logics
  - Source completeness.
  - Representing capabilities of sources:
  - limited capabilities: binding pattern limitations.
  - additional capabilities: sources that can answer complex queries and have local processing power.
  - Identifying objects across different sources: object fusion, semantic oid's.
  - Probabilistic information: degrees of overlap between sources, degrees of source coverage, probabilistic information in the mediated schema.
- Query processing and optimization
  - Finding relevant sources.
  - Computing query plans: exploiting source capabilities, cost estimation, plan evaluation in the lack of accurate cost estimates.
  - Interleaving planning and execution
  - Actively seeking additional information
- Semi-structured data
  - appropriate data models and query languages
  - query evaluation and optimization methods
  - queries over data with loose schema
- Wrapper generation
  - the purpose of the wrapper
  - automatic generation of wrappers
  - using machine-learning techniques
- Perspectives and Conclusions
  - Current implemented prototypes
  - Open problems: solutions that work and those that are still premature
  - Bringing information integration to the market: problems, products, services, data integration for what? applications of data integration (WWW, web-site management)

Managing Multimedia Information in a Database Environment – A Tutorial

William I. Grosky

Computer Science Department, Wayne State University, Detroit, Michigan 48202 USA
grosky@cs.wayne.edu

Abstract. In this tutorial, we discuss how the various aspects of database design and the modules of a database system have changed over the years so that multimedia information can be better managed.

1 Introduction

The process of managing multimedia data in a database environment has had an interesting evolution. In this tutorial, we discuss how the various aspects of database design and the modules of a database system have changed over the years so that multimedia information can be better managed. We first examine the nature of multimedia data and the field of multimedia data modeling. We then discuss how multimedia has influenced the evolution of various modules of standard database systems. Finally, we consider the various commercial systems that have recently appeared which manage multimedia information.

2 The Nature of Multimedia Data

Multimedia data is quite different from standard alphanumeric data, both from a presentation as well as from a semantics point of view. From a presentation viewpoint, multimedia data is quite huge and has time dependent characteristics that must be adhered to. From a semantics viewpoint, metadata and information extracted from the contents of a multimedia object is quite complex and affects both the capabilities and the efficiency of a multimedia database system.

Besides its complex structure, multimedia data requires complex processing in order to extract semantics from its contents. Real-world objects shown in images, video, animations, or graphics, and being discussed in audio are participating in meaningful events whose nature is often the subject of queries. Utilizing state-of-the-art approaches from the fields of image interpretation and speech recognition, it is often possible to extract information from multimedia objects which is less complex and voluminous than the multimedia objects themselves and which can give some clues as to the semantics of the events being represented by these objects. This information consists of objects called *features,* which are used to recognize similar real-world objects and events across multiple multimedia objects.

3 Multimedia Data Modeling

There are many multimedia data models in the literature. However, at a high enough level of abstraction, all such data models are quite similar.

4 Multimedia and Database Systems

The architecture of a standard database system consists of modules for query processing, transaction management, buffer management, file management, recovery, and security. Implementations differ depending on whether the database system is relational/object-oriented or centralized/distributed, but the natures of these modules are basically the same.

4.1 Query Processing

Querying in a multimedia database is quite different from querying in standard alphanumeric databases. Besides the fact that browsing takes on added importance in a multimedia environment, queries may contain multimedia objects input by the user, and the results of these queries are not based on perfect matches but on degrees of similarity.

4.1.1 Access Methods

Indexes of standard database systems are designed for the standard data types. They are one-dimensional and are usually hash-based or utilize some of the B-tree variants. In most cases, they are unsuitable for similarity matching. In the literature, there have been many specialized indexes used for various types of features. These cannot be used, however, in standard database systems. Only database systems that support extensible data types and their associated access methods can be profitably used for these applications. At present, such database systems are called object-relational.

4.1.2 Query Optimization

Query optimization is the process of choosing the optimal access path to answer a query. Object-relational database systems, which support the above user-defined access methods, also need to know the associated costs involved in using these methods in order to make an intelligent decision about how to answer a query. There have not been many articles written on query optimization for multimedia database systems.

4.2 Transaction Management

For advanced applications, such as multimedia databases, conventional concurrency control algorithms can be used; the results would still be correct. However, the concurrency of the overall system would suffer, since in this environment, transactions tend to be long, compute intensive, interactive, cooperative, and refer to many database objects. In order to increase the system concurrency in such an environment, new transaction models have been defined.

Multimedia data presents another interpretation of the concept of read-only transaction management called *playout management.*

4.3 Buffer Management

Continuous media presentations for many concurrent users require sophisticated buffer management techniques in order to deliver information on demand.

4.4 Storage Management

The challenge is to serve multiple requests for multiple media streams so as to guarantee that the playout processes do not starve, while minimizing the buffer space needed and minimizing the time between an initial request for service and the time when the first bits of data become available.

4.5 Recovery

There are many advanced transaction models that have generalized recovery methods that can be used in a multimedia database environment.

4.6 Security

There are very few papers concerning multimedia specific issues in database security. Many interesting questions remain unexamined.

5 Commercial Systems for Multimedia Information Management

Currently, there are at least three commercial systems for visual information retrieval and several commercial database systems at various levels on the object-relational scale that can manage multimedia information at an acceptable level.

Association Rules... and What's Next?
– Towards Second Generation Data Mining Systems

Tomasz Imieliński and Aashu Virmani

Department of Computer Science,
Rutgers University
New Brunswick, N.J. 08903 USA
{imielins,avirmani}@cs.rutgers.edu

Abstract. In the process of rule generation from databases, the volume of generated rules often greatly exceeds the size of the underlying database. Typically only a small fraction of that large volume of rules is of any interest to the user. We believe that the main challenge facing database mining is what to do with the rules after having generated them. *Rule post-processing* involves selecting rules which are relevant or interesting, building applications which use the rules and finally, combining rules together to form a larger and more meaningful statements. In this paper we propose an application programming interface which enables faster development of applications which rely on rules. We also provide a rule query language which allows both selective rule generation as well as retrieval of selected categories of rules from the pre-generated rule collections.

1   Introduction

Since the original paper on generating association rules appeared in 1993 [1], a large volume of papers have been published proposing more efficient solutions to the problem of association rule generation ([2, 5, 15, 14, 4, 9, 12]). Additionally, a number of products generating association rules from the underlying database are already available on the market.

The main focus of attention so far has been on improving performance of the rule generation algorithms. Unfortunately, performance, while technically important, is not a bottleneck preventing the wide spread use of association rules. The sheer volume of association rules which are generated even from relatively small databases often greatly exceeds the size of the underlying database. Typically only a small fraction of that large volume of rules is of any interest to the user who is very often overwhelmed with the massive dose of "look-alike" rules. Thus, a real bottleneck is a "cognitive bandwidth" of the user - cognitive processing of thousands of rules takes much more time then generating them even by a less efficient tool. In a way, whether it takes 10 or 20 hours to produce 100,000 rules, is probably irrelevant from the point of view of the user who would have to spend much more time to "digest" the obtained volume of data.

We believe that the main challenge facing database mining is what to do with the rules further. *Rule post-processing* involves selecting rules which are relevant or interesting, building applications which use the rules and finally, combining rules together to form a larger and more meaningful patterns and relationships. In this paper we propose an application programming interface which enables faster development of applications which rely on rules. The proposed API includes a library of primitives to manipulate, compare and manage collections of rules and embed rules in the host language programming interface. It also provides a rule query language which allows both selective rule generation as well as retrieval of selected categories of rules from the pre-generated rule collections.

While rules are useful building blocks for aggregate metadata, they are rarely of interest by themselves. Indeed, in order to assess importance of a rule, it has to be put in the context of other rules. Analysts are typically interested in functional, dynamic characterizations of relationships between attributes, rather than isolated "data points" which correspond to "static" rules. Finally, aggregations upon sets of rules may be more informative then rules themselves, especially when the number of rules is very large. Often, mapping the discovered information back to the original database in form of new attributes (such as predicted attribute values, typicality/atypicailty of a given record etc) provides an analyst with a better, more clear picture than analyzing rules.

The following examples which illustrate the above points are taken from the insurance domain:

- Characterize the seniors market (people $\geq$ 50 in age) in terms of what they own; the other defines the market in terms of what purchases someone 50 or older tends to make.
- How does what someone buys differ as they age - especially as they pass 50 and as they age beyond that?
- Does the combination of products, the riders on those products, the face amount of the products, etc. differ by age, gender, etc. for seniors (controlling for marital status - fewer men are still alive at the older age categories)?
- What are the characteristics of agents that sell best to what customers (further characterized by census attributes)
- What are natural market segments - what subgroups behave similarly with respect to the products they have or products they buy? Are there gender differences in purchasing behavior for those 50 or older? How does this differ from younger persons? When does it change?
- What is the relationship between what one spouse has and what the other has?
- What are differences and what are the similarities between acquiring car and home insurance. How about life insurance?

The reason why database systems are so successful today is that they provide a number of primitives (queries, transactions, storage management etc) which are sufficient to quickly develop and efficiently execute business applications dealing with large collections of data. Unfortunately, as already indicated, they fall short with respect to knowledge discovery applications. Thus, our goal is to *provide the same level of support for knowledge discovery applications as is currently offered by the DBMS for business applications*. In many ways, we are today, where database systems were 30+ years ago. So lets follow their path to success!

We have characterized second generation data mining systems using three basic requirements (three A's):

1. **Ad hoc application support**
   One of the keys to the success of relational DBMS was the establishment of the simple primitive operations which led to the development of SQL. Using SQL, queries which used to take pages of code to write, can be written in just a few lines of "declarative" code allowing fast development of new "ad hoc" applications. This led to the order of magnitude increase in programmer's productivity by relying on efficient system support for the basic operations and offering data independence. The key question here is whether such a set of primitives can be defined for knowledge discovery applications in such a way that new, "ad hoc" applications can be easily developed, and efficiently evaluated? Later in the paper, we present as proof, the design of the API used in the *Discovery Board* system [16], and enlist some applications that have been successfully developed using this API.

2. **Accumulation, Management and Building upon Discovered Knowledge.**
   The next feature deals with storage and management of the previously discovered knowledge.
   Today, data mining is viewed as "session driven" activity. That is, the mining results are typically displayed on the screen, viewed by the user and subsequently, either completely discarded or stored in a file. Thus, the typical lifetime of the discovered knowledge is the duration of the mining session. There is little or no support for the future "data miner" to rely on the results of the previous mining sessions. There are no tools to accumulate the discovered knowledge, query it later and perhaps further "mine around" the discovered knowledge treating it as the departure point for further discovery. With such little support for "persistence" of the discovered knowledge, it is very difficult to analyze often massive volumes of discovered knowledge. For example, a typical output of association rule mining can exceed tens of thousands of rules and often the original database is smaller in size than the discovered knowledge. Without ability to store and further query such large volumes of rules, the result is often overwhelming and impossible to penetrate during a single session.
   Thus, we postulate a strong need for a **Knowledge Discovery Management System (KDMS)** – a system which would provide storage, querying and further mining on previously discovered knowledge. In such a system, the discovered knowledge from possibly many mining sessions (and different data miners) can be stored and queried using the M-SQL features. Furthermore, one can build upon the knowledge, or "collective wisdom", accumulated over time.

3. **Aggregation and Summarization of results**

One of the data analysts who evaluated various data mining systems for the potential use in his company made the following comment: *"A rule seems to be very impressive when you see it in isolation, but when you see many rules they all look alike."*

In fact, seeing a large volume of rules makes the user increasingly confused and doubtful about the real value of the data mining results. The advantage of the rules being "atoms" of knowledge is also, in the same time, their disadvantage. They are often too specific, missing the "bigger picture". Rules look alike, and it is not clear which rules are important, interesting or valuable. The "context" of a rule is also missing, for example, a rule with high confidence may not be that interesting if a more general rule (same consequent but smaller body) has a similar confidence.

Consequently, it is not enough to simply present rules which answer user's query. More work is necessary in presenting rules in the fashion which keeps the user interested in further analysis and also attempts to offer a "bigger picture" along with the detailed view of the rules.

This requirement is perhaps the most difficult to specify formally. Rules should be provided with extra attributes which can reflect the "context" of the rule better by comparing the rule's confidence and support with the "similar" or "relative" rules. Rules may not even be presented to the user directly at first but grouped together into "cubes". Thus, along the lines of SQL reporting, efficient reporting and presentation primitives should also be developed for rules. This summarization and aggregation feature will provide an "ice-breaker" for an analyst, who starts to take a look at the output of a long mining session.

Discovery board system developed at Rutgers [7] is a research prototype implementing second generation data mining concepts. The concepts of API and the query language which are presented below, have been implemented in this system.

2   Basic notions

In this section, we formalize some notions used throughout the remainder of the paper.

A **descriptor** is an expression of the form $(A_i = a_{ij})$, where a_{ij} belongs to the domain of A_i. For continuous valued attributes, a descriptor of the form $(A_i = [lo, hi])$ is allowed, where $[lo, hi]$ represents a range of values over the domain of A_i. A **conjunctset** stands for a conjunction of an arbitrary number of descriptors, such that no two descriptors are formed using the same attribute. The **length** of a conjunctset is the number of descriptors which form the conjunctset. A descriptor is thus the special case of a singleton conjunctset. A record (tuple) in R is said to **satisfy** a descriptor $(A_i, = v_{ij})$, if the value of A_i in the record equals v_{ij}. To satisfy a conjunctset, a record must satisfy **all** k descriptors forming the conjunction.

Example: Let R be a relation represented by the table shown below:

EmpId	Job	Sex	Car
1	Doctor	Male	BMW
2	Lawyer	Female	Lexus
3	Consultant	Male	Toyota
4	Doctor	Male	Volvo

Then (**Job** = Doctor) is an example of a descriptor in the above data, satisfied by records with EmpId values 1 and 4. Along the same lines, (**Sex** = Female) $\wedge$ (**Car** = Lexus) is an example of a conjunctset of length 2 in the above data.

By a **propositional rule** over R, we mean a tuple of the form $\langle B, C, s, c \rangle$, where B is a conjunctset called the **Body** of the rule, C is a descriptor called the **Consequent** of the rule, s is an integer called the **support** of the rule, and c is a number between 0 and 1 called the **confidence** of the rule. Support is defined as the number of tuples in R which satisfy the body of the rule, and **confidence** is defined as the ratio of the number of tuples satisfying both the body and the consequent to the number of tuples which satisfy just the body of the rule.

Intuitively, rules are if-then statements of the form "if Body then Consequent", with s and c being their quality measures computed in R. We will usually represent rules in the following syntactic form:

$$Body \implies Consequent \quad [support, confidence]$$

For instance, the following is a rule over the example relation shown earlier:

$$(\textbf{Job} = \text{Doctor}) \wedge (\textbf{Sex} = \text{Male}) \implies (\textbf{Car} = \text{BMW}) \quad [2, 0.5]$$

A rule in our case is thus a generalization of the association discussed in [1]. Since we allow user defined procedures and functions in our API, the expressive power of propositional rules is actually, for all practical reasons equivalent to non-recursive predicate rules.

A rule can also be viewed as a query when applied to a relation. We say a a relation R **satisfies** a rule $r = \langle B, C, s, c \rangle$ if there are at least s tuples in R which satisfy B and at least a fraction c of them satisfy the conjunction $B \wedge C$. This is also expressed by saying that r **holds** in R. If R does not satisfy r, then we say that R **violates** r, or alternately, r **does not hold** in R.

Since rules represent aggregates over a set of tuples, the relationship between a rule and an individual tuple cannot be similarly defined. However if we only consider the rule-pattern $\langle B, C \rangle$ without the associated support and confidence, we can define the following relationships between them.

A tuple t **satisfies** a rule pattern $\langle B, C \rangle$, if it satisfies the conjunction $B \wedge C$, and it **violates** the above pattern if it satisfies B, but not C.

3 What are rules good for?

Once the large effort of generating rules have been invested we can amortize the cost of rule generation by building multiple applications. This is different from other situations when knowledge generation in driven just by one application (for example classification). Here, knowledge generated can serve multiple applications. Below, we list some examples:

- **"Typicality"**: What are the typical vs atypical records in the database? A typical record can be defined as one satisfying most of the strong (high confidence, high support) rules for which it satisfies the body, and atypical record as one that violates most such rules. Other measures can be defined as well. This is an example of an application which would "map rules back to the data"
- **"Characteristic of"**: Given a data cube (records satisfying a conjunction of descriptors) find out rules which make this data cube different from the other data cubes, rules which are particularly strong or particularly weak. This can be further used in fine grained clustering of different data cubes together.
- **"Changing patterns"**: How changing values of an attribute(s) changes the support and confidence of a rule(s)
- **"Best N"**: Find best rules which "cover" N individuals or records. This is very useful in marketing applications when looking for best candidates to send a "marketing package"
- **"Clustering"**: Group cubes into structures which are similar in terms of patterns of rules which they satisfy or violate. This can, for example, provide market or product segments.
- **"What if"**: These applications involve the best hypothetical scenario of best actions which have to be undertaken in order to achieve a certain goal. For example, what should a given individual do in order to make more money in a given number of years.
- **"Knowledge summarization"**: Find out about all rules which deal with particular category, descriptor, such as all rules which characterize or are characterized in terms of "smokers". This is an example of "meta-querying" where rules are query subjects.
- **Cross Verification:** This involves comparing sets of rules by renaming attributes: for example are rules predicting car insurance switch are "similar" to those predicting "home insurance" (rules which are or are not isomorphic under renaming attributes)
- **Second Opinion:** Take the output from another discovery method like classification tree, or a neural net. Characterize the records on which the method generates high percentage of error.
- **Interesting Rules:** A common question arises in mining regarding the "novelty" of a rule. For instance, a rule may say: "39% of all graduate students in NJ drive a used American car". But what if all graduate students in the US (as opposed to NJ), or worse, all students (graduate or otherwise) in the country behaved similarly? A rule is interesting only if it is a substantial "winner" in terms of confidence over its predecessors. (A rule $A \implies B$ is considered a predecessor of $AC \implies B$). This application finds all interesting rules in a rulebase, given a measure of what a "substantial win" over a predecessor is.

4   Query language

In [8] we have argued that due to the tremendous number of association rules which are generated by data mining there is a pressing need to provide rule querying, both to selectively generate rules from data as well as query the rule-base of rules which were previously generated. Several such query languages have been proposed in the literature [6, 10]. Other similar efforts were also recently noticed in literature, either to generate rules satisfying some constraints in the database [11], or to integrate mining closely with relational databases [13].

In our view, these proposals are a step in the right direction. Following is the set of prerogatives which a rule query language should, in our view, satisfy:

- **Ability to nest SQL:** Since SQL is a well accepted interface to relational databases, and allows for declarative, set level, expressions which are optimized substantially, it is desirable if users can utilize SQL primitives such as sorting, group-by, and others like these within MSQL, and be able to express nested queries using the SQL nested query constructs like [NOT] IN, [NOT] EXISTS etc.
- **Closure:** Mining is essentially an iterative task, which often involves refinement of existing queries and regenerating results. The language must provide for operations to further manipulate the results of the previous MSQL query.
- **Cross-over between data and rules:** To permit the "iterative refinement" as mentioned in the previous item, the language must allow primitives which can map generated rules back to the source data, and vice-versa.
- **Generation versus querying:** Given the enormous size of rulebases, it may not always be possible to "extensionally" maintain rulebases. The language should allow a user to express rule-generation vs. rule-querying using the same expression syntax.

Keeping the above guidelines in mind, MSQL, the language developed in [16] starts with the SQL92 standard and adds support for rule-manipulation operations in a familiar SQL-like syntax. Due to space restrictions, we present an overview and some examples of the query language here. For a more complete treatment of the language, including its evaluation and optimizations, we refer the reader to the above reference.

MSQL can be described under four main subsections, as shown below.

```
<MSQL Stmt> ::=        <GetRules-Query>
              |        <SelectRules-Query>
              |        <Sat-Violate-SubQuery>
              |        <Encode-Stmt>
```

A quick overview of these constructs is as follows. The GetRules query is used for rule-generation, and the SelectRules query, which follows the same syntax (covered under GetRules-Query syntax), is used to query rules from an existing rulebase. In addition, a standard SQL query on a database table can have a nested GetRules sub-query in its "where" clause connected via the Satisfy or Violate keyword. Syntax for this clause is covered under the Sat-Violate-SubQuery statement. The Encode statement provides pre- and post-processing support for continuous valued attributes, and is not discussed further because of space reasons. Since these primitives are also supported under our object oriented API, (discussed later) where a relational table corresponds to a class, we may use the terms "table" and "class" interchangeably.

4.1 General query syntax

The most general formulation of the GetRules Query is as follows:

```
[Project Body, Consequent, confidence, support]
GetRules(C) [as R1]
[into <rulebase_name>]
[where <conds>]
[sql-group-by clause]
[using-clause]
```

where C is a database table, and R1 is an alias for the rulebase thus generated. In addition, ⟨Conds⟩ may itself contain:

```
<Rule Format Conditions RC> |
<Pruning Conditions PC> |
<Mutex Conditions MC> |
<Stratified Subquery Conditions SSQ> |
<Correlated Subquery Conditions CSQ>
```

The GetRules operator generates rules over elements of the argument class C, satisfying the conditions described in the "where" clause. The results are placed into a rule class optionally named by the user, else named by suffixing 'RB' to the name of the source class. (So for instance, the class Emp generates the rulebase EmpRB). The projection and group-by operations can optionally be applied, and their meaning is the same as defined in SQL. Since they basically post-process the generated rules, they do not affect the semantics of rule generation.

Another important thing to note is that the GetRules query operates on the complete class C, rather than a subset of it. There is a difference. All rules from the subset of data with $(A_1 = a)$ in them is not the same as all rules on the whole data with $(A_1 = a)$ in the Body, since if we subset and then mine for rules, the confidence and support in the rules generated will change. Besides, if one mines for rules about a subset of the data, then technically, it is a different class and therefore, there should be a different rulebase corresponding to it.

Given the above reasoning, the GetRules operator disallows any "where" clause conditions on pure attributes of the source class C. These can always be performed by creating a view on C with the appropriate selections/projections and then using GetRules on the view. The only conditions allowed are the ones on rule components: Body and Consequent. Note that the evaluation of GetRules internally may involve selecting/projecting the data for efficiency, but it will preserve the query semantics.

Conditions in the "where" clause To understand the complete syntax of the query, let us first examine the different types of conditions possible in the "where" clause. They have been categorized in the following groups to facilitate understanding of the evaluation plan. Each type of condition affects the execution plan in a different way.

- ⟨**Rule Format Conditions RC**⟩ Rule format conditions occur on the Body and the Consequent, and have the following format:

  ```
  Body { in | has | is } <descriptor-list>
  Consequent { in | is } <descriptor-list>
  ```

  The operators **in, has** and **is** represent the subset, superset and set-equality conditions respectively. A few examples below explain their usage. Note that one or both operands could be constants.

  ```
  r.body has {(Job='Doctor'), (State='NJ')}
  r1.consequent in r2.body
  r.body in {(Age=[30,40]), (Sex='Male'), (State=*)}
  r.consequent is {(Age=*)}
  ```

  The first condition above is true for all rules which have at least the predicate (Job='Doctor') ∧ (State='NJ') in their bodies. Similarly, the second condition above is true for all pairs of rules (r1, r2), such that r1's Consequent is an element of r2's Body. The third clause above, when present in a GetRules query, specifies that the bodies of rules produced may only belong to a subset of the set of combinations generated by the expression "(Age=[30,40]) (Sex='Male') (State =*)". The fourth condition restricts the Consequent attribute to Age, without restricting its values. In general, the "where" expression can have several of these conditions connected via AND and OR logical operators.

  In MSQL, a descriptor pattern of the form $(A_i = *)$, can be used anywhere a descriptor is allowed. In the above case of $(Age = *)$, any descriptor of the form $(Age = [lo, hi])$ satisfies the pattern.

- ⟨**Pruning Conditions PC**⟩ These are conditions involving support, confidence and lengths of Body and Consequent, which can be used to control the algorithm. These have the format:

  ```
  confidence <relop> <float-val in [0.0,1.0]>
  support <relop> <integer>
  support <relop> <float-val in [0.0,1.0]>
  length <relop> <integer>
  relop ::= { < | <= | = | >= | > }
  ```

  Confidence is specified as a fraction between 0 and 1, while support can be specified either as a fraction of the database, or as an absolute number of records.

- ⟨**Mutex Conditions MC**⟩ These conditions define sets of two or more attributes such that, in a given rule, if there is an attribute from one of these sets, then that rule doesn't have any other attribute from that set. The syntax is:

```
Where <other-conditions>
        { AND | OR } mutex(method, method [, method])
        [{ AND | OR } mutex(method, method [, method])]
```

For instance, the condition "`mutex(zipcode, county, phone_area_code)`" can be used in the "where" clause of the GetRules operator to avoid expansion of any rule containing one of the above attributes with another attribute from the same set.
- ⟨**Subquery Conditions SSQ**⟩ These are subqueries which are connected to the "where" clause using either EXISTS, NOT EXISTS, or the IN connectives. The connectives used to join outer and inner queries preserve their SQL semantics. Subqueries are dealt with in more detail in section 4.4.

4.2 Generating and retrieving rules

All examples in this section assume the presence of data about employees in the following schema:

```
Emp(emp_id, age, sex, salary, nationality, position, smoker, car)
```

To generate rules from the Employee table, one uses the GetRules command as follows:

```
GetRules(Emp)
where Consequent in { (Age=*), (Salary=[30000,80000]) }
and Body has { (Job=*) }
and confidence > 0.3
and support > 0.1
```

The above query would generate rules having at least Job in the antecedent and either Age or Salary as the Consequent methods with values of salary within the ranges specified. Also note that there is an implicit line:
`Project Body, Confidence, Confidence(Emp), support(Emp)`
before the GetRules command. Later we will show how this can be altered to evaluate existing rules on different sets.

The typical mechanism observed to be most commonly used in query based mining is for users to first do a fairly general GetRules query and store the result persistently, and to follow this with a series of SelectRules queries, each of which selects a small subset of the entire rulebase.

To generate rules for a given database table, the **GetRules** operator must be used with a table argument as follows:

```
GetRules(T)
into R
where confidence > 0.3
and support > 0.1
```

This will generate all rules existing in table T matching the confidence and support requirements, and put them in a persistent rulebase named R.

For future selections of these rules, the language has the **SelectRules** command. SelectRules will not generate any new rules, but rather rely on the contents of the argument rulebase for providing results. For instance, the following query retrieves rules with at least Age and Sex in the Body and the car driven as a Consequent.

```
SelectRules(R)
where Body has { (Age=*), (Sex=*) }
  and Consequent is { (Car=*) }
```

Note that by default, the lowest confidence and support of the rules produced by this query will be 30 percent and 10 percent respectively, since those were the parameters R was mined with.

So far we have used the Project operator implicitly. One can use the Projection to explicitly evaluate different rule patterns over various similar databases. For instance, if NJ_Emp and NY_Emp are two views defined on the Emp table, one might be interested in knowing how the two data sets compare with respect to the above rule pattern. The following query, in this case,

```
Project Body, Consequent, Confidence(NJ_Emp), Support(NJ_Emp),
                          Confidence(NY_Emp), Support(NY_Emp),
SelectRules(R)
where Body has { (Age=*), (Sex=*) }
  and Consequent is { (Car=*) }
```

will select the Bodies and Consequents of rules from R, and evaluate them over the two views. SelectRules, by definition, *does not* generate new rule patterns.

The above example brings up an interesting issue: What if R is not a rulebase generated by the Emp table, but rather, by some other table? There are two possible scenarios. In the simpler case, R could be a rulebase not containing the attributes required in the query (in this case, Age, Sex and Car). In that case, the query will be syntactically incorrect and will return an error. In a more complicated case, the rule table and the other data tables in the above type of SelectRules query could both contain the attributes required by the "where" clause, even when they semantically meant something totally different. Should the language be enforcing this "typing" between rulebases and databases?

Our design decision has been to follow strong typing between rulebases and databases in our API, implemented in C++, but to treat both rulebases and datasets as untyped relational tables in MSQL. In a typical relational environment, it is quite possible for someone to join two tables A and B on two integer fields A.length and B.speed thus yielding a senseless result. Similarly, it is extremely hard to police the proper use of these operators once the queries span more than one table. The onus in both cases lies on the user and the data dictionary to ensure correct semantics in the operations. In [16], we have described our proposed catalog enhancements as part of the *Discovery Board* system to ensure that there is enough metadata kept in the DBMS catalogs to allow the user to correctly identify the rulebases developed from a given data table.

4.3 Using Satisfy and Violate

An extremely important feature in a database mining system is the ability to correlate the generated knowledge (rules in this case) with the source data which produced that knowledge. The **Satisfy** and **Violate** operators in MSQL provide this capability of connecting the rules with the data. A tuple is said to satisfy a rule if it satisfies the boolean condition formed by logically and-ing the rule body and the consequent. To violate a rule, a tuple must satisfy the rule body, but not its consequent.

Both Satisfy and Violate operators take a tuple and a set of rules and return true if the tuple satisfies (violates) any (or all) the rules in the set. Syntactically, their usage is much like the EXISTS operator in SQL:

```
Select  ...
From    ...
Where { SATISFIES | VIOLATES } { ALL | ANY } (
            GetRules | SelectRules Subquery
        )
```

Example 41 *Find all records in Emp table which violate all rules of the form* "age ⟹ salary" *above a 30% confidence.*

```
Select *
from    Emp
where   VIOLATES ALL (
            GetRules(Emp)
            where Body is { (Age=*) }
            and Consequent is { (Salary=*) }
            and confidence > 0.3
            )
```

4.4 Nesting the GetRules operator

The Satisfy and Violate connectives discussed above show one form of nesting within GetRules queries. Interesting queries can also be formulated using SQL-like nesting of multiple GetRules queries. The semantics for such queries is exactly the same as in SQL if we first generate both the rulebases in the inner and outer query, and treat them as two classes in SQL. However, this may not be the best approach for evaluation, as shown in [16].

For evaluation purposes, one can distinguish nested queries in which the inner query makes a reference to the data or rule objects of the outer query, from queries where there is no cross-referencing of data. Using SQL terminology, the former can be called **correlated queries**, and the latter, **stratified queries**. For instance, the following is an example of a correlated query, since the rule class generated in the outer query, R1, is referenced in the inner query.

```
GetRules(C) R1
where <pruning-conds>
and not exists ( GetRules(C) R2
                 where <same pruning-conds>
                 and R2.Body HAS R1.Body )
```

The above query finds rules that are "on the border", i.e. if they are expanded any more, they will drop out of support. The next query is an example of nesting a SelectRules within a GetRules operator. It generates all rules where the Consequent exists in a prior set of rules. It is stratified, since no references to R1 are made in the nested subquery.

```
GetRules(C) R1
where <pruning-conds>
  and Consequent is {(X=*)}
  and Consequent in ( SelectRules(R2)
                      where Consequent is {(X=*)} )
```

5 API

A rule query language alone is not sufficient to create applications described in the section 3. It is necessary to provide features to embed queries in a host programming language, just as SQL queries are embedded in their host programming environments.

We assume here an object oriented host language environment such as C++. To embed rule queries into such environment it is necessary to introduce the following features:

– Adding a class of rules to the standard library of classes
– Implementing a signature of the rule class to allow the basic rule operations such as selection of a body, consequent, support and confidence as well as ability to compare sets of rules, cross reference the underlying database etc.
– Embedding MSQL in the host language, in a similar fashion as SQL embedding in a host language.
– Providing summarizing operators, OLAP like operators to summarize the sets of rules

In our considerations we have throughly compared possible approaches based on pure object-oriented, object-relational and finally, fully relational approaches.

For reasons explained in detail in [16], we chose to go with the ODMG 2.0 standard [3], and enhance it to support rules as first class objects.

We enhanced the class framework with another class called **dm_Rule** to represent a rule, and along the lines of OQL C++ binding, provided primitives for supporting various collections of rules. We provided support for embedded mining in OQL in two ways:

- By providing a *Mine()* method on the **dm_DBTable** and **dm_RBTable** classes, (which model a database and a rulebase respectively), that accepts the where clause of the GetRules and SelectRules commands respectively, as its input, and applies the query on the class it was invoked from.
- By providing a new class **dm_MSQL_query**, similar to the existing class **d_OQL_query**, which allows one to embed a complete MSQL query, possibly involving multiple tables, within an application program.

Thus, in our environment, rules become *first class programming objects* for knowledge discovery applications just as records are first class objects for business database applications. We later demonstrate the benefits of this procedural framework by writing several knowledge discovery applications, which would have not been expressible using a purely declarative database language.

A rule object r is composed of the following components:

- *Body*, which the left hand side of the rule, and is of the type Set⟨**dm_Desc**⟩.
- *signature*, which is a number uniquely determined by the set of attributes which make up the descriptors in the Body. *c_signature* is the corresponding member determined by the consequent attribute.
- *length*, which returns the number of descriptors which make up the Body.
- *Consequent*, which is the right hand side of the rule, and is an element of the **dm_Desc** class.
- *support(C)*, which takes a class C, and returns the number of type-compatible (defined below) objects in C which satisfy all the descriptors in $r.Body$. Without any arguments, it simply returns the value of support pre-computed on the source table.
- *confidence(C)*, which is the ratio of the number of objects in C which satisfy both $r.Body$ and $r.Consequent$ to the number of objects that satisfy only $r.Body$. Confidence is overloaded similar to the support member.

Further, an object of the tuple class is said to be *compatible* with a rule object, if the set of methods present in the rule object is a subset of the set of methods present in the tuple object, and for all the methods in the rule object, the type matches with the type of the corresponding tuple method.

As a convention, from now on we will use the uppercase symbols R, S for collections of rules, T, U for collections of tuples, r, s etc. for instances of rules, and t, u etc. for individual tuple instances.

The rule class supports several other methods in addition to the above, which include iterators over the descriptors in the rule body, methods to get and set the members of the rule class, and functions to check containment of a particular attribute, value, or a descriptor within a rule. A complete listing for these is provided in [16]. Further, the *Satisfy* and *Violate* primitives verify if a tuple satisfied or violated a rule pattern. These are discussed in more detail below.

5.1 Representing relationships with data

The satisfy and violate methods which are defined on rules and collections of rules, allow one to map between rules and their source data.

In a relational environment, relationships indicating if a tuple satisfied or violated a rule-pattern $\langle B, C \rangle$ would be extensionally represented as a table *Satisfies* containing (rule-id, tuple-id) pairs and a table *Violates* with an identical structure. Since the relationship is many-to-many, in OQL, this would be represented as Set$\langle$Ref$\langle$dm_Tuple$\rangle\rangle$ in the rule class and a Set$\langle$Ref$\langle$dm_Rule$\rangle\rangle$ in the tuple class. However, we discovered that in practice, either representation suffers from the following drawbacks:

- With data sizes well into hundreds of thousands of tuples, the number of generated rules could run into millions. Representing this relationship extensionally (which is of the order of the product of rulebase and database size) becomes almost impractical storage-wise.
- Rules generated from a given dataset can be semantically related to various other sets of similar data (e.g. Jan97_sales and Feb97_sales for the same company). In this case, one must represent this relationship multiple times, once per related pair, making the storage problem even worse, and forcing all queries to correctly resolve the correct table representing the relationships – a potential source of errors.

We therefore decided to discard both approaches and represent the satisfy and violate as methods which are evaluated at run-time. This also allows us to overload them to accept either a single tuple and return a boolean value, or a collection of tuples and return the ones which were satisfied (or violated) by the given rule.

In general, *Satisfy* is an overloaded method, which works as follows: if t is a tuple, then $r.satisfy(t)$ returns true iff t is compatible with r and satisfies the conjunction of descriptors in $r.body$ and $r.consequent$. If t is not compatible with r, it doesn't generate an error but returns false.

On the other hand, if the argument is T of type **dm_DBTable**, then $r.satisfy(T)$ returns the subset of all Tuples t in T such that $r.satisfy(t)$ is true.

The *Violate* method is overloaded in a similar manner, but behaves in an opposite fashion.

5.2 Comparing rules

Rules and rule bodies can be compared for equality at two different levels - at the *signature* level, which only compares which tuple methods make up the conjunctsets and at the *value* level, which not only checks the methods used to formulate the conjunctset, but also their respective values. Given two rules $r1$ and $r2$, we can find out:

- if the methods that make up the body of $r1$ are the same ones as the body methods of $r2$ (their respective values could be different). This can be expressed as: `r1.signature = r2.signature`
- if the two bodies are identical not only in the methods that comprise them but also in their respective values. This is expressed as: `r1.body = r2.body`

Similar comparisons can be made for the Consequent. To check if two rules $r1$ and $r2$ have same consequents, one uses the expression: `r1.consequent = r2.consequent`. To check if the consequent attributes are the same (their respective values could differ) for $r1$ and $r2$, one can say: `r1.c_signature = r2.c_signature`

In addition, the signature comparisons for Body also allow the **has, in** or **is** operators to permit set-containment checking. For instance, the expression to check if the set of attributes in $r1$'s body is a superset of the set of attributes in $r2$'s body, can be written as: `r1.signature has r2.signature`.

5.3 Collections of rules

The **dm_RBTable** type represents a Set of rules, and supports the usual collection type methods. In addition, we define on this class the methods **Mine()**, similar to the one defined on the **dm_DBTable** class, except that this operator takes as its input the where clause of the **SelectRules** query and returns a subset of rules satisfying the given query. The **SelectRules** query performs what we call *rule-mining*, as opposed to the **GetRules** query which performs *data-mining*. Both these queries were described earlier in the section dealing with MSQL - our query language extension.

5.4 An example application: Typicality/Atypicality

We have developed several applications using this API, and they are part of the *Discovery Board* system. However due to space restrictions, we just present the pseudo-code for one such application, and describe the others briefly in the next section.

The typicality application deals with taking a given predicate, and selecting the best few "representative data items" satisfying that given predicate. For instance, when mining on a car dealership data, the sales staff might want to know: "Who are the most typical buyers of BMW?" or when looking at the historical voting data for the states in the US presidential and gubernatorial elections, one might ask: "What is an example of a typical Democrat state?".

For a given predicate X, the algorithm finds rules of the form "$X \implies Y$" and then looks at data items which satisfy X. It then ranks these data items based on how many of the above rules they satisfy. Using the previous example, a BMW buyer satisfying most of the properties of (rules about) BMW buyers is a typical BMW buyer. Conversely, a person who buys a BMW, but has none of the properties of usual BMW buyers is an "atypical" person.

The notion of Atypicality can be used in a wide variety of forensic analysis applications, e.g. by insurance companies who would like to detect fraudulent claims. The advantage here is that the model of what is typical is built by looking at the data itself, and doesn't require pre-classified data, or any preprocessing.

The example shown in figure 1 finds top 'N' typical members in database 'DB' satisfying the predicate 'typPat'. It first finds rules of the form $typPat \implies *$, and stores them temporarily in tmpRB. It then loops over all data elements satisfying the pattern typPat, and computes a total weight for them based on how many, and which of the rules in tmpRB they satisfy. The top N such data elements are returned to the caller.

5.5 Other primitives and applications

We now describe some of the other high level primitives that normally could have been built using the low level access methods supported on rules, but for for the sake of efficiency require that they be supported natively within the API. These include:

- **Diff:** This takes two different rulebases with similar schemas and returns an aggregate number (based on a choice of user specified metrics) between 0 and 1 indicating how "far apart" two rulebases are. By default, the value computed is an aggregate of support-weighted confidence difference between rules from the two sets identical in their bodies and consequents.
- **IncrUpdate:** Rule generation can be a costly step, especially if the data hasn't changed substantially. This primitive takes an existing database, a rulebase, and an additional set of records to be added and deleted, and updates the support and confidence of rules in a more efficient manner, without dropping and recreating the rulebase again.
- **PredictedVal:** This primitive returns a set of most likely values, in order of preference, for a missing attribute in a tuple. The primitive looks at other similar records in the database, and using the rules derived from those, tries to come up with a set of "plausible" values for the argument tuple. This primitive is useful in determining missing values for records which are being used in some higher aggregation primitives.

Our API allows fast implementation of most of the applications listed in the section 3, It still remains to be seen whether our set of primitives is sufficient to support a rich set of data mining applications. We are currently evaluating *DiscoveryBoard* through industrial trials to verify its API in the real world setting.

6 Conclusions

We have argued that the main obstacle in wide spread use of data mining technology is not insufficient performance but lack of tools and environments to develop data mining applications. Typically, the volume of (association) rules generated

//: Finds 'N' most typical tuples in database 'DB', satisfying the pattern 'typPat'.
//: Returns the result in a temprary DBTable, 'answer', pre-allocated by caller
//: 'conn' is the database connection handle.
//: 'compute_weight' could be a user defined function which determines the
//: importance of a rule. The **default** is to use confidence*suppport as the weight.

```
dm_DBTable&
N_most_Typical(dm_dbConnect &conn,
                dm_DBTable& DB,
                dm_DescriptorList typPat,
                int N,
                dm_DBTable& answer)
{
    char *qryPat;

    create_rule_qry(typPat, qryPat); // generates "typPat ==> *" pattern
    dm_RBTable tmpRB = DB.mine(typPat); // Get all rules using above pattern
    dm_RBTableIterator R_Iter(tmpRB);

    // iterate over the subset of tuples in DB database which satisfy typPat
    dm_DBTableIterator Iter(DB);
    dm_Tuple tup = Iter.initTuple(typPat);

    while (!Iter.done()) {
        int wt = 0;
        dm_Rule r = R_Iter.initRule();

        while (!R_Iter.done()) {
            if r.satisfy(tup) {
                if (exists_in(answer, tup)) {
                    add_to_weight(answer, tup, compute_weight(r));
                } else {
                    insert_weight(answer, tup, compute_weight(r));
                }
            }
            r = R_Iter.next_rule();
        }
        tup = Iter.next_tuple();
    }
    retain_topN(answer);
    return answer;
}
```

Fig. 1. The "Typicality" Application

by data mining algorithms is larger than the size of the underlying data itself. Such a rulebase can be invaluable source of insight, but only if it is offered in conjunction with application building and querying tools and is overwhelming and frustrating to use otherwise. Thus, we have argued for Knowledge Discovery Management System, which would provide application support similar in scope to that provided by DBMS for management of record oriented data. To this end we have described the concepts of a rule query language and the application programming interface to develop new, ad hoc, data mining applications.

Developing a *second generation of data mining systems* to offer the KDMS features is an ambitious research program. *Discovery Board* system is the first prototype of a second generation data mining system, which not only generates rules from the underlying database, but also provides support for building sophisticated data mining applications which use rules.

References

1. Rakesh Agrawal, Tomasz Imielinski, and Arun Swami. Mining associations rules between sets of items in large databases. In *Proceedings of ACM SIGMOD Conference on Management of Data (SIGMOD'93)*, pages 207 – 216, Washington D.C., May 1993.
2. Rakesh Agrawal and R. Srikant. Fast algorithms for mining association rules. In *vldb94*, pages 487 – 499, Santiago, Chile, 1994.
3. Dirk Bartels, Mark Berler, Jeff Eastmane, Sophie Gamerman, David Jordan, Adam Springer, Henry Strickland, and Drew Wade. *The Object Database Standard: ODMG 2.0*. Morgan Kaufmann, San Francisco, CA, 1997.
4. Sergey Brin, Rajeev Motwani, Jeffrey Ullman, and Shalom Tsur. Dynamic itemset counting and implication rules for market basket data. In *Proceedings of ACM SIGMOD Conference on Management of Data (SIGMOD'97)*, pages 255 – 264, Tuscon, Arizona, May 1997.
5. J. Han and Y. Fu. Discovery of multiple level association rules from large databases. In *Proceedings of the 21st International Conference on Very Large Data Bases (VLDB'95)*, pages 420 – 431, Zurich, Switzerland, Sept 1995.
6. J. Han, Y. Fu, K. Koperski, W. Wang, and O. Zaiane. DMQL: A data mining query language for relational databases. In *DMKD-96 (SIGMOD-96 Workshop on KDD)*, Montreal, Canada, June 1996.
7. T. Imielinski, A. Virmani, and A. Abdulghani. Datamine: Application programming interface and query language for database mining. In *Proceedings of the Second International Conference on Knowledge Discovery and Data Mining (KDD'96)*, Portland, Oregon, August 1996.
8. Tomasz Imielinski and Heikki Mannila. A database perspective on knowledge discovery. *Communications of the ACM*, 39(11):58 – 64, november 1996.
9. Heikki Mannila, Hannu Toivonen, and A. Inkeri Verkamo. Discovering frequent episodes in sequences. In Usama M. Fayyad and Ramasamy Uthurusamy, editors, *Proceedings of the First International Conference on Knowledge Discovery and Data Mining (KDD'95)*, pages 210 – 215, Montreal, Canada, August 1995. AAAI Press.
10. Rosa Meo, Giuseppe Psaila, and Stefano Ceri. A new sql-like operator for mining association rules. In *Proceedings of the 22nd International Conference on Very Large Data Bases (VLDB'96)*, pages 122 – 133, Bombay, India, Sept 1996.

11. Raymond T. Ng, Laks V. S. Lakshmanan, Jiawei Han, and Alex Pang. Exploratory mining and pruning optimizations of constrained associations rules. In *Proceedings of ACM SIGMOD Conference on Management of Data (SIGMOD'98)*, Seattle, Washington, June 1998.

12. Jong Soo Park, Ming-Syan Chen, and Philip S. Yu. An effective hash based algorithm for mining association rules. In *Proceedings of ACM SIGMOD Conference on Management of Data (SIGMOD'95)*, pages 175–186, San Jose, California, may 1995.

13. Sunita Sarawagi, Shiby Thomas, and Rakesh Agrawal. Integrating association rule mining with relational database systems: Alternatives and implications. In *Proceedings of ACM SIGMOD Conference on Management of Data (SIGMOD'98)*, Seattle, Washington, June 1998.

14. Ashok Savasere, Edward Omiecinski, and Shamkant Navathe. An efficient algorithm for mining association rules in large databases. In *Proceedings of the 21st International Conference on Very Large Data Bases (VLDB'95)*, pages 432 – 444, Zurich, Switzerland, Sept 1995.

15. Ramakrishnan Srikant and Rakesh Agrawal. Mining generalized association rules. In *Proceedings of the 21st International Conference on Very Large Data Bases (VLDB'95)*, pages 407 – 419, Zurich, Switzerland, Sept 1995.

16. Aashu Virmani. Second generation data mining: Concepts and implementation. *PhD Thesis, Rutgers University*, April 1998.

Workflow Management in the Internet Age

C. Mohan

IBM Almaden Research Center
650 Harry Road, K01/B1
San Jose, CA 95120, USA
Institute National de Recherche en Informatique et en Automatique (INRIA)
Rocquencourt, B.P. 105
78153 Le Chesnay Cedex
France
mohan@almaden.ibm.com, mohan@rodin.inria.fr
http://www.almaden.ibm.com/u/mohan/

Abstract. For the last many years, workflow management (WFM) has been the focus of intense activity in terms of products, standards and research work worldwide. WFM integrates concepts from many areas of computer science. Numerous workflow companies, and industrial and academic research groups are in existence now. Several conferences and workshops relating to WFM are being held regularly. The popularity of the worldwide web, extranets and electronic commerce is further increasing the desirability of standards in the workflow arena to enable interoperability. The recent emphasis on supply chain reengineering as a means of reducing costs and improving responsiveness is also a factor in this regard. In this extended abstract, which is a condensed version of a paper which appears in the proceedings of the NATO Advanced Study Institute in Workflow Management and Interoperability held in Istanbul in August 1997, I briefly summarize the recent trends in WFM products, standards and research. I address technical as well as business trends.

1 Introduction

While workflow management (WFM) as a concept has existed for many years, it is only in the last few years that it has become very popular in the commercial as well as research world. Several workflow companies, and industrial and academic research groups are currently in existence, especially in Europe and North America. Numerous products with varying functionalities have been released in the last few years. Efforts on standardizing workflow concepts and interfaces are in progress under the auspices of the Workflow Management Coalition (WFMC) and the Object Management Group (OMG).

Over the years, various definitions have been proposed for concepts relating to WFM. For example, Giga Group (http://www.gigaweb.com/) has given the following definition: *"we call the operational aspects of a business process — the sequence of tasks and who performs them, the information flow to support the tasks, and the tracking and reporting mechanisms that measure and control them*

— *the workflow*". It should be noted that the aim of WFM is not to automate necessarily all the tasks of a workflow process. Some tasks (also called activities) might continue to involve humans and even for automated tasks the determination of when to initiate them and/or determining whether such automated tasks have successfully completed might be left to humans. The emphasis is much more on automating the tracking of the states of the tasks of a workflow, and allowing specification of preconditions to decide when tasks are ready to be executed (intertask dependencies) and of information flow between tasks.

One of the chief goals of WFM is to separate process logic from task or activity logic which is embedded in individual user applications. This separation allows the two to be independently modified and the same task logic to be reused in different processes, thereby promoting software reuse as in object-oriented programming, and the integration of heterogeneous applications which were developed in isolation.

The focus in the last few years on business process reengineering, especially with regard to the supply chain, by enterprises as a cost saving and service improvement measure has contributed significantly to the recent popularity of WFMSs. The emergence of the worldwide web as the means for carrying out electronic commerce is also contributing to this trend. EDI (electronic data interchange) on the internet and the emerging XML (extended markup language) standard are also going to be playing significant roles in the emergence of web-based workflows. So far WFMSs have been widely deployed in the following types of businesses/organizations: banking, accounting, manufacturing, brokerage, insurance, healthcare, government departments, telecommunications, university administration and customer service.

Traditionally, WFMSs and workflow applications have been divided into four broad categories: *production, administrative, collaborative* and *ad hoc*. While this is not a very strict categorization, it helps to distinguish the design points of different products somewhat reasonably. Over the years, vendors have tried to reposition/redesign their products to cover more of this spectrum of applications.

2 Market Trends and Business Considerations

The WFM market has grown steadily in the last few years, although the rate of growth has slowed down a bit in the recent past. Depending on the definition of what constitutes workflow software, different market analysis firms come up with different numbers for the size of the market. But, there is general agreement that commercially workflow is a very significant market with a lot more potential in store.

FileNet (http://www.filenet.com/) is widely believed to be the current market leader, although the company has suffered losses in the recent past and has been forced to restructure its operations. In keeping with the trends in the PC arena, some of the workflow vendors have recently reduced their products' per seat prices dramatically. This is the case especially for products which operate with Microsoft's messaging product Exchange (http://www.microsoft.com/exchange/). The increase in the popularity of the web has also contributed to the downward trend in prices.

Unlike in the case of some other products, WFMSs involve a longer sales cycle, since their adoption requires executive approval and end user commitment. Adopting a WFMS necessitates a cultural change in the way an organization does its business. It requires group consensus and retraining. Typically, implementing a workflow solution involves the hiring of consultants for advice. VARs (Value-Added Resellers), tool vendors and consultants stand to benefit economically from the complexities involved in implementing WFM applications.

The WFM market has been undergoing a great deal of consolidation in the last couple of years. There have been many mergers and partnerships involving companies that produce workflow and related products (document management, imaging, text search, e-mail, forms management and groupware). It is anticipated that in the next few years there will be a shakeout in the market and some of the smaller companies will disappear due to inadequate revenues and their inability to keep up with the competition. All the same, new players are still entering the market: application development tools vendor Forte recently introduced its Conductor workflow product (http://www.forte.com/Product/conductor/index.htm) and Oracle has included workflow functionality in its InterOffice product (http://www.oracle.com/products/interoffice/html/features.html).

One of the major consequences of the above partnerships/acquisitions is that several product suites, where each suite consists of many related products, have been released. This has resulted in improvements in the interoperability amongst the products within a suite. More synergy has been brought about amongst imaging, document/forms management, and workflow products.

Users have demanded better tools to help them in using WFMSs effectively. They have also asked for better synergy between related products produced by different vendors. In response, companies that have specialized in business process and data modelling have begun to work with workflow vendors to better integrate their products.

Several information sources on WFM exist on the internet. Workflow And Reengineering International Association (WARIA) is a non-profit organization whose mission is to make sense of what's happening at the intersection of business process reengineering (BPR), workflow and electronic commerce, and reach clarity through sharing experiences, product evaluations, networking between users and vendors, education and training. The WARIA web site (http://www.waria.com/) has a listing of BPR, groupware, and workflow vendors and consultants. The Concordium web site (http://www.concordium.co.uk/) also includes a list of WFMS products.

3 Workflow Standards

The Workflow Management Coalition (WFMC) is the main organization that is involved in workflow management standardization efforts (http://www.aiai.ed.ac.uk/project/wfmc/). WFMC defined a reference model for a WFMS's architecture. This model has 5 interfaces and application program interfaces (APIs) relating to those interfaces are intended to be standardized. The interfaces/APIs are: (1) Process definition model and interchange APIs, (2) Client APIs, (3) Application invocation interface, (4) Workflow interoperability, and (5) Administration and monitoring.

As WFMC releases its specifications for the various interfaces, vendors have been releasing new versions of their products to support those standards. The latest version (1.2) of the workflow API (interface 2, WAPI) specification was released in October 1996. In October 1996, an interoperability abstract specification (interface 4) which is designed to ensure that businesses can exchange and process work from two or more workflow engines was published. A specific binding for the requests and responses of the abstract specification was also released at the same time (WFMC-TC-1018). This binding uses internet mail for transport, and MIME (Multipurpose Internet Mail Extension) and CGI (Common Gateway Interface) for content encoding. In November 1996, an audit data specification (interface 5) was unveiled. WFMC published "Workflow Handbook 1997" in January 1997.

While users find it very convenient to define process models using graphical tools, different products provide the graphical support differently. As a result, WFMC decided that it would be too difficult to arrive at a graphical standard for process definitions. Consequently, a language based standard is being worked on for this purpose. Products like FlowMark already support such a language (FlowMark Definition Language, FDL) to allow the convenient export and import of process definitions between different workflow installations.

WFMC and OMG are trying to coordinate their activities to marry workflow and CORBA object technologies. In July 1997, OMG released a call for proposals for a workflow management facility within OMG's object management architecture (http://wwwdb.inf.tu-dresden.de/wf-wg/documents.html). The plan is to define the interfaces and semantics required for manipulating and executing interoperable workflow objects and metadata. Currently, the submitters of different proposals made in response to the RFP are merging their proposals to create an OMG Workflow Facility called jFlow.

In June 1998, WFMC released a white paper which presents arguments for thinking of the internet and workflow as catalysts for radical change (http://www.aiim.org/wfmc/pr/finalwp.pdf). It shows how the WFMC specifications can be mapped onto the internet technologies.

As a result of an initiative taken by Netscape, Sun and HP in April 1998, the Internet Engineering Task Force (IETF) is involved in developing a standard called Simple Workflow Access Protocol (SWAP) for producing interoperable workflow products from multiple vendors (http://search.netscape.com/newsref/pr/newsrelease597.html).

4 Technical Trends

From a technical perspective, WFM is very interesting since it brings together principles, methodologies and technologies from various areas of computer science and management science: database management, client server computing, programming languages, heterogeneous distributed computing, mobile computing, graphical user interfaces, application (new and legacy) and subsystem (e.g., CICS and MQSeries) integration, messaging, document management, simulation, and business practices and reengineering. Integrating different concepts from these areas poses many challenges. Factors like scalability, high availability, manageability, usability and security also further aggravate the demands on the designs of WFMSs.

Functionality Evolution. At the beginning, many of the WFMS products were designed for imaging-based applications. Of late, imaging is being made an optional component of WFMSs, thereby broadening the utility of such systems for a wider set of applications. This is also a consequence of more and more information being digitally captured via online data entry rather than such information having to be extracted from paper documents via imaging technologies like optical character recognition (OCR).

There are a number of similarities between WFMSs and transaction processing monitors (TPMs) since both manage a collection of applications with a significant number of similar requirements in terms of performance, industrial-strength features, interoperability, etc. While, for this reason, WFMSs can be thought of as the next stage in the evolution of TPMs, as a matter of fact none of the existing WFMS products that I know of came about as a result of enhancing any TPM!

Embedded Workflow. In the last few years, many general purpose business application packages have been developed for managing human resources, manufacturing, sales, accounting, etc. by companies like Baan, Oracle, People-Soft and SAP. The market for such products has grown tremendously as customer organizations try to avoid producing home-grown solutions. Developers of such packages — like SAP (http://www.sap.com/workflow/wrkflow.htm), Baan (http://www.baan.com/3_Solutions/Concepts/work/default.htm) and People-Soft (http://www.peoplesoft.com/) — have incorporated workflow functionality into their products.

Web-based Workflow. With the widespread and rapid popularity of the worldwide web, very quickly many WFMS products have been adapted to work in the context of the web. The degree of sophistication of web support varies from product to product. Some products permit workflows to be initiated or controlled from a browser. Worklist handling via the web is another form of support that is provided by a few products. In summary, it is the client side WFMS functionality that has been made available through a web browser. The advantage of web support is that no specialized WFMS-specific client software needs to be installed to invoke workflow functionality at a workflow server. In the future, more sophisticated support can be anticipated which would allow the execution of inter-enterprise workflows spanning the internet and involving multiple web/workflow servers. ActionWorks Metro 3.0 comes with over 20 ready-to-run administrative applications that support key human resources, sales/marketing and support processes.

Distributed Workflows. WFMS architectures have evolved from supporting mostly single workgroup type environments to providing enterprise-wide (and even inter-enterprise level) functionality. With such enhancements, a single workflow is allowed to span servers and clients across wide area networks. This provides additional scalability, availability and manageability since more servers can be involved in a single workflow and the impact of server failures can be minimized.

Ad Hoc Workflows. In the last couple of years, production WFMSs have been enhanced to provide support for ad hoc workflows with different levels of flexibility. Also, new products which are specifically intended for ad hoc workflows have been introduced recently. Novell released Groupwise Workflow (http://www.novell.com/groupwise/) which is based on messaging. It uses as its core workflow engine FileNet's Ensemble (http://www.filenet.com/prods/ensemble.html). Several e-mail based WFMS products have been developed recently on top of Microsoft's Exchange messaging product.

Process Modeling. Business process and data modelling companies like HOLOSOFX (http://www.holosofx.com/) and IDS-Scheer (http://www.ids-scheer.de/english/index.htm) are enhancing their respective products Workflow-BPR and ARIS Toolset to generate workflow schema definitions (e.g., FlowMark Description Language versions of workflow definitions for use with FlowMark). This is analogous to, in the relational DBMS world, 4GLs being used to generate SQL programs rather than forcing users to hand code SQL.

Groupware. The groupware product Lotus Notes has been around for many years. Recently, the Notes server has been renamed to be Domino and the name Notes is now associated with the client. Domino provides some basic workflow functionality and permits building workflow applications with both database-based and mail-based architectures. Recent releases of Domino provide support for advanced concepts such as agents, field-level replication, integrated web access, web serving, etc. Domino has been ported to run even on the IBM mainframe operating system Posix-compliant OS/390. Other vendors have built products which provide high-level process definition capabilities on top of Domino/Notes. Some of these products are Action Technology's Action Workflow, Pavone's GroupFlow (http://www.pavone.de/wpub_pav/21de.htm) and ONEstone Information Technologies' ProZessware (http://www.onestone.de/). FlowMark 2.3 supports runtime clients based on Lotus Notes, thereby allowing users to take advantage of the replication and disconnected operation features of Notes. With such a client, worklist items and process definitions are made available as Notes documents.

WFMS State Repository. Most WFMSs' servers use a relational DBMS as the repository for keeping track of workflow process definitions, organization structure, runtime information on process and activity instances, workflow data, etc. Typically, installations are allowed to choose a DBMS from a variety of different RDBMS products. As described before, some products use Lotus Notes/Domino as the repository. FlowMark currently uses ODI's ObjectStore OODBMS as the repository but work is in progress to make DB2 available as a repository in Release 3.0. The usage characteristic of a DBMS by a WFMS is very different from the usual assumptions made about most database accesses being read-only. As a matter of fact, most accesses made by a workflow server to its repository will be in the form of update transactions. This is because most of the time the server accesses the repository to perform state transitions in the workflow process graph at the time of activity/process instance completions/initiations. Such actions have to be recorded persistently. The update transactions executed by the workflow servers tend to be of short duration. The locking granularity that the DBMS supports can have a significant impact on the number of workflow clients that can be supported. High availability features in the repository DBMS are crucial since any failure of the DBMS would make the WFMS's operations come to a standstill since the workflow server needs access to it to do its process navigation on an activity completion.

Transaction Concepts. While much research has been done in the area of advanced transaction models, none of the current WFMS products supports the transaction concept in any explicit fashion. Typically, the products do not even guarantee that if an activity's execution is an ACID transaction that the execution of that activity and the recording of that activity's completion in the workflow server's repository will be done atomically. The consequence is that the activity may complete successfully but the client node where the activity executed may crash before the activity completion notification is sent to the server and then the server will continue to think that the activity is still in progress. Human intervention will be needed to resolve this situation. This scenario becomes especially difficult to handle where the activity program is a legacy application which was written without its usage in a workflow context in mind.

Application Development. A number of vendors have added support for Microsoft's Object Linking and Embedding (OLE) technology. This allows OLE-enabled applications to be very easily invoked by a WFMS as a consequence of starting executions of activities. Activity implementations become much easier to code since passing of data from the workflow engine to the invoked applications is automated. Support for OMG's CORBA has not been forthcoming as much as for OLE in WFMS products.

Document Handling. Different WFMSs provide different degrees of support for handling documents. Some WFMSs have built-in document management. Examples of such systems are Eastman Software's OPEN/workflow 3.1 and Keyfile's Keyfile. Certain WFMSs have tight coupling with external document management products. Products built on top of Lotus Notes/Domino, for example, belong to this category. Some products (like FlowMark) have a loose coupling with a document management system (e.g., ImagePlus Visual-Info (http://www.software.ibm.com/is/image/vi21.html)).

Intercomponent Communication. Some products like FlowMark currently use their own home-grown messaging mechanisms for communication between their components. In the case of FlowMark, work is in progress to replace the special purpose messaging scheme with IBM's MQSeries which provides persistent messages and transaction support across a wide variety of platforms. The next release of FlowMark will be called MQSeries Workflow. It will constitute a part of IBM's Business Integration series of products (http://www.software.ibm.com/ts/mqseries/workflow/). Products based on Exchange and Groupwise use the mail system for almost all their communications needs. WFMS products based on Lotus Notes/Domino use that groupware product's native support for messaging. As far as I know, CORBA is not yet supported by WFMS products for this purpose.

5 Research Projects

Overall, the workflow research community has not had enough impact on workflow products. There are a few exceptions, of course. Action Technology's Action Workflow originated from research done at Stanford University. InConcert's InConcert grew out of office automation research performed at the Computer Corporation of America. Pavone's GroupFlow came out of research work carried out at the University of Paderborn in Germany. Some of the ideas from the Intelligent Control Nets project at Xerox PARC were commercialized in the now-defunct FlowPath product of Bull which was sold to Wang.

Much of the research work on workflow management has concentrated on workflow specification (e.g., intertask dependencies) and verification, transactional workflows (e.g., advanced transaction models) and extensions of ideas from active database management to workflow management. There are only a few workflow research groups which are engaged in seriously prototyping their research results using either home-grown WFMSs or commercially available WFMS products. At least some of the prototypes replicate functionality that is already widely available in one or more products.

A number of issues deserve serious attention from researchers: modeling of external events, exception handling (combining production and ad hoc workflows), interoperability, process schema inference, supporting object-oriented views of workflow definitions (e.g., inheritance), fault tolerance, benchmarks, load balancing.

6 Conclusions

As I briefly outlined in this extended abstract, workflow management is a very active field with numerous products and research groups. Technically it is an exciting field since it amalgamates technologies, principles and methodologies from numerous areas of computer science. The product landscape is being transformed significantly due to the absorption of emerging technologies like the worldwide web, and due to mergers and partnerships involving numerous companies which produce complementary products. With the emergence of support for workflow management in process modeling and application development tools, WFMSs are becoming a little easier to use. There is a significant amount of hope riding on the work of the Workflow Management Coalition in order to achieve interoperability across different vendors' products and to make inter-enterprise workflows a reality. Workflow management has a very significant role to play in disparate organizations' drive to improve their efficiency and customer service.

A more comprehensive tutorial presentation on which this extended abstract is based is available at http://www.almaden.ibm.com/u/mohan/nato97.eps

Untyped Queries, Untyped Reflective Machines and Conditional Quantifiers * **

Jose Maria Turull Torres

Universidad Nacional de San Luis
Universidad Tecnológica Nacional, F.R.B.A.
Peron 2315, piso 4, depto. P
1040 Capital Federal, ARGENTINA
email: turull@iamba.edu.ar   turull@unsl.edu.ar

Abstract. In the definition of the class CQ of computable queries, Chandra and Harel ([7]) included *untyped queries*, that is, queries whose answers are relations of possibly different arities on different databases. However, it seems that in the work which followed on the subject, untyped queries were not considered at all, neither in the abstract machines side nor in the logic framework. We propose to re-introduce these queries in the study of Query Computability, and also in the construction of Industry query languages, without leaving the Relational Model. So, we define an extension of the Reflective Relational Machine of [2], which we call *untyped Reflective Relational Machine*. In the logic framework, we define a new quantifier, which we call *conditional quantifier*, and we build with it an infinitary logic which we denote by $\mathcal{L}^c_{\omega_1\omega}$. Then we prove completeness results regarding both formalisms considering both typed and untyped queries.

1   Introduction

The class of *Computable Queries*, denoted by CQ, was first defined in [7] in order to start the construction of a theoretical framework in which the computability and the complexity of queries to databases (db) could be studied. Roughly, a *computable query* is a partial function from classes of finite relational structures (or db) of a given finite relational signature (or db schema) to classes of relations on the corresponding structure, such that it is partial recursive and it preserves isomorphisms. Chandra and Harel defined a formal programming language for computing queries in that article, called QL, and they proved that this language is *complete*, that is, the set of QL programs computes (or "expresses") the whole class CQ. After that, in 1991, Abiteboul and Vianu defined in [3] another kind of formalism to characterize computable queries. They defined an abstract machine,

---

* The work presented here was done during a visit to the Department of Mathematics of the University of Helsinki.
** This work has been partially supported by Grant 1011049 of the Academy of Finland and by a Grant of Universidad CAECE, Argentina.

which they called *Generic Machine*, denoted as GM^{loose}, and they proved that it is strictly included in QL, considering the class of queries which may be computed by programs or machines in each formalism. This computational model was renamed as *Relational Machine* in [4] (*RM* from now on). Recall that a *RM* is a Turing Machine (*TM*) with the addition of a *relational store*, where a countable set of relations of bounded arity can be stored. The interaction with the relational store is done only through *FO* (First Order Logic) formulae in the finite control of the machine, and the input db as well as the output relation are in the relational store. They defined later the so called *Reflective Relational Machine*, together with Papadimitriou in [2]. Recall that a reflective relational machine, which we will denote as *RRM*, is a *RM* with an additional *query tape* where *FO* queries, which are called *dynamic queries*, may be written during a computation of the machine, and are then evaluated in one step. And they noted that the class of *RRM* "behaves" as complete if dynamic queries with $O(n)$ variables are allowed. Let's denote it by RRM^n. In the meantime, and from the field of Logic, Gurevich defined in 1984 the concept of *global predicate* ([11]), which as he pointed out is the same to that of a query (not a *computable* query since in his definition he doesn't require for the function to be partial recursive). In this way, the notion of a *logic*, in an abstract sense, turned into a different kind of formalism for computing queries. This is because every formula of a given logic with, say, r free variables can be considered to express a query to relational db, whose answer is a relation of arity r (in the spirit of Codd's *Relational Calculus*, see [1], but not restricted to *FO*). There are by now a lot of results characterizing different subclasses of the class of computable queries by different logics. And one of them is the well known fact that the *infinitary logic* $\mathcal{L}_{\omega_1\omega}$ (which extends *FO* by allowing disjunction and conjunction over countably infinite sets of formulae) strictly includes the whole class $total(\mathcal{C}\mathcal{Q})$ (i.e., $\mathcal{C}\mathcal{Q}$ restricted to total functions).

Now, there are some aspects in the relation among the three different formalisms which we mentioned, which are worthwhile to be noted:

1. In the definition of computable query in [7] the result of applying a query to different db are relations which are *not* restricted to be of the same arity. Moreover, the authors point out this fact in the article, and they briefly describe a slight modification to the definition of the language QL, so that it can include only the queries of fixed arity (which they call *typed queries*), excluding what we will call *untyped queries* from now on.

2. In [3] the authors define computable queries as *fixed arity* queries, while maintaining the other properties defined in [7]. They make explicit reference to the work of Chandra and Harel, and they mention the language QL (which they call *while*^{unsorted} in their paper) pointing out that this was the first *complete* language. And the consideration of *only* the queries of fixed arity seems to be the general feeling in the literature among the authors who come from the field of Computer Science, as well (as in [4], [5], [2], [12], [13], among others). One exception is in [1], where a formal programming language called *while*^{untyped} is exhibited (it is quite similar to QL but much easier, since both integer variables and relation variables can be used in a

program) though it seems that all the study on query languages for queries in CQ in the book is devoted to typed queries.

3. The concept of global predicate by Gurevich requires also a *fixed arity* of the resulting relation for the whole class of structures where it is defined. And it seems to be the case that all the logicians who work in this area consider the same restriction as to the arity of the global predicates or queries.

Let us summarize the situation of the field to this regard as follows (from now on and regarding abstract machines, we will use the same notation for the model itself and for the class of queries which can be computed by that model), where by *total-typed(CQ)* we mean the subclass of computable queries which are total and typed:

1. $QL = CQ$ and $CQ \supset typed(CQ) \supset total\text{-}typed(CQ)$;
2. $RM \subset typed(CQ) = RRM^n$;
3. $\mathcal{L}_{\omega_1\omega} \supset total\text{-}typed(CQ)$;
4. $\mathcal{L}_{\omega_1\omega} \not\supset total(CQ)$, because it cannot express untyped queries.

Note that there are interesting untyped queries which are meaningful in the Model Theory setting (that is, without considering any specific semantics for the given db). Recall that an automorphism is a bijection defined in the domain of the db, which preserves every relation in its schema. One example is *the set of automorphisms of a db*, defined as a query which induces a $2n$-ary relation in every db I whose domain is of size n. In this query, every $2n$-tuple represents one ordering of the domain of I, in the first n-subtuple, together with one of the automorphisms in I for that ordering, in the second n-subtuple. In the Example 1 we show how to express this query in the formalism which we propose and which we define later.

In a query language which is widely used in the Industry, SQL, and regarding relational db, untyped queries of *unbounded arity* (that is, the arity of the resulting relation is not bounded by any constant) such as the example given above cannot be expressed. Though they can certainly be expressed in a programming language (like C) with *embeded SQL*, the point is that we think that the query language by itself should be capable to express queries whose answer is a relation of varying arity, *as naturally* as it can express queries whose answer is a relation of varying length. And it seems that this is the general case for the query languages which are being used for relational db. One important reason why this situation is highly inconvenient is that in "combined" languages like $(C + SQL)$ it is possible to express queries which don't preserve isomorphisms. Consider the query "*give me the name of 3 clients whose balance is negative*". It can be computed by a program in that language but its result depends on the physical order of the tuples in the files where the relations are stored (there may be more than 3 clients in that situation). It is *representation dependent*, and this sort of queries are not considered as computable ([7], [3]). On the other hand, in SQL such a query is clearly not expressible. Since [7], among others, it is well known that Turing Machines do not preserve isomorphisms. They are sensible to the representation of the input data. And it is widely accepted that the result of the evaluation of a query should not depend on the way the db is represented. Query languages should work like QL programs, RM or RRM, or whatever model whose class of expressible queries is contained in CQ. So that the consideration of only typed queries is far from being just a theoretical issue.

On the other hand, in real world data bases it is quite usual to ask *numerical queries*, that is, queries whose answers are expected to be (natural) numbers, instead of relations. Consider queries like *"which is the total amount that is being paid in salaries in a month?"*. They should be considered as computable queries, but they are *not* because, according to the definition, a query is expected to range over relations defined on the input structure (or db), and not over an infinite set of numbers. Some extensions to the formalism of [7] have been defined to consider these kind of queries. One was defined in the same article (the language EQL) and another was recently defined by Gurevich and Grädel in 1995 ([10]). Roughly speaking, both of them propose to extend the finite relational structures which represent data base instances with the infinite domain of the natural numbers. And, of course, this trend takes us out of the field of Finite Model Theory, a theoretical framework which is becoming more and more solid in the present decade.

So, in order to remain within the current framework of FMT, and in the consideration of the mismatch which was exposed above, we propose to extend the concept of computable query which is being used both in the formalism of abstract machines and in the formalism of abstract logic. The idea is to consider also *untyped queries*, and in particular a subclass of them as what we call *numerical queries*. That is, queries which range over the Naturals. We will do this by encoding the resulting number as the arity of the output relation of an untyped query (as it was done in [7] regarding QL). For the purpose of computing both typed and untyped queries, and including numerical queries, we extend the Reflective Machine to what we call Untyped Reflective Machine (RRM_u). Then we prove that it computes exactly the *whole* class CQ, including untyped queries. As to the Logic Formalism, we introduce a new kind of quantifier, which we call *conditional quantifier*, which allows the same formula to induce relations of different arities on different structures or db. So, we define the infinitary logic $\mathcal{L}^c_{\omega_1\omega}$, augmenting the well known logic $\mathcal{L}_{\omega_1\omega}$, and we prove that it strictly includes the *whole* sub-class $total(CQ)$, including the untyped queries and, hence, the numerical queries. Finally, we define a fragment of $\mathcal{L}^c_{\omega_1\omega}$, which we denote by $\mathcal{L}^c_*$, and we prove that it captures exactly the sub-class $total(CQ)$, but unfortunately it is undecidable. And we also get, as a Corollary to the former, an undecidable fragment $\mathcal{L}_*$ of the logic $\mathcal{L}_{\omega_1\omega}$ which exactly captures the sub-class $total\text{-}typed(CQ)$, solving a long standing open problem.

A preliminary, and more extended version of the present work is in [15].

2 Numerical Queries

As we said in Sect. 1, we want to consider a part of the subclass of the *untyped queries* as what we call *numerical queries*. That is, queries which range over the

Naturals. We will do this by encoding the resulting number as the arity of the output relation of an untyped query. We will restrict the content of the output relations so that their cardinality will be minimal. In the present article we will use the standard notation for Finite Model Theory, as in [9], unless otherwise stated. By $S_{\sigma,fin}$ we will refer to the class of finite structures with signature σ (equivalently, the class of db with schema σ).

Definition 1. *A numerical query is a function* $q : S_{\sigma,fin} \to \bigcup_{r \in \omega} S_{\langle R^r \rangle,fin}$, *for some finite relational signature* σ, *such that:*

1. *q is partial recursive in some codification;*
2. *q preserves isomorphisms;*
3. *for all $I \in S_{\sigma,fin}$, if $q(I)$ is defined then $|q(I)| = |dom(I)|$ and every tuple of the relation $q(I)$ is formed with only one element of $dom(I)$ by repeating it according to the arity of the relation. If the arity of $q(I)$ is 0 then it will be a 0-ary relation with the value TRUE.*

We will denote the class of numerical queries as NQ. Then, it is clear that $NQ \nsubseteq typed(CQ)$ and $NQ \subset CQ$. Note that there are also interesting numerical queries which naturally arise in the Model Theory setting. Just consider any numerical invariant of finite relational structures, such as the size of a structure, the size of its automorphisms group, the diameter of a graph, the size of the maximal complete subgraph in a graph, etc.

3 The Abstract Machine Formalism

We will define an extension of the reflective relational machine RRM^n, considered as a transducer (see [14]).

Definition 2. *An untyped reflective machine, denoted by RRM_u, is a transducer reflective machine which allows dynamic queries in FO (see [2]) with any number of variables, with the following characteristics:*

1. *The signature of the output structure, ρ, is countably infinite, having exactly one relation symbol T_i for every $i \in \omega$. Note that this includes a 0-ary relation symbol T_0.*
2. *There are countably many relation symbols of each finite arity in the relational store. So that the signature of the relational store, σ, is countably infinite.*
3. *The output structure of every computation has at most one relation symbol T_i whose content at the end of the computation is non empty (for some $i \geq 0$). In the case of $i = 0$, this means that the content of the relation symbol T_0 is a 0-ary relation with the value TRUE.*
4. *The machine has a distinguished halting state which indicates that in the output structure all the relations T_i are empty, for $i \geq 0$. In the case of $i = 0$, this means that the content of the relation symbol T_0 is a 0-ary relation with the value FALSE.*

Theorem 1. $RRM_u = CQ$.

Proof. One direction is trivial. As to the other direction, for a given $q \in CQ$ we can build a RRM_u machine which first builds a *canonical encoding* of the input structure on the TM tape by using dynamic queries with every possible configuration of the input structure. Then the machine computes q in the TM tape and finally it decodes the result into the relational store. □

Corollary 1. $RRM_u \supset NQ$.

□

The Proof of Theorem 1 gives us a *Normal Form* for computations of queries in the whole class CQ, consisting of three stages. The first stage is the construction of a canonical representation of the input db in the TM tape of the machine. The second stage is a pure TM computation, in which the relational store is not used at all, and leaves an encoding of the resulting relation in the TM tape. Finally, the third stage consists just of the decoding of the output relation from the tape, and its storage in the relational store. However, we should point out that this is important as a matter of expressibility or computability, but not as a matter of complexity, since the canonical encoding requires exponential time. This should be contrasted with the Normal Form of [3] for RM, where an encoding which is built in the TM tape in the first stage of the computation can be computed in polynomial time, though this model is not complete.

4 The Logic Formalism

According to Tarski semantics for FO, which in turn has been usually followed in the construction of other logics, every formula with, say, r free variables defines an r-ary relation in every structure of the corresponding signature. This means that we cannot express untyped queries with the usual semantics and syntax. So, we will change the notion of free variable in a formula by making the property of an occurrence of a variable being free or bounded be a semantic notion, instead of a purely syntactic one. To this regard, we will introduce a new kind of quantifier, which we will call *conditional quantifier*. The main idea behind it is that the structure which in a given moment interprets a formula is which actually defines which variables are free and which are bound in that formula and for that structure. Then, as the set, and hence the number, of free variables of a given formula will depend on the structure, the formula will define in that structure a relation whose arity will depend on the structure as well, and not only on the formula. One important restriction to note at this point is that if we use finitary logics then the arities that the untyped queries can take will be bounded by a constant. So we will add the conditional quantifier to an infinitary logic, namely $\mathcal{L}_{\omega_1\omega}$.

Definition 3. *Let $\mathcal{L}^c_{\omega_1\omega}$ be the infinitary logic $\mathcal{L}_{\omega_1\omega}$ augmented with the following formation rule for formulae: if δ is a sentence of $\mathcal{L}_{\omega_1\omega}$, φ is a formula of $\mathcal{L}^c_{\omega_1\omega}$ and x_i is a variable, then $\exists^c x_i(\delta, \varphi)$ is also a formula of $\mathcal{L}^c_{\omega_1\omega}$. We will* *usually write* $\exists^c x_i(\delta, \varphi(x_i))$ *to emphasize the fact that the variable* x_i *is free in* φ *in the purely syntactic sense (i.e., in the classical sense).*

Definition 4. *The semantics of the conditional quantifier is as follows. Recall that a valuation* v *is a total function from the countable set of variables in a logic to the domain of a structure. We say that two valuations* v *and* v' *are i-equivalent, for an arbitrary positive integer* i, *if it is the case that* $v(x_j) = v'(x_j)$ *for every positive integer* $j \neq i$. *Then, if* I *is a structure of the same signature that* δ *and* φ, *and* v *is a valuation on the domain of* I, *we say that* $I, v \models \exists^c x_i(\delta, \varphi(x_i))$ *iff either* $I \models \delta$ *and for some valuation* v' *which is i-equivalent to* v *it is* $I, v' \models \varphi(x_i)$ *or* $I \not\models \delta$ *and* $I, v \models \varphi(x_i)$.

Now we will define the relation induced in a structure by a formula of the logic $\mathcal{L}^c_{\omega_1 \omega}$. For that purpose, for every formula $\psi \in \mathcal{L}^c_{\omega_1 \omega}$ with signature σ, and for every σ-structure I, we will denote by $\hat{\psi}_I$ the formula in $\mathcal{L}_{\omega_1 \omega}$ which we get from ψ by replacing every subformula of the form $\exists^c x(\delta, \varphi(x))$ in ψ, either by the subformula $\exists x(\varphi(x))$, if $I \models \delta$, or by the subformula $\varphi(x)$ (with x as a free variable) if $I \not\models \delta$. Next, we will define it formally, by induction.

Definition 5. *For every formula* $\psi \in \mathcal{L}^c_{\omega_1 \omega}$ *with signature* σ, *and for every* σ-*structure* I, *we define* $\hat{\psi}_I$ *as follows:*

1. *if* ψ *is atomic, then* $\hat{\psi}_I = \psi$;
2. *if* $\psi \equiv \psi_1 \wedge \psi_2$, *then* $\hat{\psi}_I = \hat{\psi}_{1,I} \wedge \hat{\psi}_{2,I}$;
3. *if* $\psi \equiv \psi_1 \vee \psi_2$, *then* $\hat{\psi}_I = \hat{\psi}_{1,I} \vee \hat{\psi}_{2,I}$;
4. *if* $\psi \equiv \neg\psi_1$, *then* $\hat{\psi}_I = \neg\hat{\psi}_{1,I}$;
5. *if* $\psi \equiv \exists x(\psi_1)$, *then* $\hat{\psi}_I = \exists x(\hat{\psi}_{1,I})$;
6. *if* $\psi \equiv \exists^c x(\delta, \psi_1(x))$, *then* $\hat{\psi}_I = \exists x(\hat{\psi}_{1,I}(x))$, *if* $I \models \delta$, *and* $\hat{\psi}_I = \hat{\psi}_{1,I}(x)$, *with* x *as a free variable in* $\hat{\psi}_{1,I}$, *if* $I \not\models \delta$.

Then, if $\hat{\psi}_I$ is t-ary, for some $t \geq 1$, the relation induced in I by ψ is defined as follows: $\psi^I = \{(v(x_1), \ldots, v(x_t)) : v$ is a valuation on the domain of I and $I, v \models \hat{\psi}_I(x_1, \ldots, x_t)\}$. Otherwise, if $\hat{\psi}_I$ is 0-ary, i.e, if it is a sentence, then $\psi^I = \text{TRUE}$ iff $I \models \hat{\psi}_I$. Note that $\hat{\psi}_I$ may have countably many free variables, though we have considered above only the case where it has a finite number of them (see Definition 6 to this regard). The same kind of extension can be defined over FO, getting the logic FO^c. We will refer to this logic in Definition 6 in Sect. 5.

Example 1. We will show how to express the query which we mentioned as an example in Sect. 1 in the logic $\mathcal{L}^c_{\omega_1 \omega}$. That is, for a given signature σ, and for every σ-structure or db I, we want the set of automorphisms of I. For this matter we will define a $2n$-ary relation, with n being the size of the domain of I, such that every $2n$-tuple t represents one automorphism on one of the possible orderings of $dom(I)$. The first n-subtuple of t will represent an ordering, and the second n-subtuple of t will represent one automorphism f as follows: for every

$1 \leq i \leq n$ $f(t_i) = t_{n+i}$, where t_i denotes the i-th component of the tuple t. Let $\sigma = \langle R_1^{r_1}, \ldots, R_k^{r_k} \rangle$. Then the following formula Ψ of $\mathcal{L}_{\omega_1 \omega}^c$ expresses the query:

$$\Psi \equiv \bigvee_{n \in \omega} \exists^c z_1 \ldots z_{2n} ($$

$$\neg(\exists x_1 \ldots x_n (x_1 \neq \ldots \neq x_n \wedge \forall x_{n+1}(x_{n+1} = x_1 \vee \cdots \vee x_{n+1} = x_n))),$$

$$\bigwedge_{i=1}^{k} \bigwedge_{(y_1, \ldots, y_{r_i}) \in \{z_1, \ldots, z_n\}^{r_i}} R_i(y_1, \ldots, y_{r_i}) \Longleftrightarrow R_i(y'_1, \ldots, y'_{r_i}))$$

where for $1 \leq j \leq r_i$ and for $1 \leq l \leq n$, if $y_j = z_l$, then $y'_j = z_{l+n}$.

$\square$

Theorem 2. $\mathcal{L}_{\omega_1 \omega}^c \supset (\mathcal{N}\mathcal{Q} \cup total(\mathcal{C}\mathcal{Q}))$.

Proof. Let $f \in \mathcal{C}\mathcal{Q}$, then by Theorem 1 there is a RRM_u $\mathcal{M}_f$ which computes it, as in the proof of the theorem. We add four constants to the vocabulary of f, say $\{@, -, 1, *\}$, and we modify $\mathcal{M}_f$ by definning two additional distinguished states, q_I and q_T, in such a way that we can encode in a structure of the new vocabulary, say σ', the "pure" TM part of the computation of $\mathcal{M}_f$ on a given input structure I, together with the transition function of the corresponding TM. We will build now a formula $\Psi_f \in \mathcal{L}_{\omega_1 \omega}^c$ which expresses the query f. The formula will affirm the existence of a Turing Machine which computes the query f, and which is actually the pure TM part of $\mathcal{M}_f$. In Ψ_f we will use second order variables, to write it in a simpler way. This is well known to be possible in the infinitary logic $\mathcal{L}_{\omega_1 \omega}$ on finite models, and hence in $\mathcal{L}_{\omega_1 \omega}^c$. The SO variables which will be used in the definition of Ψ_f are $C_1^p, \ldots, C_p^p$ and F^b. $C_1^p, \ldots, C_p^p$ are p-ary relations with only one tuple which represent the content of the p cells of the TM tape of $\mathcal{M}_f$ which might have been used, *before* steps $1, \ldots, p$, respectively, in a computation of the machine which reaches the state q_T after $(p-1)$ steps. The tuple also represents the current state of $\mathcal{M}_f$ and the current position of its TM tape head. F^b is a b-ary relation which encodes the transition function of $\mathcal{M}_f$, restricted to the part of the computation defined by the states q_I and q_T as beginning and ending states, respectively. The formula Ψ_f when interpreted by some $I_l \in S_{\sigma', fin}$ generates a relation of some arity $t \geq 0$:

$$\Psi_f \equiv \exists F^b (\varphi_F \wedge \bigvee_{I_l \in S_{\sigma', fin}} \bigvee_{n \geq 4} \exists x_1 \ldots x_n (x_1 \neq \cdots \neq x_n \wedge$$

$$\forall x_{n+1}(x_{n+1} = x_1 \vee \cdots \vee x_{n+1} = x_n) \wedge \psi_{n, I_l}(x_1, \ldots, x_n) \wedge * \neq 1 \neq - \neq @ \wedge$$

$$\bigvee_{p \in \omega} \exists C_1^p \ldots C_p^p (\gamma_{I_l, C_1^p} \wedge \alpha_{C_1, p} \wedge$$

$$\left(\left(\bigvee_{t\geq 1}\bigvee_{(i_1,\ldots,i_t)\in\{1,\ldots,n\}^t}\phi^c_{p,(i_1,\ldots,i_t)}(x_{i_1},\ldots,x_{i_t})\right)\vee\phi_{p,0})\cdots\right)$$

The actual meaning of the expression $I_l\in\mathcal{S}_{\sigma',fin}$ in the infinitary disjunction is taking every possible string of the appropriate length from $\{1,\ldots,n,*\}$, for every $n\geq 4$ (this is due to the second infinitary disjunction), as we did in the Proof of Theorem 1, where $*$ is used to separate the positive atomic formulae from the negative atomic formulae in the diagram of the input structure. And we take these strings in lexicographical order. φ_F means F *is well formed for* $\mathcal{M}_f$. $\psi_{n,I_l}(x_1,\ldots,x_n)$ means *the input* σ'-*structure is* I_l *and its size is* n. γ_{I_l,C_1^p} means *the state encoded in* C_1^p *is* q_I *and the input structure encoded in* C_1^p *is* I_l. $\alpha_{C_{1,p}}$ means $C_1^p,\ldots,C_p^p$ *are well formed.*

$$\phi^c_{p,(i_1,\ldots,i_t)}(x_{i_1},\ldots,x_{i_t})\equiv\exists^c z_1\ldots z_t(\neg\bar{\delta}_{l,t},\delta_{l,(i_1,\ldots,i_t)}(z_1,\ldots,z_t,x_{i_1},\ldots,x_{i_t}))$$

Note that the variables $\{x_{i_1},\ldots,x_{i_t}\}$ are bounded in Ψ_f, while $\{z_1,\ldots,z_t\}$ will be free in Ψ_f for I_l iff $I_l\models\bar{\delta}_{l,t}$. Where:

$$\delta_{l,(i_1,\ldots,i_t)}(z_1,\ldots,z_t,x_{i_1},\ldots,x_{i_t})\equiv z_1=x_{i_1}\wedge\ldots\wedge z_t=x_{i_t}\wedge$$

$$\bigwedge_{1\leq j<p}\beta_{p,j}\wedge\pi_p\wedge\rho_{p,t}\wedge\tau_{n,p,(i_1,\ldots,i_t)}$$

and $\bar{\delta}_{l,t}$ is a sentence, which is a sub-formula of $\delta_{l,(i_1,\ldots,i_t)}$: $\bar{\delta}_{l,t}\equiv\bigwedge_{1\leq j<p}\beta_{p,j}\wedge\pi_p\wedge\rho_{p,t}$.

$\beta_{p,j}$ means *the transition from* C_j^p *to* C_{j+1}^p *corresponds to* F. π_p means *the state encoded in* C_p^p *is* q_T. $\rho_{p,t}$ means *the resulting relation encoded in* C_p^p *is of arity* t. $\tau_{n,p,(i_1,\ldots,i_t)}$ means *the* t-*tuple* $(i_1,\ldots,i_t)$ *belongs to the resulting relation in* C_p^p. It is clear that all this sub-formulae can be expressed in $\mathcal{L}_{\omega_1\omega}$, with the exception of the sub-formula $\phi^c_{p,(i_1,\ldots,i_t)}$, which can be expressed in $\mathcal{L}^c_{\omega_1\omega}$. □

5 An Undecidable Characterization of the Total Computable Queries

It would be very interesting to characterize the fragment of the logic $\mathcal{L}^c_{\omega_1\omega}$ which captures *exactly* the class $total(\mathcal{CQ})$. As to the logic $\mathcal{L}_{\omega_1\omega}$, no fragment that captures exactly $total\text{-}typed(\mathcal{CQ})$ is known either. So, in this Section we define such fragments for both of these logics. Unfortunately, our characterization defines a formalism which is clearly undecidable in both cases, but we hope it can still be of interest, at least by giving some intuition for the search of a decidable formalism, if such a formalism exists. We think that for the case of $total(\mathcal{CQ})$ it most probably doesn't exist, because it is closely related to the class of Turing Machines which compute total functions, which is well known to be not even recursively enumerable (see [8], among others).

Definition 6. *Let's denote by* $\mathcal{L}$ *the sub-logic of the logic* $\mathcal{L}^c_{\omega_1\omega}$ *defined as the set of formulae* Ψ *of signature* σ, *for every finite relational signature* σ, *such that the following holds:*

1. Ψ is of the form $\bigvee_{p_1 \in P_1} \cdots \bigvee_{p_h \in P_h} \alpha_{p_1, \ldots, p_h}$, where:
   (a) for every $1 \leq i \leq h$, the set P_i is recursive;
   (b) for every $1 \leq i \leq h$, every element in the set P_i can be encoded with a finite string over a finite alphabet;
   (c) for every h-tuple $(p_1, \ldots, p_h) \in P_1 \times \cdots \times P_h$, the formula $\alpha_{p_1, \ldots, p_h}$ is in FO^c (see the remark after Definition 5 in Sect. 4).

2. For every σ-structure I, and denoting the set of free variables in the formula φ by $FV(\varphi)$, the set $\bigcup_{(p_1, \ldots, p_h) \in P_1 \times \cdots \times P_h} FV(\hat{\alpha}_{I, p_1, \ldots, p_h})$ must be finite. Where $\hat{\alpha}$ is as in Definition 5. That is, for every σ-structure I the resulting relation of the query expressed by Ψ must be of a finite arity.

3. There exists a TM M_Ψ which is total, and which with input $(p_1, \ldots, p_h) \in P_1 \times \cdots \times P_h$ and an encoding of a σ-structure I writes in its output tape the arity of the formula $\hat{\Psi}_I$ and the formula $\hat{\alpha}_{I, p_1, \ldots, p_h}$. Further, M_Ψ must preserve isomorphisms, so that the output does not depend on the encoding of the structure I. Thus, M_Ψ builds the formula in FO corresponding to $\alpha_{p_1, \ldots, p_h}$ for the structure I according to the Definition 5, and it also computes the arity of the output relation of the query expressed by Ψ on the structure I.

Now we define $\mathcal{L}_*^c$ as the fragment of $\mathcal{L}$ which is closed under complement, that is, for every $\Psi \in \mathcal{L}_*^c$ there is a formula equivalent to $\neg\Psi$ in $\mathcal{L}_*^c$.

Theorem 3. Let $\mathcal{L}_*^c$ be as in Definition 6, then it captures exactly the class $total(\mathcal{CQ})$.

Proof. a) $total(\mathcal{CQ}) \subseteq \mathcal{L}_*^c$: Let $f \in total(\mathcal{CQ})$. Then, by Theorem 2, there exists a formula Ψ_f which expresses f, and which can be clearly rephrased according to Definition 6. Considering that formula, it is also clear that there exists a TM M_Ψ like the one required by that Definition. b) $\mathcal{L}_*^c \subseteq total(\mathcal{CQ})$: Given a formula Ψ we build a RRM_u machine $\mathcal{M}_\Psi$ which runs the TM machines M_Ψ and $M_{\neg\Psi}$ for every h-tuple of parameters, until the arity of the two output relations is equal to the resulting arity of the evaluation of Ψ on the given input, say r, and the union of the two output relations is $(dom(I))^r$. □

Regarding the logic $\mathcal{L}_{\omega_1\omega}$ and the class $total\text{-}typed(\mathcal{CQ})$, we can also define an analogous fragment. Let's define the fragment $\mathcal{L}_*$ of the logic $\mathcal{L}_{\omega_1\omega}$ in almost the same way as in Definition 6. Just consider that for every σ-structure I the arity of the relation induced by a given $\mathcal{L}_{\omega_1\omega}$ formula Ψ of the same signature when interpreted by I, is the same. Besides, the corresponding formula $\hat{\Psi}_I$ by Definition 5 is the formula Ψ itself. So, for the TM M_Ψ we don't need the structure I as input, and it will just build the FO sub-formula $\alpha_{p_1, \ldots, p_h}$, for every input $(p_1, \ldots, p_h) \in P_1 \times \cdots \times P_h$. Then the following Corollary is straightforward.

Corollary 2. The fragment $\mathcal{L}_*$ of the logic $\mathcal{L}_{\omega_1\omega}$ captures exactly the class $total\text{-}typed(\mathcal{CQ})$.

□

Acknowledgements: My deep gratitude to Lauri Hella and Jouko Väänänen for letting me visit the Department of Mathematics of the University of Helsinki, as well as for their partial funding.

References

1. Abiteboul, S., Hull, R. Vianu, V.: Foundations of Databases. Addison-Wesley (1995)
2. Abiteboul, S., Papadimitriou, C. and Vianu, V.: The Power of the Reflective Relational Machine. Proc. of 9th IEEE Symposium on Logic in Computer Science (1994)
3. Abiteboul, S. and Vianu, V.: Generic Computation and its Complexity. Proc. of 23th ACM Symposium on Theory of Computing (1991) 209–219
4. Abiteboul, S., Vardi, M. and Vianu, V.: Fixpoint Logics, Relational Machines, and Computational Complexity. Proc. of 7th IEEE Conference on Structure in Complexity Theory (1992) 156–168
5. Abiteboul, S., Vardi, M. and Vianu, V.: Computing with Infinitary Logic. Proc. of International Conference on Database Theory (1992)
6. Balcázar, J., Díaz, J., Gabarró, J.: Structural Complexity II. Springer Verlag (1990)
7. Chandra, A. and Harel, D.: Computable Queries for Relational Data Bases. Journal of Computer and System Sciences 21 (1980) 156–178
8. Davis, M. and Weyuker, E.: Computability, Complexity and Languages. Corrected printing, Academic Press (1983)
9. Ebbinghaus, H., Flum, J.: Finite Model Theory. Springer Verlag (1995)
10. Grädel, E., Gurevich, Y.: Meta Finite Model Theory. To appear in Information and Computation. Preliminary version in Logic and Computational Complexity, International Workshop LCC'94, USA (1995)
11. Gurevich, Y.: Toward Logic Tailored for Computational Complexity. Computation and Proof Theory. Lecture Notes in Mathematics, Vol 1104. Springer-Verlag (1984) 175–216
12. Immerman, N.: Relational Queries Computable in Polynomial Time. Information and Control 68 (1986) 86–104
13. Kanellakis, P.: Elements of Relational Database Theory. Handbook of Theoretical Computer Science, Volume B. Elsevier and The MIT Press (1990) 1073–1156
14. Turull Torres, J.M.: Query Completeness, Distinguishability and Relational Machines. Proc. of the X Latin American Symposium on Mathematical Logic, Bogotá (1995)
15. Turull Torres, J.M.: Untyped Queries, Untyped Reflective Machines and Conditional Quantifiers. Research Report 146 of the Department of Mathematics of the University of Helsinki (1997)

Containment of Conjunctive Queries with Built-in Predicates with Variables and Constants over Any Ordered Domain[*]

Nieves R. Brisaboa[1], Héctor J. Hernández[2], José R. Paramá[1], and Miguel R. Penabad[1]

[1] Departamento de Computación, Universidade da Coruña, 15071 A Coruña, Spain.
{brisaboa,parama,penabad}@udc.es

[2] Laboratory for Logic, Databases, and Advanced Programming, New Mexico State University, Las Cruces, NM 88003-8001, USA.
hector@cs.nmsu.edu

Abstract. In this paper, we consider conjunctive queries with built-in predicates of the form $X < Y$, $X \leq Y$, $X = Y$, or $X \neq Y$, where X and Y are variables or constants from a totally ordered domain. We present a sufficient and necessary condition to test containment among these kinds of queries. Klug [8] left the problem open for the case when the domain is nondense, like the integers. Ullman [11] gave only a sufficient condition for the containment of conjunctive queries with built-in predicates and integer variables. Our test is based in a method that uses a new idea: the representation of an infinite number of databases by a finite set of, what we call, canonical databases, that use variables that denote uninterpreted constants.

1 Introduction

A *conjunctive query* is a safe, nonrecursive datalog rule [11] (with subgoals defined exclusively on extensional database predicates); it is equivalent to a relational algebra expression that uses the selection, projection, and Cartesian product operators. A conjunctive query Q is contained in a conjunctive query Q', denoted $Q \subseteq Q'$, if for any input database D, $Q(D)$, the output of Q when D is its input, is contained in $Q'(D)$.

Testing equivalence of conjunctive queries is a basic problem that query optimizers must be able to solve. Their main goal of finding a plan to execute a query as efficiently as possible could benefit from the ability to chose between two equivalent queries, in the very likely case that one of them is more expensive to process than the other one. Since checking equivalence of two queries can be done by testing the mutual containment of the queries involved, this latter problem has been studied. Because of its importance, the problem of testing

---

[*] This work was partially supported by CICYT grant TEL96-1390-C02 and by NSF grant HRD-9628450.

containment of two conjunctive queries has been studied extensively, and it is well understood [1,2,5]. In particular, there is an exact condition to test it.

However, testing containment of conjunctive queries with built-in predicates is a problem that has not been fully solved. Klug [8] solves it for totally ordered dense domains, but not for nondense domains such as the integers. Ibarra and Su [7] show that this problem is decidable for linear constraints, but no effective procedure to test it is given. For built-in predicates of the form $X < Y$, $X \leq Y$, $X = Y$, or $X \neq Y$ over a nondense domain, we only know a sufficient condition [11]. The following example, adapted from Example 14.7 from [11], shows where that condition fails to be necessary[1].

Example 1. Let Q_1 and Q_2 be the following conjunctive queries.
$Q_1 : p(X,Y) : -q(X,Y), r(U,V), r(V,U), X \geq Y.$
$Q_2 : p(X,Y) : -q(X,Y), r(U,V), U \leq V.$
We want to know if $Q_1 \subseteq Q_2$. The test in [11] requires a containment mapping from Q_2 to Q_1 and that the built-in predicates of Q_2 be implied by the ones in Q_1. For this couple of queries, there are two ways to map the ordinary subgoals of Q_2 to the ones in Q_1: $h_1(X) = h_2(X) = X$, $h_1(Y) = h_2(Y) = Y$, $h_1(U) = h_2(V) = U$, $h_1(V) = h_2(U) = V$. Under any of the two mappings, $h_i(U \leq V)$ is not implied by $X \geq Y$, the built-in predicate of Q_1, and thence that test cannot tell whether the containment holds even though Q_1 is contained in Q_2. □

In [4] we showed with success that the idea of *canonical databases* can be used in testing containment of conjunctive queries under bag-semantics. The canonical database set built form the body of a query Q, $CDBS(Q)$, is a finite set of databases, whose tuples contain *uninterpreted constants* that represent in a finite way the infinite number of possible databases that one has to consider in a solution to containment problems. In this paper we use those kinds of databases to present a necessary and sufficient condition to test containment of two conjunctive queries with built-in predicates. Our condition solves the open problem [8] of finding an exact test for nondense domains like the integers.

The plan for the rest of the paper is as follows. In Section 2, we give some definitions. In Section 3, we define canonical databases. In Section 4 we present our condition together with an example of its application. The last section contains our conclusions.

2 Definitions and Notation

We assume the definitions in [11] and only give some nonstandard definitions.

A *conjunctive query* is a safe, nonrecursive datalog rule [11]. We consider conjunctive queries with built-in predicates of the form $X < Y$, $X \leq Y$, $X = Y$, and $X \neq Y$, where X, Y, and Z are variables or constants from a totally ordered domain.

---

[1] The conditions required to have an exact characterization of the containment among two conjunctive queries with built-in predicates are so subtle that in Theorem 8.1 of [10] a wrong necessary condition is given.

A *database schema* is a finite set of predicate names. We assume that all predicates used in this paper are implicitly in $\mathcal{U}$, a fixed database schema, and that there is a set of constants called the *Herbrand universe*, which in this paper is any totally ordered domain. The *Herbrand base* $B_{\mathcal{U}}$ for $\mathcal{U}$ is the set of all ground atoms that can be formed by using predicate names in $\mathcal{U}$ and constants from the Herbrand universe [9].

A *database* is a finite subset of the Herbrand base. In the examples, we shall represent databases as tables showing the tuples defined on each predicate.

Two databases are *isomorphic* if they are identical up to a consistent renaming of constants. For example, the databases $D = \{ r(a,b), p(b,a), r(b,b) \}$ and $D' = \{ r(1,2), p(2,1), r(2,2) \}$ are isomorphic.

The semantics for conjunctive queries is defined in terms of assignment mappings [6]. An *assignment mapping* of a conjunctive query Q into a database D is an assignment of the constants in the facts in D to the variables of Q such that every atom in the body of Q is mapped to a fact that is in D.

Example 2. Let $Q = q(X,Y) : - r(X,U), r(V,U), r(Y,U)$, let $D = \{ r(a,b), r(c,b)\}$, and let α be the following assignment mapping of Q into D: $\alpha(X) = a$, $\alpha(U) = b$, $\alpha(V) = a$, $\alpha(Y) = c$. Then $q(a,c) \in Q(D)$, since α maps $r(X,U)$ and $r(V,U)$ to $r(a,b)$, and it maps $r(Y,U)$ to $r(c,b)$. □

3 Canonical Databases

In this section we introduce canonical databases, which are a finite representation of the infinite number of databases that can be the input to a conjunctive query. In the rest of this section, we will show an example of the canonical databases set for a query Q, denoted by $CDBS(Q)$; an algorithm that builds $CDBS(Q)$ for any conjunctive query Q; and how to apply a conjunctive query to a canonical database

3.1 Example of Building $CDBS(Q)$

The objective of building the set of canonical databases for a specific query Q is to cover all the possible mappings between that query and any database. The next example illustrates this. After the example, we give the formal definition of $CDBS(Q)$.

Example 3. Let us consider the query $Q = q(X,Y,Z) : - r(X,U), r(U,Z), p(U,Y), X > Y$. We shall use the atoms in the body of Q to build $CDBS(Q)$. To do that it is necessary to consider all the different possible mappings of variables in Q to any database. We use the letters A, B, C, D (which represent uninterpreted constants) to identify the values to which the variables in Q could be mapped.

The following cases list the different possible mappings; each case shows several d_i's, where each d_i represents an element of $CDBS(Q)$. Each canonical database d_i has attached two sets of constraints. The first set contains constraints to enforce that each uninterpreted constant is different of any other in $d_i{}^2$. The second set contains a constraint for each built-in predicate in Q, but the variables in the built-in predicates are transformed in the corresponding uninterpreted constants. These constraints will be denoted by $constraints(d_i)$; for d_1, $constraints(d_1) = (A \neq B \wedge A \neq C \wedge A \neq D \wedge B \neq C \wedge B \neq D \wedge C \neq D) \wedge (\theta_1(X) > \theta_1(Y))$; for d_2, $constraints(d_2) = A \neq B \wedge (\theta_2(X) = A) > (\theta_2(Y) = A)$, which means that such a database is not consistent with the constraints; d_3, d_6, d_9, and d_{15} are also not consistent with their constraints and, hence, it is not possible to build an extensional database isomorphic to them.

Case 1: Each variable in Q is mapped to a different value. Then a canonical database, like the one shown on Table 1, is generated.

Table 1. Canonical Database for Case 1 of Example 3.1

NAME	CDB		MAPPING	$constraints(d_1)$
	r	p		$A > B \wedge$
d_1	(A,D) (D,C)	(D,B)	$\theta_1(X) = A;\quad \theta_1(Y) = B;$ $\theta_1(Z) = C;\quad \theta_1(U) = D$	$A \neq B \wedge\ A \neq C \wedge\ A \neq D \wedge$ $B \neq C \wedge\ B \neq D \wedge\ C \neq D$

Case 2: Three variables are mapped to the same value, the other one is mapped to a different value. Table 2 shows the canonical databases for this case.

Table 2. Canonical Databases for Case 2 of Example 3.1

NAME	CDB		MAPPING	$constraints(d_i)$
	r	p		
d_2	(A,B) (B,A)	(B,A)	$\theta_2(X) = \theta_2(Y) = \theta_2(Z) = A;\quad \theta_2(U) = B$	$A > A \wedge A \neq B$ d_2 is not consistent
d_3	(A,A) (A,B)	(A,A)	$\theta_3(X) = \theta_3(Y) = \theta_3(U) = A;\quad \theta_3(Z) = B$	$A > A \wedge A \neq B$ d_3 is not consistent
d_4	(A,A)	(A,B)	$\theta_4(X) = \theta_4(Z) = \theta_4(U) = A;\quad \theta_4(Y) = B$	$A > B \wedge A \neq B$
d_5	(B,A) (A,A)	(A,A)	$\theta_5(Y) = \theta_5(Z) = \theta_5(U) = A;\quad \theta_5(X) = B$	$B > A \wedge A \neq B$

Case 3: Two variables are mapped to the same value and the other two are mapped to another value. Table 3 shows the three canonical databases generated in this case.

---

^{2} There are canonical databases for each of the possible equalities among the variables in Q.

Table 3. Canonical Databases for Case 3 of Example 3.1

NAME	CDB		MAPPING	constraints(d_i)
	r	p		
d_6	(A,B) (B,B)	(B,A)	$\theta_6(X) = \theta_6(Y) = A;\quad \theta_6(Z) = \theta_6(U) = B$	$A > A \wedge A \neq B$ d_6 is not consistent
d_7	(A,B) (B,A)	(B,B)	$\theta_7(X) = \theta_7(Z) = A;\quad \theta_7(Y) = \theta_7(U) = B$	$A > B \wedge A \neq B$
d_8	(A,A) (A,B)	(A,B)	$\theta_8(X) = \theta_8(U) = A;\quad \theta_8(Y) = \theta_8(Z) = B$	$A > B \wedge A \neq B$

Case 4: Two variables are mapped to the same value and the other two are mapped to different values. The canonical databases generated in this case are shown on Table 4.

Table 4. Canonical Databases for Case 4 of Example 3.1

NAME	CDB		MAPPING	constraints(d_i)
	r	p		
d_9	(A,C) (C,B)	(C,A)	$\theta_9(X) = \theta_9(Y) = A;$ $\theta_9(Z) = B;\quad \theta_9(U) = C$	$A > A \wedge$ $A \neq B \wedge A \neq C \wedge B \neq C$ d_9 is not consistent
d_{10}	(A,C) (C,A)	(C,B)	$\theta_{10}(X) = \theta_{10}(Z) = A;$ $\theta_{10}(Y) = B;\quad \theta_{10}(U) = C$	$A > B \wedge$ $A \neq B \wedge A \neq C \wedge B \neq C$
d_{11}	(A,A) (A,C)	(A,B)	$\theta_{11}(X) = \theta_{11}(U) = A;$ $\theta_{11}(Y) = B;\quad \theta_{11}(Z) = C$	$A > B \wedge$ $A \neq B \wedge A \neq C \wedge B \neq C$
d_{12}	(B,C) (C,A)	(C,A)	$\theta_{12}(Y) = \theta_{12}(Z) = A;$ $\theta_{12}(X) = B;\quad \theta_{12}(U) = C$	$B > A \wedge$ $A \neq B \wedge A \neq C \wedge B \neq C$
d_{13}	(B,A) (A,C)	(A,A)	$\theta_{13}(Y) = \theta_{13}(U) = A;$ $\theta_{13}(X) = B;\quad \theta_{13}(Z) = C$	$B > A \wedge$ $A \neq B \wedge A \neq C \wedge B \neq C$
d_{14}	(B,A) (A,A)	(A,C)	$\theta_{14}(Z) = \theta_{14}(U) = A;$ $\theta_{14}(X) = B;\quad \theta_{14}(Y) = C$	$B > C \wedge$ $A \neq B \wedge A \neq C \wedge B \neq C$

Case 5: The four variables are mapped to the same value. Table 5 shows the canonical database generated in this case.

Thus there are 15 canonical databases for Q, but not all of them are consistent with their constraints. Notice that not all the possible canonical databases are required. For example, the mapping of X and Y to B and U and Z to D would produce a canonical database that has the same equalities as d_6 (it would be isomorphic to d_6). With four variables there are 256 different possible canonical databases, but there are only 15 different (nonisomorphic) ones. In [3], the reader

Table 5. Canonical Database for Case 5 of Example 3.1

NAME	CDB		MAPPING	constraints(d_i)
	r	p		
d_{15}	(A,A)	(A,A)	$\theta_{15}(X) = \theta_{15}(U) = \theta_{15}(Y) = \theta_{15}(Z) = A$	$A > A$ d_{15} is not consistent

can find a procedure to compute the number of canonical databases in terms of the number of variables in the conjunctive query. □

3.2 Algorithm to Build *CDBS(Q)*

Definition of Canonical Databases

Before describing the algorithm it is necessary to define some concepts.
Let Q be a conjunctive query. Then, $db(Q)$ is the set of atoms

$$db(Q) = \{p_i(V_1, \cdots, V_{k_i}) \mid p_i(V_1, \cdots, V_{k_i}) \text{ is an ordinary atom in the body of } Q\}$$

We shall use $db(Q)$ to construct $CDBS(Q)$. The idea is to define below a set of mappings that will be applied to $db(Q)$: for each mapping that we define, an element of $CDBS(Q)$ will be generated along with the restriction that all its variables are distinct. The mappings will be defined on the set of variables found in the atoms in $db(Q)$. We define these next.

Let $V_Q = \langle V_1, \cdots, V_q \rangle$ be an ordering of all the variables that appear in the atoms in $db(Q)$. Let $A_Q = \{A_1, \cdots, A_q\}$ be q new, distinct identifiers ($A_i \neq A_j$ if $i \neq j, 1 \leq i, j \leq q$); they represent uninterpreted constants. We now define the mappings mentioned above, called Q-mappings, from V_Q to A_Q. A Q-mapping θ is a q-tuple $\theta = (A_{i_1}, ..., A_{i_q})$ where $1 \leq i_1, i_2, ..., i_q \leq q$. This tuple denotes the mapping $\theta(V_1) = A_{i_1}, ..., \theta(V_q) = A_{i_q}$. Thus Q-mappings are shorthands for the mappings we need to use to produce the canonical databases.

These Q-mappings can be applied to an atom or to $db(Q)$. Let θ be a Q-mapping. Let $p_i(U_1, ..., U_{r_i})$ be an atom. The application of θ to $p_i(U_1, ..., U_{r_i})$ is defined as $\theta(p_i(U_1, ..., U_{r_i})) = p_i(\theta(U_1), ..., \theta(U_{r_i}))$. The application of θ to $db(Q)$ is defined as the canonical database $\theta(db(Q)) = \{p_i(\theta(U_1), \ldots, \theta(U_{r_i})) \mid p_i(U_1, \ldots, U_{r_i}) \in db(Q)\}$.

The following example demonstrates these definitions.

Example 4. Let us consider the query $Q = q(X, Y, Z) : -r(X, U), r(U, Z), p(U, Y), X \geq Y$. Then $V_Q = \langle X, Y, Z, U \rangle$ is an ordering of the variables in Q; and $A_Q = \{A_1, A_2, A_3, A_4\}$; $db(Q)$ in this example is $\{r(X, U), r(U, Z), p(U, Y)\}$. Let the Q-mapping θ be (A_4, A_3, A_4, A_4); θ denotes the mapping $\theta(X) = \theta(Z) = \theta(U) = A_4$ and $\theta(Y) = A_3$. Then $\theta(db(Q)) = \{r(A_4, A_4), p(A_4, A_3)\}$; with this database the constraints $A_3 \neq A_4$ and $A_3 \leq A_4$ will be associated. We will show later how to deal with this pairs of constraints. □

Isomorphic Q-mappings, which are used to define a minimal number of canonical databases, are defined as follows. Two Q-mappings $\theta_1 = (A_{i_1}, ..., A_{i_q})$ and $\theta_2 = (A_{j_1}, ..., A_{j_q})$ are *isomorphic* if there are two mappings γ_1 and γ_2 (from A_Q to A_Q) such that $(\gamma_1(A_{i_1}), ..., \gamma_1(A_{i_q})) = \theta_2$, and $(\gamma_2(A_{j_1}), ..., \gamma_2(A_{j_q})) = \theta_1$.

Example 5. The Q-mapping $\beta = (A_3, A_3, A_1, A_3)$ is isomorphic to $\alpha = (A_4, A_4, A_3, A_4)$; and (A_1, A_1, A_1, A_1) is isomorphic to (A_2, A_2, A_2, A_2). □

We now define some concepts associated to the canonical databases.

Let Q_1 be the following conjunctive query. $Q_1 : I : -J_1, \cdots, J_q, K_1, \cdots, K_n$, where the K_i's are the built-in predicates of Q_1. Then for all d in $CDBS(Q_1)$, we define:

1. θ_d to be the Q-mapping that we used to build d (from Q_1);
2. t_d to be the fact $\theta_d(I)$;
3. *constraints*(d) to be the constraints that d has to satisfy, i.e: $\theta_d(K_1 \wedge \cdots \wedge K_n)$ $\wedge (A_i \neq A_j, \forall i, j, 1 \leq i \neq j \leq q_d)$, where $A_1, ..., A_{q_d}$ are the variables used to construct d.

Algorithm to build $CDBS(Q)$

Using the above definitions, we can now show an algorithm that builds the canonical databases of Q.

Algorithm to build $CDBS(Q)$
Input: $Q = q(X) : -p_1(X_1), ..., p_n(X_n), K_1(Y_1), ..., K_m(Y_m)$,
        where the K_i's are the built-in predicates.
Output: $CDBS(Q)$
Method:
Step 1: Let $db(Q) = \{p_1(X_1), ..., p_n(X_n)\}$;
        Let $V_Q = \langle V_1, ..., V_q \rangle$ be an ordering of all the variables that appear in $db(Q)$;
        Let $A_Q = \{A_1, ..., A_q\}$ be q new, distinct (uninterpreted) constants
        $(A_i \neq A_j,$ if $i \neq j, 1 \leq i, j \leq q)$;
        Let $j = 1$;
        Let $Mappings = \emptyset$;
        //
Step 2: // Definition of Q-mappings (using C syntax).
        for$(i_1 = 1; i_1 \leq q; i_1 + +)$
          for$(i_2 = 1; i_2 \leq q; i_2++)$

            $\vdots$

            for$(i_q = 1; i_q \leq q; i_q++)\{$
            $\theta_j = (A_{i_1}, A_{i_2}, ..., A_{i_q})$;
            if (there is no Q-mapping in $Mappings$ that is isomorphic to $\theta_j)\{$
                $Mappings = Mappings \cup \{\theta_j\}$;
                $j++$;
            $\}$
        $\}$
Step 3: // Now using the Q-mappings we generate the $j - 1$ databases $d_i \in CDBS(Q)$

```
//
    for(l = 1; l < j; l++)
        if( θ_l(K_1(Y_1)) ∧ ··· ∧ θ_l(K_m(Y_m)) is unsatisfiable CDB_l = ∅;
        else CDB_l = θ_l(db(Q));
```

Step 4: return $\{CDB_1, ..., CDB_{j-1}\}$;
Each CDB_i has attached to it the constraints
$$(\theta_i(K_1(Y_1)) \wedge \cdots \wedge \theta_i(K_m(Y_m))) \wedge (A_j \neq A_k, \forall j, k \; 1 \le j \neq k \le q)$$

3.3 Applying Q_2 to a Canonical Database

Our method to test whether $Q_1 \subseteq Q_2$ first builds $CDBS(Q_1)$, the set of canonical databases, d_i, for Q_1, and then it applies Q_2 to these databases. Let us describe how to apply a query (Q_2) to a canonical database d_i.

First, we have to define what it means that a tuple, defined on the variables used to construct canonical databases, belongs to $Q_2(d)$, where d is a canonical database in $CDBS(Q_1)$.

Definition 1. *Let d be a database in $CDBS(Q_1)$. We say that $t \in Q_2(d)$ if for all ground substitutions α, defined on the variables in d, $\alpha(t) \in Q_2(\alpha(d))$.*

The following lemma gives a condition to test membership of a tuple in $Q_2(d)$.

Lemma 1. *Let Q_1 and Q_2 of the form [11]*
$Q_1 : I :\text{-} J_1 \wedge J_2 \wedge \cdots \wedge J_l \wedge K_1 \wedge K_2 \wedge \cdots \wedge K_n.$
$Q_2 : H :\text{-} G_1 \wedge G_2 \wedge \cdots \wedge G_r \wedge F_1 \wedge F_2 \wedge \cdots \wedge F_m.$
where J_i's and G_i's are ordinary subgoals, and K_i's and F_i's are the built-in predicates.
Let $d \in CDBS(Q_1)$. Then $t \in Q_2(d)$ if and only if

1. *There are assignment mappings $\tau_1, \ldots, \tau_k$ from the ordinary subgoals of Q_2 to d such that $\tau_1(H) = \cdots = \tau_k(H) = t$, and*
2. *The formula $F = constraints(d) \wedge \neg(\tau_1(F_1) \wedge \cdots \wedge \tau_1(F_m)) \wedge \cdots \wedge \neg(\tau_k(F_1) \wedge \cdots \wedge \tau_k(F_m))$ is not satisfiable.*

Proof. only-if part: Condition 1 must be true, otherwise t cannot be in $Q_2(d)$. Now by contradiction we prove that condition 2 is also necessary. Consider all such assignment mappings from Q_2 to d. Suppose that F is satisfiable. Then there is a ground substitution α for the variables of F, such that for all j, $1 \le j \le k$, $\alpha(\tau_j(F_1) \wedge \cdots \wedge \tau_j(F_m))$ is *false*. Using the constants in the substitution, we can define a database D such that $\alpha(t) \notin Q_2(D)$. Thus, $t \notin Q_2(d)$.
if-part: Assume conditions 1 and 2 hold. Therefore, F is not satisfiable. Since F is not satisfiable, for any substitution α that grounds d, there is a $j, 1 \le j \le k$ such that $\alpha(\tau_j(F_1) \wedge \cdots \wedge \tau_j(F_m))$ is *true*; that is, the built-in predicates in Q_2 always hold under this condition. Then for any such α, $\alpha(t) \in Q_2(\alpha(d))$, and hence this part of the lemma follows. □

The following example illustrates the test of membership of a tuple in $Q_2(D)$.

Example 6. Let Q_1 and Q_2 be as defined in Example 1.

One of the canonical databases that we build from Q_1 is $d = \{q(A,B),$ $r(C,D),\ r(D,C)\}$, where A, B, C, D are uninterpreted constants that satisfy $constraints(d) = (A \neq B) \wedge (A \neq C) \wedge (A \neq D) \wedge (B \neq C) \wedge (B \neq D) \wedge (C \neq D) \wedge (A \geq B)$; this represents a situation where X, Y, U, and V are mapped to different values in the database; another canonical database, $d' = \{q(A,A), r(A,A)\}$, will capture the case when the variables of Q_1 are mapped to the same constant; for this query there are 15 different canonical databases.

For this canonical database d, Q_2 can obtain the tuple $p(A,B)$. There are two ways to map the ordinary subgoals of Q_2 to d to obtain $p(A,B)$: $h_1(X) = h_2(X) = A$, $h_1(Y) = h_2(Y) = B$, $h_1(U) = h_2(V) = C$, $h_1(V) = h_2(U) = D$. Then we use both mappings to test whether $p(A,B)$ belongs to $Q_2(d)$, checking if the following formula is not satisfiable:

$$constraints(d) \wedge \neg(h_1(U \leq V)) \wedge \neg(h_2(U \leq V))$$

If it is not satisfiable, and since we assume that d satisfies $constraints(d)$, it means that at least one of the two constraints $(h_1(U \leq V))$, $(h_2(U \leq V))$ is true.

The above formula is not satisfiable, since

$$constraints(d) \wedge \neg(h_1(U \leq V)) \wedge \neg(h_2(U \leq V))$$

$$=$$

$$constraints(d) \wedge \neg(h_1(U) \leq h_1(V)) \wedge \neg(h_2(U) \leq h_2(V))$$

$$=$$

$$constraints(d) \wedge \neg(C \leq D) \wedge \neg(D \leq C)$$

$$\equiv$$

$$constraints(d) \wedge (C > D) \wedge (D > C)$$

The unsatisfiability of the formula means that either $C \leq D$ or $D \leq C$ is true when we map Q_2 to any grounding of d. Therefore $p(A,B) \in Q_2(d)$. $\qquad\square$

3.4   Testing the Satisfiability of a Formula

The full version of this paper provides the complete and detailed algorithm to test the satisfiability of a formula F of the form:

$$F = constraints(d) \wedge \neg(\tau_1(F_1) \wedge \cdots \wedge \tau_1(F_m)) \wedge \cdots \wedge \neg(\tau_k(F_1) \wedge \cdots \wedge \tau_k(F_m)) \ .$$

Basically, the algorithm performs the following steps:

1. Normalize the formula, obtaining an equivalent formula in Conjunctive Normal Form without negated atoms.
2. Build a directed graph for each element of the conjunction in the formula. These graphs are similar to the ones produced by the algorithm in [11].

3. Check the satisfiability of each graph. For a graph to be satisfiable, it cannot have cycles of solid arcs and, if the variables range over nondense domains, we must be able to find an ordering of the variables that satisfy the constraints represented by the graph.
4. If none of the graphs is satisfiable, the formula F is unsatisfiable, otherwise it is satisfiable.

4 Main Theorem

The following result is crucial for our test.

Lemma 2. *Let* $Q : I : -J_1, \cdots, J_q, K_1, \cdots, K_n$ *be a conjunctive query, where the* K_i *'s are its built-in predicates. Let* τ *be an assignment mapping of* Q *into a database* D, *such that* $(\tau(K_1) \wedge \cdots \wedge \tau(K_n))$ *is true. Let* $sd = \{\tau(J_1), \cdots, \tau(J_q)\}$; *i.e.,* sd *is the subset of* D *on which* τ *maps the ordinary subgoals of* Q. *Then* sd *is isomorphic to a database* d, *where* $d \in CDBS(Q)$.

Proof. The reader can find a complete proof of this lemma in [3,4]. It takes advantage of the way the canonical databases are built. Given that $CDBS(Q)$ covers all the possible inequalities among variables, the subset sd of D obtained by a mapping of Q will be isomorphic to a canonical database.   □

The following theorem shows our condition to test containment of two conjunctive queries with built-in predicates.

Theorem 1. $Q_1 \subseteq Q_2$ *if and only if* $\forall d \in CDBS(Q_1)$ ($t_d \in Q_2(d)$).

Proof. only-if-part: By contradiction. Assume that there is a d, $d \in CDBS(Q_1)$, such that $t_d \notin Q_2(d)$. Then, by definition 1, there exists an α such that $\alpha(t_d) \notin Q_2(\alpha(d))$. Since, by construction of each $d \in CDBS(Q_1)$, $t_d \in Q_1(d)$, then $\alpha(t_d) \in Q_1(\alpha(d))$. Therefore, $Q_1 \not\subseteq Q_2$,
if-part: Let D be an arbitrary database. Let $t \in Q_1(D)$. We have to prove that $t \in Q_2(D)$.

We have that $t \in Q_1(d)$, so there exists an assignment mapping θ that maps the ordinary predicates of Q_1 to some atoms in D, such that $\theta(I) = t$.

Let $sd = \{\theta(J_1), \cdots, \theta(J_q)\}$, that is, sd is the subset of facts in D mapped by the ordinary subgoals in the body of Q_1 through the assignment mapping θ. By Lemma 2, sd is isomorphic to a database d in $CDBS(Q_1)$. Let α be the mapping that shows that isomorphism. Then $\alpha(t_d) = t$ and $\alpha(d) = sd$. From hypothesis, $t_d \in Q_2(d)$. Then $t \in Q_2(sd)$. Hence $t \in Q_2(D)$.

So for any database D and for any t in $Q_1(D)$, $Q_2(D)$ contains t. Therefore $Q_1 \subseteq Q_2$.   □

4.1 Testing the Containment of Conjunctive Queries with Built-in Predicates

Our procedure to test the containment of two conjunctive queries with built-in predicates Q_1 and Q_2 consists of the following steps:

1. Build $CDBS(Q_1)$, using the algorithm shown in Section 3.2.
2. Apply Q_2 to all consistent databases d in $CDBS(Q_1)$. Using the different mappings that can reach d from Q_2, and using also $constraints(d)$, build the formula F corresponding to each database.
3. Test if $t_d \in Q_2(d)$ for all d in $CDBS(Q_1)$. To do so, it is only needed to check the unsatisfiability of every formula F. If all formulas are not satisfiable, then $Q_1 \subseteq Q_2$.

Let us illustrate the procedure with an example:

Example 7. Let Q_1 and Q_2 be the following queries:
$Q_1 : q(X,Y) : -p(X,Y), p(Y,Z), X \geq Y, Y > Z$
$Q_2 : q(X,Y) : -p(X,Y), p(X,W), X > W$

There is only one mapping τ from Q_2 to Q_1: $\tau(X) = X; \tau(Y) = Y; \tau(W) = Y$. Using the results from Ullman [10, 11], it is not possible to imply $\tau(X > W)$ from the built-in predicates in Q_1, $X \geq Y$ and $Y > Z$. Considering X, Y and Z belonging to a nondense domain like the integers, the results of [8] are not useful either.

However, applying our procedure, which is summarized in Table 6, we can conclude that $Q_1 \subseteq Q_2$. The canonical databases that are possible, consistent with their constraints, are d_2 and d_5. We can apply assignment mappings from Q_2 to each database, and the resulting formulas are not satisfiable. By Lemma 1, we can conclude that $t_{d_2} \in Q_2(d_2)$ and $t_{d_5} \in Q_2(d_5)$. Therefore, we have that for all (consistent) d in $CDBS(Q_1)$, $t_d \in Q_2(d)$. Then, using Theorem 1, we can conclude that $Q_1 \subseteq Q_2$. □

Table 6. Example of our procedure

Q-map.		$CDBS(Q)$	t_d	Mappings	Formula
X Y Z	d_i	p	p		
A A A	d_1	AA			
		$A \geq A \wedge A > A$		d_1 is not consistent	
A A B	d_2	AA	AA	$\tau_1(X) = \tau_1(Y) = A;$	$A \neq B \wedge A > B \wedge$
		AB		$\tau_1(W) = B$	$\neg(A > B) \wedge \neg(A > A)$
		$A \neq B \wedge A \geq A \wedge A > B$		$\tau_2(X) = \tau_2(Y) = A$	*(Not satisfiable)*
				$\tau_2(W) = A$	
A B A	d_3	AB			
		BA		d_3 is not consistent	
		$A \neq B \wedge A \geq B \wedge B > A$			
B A A	d_4	BA			
		AA		d_4 is not consistent	
		$A \neq B \wedge B \geq A \wedge A > A$			
A B C	d_5	AB	AB	$\tau_1(X) = A;$	$A \neq B \wedge B \neq C \wedge$
		BC		$\tau_1(Y) = \tau_1(W) = B$	$A \neq C \wedge A \geq B \wedge$
		$A \neq B \wedge B \neq C \wedge A \neq C$			$B > C \wedge \neg(A > B)$
		$\wedge A \geq B \wedge B > C$			*(Not satisfiable)*

5 Conclusions

We have given an exact characterization to test containment of conjunctive queries with built-in predicates. This solves the long-standing open problem of finding an exact characterization to test this kind of containment over nondense domains.

This result is possible due to our definition and use of Canonical Databases. It is a tool that clearly helps in problems related to containment of queries, as it was already shown in [3, 4] where they had been used to test containment of conjunctive queries under bag-semantics.

References

1. A.V. Aho, Y. Sagiv, and J.D. Ullman. "Equivalence of Relational Expressions". *SIAM J. of Computing 8:2*, pp. 218-246.
2. A.V. Aho, Y. Sagiv, and J.D. Ullman. "Efficient Optimization of a Class of Relational Queries". *ACM TODS 4:4*, pp. 435-454.
3. Brisaboa, N.R., "Inclusión de Consultas Conjuntivas en la semántica de bolsas", Ph.D. Dissertation, Departamento de Computación, Facultade de Informática, Universidade da Coruña, A Coruña, Spain, May 1997.
4. Brisaboa, N.R., Hernández, H.J. Testing bag-containment of conjunctive queries, *Acta Informatica*, 34, 1997. Springer-Verlag, Munich, Germany,pp. 557-578.
5. A.K. Chandra and P.M. Merlin. "Optimal implementation of conjunctive queries in relational databases". *Proc. of 9th ACM Symposium on Theory of Computing*, New York, NY, 1977, pp. 77-90.
6. S. Chaudhuri, M Vardi. "Optimization of Real Conjunctive Queries," *Proc. Twelfth ACM SIGACT-SIGMOD-SIGART Symp. on Principles of Database Systems*, Washington, DC, May 1993, pp. 59-70.
7. O. Ibarra, J. Su. "On the containment and equivalence of database queries with linear constraints".*PODS'97*, Tucson, Arizona, 1997,pp. 32–43.
8. Klug, A., "On conjunctive queries containing inequalities," J. ACM **35**:1, 1988, pp. 146-160.
9. J. W. Lloyd. *Foundations of Logic Programming*, Second, Extended edition, Springer-Verlag 1987.
10. Ullman, J. D.: Principles of Database Systems, Second Edition, Computer Science Press, 1982.
11. Ullman, J. D.: Principles of Database and Knowledge-base Systems, Vols. 1-2, Computer Science Press, 1988-1989.

Using Queries with Multi-directional Functions for Numerical Database Applications

Staffan Flodin, Kjell Orsborn, and Tore Risch

Department of Computer and Information Science
Linköping University, Sweden
stafl@ida.liu.se, kjeor@ida.liu.se, torri@ida.liu.se

Abstract. Object-oriented database management systems are often motivated by their support for new emerging application areas such as computer-aided design and analysis systems. The object-oriented data model is well suited for managing the data complexity and representation needs of such applications. We have built a system for finite element analysis using an object-relational database management system. Our application domain needs customized numerical data representations and an object-oriented data model extended with multi-methods where several arguments are used in type resolution. To efficiently process queries involving domain functions in this environment without having to copy data to the application, support is needed for queries calling multi-methods with any configuration of bound or unbound arguments, called multi-directional functions. We show how to model multi-directional functions views containing matrix algebra operators, how to process queries to these views, and how to execute these queries in presence of late binding.

1   Introduction

Object-oriented database management systems (OODBMSs) [8][3][34] are often motivated by applications such as systems for computer-aided design and analysis [4][5][19]. The object-oriented data model is well suited for managing the complexity of the data in such applications. We have built a system for finite-element analysis (FEA) storing numerical data in an object-relational DBMS [25][26][27]. The performance requirements on the numerical data access in an FEA model are very high, and special methods have been developed for efficient representation of, e.g., matrices used in FEA. For instance, a fundamental component in an FEA system is a equation solving sub-system where one is interested in solving linear equation systems such as $K \times a = f$ where a is sought while K and f are known. Special representation methods and special equation solving methods must be applied that are dependent on the properties of the matrices. To get good performance in queries involving domain operators it is desirable to store both domain-oriented data representations and functions in the database. It is desirable to be able to evaluate the functions in the database server in order to avoid data shipping to the client. For this modern Object-Relational DBMS therefore provide User Defined Functions (UDFs) [20].

View in an object-oriented data model can be represented as functions (or methods) defined using queries containing operators from the domain, e.g. for matrix algebra [23]. Such *derived functions* expressed by side-effect free queries have a high abstraction level which is problem oriented and reusable. Query optimization techniques can be used to optimize such function definitions. To represent the model, an object-relational DBMS with extensible storage representation and query optimization is needed. The query optimizer needs to have special optimization methods and cost formulae for the FEA domain operators.

In pure object-oriented models the function (method) invocation is based on the *message-passing* paradigm where only the receiver of the message (the first argument of a function) participate in *type resolution*, i.e. selecting which *resolvent* (variant of an overloaded method or function name) to apply. The message-passing style of method invocation restricts the way in which relations between objects can be expressed [2].

In order to model a computational domain such as the FEA domain it is desirable to also support *multi-methods* [2] corresponding to functions with more than one argument. With multi-methods all arguments are used in type resolution. Thus, by extending the data model to incorporate multi-methods e.g. matrix operators applied on various kinds of matrix representations can be expressed in a natural way. In Sect. 4 we show how matrix operators are modeled as multi-methods in our application.

```
DECLARE mx1 AS matrix_type_1
DECLARE mx2 AS matrix_type_2
SELECT x FROM Matrix x
         WHERE mx1 * x = mx2 AND x IN f();
```

Fig. 1. A sample query exemplifying a multi-directional method

High level declarative queries with method calls do not specify exactly how a function is to be invoked in the query. We will show that *multi-directional functions* are needed in the database query language [15][16] for processing of queries involving inverses of functions. A function in the database query language is multi-directional if, for an arbitrary function invocation $m(x) = y$, it is possible to retrieve those arguments x that are mapped by the function m to a particular result, y. Multi-directional functions can furthermore have more than one argument. This ability provides the user with a declarative and flexible query language where the user does not have to specify explicitly how a function should be called. To exemplify a multi-directional function, consider the AMOSQL [17] query in Fig. 1 that retrieves those matrices which, when multiplied by the matrix bound to the variable mx1, equals the matrix bound to the variable mx2.

This query is a declarative specification of the retrieval of the matrix x from the result set of the function f() where x solves the equation system mx1 * x = mx2 (mx1 and mx2 are assumed given). It is the task of the query processor to find an efficient execution strategy for the declarative specification, e.g. by using the inverse of the * method (matrix multiplication) that first solves the equation system to get a value for x. An alternative execution strategy is to go through all matrixes x in $f(x)$

and multiply them with mx1 to compare the result with mx2. The first strategy is clearly better.

To provide a query optimizer with all possible execution plans it must be able to break encapsulation to expand the definitions of all referenced views [32]; thus the optimization is a *global optimization* method. In global optimization the implementations of all referenced views are substituted by their calls at *compile time*. For ORDBMS this means that the definitions of derived functions must be expanded before queries can be fully optimized, a process called *revelation* [12]. With revelation the query optimizer is allowed break encapsulation while the user still cannot access encapsulated data.

The object-oriented features include *inheritance, operator overloading, operator overriding* and *encapsulation* [3]. The combination of inheritance in the type hierarchy and operator overriding results in the requirement of having to select at run-time which resolvent to apply, i.e. *late binding*.

A function which is late bound obstructs global optimization since the resolvent cannot be selected until *run-time*. This may cause indexes and other properties that are important to achieve good performance to be hidden for the optimizer inside function definitions and remain unused during execution. Thus, late bound functions may cause severe performance degradation if not special query processing techniques are applied. This is why providing a solution that enables optimization of late bound functions is an important issue in the context of a database [12].

A special problem is the combination of late bound functions and multi-directional functions. This problem is addressed in [16] where late bound function calls are represented by a special algebra operator, DTR, in the execution plan. The DTR operator is defined in terms of the *possible resolvents*, i.e. the resolvents eligible for execution at run-time. Each resolvent is optimized with respect to the enclosing query plan. The cost model and selectivity prediction of the DTR operator is defined in terms of the costs and selectivities of the possible resolvents. The DTR-approach in [16] has been generalized to handle multi-methods [15].

In this paper we show, by using excerpts from our FEA application, that extending a pure object-oriented data model with multi-directional functions results in a system where complex applications can be modeled easily compared to modeling within a pure object-oriented data model. We furthermore show how such queries are translated into an algebraic representation for evaluation.

2   Related Work

Modeling matrix computations using the object-oriented paradigm has been addressed in e.g. [28][29]. In [21] an algebra for primitive matrix operations is proposed. None of those papers address late binding, multi-methods, or multi-directional functions. We will show the benefits of having these features when modeling complex applications.

OODBMSs have been the subject of extensive research during the last decade, e.g. [3][4][5][34]. Several OO query languages [9][24][23] have been proposed. However, to the best of our knowledge processing queries with multi-directional functions in OODBMSs has not yet been addressed.

Multi-methods require generalized type resolution methods compared to the type resolution of pure object-oriented methods [1][2]. In the database context good query optimization is another important issue.

Advanced applications, such as our FEA application, require domain dependent data representations of matrixes and an extensible object-relational query optimizer [33] to process queries over these representations. For accessing domain specific physical representations we have extended the technique of multi-directional foreign functions described in [22].

In [15][16] the optimization of queries with multi-directional late bound functions in a pure object-oriented model is addressed and the DTR operator is defined and proven to be efficient. In this paper that approach is generalized to multi-methods.

3   Background

In this section we first give a short introduction to the data model we use. Then properties of multi-directional functions are discussed followed by an overview of the issues related to late binding.

3.1   The Functional Data Model

The functional data model DAPLEX [31] has the notions of *entity* and *function*. A function is a mapping from entities to sets of entities. Based on DAPLEX the AMOS [13] data model contains *stored functions* and *derived functions*. Stored functions store properties of objects and correspond to attributes in the relational model and the object-oriented model. Derived functions are used to derive new properties which are not explicitly stored in the database. A derived function is defined by a query and corresponds to a view in the relational model and to a function (method) in the object-oriented model. In addition to stored and derived functions AMOS also has *foreign functions* which are defined using an auxiliary programming language such as C++ and then introduced into the query language [22]. In Fig. 1 the operator * is implemented by foreign functions. The only way to access properties of objects is through functions, thus functions provide *encapsulation* of the objects in the database.

3.2   Multi-directional Functions

Multi-directional functions are functions which may be called with several different configurations of bound or unbound arguments and result, called *binding-patterns*. The query compiler must be capable of generating an optimal execution plan choosing among the possible binding-patterns for each multi-directional function. Sometimes such an execution plan may not exist and the query processor must then report the query as being unexecutable.

To denote which binding-pattern a function is called with, the arguments, a_i, and result, r, are annotated with b or f meaning bound or free as a^b_i or a^f_i if a_i is bound or free, respectively. In Fig. 1 the function * is called with its second argument unbound and with the first argument and the result bound. Thus, the call to * in that example will be denoted as $x^b \times y^f \rightarrow r^b$.

```
CREATE FUNCTION times(SymmetricMx x, ColumnMx y) -> ColumnMx r AS
            MULTIDIRECTIONAL
            'bbf' FOREIGN MatrixMultiplication COST MultCost
            'bfb' FOREIGN GaussDecomposition COST GaussCost;
```

Fig. 2. Creation of a multi-directional foreign function

Recall the three types of functions in the AMOS data model; stored, foreign and derived functions. Stored functions are made multi-directional by having the system automatically derive access plans for all binding-pattern configurations. Derived functions are made multi-directional by accessing their definitions and finding efficient execution plans for binding-patterns when needed. For multi-directional foreign functions the programmer has to explicitly assign each binding-pattern configuration an implementation, as illustrated in Fig. 2.

```
SELECT x FROM ColumnMx x WHERE mx1 * x = mx2;
```

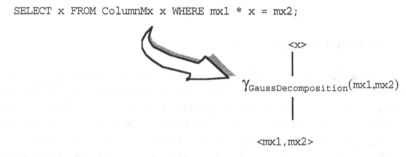

Fig. 3. Multi-directional function execution

In Fig. 2 the function `times` (implements *) is defined for two arguments and made multi-directional by defining which implementation to use for a certain binding-pattern. For $times(a^b, b^f) \rightarrow r^b$ the foreign function definition `GaussDecomposition` implements `times`, while `MatrixMultiplication` will be used for $times(a^b, b^b) \rightarrow r^f$. The functions `GaussDecomposition` and `MatrixMultiplication` are implemented in a conventional programming language such as C++. The implementor also provides optional cost functions, `MultCost` and `GaussCost`, which are applied by the query optimizer to compute selectivities and costs.

The query processor translates the AMOSQL query into an internal algebra expression. Fig. 3 gives an example of a query with a multi-directional function and the corresponding algebra tree. Here the query interpreter must use $times(a^b, b^f) \rightarrow r^b$ which is a multi-directional foreign function (Fig. 2). The chosen implementation of `times`, i.e. `GaussDecomposition`, depends on the types of `mx1` and `mx2`. It will be called by the `apply` algebra operator, γ, which takes as input a tuple of objects and applies the subscripted function (here `GaussDecomposition`) to get the result.

Multi-directional functions enhance the expressive power of the data model but the query processor must include algorithms for type resolution of multi-methods [2] and for handling ambiguities [1].

3.3 Function Overloading and Late Binding

In the object-oriented data model [3] types are organized in a hierarchy with inheritance where subtypes inherit properties from their supertypes. *Overloading* is a feature which lets the same name denote several variants. For function names such variants are called *resolvents*. Resolvents are named by annotating the function name with the type of the arguments and result. The naming convention chosen in AMOS (and in this paper) is: `t1.t2.....tn.m -> tr` for a function m whose argument types are `t1,t2,...,tn` and result type is `tr`.

When names are overloaded within the transitive closure of a subtype-supertype relationship that name is said to be *overridden*.

In our object-oriented model an instance of type t is also an instance of all supertypes to that type, i.e. *inclusion polymorphism* [7]. Thus, any reference declared to denote objects of a particular type, t, may denote objects of type t or any subtype, t_{sub}, of that type. This is called *substitutability*. As a consequence of substitutability and overriding, functions may be required to be *late bound*.

For multi-directional functions the criteria for late binding is similar as for pure object-oriented methods [16] with the difference that for multi-directional functions, *tuple types* are considered instead of single types.

The query compiler resolves which function calls require late binding. Whenever late binding is required a special operator, DTR, is inserted into the calculus expression. The optimizer translates each DTR call into the special algebra operator γ_{DTR} which, among a set of possible resolvents, selects the subplan to execute according to the types of its arguments. This will be illustrated below. If the call does not require late binding it is either substituted by its body if a stored or derived function is called, or to a function application if a foreign function is called.

Special execution sub-plans are generated for the possible resolvents of the specific binding-patterns that are used in the execution plan. Thus available indexes will be utilized or other useful optimization will be performed on the possible resolvents. If any of the possible resolvents are unexecutable the enclosing DTR will also be unexecutable. The cost and selectivity of the DTR operator is calculated based on the costs and selectivities of the possible resolvents as their maximum cost and minimum selectivity, respectively. Hence, DTR is used by a cost-based optimizer [30] to find an efficient execution strategy [16].

4 A Finite Element Analysis Example

A finite element analysis application has been modeled using the AMOS object-relational (OR) DBMS prototype. The purpose of this work is to investigate how a complex application can be built using the queries and views of an ORDBMS, and to develop suitable query processing algorithms.

4.1 Queries for Solving Linear Equations

A fundamental component in an FEA system is a linear equation solving sub-system. To model an equation solving system we define a type hierarchy of matrix types as illustrated in Fig. 4. Furthermore, the matrix multiplication operator, ×, is defined as functions on this matrix type hierarchy for several combinations of arguments. Fig. 5 illustrates how each variant of the multiplication function takes various matrix types (shapes) as arguments.

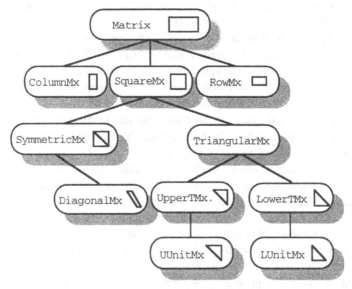

Fig. 4. A matrix type hierarchy for linear matrix algebra

The functions for multiplication are used to specify linear equation systems as matrix multiplications as $\mathbf{K} \times \mathbf{a} = \mathbf{f}$, where $\mathbf{a}$ is sought while $\mathbf{K}$ and $\mathbf{f}$ are known. Special representation methods and special equation solving methods have been developed that are dependent on the properties of the matrices. In our system, the function times (= infix operator *) is overloaded on both its arguments and has different implementations depending on the type (and thus representations) of the matrices used in its arguments. For example, when $\mathbf{K}$ is a symmetric matrix, i.e. ◩ × ◻ = ◻, it can be solved by a method that explores the symmetric properties of the first argument. One such method, $\mathbf{LDL^T}$ decomposition [18] illustrated in Fig. 6, substitutes the equation system with several equivalent equation systems that are simpler to solve.

The linear equation system is solved by starting with the factorization, $\mathbf{K} = \mathbf{U}^T \times \mathbf{D} \times \mathbf{U}$, that transforms K into the three matrices $\mathbf{U}^T$, $\mathbf{D}$, and $\mathbf{U}$. Then the upper triangular equation system $\mathbf{U}^T \times \mathbf{y} = \mathbf{f}$ is solved to get $\mathbf{y}$. The diagonal equation system $\mathbf{D} \times \mathbf{x} = \mathbf{y}$ is then solved to get $\mathbf{x}$, and finally the solution of the lower triangular equation system $\mathbf{U} \times \mathbf{a} = \mathbf{x}$ gets $\mathbf{a}$. If the equation on the other hand is typed as $\Box \times \Box = \Box$ some other method to solve it must be used, e.g. Gauss decomposition.

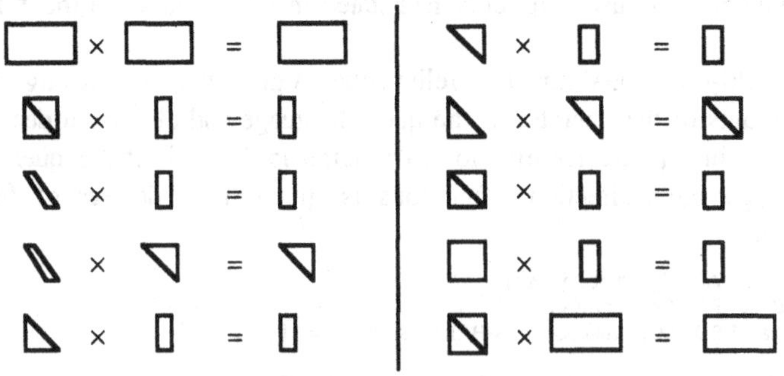

Fig. 5. A graphical notation for various matrix multiplication operators

The rationale for having these different overloaded matrix multiplication functions is efficiency and reusability. Efficiency because mathematical properties of the more specialized matrix types can be considered when implementing multiplication operators for them. Furthermore, specialized physical representations have been developed for many of the matrix types, e.g. to suppress zeroes or symmetric elements, and the matrix operators are defined in terms of these representations. The more specialized operators will in general have lower execution costs than the more general ones. The overloading provides reusability because every multiplication operator may be used in different contexts. To exemplify this consider the example in Fig. 7 over the type hierarchy in Fig. 4 and the multiplication operators from Fig. 5.

$$(\mathbf{K}^b \times \mathbf{a}^f = \mathbf{f}^b) \rightarrow \left\{ \begin{array}{l} \mathbf{K}^b = (\mathbf{U}^T)^f \times \mathbf{D}^f \times \mathbf{U}^f \\[6pt] \mathbf{U}^b \times \mathbf{a}^f = \mathbf{x}^b \\[6pt] \mathbf{D}^b \times \mathbf{x}^f = \mathbf{y}^b \\[6pt] (\mathbf{U}^T)^b \times \mathbf{y}^f = \mathbf{f}^b \end{array} \right\}$$

Fig. 6. The rewrite of a matrix multiplication expression to solve the equation system using $\mathbf{LDL}^T$ decomposition.

In this example a query is stated that solves an equation system by taking one square and one column matrix as arguments and calculating the solution by using the multiplication function. Depending on the type of the arguments the appropriate function from the type hierarchy below SquareMx will be selected at run-time, i.e. late binding. Also note that here the multiplication function (*) is used with the first argument and the result bound and the second argument unbound. This is only possible when multi-directional functions are supported by the system.

With multi-directional functions the equation system in Fig. 7 can be written as **K** × **a** = **f** which is a more declarative and reusable form than if separate functions were needed for matrix multiplication and equation solving, respectively. It is also a more optimizable form since the optimizer can find ways to execute the statement which would be hidden if the user explicitly had stated in which direction the * function is executed.

Hence, multi-directional functions relieve the programmer from having to define all different variants of the operator in the query language and also from deciding which variant to use in a particular situation. The latter is the task of the query optimizer which through multi-directional functions is given more degrees of freedom for optimization.

```
DECLARE K AS SymmetricMx;
DECLARE f AS ColumnMx;
SELECT a FROM ColumnMx a WHERE K * a = f;
```

Fig. 7. A simple query illustrating function overloading.

The implementor can often define different implementations of * depending on if an argument or the result is unknown. For square matrices, $\square \times \square = \square$, two variants are required. The first variant does matrix multiplication when both arguments are known and the result is unknown. When the first argument and the result are known and the second argument is unknown, * will perform equation solving using Gauss decomposition. There are also two variants for symmetric matrices, $\blacksquare \times \square = \square$, the difference is that instead of using Gauss decomposition when the second argument is unknown, the more efficient **LDL**$^\text{T}$ decomposition is used.

Late binding relieves the programmer from having to decide when any of the more specialized multiplication operators can be used since the system will do this at run-time. Thus, the general matrix multiplication will at run-time be selected as the most specialized variant possible, e.g. $\blacksquare \times \square = \square$, when the first argument is a symmetric matrix. Note that the types of all arguments participate in type resolution to select which resolvents of the multiplication operator to use from all the possible multiplication operators in Fig. 5. Contrast this with a pure object-oriented data model without multi-methods where the system cannot select the correct resolvent when the type of another argument than the first one has to be considered. This imposes restrictions on how object relations can be expressed in a pure object-oriented data model.

Our example shows that multi-directional functions are useful to support the modeling of complex applications. A system that supports both late binding and multi-directional multi-methods offers the programmer a flexible and powerful modeling tool. It is then the challenge to provide query processing techniques to support these features. This will be addressed next.

5   Processing Queries with Multi-Directional Functions

We will show through an example how queries with multi-directional functions are processed in AMOS for a subset of the functions in Fig. 5. In Fig. 8 the function definitions in AMOSQL are given that are needed for the previous example in Fig. 6.

```
CREATE FUNCTION factorise(SymmetricMx K) ->
                  <DiagonalMx D, UUnitMx U> AS
                  FOREIGN Factorise;
CREATE FUNCTION transpose(UUnitMx U) -> LUnitMx L AS
                  FOREIGN Transpose;
CREATE FUNCTION times(LUnitMx L, ColumnMx y) -> ColumnMx f AS
                  MULTIDIRECTIONAL
                  'bbf' FOREIGN LUnitMult
                  'bfb' FOREIGN LUnitSolve;
CREATE FUNCTION times(DiagonalMx D, ColumnMx x) -> ColumnMx y AS
                  MULTIDIRECTIONAL
                  'bbf' FOREIGN DiagonalMult
                  'bfb' FOREIGN DiagonalSolve;
CREATE FUNCTION times(UUnitMx U, ColumnMx a) -> ColumnMx x AS
                  MULTIDIRECTIONAL
                  'bbf' FOREIGN UUnitMult
                  'bfb' FOREIGN UUnitSolve;
CREATE FUNCTION times(SymmetricMx K, ColumnMx a) -> ColumnMx f AS
                  MULTIDIRECTIONAL
                  'bbf' FOREIGN SymmetricMult,
                  'bfb' AMOSQL SymmetricSolve;
CREATE FUNCTION SymmetricSolve(SymmetricMx K,ColumnMx f)->ColumnMx
                  AS SELECT a
                  FROM UUnitMx U,DiagonalMx D,ColumnMx x,ColumnMx y
                  WHERE
                      factorise(K) = <U,D> AND
                      transpose(U) * y = f AND
                      D * x = y AND
                      U * a = x;
```

Fig. 8. Multi-method function definitions needed in the example

The multi-directional function times is overloaded and defined differently depending on the shape and representation of the matrixes. It is multi-directional to handle both matrix multiplication and equation solving. The primitive matrix operations are implemented as a set of User Defined Functions (UDFs) in some programming language (i.e. C). For symmetric matrixes the multiplication is implemented by the UDF SymmetricMult while equation solving uses the LDL method (SymmetricSolve) above.

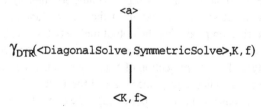

Fig. 9. The top level query algebra tree for the query in Fig. 7

The query optimizer translates the query into an optimized execution plan represented as an algebra tree (Fig. 9). During the translation to the algebra the optimizer will apply type resolution methods to avoid late binding in the execution plan when possible. In cases where late binding is required the execution plan may call subplans.

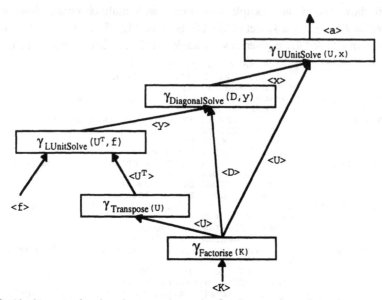

Fig. 10. Algebra tree showing the execution order for the transformed matrix expression

In the example query of Fig. 7 there are two possible resolvents of the name times:
1. DiagonalMx.ColumnMx.times→ColumnMx
2. SymmetricMx.ColumnMx.times→ColumnMx

The example thus requires late binding where resolvent 2 will be chosen when the first argument is a SymmetricMx and 1 will be chosen otherwise. When resolvent 2 is chosen the system will be solved using the **LDL^T**-decomposition, while a trivial diagonal solution method is used for case 1. The optimizer translates the query into the algebra tree in Fig. 9, where the algebra operator γ_{DTR} implements late binding. It selects at run time the subplan to apply on its arguments K and f based on their types. In the example there are two subplans, DiagonalSolve and SymmetricSolve. DiagonalSolve is implemented as a foreign function in C (Fig. 8), while SymmetricSolve references the subplan performing the **LDL^T**-decomposition in Fig. 10.

The subplan in Fig. 10 has K and f as input parameters (tuples) and produces a as the result tuple. K is input to the application of the foreign function factorise that does the **LDL^T** factorization producing the output tuple <D, U>. The U part is projected as the argument of the functions transpose and UUnitSolve (the projection operator is omitted for clarity), while the projection of D is argument to DiagonalSolve. The application of LUnitSolve has the arguments f and the result of transpose(U), i.e. U^T. Analogous applications are made for DiagonalSolve and UUnitSolve to produce the result tuple <a>.

6 Summary and Future Work

Domain-oriented data representations are needed when representing and querying data for numerical application using an ORDBMS, e.g. to store matrices. To avoid unnecessary data transformations and transmissions, it is important that the query language can be extended with domain-oriented operators, e.g. for matrix calculus. For high-level application modeling and querying of, e.g., matrix operators multi-directional functions are required.

Although multi-directional functions require generalized type checking, the benefits gained as increased naturalness and modeling power of the data model are important for many applications, including ours.

Our example illustrates how multi-directional functions can be utilized by the query optimizer. This is a new area for query optimization techniques.

We also showed that the system must support late binding for multi-directional functions. In our approach each late bound function in a query is substituted with a DTR calculus operator which is defined in terms of the resolvents eligible for execution. Each DTR call is then translated to the algebra operator γ_{DTR} that chooses among eligible subplans according to the types of its arguments. Local query execution plans are generated at each application of γ_{DTR} and optimized for the specific binding-patterns that will be used at run-time, as illustrated in our examples.

Further interesting optimization techniques to be investigated include the identification of common subexpressions among the possible resolvents, transformations of DTR expressions, and performance evaluation.

References

1 Amiel, E., Dujardin, E.: Supporting Explicit Disambiguation of Multi-Methods. Research Report n2590, Inria, 1995. ECOOP96, 1996.
2 Agrawal, R., DeMichiel, L.G., Lindsay, B.G.: Static Type Checking of Multi-Methods. OOPSLA Conf., p113-128, 1991.
3 Atkinson, M., Bancilhon,F., DeWitt,D., Dittrich,K., Maier,D., Zdonik,S.: The Object-Oriented Database System Manifesto. 1st. Conf. Deductive OO Databases, Kyoto, Jpn, Dec. 1989.
4 Banerjee, J., Kim, W., Kim, K.C.: Queries in Object-Oriented Databases. IEEE Data Eng. Conf., Feb. 1988.
5 Bertino, E., Negri, M., Pelagatti, Sbattella, G., L.: Object-Oriented Query Languages: The Notion and the Issues. IEEE Trans. on Knowledge and Data Eng., v4, Jun 1992.
6 Bobrow, D. G., Kahn, K., Kiczales, G., Masinter, L., Stefik, M., Zdybel, F.: CommonLoops Merging Lisp and Object-Oriented Programming. OOPSLA Conf., 1986.
7 Cardelli, L., Wegner, P.: On Understanding Types, Data Abstraction, and Polymorphism. ACM Computing Surveys, v17, 1985.
8 Cattell, R. G. G.: Object Data Management: Object-Oriented and Extended Relational Database Systems. Addison-Wesley, 1992.
9 Cattell,R.G.G. (ed.): The Object Database Standard: ODMG 2.0. Morgan Kaufmann 1997.
10 Chambers, C., Leavens, G. T.: Typechecking and Modules for Multi-Methods. OOPSLA Conf., Oct 1994.

11 Chen, W., Turau, V., Klas, W.: Efficient Dynamic Look-Up Strategy for Multi-Methods. 8th European Conf., ECOOP94, Bologna, Italy, Jul 1994, Lecture Notes in Computer Science, N821, p408-431, Springer Verlag, 1994.

12 Daniels, S., Graefe, G., Keller,T., Maier,D., Schmidt, D., Vance, B.: Query Optimization in Revelation, an Overview. IEEE Data Eng. Bulletin, v14, p58-62, Jun 1992.

13 Fahl, G., Risch, T., Sköld, M.: AMOS, an Architecture for Active Mediators. Int. Workshop on Next Generation Information Techn. and Systems, Haifa, Israel, Jun 1993.

14 Flodin, S.: An Incremental Query Compiler with Resolution of Late Binding. LITH-IDA-R-94-46, Dept of Computer and Information Science, Linköping Univ., 1994.

15 Flodin, S.: Efficient Management of Object-Oriented Queries with Late Bound Functions. Lic. Thesis 538, Dept. of Computer and Inf. Science, Linköping Univ., Feb. 1996.

16 Flodin, S., Risch, T.: Processing Object-Oriented Queries with Invertible Late Bound Functions. VLDB 1995, Sept. 1995.

17 Flodin, S., Karlsson, J., Risch, T., Sköld, M., Werner, M.: AMOS User's Guide. CAELAB Memo 94-01, Linköping Univ., 1994.

18 Golub, G.H., van Loan, C.F.: Matrix Computations 2ed, John Hopkins Univ. Pr., 1989.

19 Graefe, G.: Query Evaluation Techniques for Large Databases. ACM Computing Surveys, v25, pp 73-170, June 1993.

20 IBM: DB2 Universal Database SQL Reference Ver. 5. Document S10J-8165-00. 1997.

21 Libkin,L., Machlin,R., Wong,L: A Query Language for Multidmensional Arrays: Design, Implementation and Optimization Techniques. ACM SIGMOD, p228-239, June 1996.

22 Litwin, W., Risch, T.: Main Memory Oriented Optimization of OO Queries Using Typed Datalog with Foreign Predicates. IEEE Trans. on Knowledge and Data Eng., v4, Dec. 1992.

23 Lyngbaek, P.: OSQL: A Language for Object Databases. HPL-DTD-91-4, HP, Jan 1991.

24 Melton, J. (ed), ANSI SQL3 Papers SC21N9463-SC21N9467, ANSI SC21, NY, USA 1995.

25 Orsborn, K.: Applying Next Generation Object-Oriented DBMS to Finite Element Analysis. 1st Int. Conf. on Applications of Databases, ADB94, Lecture Notes in Computer Science, 819, p215-233, Springer Verlag, 1994.

26 Orsborn, K., Risch, T.: Next Generation of O-O Database Techniques in Finite Element Analysis. 3rd Int. Conf. on Computational Structures Technology (CST96), Budapest, Hungary, August, 1996.

27 Orsborn, K.: On Extensible and Object-Relational Database Technology for Finite Element Analysis Applications. PhD Thesis 452, ISBN9178718279, Linköping Univ., Oct. 1996.

28 Ross, T. J., Wagner, L. R., Luger, G. F.: Object-Oriented Programming for Scientific Codes. II: Examples in C++. Journal of Computing in Civil Eng., v6, p497-514, 1992.

29 Scholz, S. P.: Elements of an Object-Oriented FEM++ Program in C++. Computers & Structures, v43, p517-529, 1992.

30 Selinger, P.G., Astrahan, M.M., Chamberlin, D.D., Lorie, R.A., Price, T.G.: Access Path Selection in a Relational Database Management System. ACM SIGMOD p23-34 1979.

31 Shipman, D. W.: The Functional Data Model and the Data Language DAPLEX. ACM Transactions on Database Systems, v6, March 1981.

32 Stonebraker, M.: Implementation of Integrity Constraints and Views by Query Modification. ACM SIGMOD , San Jose, CA, May 1975.

33 Stonebraker, M.: Object-relational DBMSs, Morgan Kaufmann, 1996.

34 Straube, D. D., Özsu, M. T.: Queries and Query Processing in Object-Oriented Database Systems. ACM Transactions on Information Systems, v8, Oct. 1990.

35 Vandenberg, S., DeWitt, D.: Algebraic Support for Complex Objects with Arrays, Identity, and Inheritance. ACM SIGMOD, 1991.

Multiple Range Query Optimization in Spatial Databases *

Apostolos N. Papadopoulos and Yannis Manolopoulos

Department of Informatics, Aristotle University
54006 Thessaloniki, Greece
{apapadop,manolopo}@athena.auth.gr

Abstract. In order to answer efficiently range queries in 2-d R-trees, first we sort queries by means of a space filling curve, then we group them together, and finally pass them for processing. Initially, we consider grouping of pairs of requests only, and give two algorithms with exponential and linear complexity. Then, we generalize the linear method, grouping more than two requests per group. We evaluate these methods under different LRU buffer sizes, measuring the cache misses per query. We present experimental results based on real and synthetic data. The results show that careful query scheduling can improve substantially the overall performance of multiple range query processing.

1 Introduction

Two basic research directions exist aiming at improving efficiency in a Spatial DBMS [4, 8, 13]. The first direction involves the design of robust spatial data structures and algorithms [2], the second one focuses on the design of clever query optimizers. Most of the work in the latter area deals with the optimization of a single (possibly complex) spatial query [1].

Here, we concentrate on range/window queries defined by a rectilinear rectangle, where the answer is composed of all objects overlapping the query rectangle. We examine methods to combine many range queries (posed by one or many users) in order to reduce the total execution time, based on the reasoning of [14]. We quote from the latter work: *the main motivation for performing such an interquery optimization lies in the fact that queries may share common data.*

There are real-life cases where many requests can be present simultaneously:

- in complex disjunctive/conjunctive queries which can be decomposed in simpler subqueries,
- in spatial join processing, where if one relation participates with only a few objects, then it is more efficient to perform lookups in the second relation,
- in spatial client/server environment, where at any given time instance more than one users may request for service.

---

* Work supported by the European Union's TMR program ("Chorochronos" project, contract number ERBFMRX-CT96-0056), and the national PENED program.

– in benchmarking/simulation environments, where submitted queries are generated with analytical techniques and therefore are known in advance.

For this purpose, we use space filling curves to sort query windows and apply a simple criterion in order to group queries efficiently. We consider the original R-tree [5] as the underlying access method. However, the method is applicable to any R-tree variant or any other spatial access methods with minor modifications. Although, the discussion is based on 2-d space, the generalization to higher dimensional spaces is straightforward.

The use of buffers is very important in database systems [3], since the performance improvement can be substantial. One of the policies that is widely acceptable is the LRU (Least Recently Used) policy, which replaces the page that has not been referenced for the longest time period. The performance of the proposed methods using LRU buffers of various sizes is evaluated and results show that different methods have different performance under different buffer sizes. However, it is emphasized that a careful preprocessing of the queries can improve substantially the overall performance of range query processing.

The rest of the paper is organized as follows. In Sections 2 and 3 we give the appropriate background on R-trees and space filling curves, and analytic considerations respectively. In Section 4 we describe the various techniques in detail. Section 5 contains the experimental results and performance comparisons. Finally, Section 6 concludes the paper and gives some future research directions.

2 Background

2.1 R-trees

The R-tree [5] is a multi-dimensional, height balanced tree structure for use in secondary storage. The structure handles objects by means of their Minimum Bounding Rectangles (MBR). Each node of the tree corresponds to exactly one disk page. Internal nodes contain entries of the form *(R,child-ptr)*, where R is the MBR enclosing all the MBRs of its descendants and *child-ptr* is the pointer to the specific child node. Leaves contain entries of the form *(R,object-ptr)*, where R is the MBR of the object and *object-ptr* is the pointer to the objects detailed description. One of the most important factors that affects the overall structure performance is the node split strategy. In [5] three split policies are reported, namely exponential, quadratic and linear split policies. More sophisticated R-tree variants have been proposed [2], however here we adopt the original R-tree structure because we mainly want to emphasize on the technique to reduce the processing cost.

2.2 Space Filling Curves

A Space Filling Curve is a special fractal curve which has the following basic characteristics:

- it covers completely an area, a volume or a hyper-volume in a 2-d, 3-d or n-d space respectively,
- each point is visited once and only once (the curve does not cross itself), and
- neighbor points in the native space are likely to be neighbors in the space filling curve.

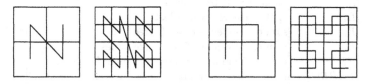

Fig. 1. Peano and Hilbert space filling curves.

In Figure 1 we present two of most important Space Filling Curves: Peano and Hilbert. We can easily observe the self-similarity property of the curves. A Peano curve can be constructed by interleaving the bits of coordinates x and y. The generation of the Hilbert curve is more complex, i.e. it is constructed by means of a process that uses rotation and mirroring. Algorithms for the generation of the 2-d Hilbert curve can be found in [6, 8]. The goodness of a space filling curve is measured with respect to its ability to preserve proximity. Although there are no analytical results to demonstrate the superiority of the Hilbert curve, experiments [6] show that it is the best distance preserving curve. Therefore, in the rest of the paper we focus on the Hilbert curve.

3 Analytical Considerations

In this section, we derive an estimate for the expected number of page references, when processing a set S of N window queries $q_1, .., q_N$. The notations used along with their description are presented in Table 1.

Assume that the query rectangle centroids obey a uniform distribution and that the dataspace dimensions are normalized to the unit square. The expected number of page references to satisfy the query q_i is [7]:

$$EPR(q_{ix}, q_{iy}) = TA + q_{ix} \cdot E_y + q_{iy} \cdot E_x + TN \cdot q_{ix} \cdot q_{iy} \qquad (1)$$

where q_{ix} and q_{iy} are the x and y extends of the window query q_i. Equation (1) is independent of the R-tree construction method as well as independent of the data object distribution. Also, the parameters used can be calculated and maintained with negligible cost.

To simplify the analysis we focus on the R-tree leaf level. However, the analysis can be applied to all the levels. We also assume that each query window is a square with side q, and each data page has a square MBR with area L_a. Setting $q_{ix}=q_{iy}=q$, $TN=LN$, $E_x=LN \cdot \sqrt{L_a}$, $E_y=LN \cdot \sqrt{L_a}$, $TA=LN \cdot L_a$, we get:

$$EPR(q) = LN \cdot (q^2 + 2 \cdot \sqrt{L_a} \cdot q + L_a)$$

Symbol	Description
N	number of pending range queries
q	query window side
Q	super window side
TN	total number of R-tree nodes
TA	sum of areas of all nodes
LN	number of R-tree leaves
L_a	area of the MBR of a leaf
E_x	sum of x extends of all R-tree nodes
E_y	sum of y extends of all R-tree nodes
$EPR(q)$	expected number of page references for query q
$TEPR(S)$	total expected number of page references for set S
$DPR(S)$	number of distinct page references for set S
$ERPP(q,Q)$	expected number of references per page

Table 1. Notations used throughout the analysis.

Since there are N requests, the total number of page references (including the redundant ones) is:

$$TERP(S) = \sum_{k=1}^{N} EPR(q) = N \cdot LN \cdot (q^2 + 2 \cdot \sqrt{L_a} \cdot q + L_a) \qquad (2)$$

We can associate to the N window queries, a super-window SW which corresponds to the MBR of all query windows. For simplicity let SW be a square with side Q. We would like to have an estimate for the number of distinct page references (i.e. excluding redundant references). We can approximate this number by the number of page references introduced when processing SW. However, this approximation is not accurate if N is small and $q \ll Q$. In this case the number of distinct page references includes a large number of pages referenced by SW, but not referenced by any q_i. Ignoring this effect we get:

$$DPR(S) = DPR(Q) = LN \cdot (Q^2 + 2 \cdot \sqrt{L_a} \cdot Q + L_a) \qquad (3)$$

We can use Formulae (2) and (3) to derive the expected number of references per page:

$$ERPP(q,Q) = \frac{TEPR(S)}{DPR(S)} = N \cdot \left(\frac{q + \sqrt{L_a}}{Q + \sqrt{L_a}} \right)^2 \qquad (4)$$

From Equation (4) we observe that as q approaches Q, $ERPP(q,Q)$ approaches N. Obviously, in the extreme case where $q=Q$, we get $ERPP(q,Q)=N$. This is exactly the case where all N query windows represent the same portion of the dataspace. Figure 2 depicts $ERPP(q,Q)$ as a function of Q for $N=100$, and $q=0$ (point queries), $q=0.1$ (small window queries), $q=0.3$ (large window queries). The value of $\sqrt{L_a}$ was set to 0.01, i.e. the area of the MBR of each leaf covers 1% of the dataspace area.

The graphs show that a single page may be references many times during the processing of the N window queries. If a page reference causes a disk access,

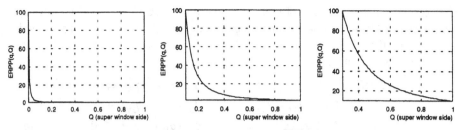

Fig. 2. Plots of $ERPP(q, Q)$ vs. Q for $N=100$, $\sqrt{L_a}=0.01$ and $q=0$, 0.1, 0.3.

the number of I/O operations increases substantially. However, with adequate cache buffers, the total processing cost may be reduced. In the following section we discuss several techniques to solve the problem.

4 Processing Multiple Requests

In this section we study several alternatives to service a number of window queries. The processing cost of a window query q_i is mainly affected by the I/O time to fetch the appropriate disk pages and the CPU time to process them. For the rest of the paper we focus on the I/O activity ignoring the CPU time as a negligible cost.

A common approach to service a number of requests is to process them in a First-Come-First-Served (**FCFS**) manner. Clearly, in case of low rate of query arrivals (e.g. one query per minute), **FCFS** is a reasonable service strategy. However, there is a major problem with this approach in other cases (see Section 1). If the order of processing follows the arrival order, then the probability to have a cache hit is very small, leading to poor cache utilization. However, we can take advantage of the fact that we have knowledge of all pending requests and improve the performance.

Our first attempt is to perform a quick preprocessing of all pending query windows, in order to increase the probability that a page required is residing into the cache buffer. The first algorithm **HS** (Hilbert Sorting) has as follows:

Algorithm HS

[HS1] For each $q_i \in S$ calculate the Hilbert value of the window's centroid.

[HS2] Sort the Hilbert values in increasing order to obtain a total order of the query windows, $q_{i1}, .., q_{iN}$.

[HS3] For all q_{ij}, $j=1..N$ execute query q_{ij}.

The method guarantees (up to a point) that nearby requests will be executed sequentially, thus enhancing the locality of references. The main observation is that the method depends heavily on the size of the cache buffer. Moreover, if there is no buffer space, the algorithm has the same performance with the **FCFS** method. This drawback motivates us to go one step further.

Consider two requests q_i and q_j. If these requests share common pages, we could execute them as one. What we need is a criterion to decide when to group these queries and when to execute them individually. We can use Equation (1) to determine if the grouping of queries q_i and q_j is advantageous or not. Let Q denote the MBR of the query windows q_i and q_j and Q_x, Q_y its x and y extend respectively. If we execute Q instead of both q_i and q_j, there will be a reduction in disk accesses if and only if:

$$EPR(Q_x, Q_y) \leq EPR(q_{ix}, q_{iy}) + EPR(q_{jx}, q_{jy}) \Leftrightarrow$$
$$E_y \cdot (Q_x - q_{ix} - q_{jx}) + E_x \cdot (Q_y - q_{iy} - q_{jy}) +$$
$$TN \cdot (Q_x \cdot Q_y - q_{ix} \cdot q_{iy} - q_{jx} \cdot q_{jy}) - TA \leq 0 \tag{5}$$

In Inequality (5) above we observe that:

- the factors $E_y \cdot (Q_x - q_{ix} - q_{jx})$ and $E_x \cdot (Q_y - q_{iy} - q_{jy})$ are negative if the two query rectangles overlap in space.
- the value of the factor $TN \cdot (Q_x \cdot Q_y - q_{ix} \cdot q_{iy} - q_{jx} \cdot q_{jy})$ decreases as the overlap increases.

However, two queries may share common pages even if they do not intersect. Consequently, as the distance between the two query rectangles in the native space decreases, the gain in disk accesses increases. If two range queries satisfy Inequality (5), this is a clear criterion that with high probability there will be a reduction in the number of disk accesses.

Based on this simple grouping criterion, let us proceed with the construction of efficient algorithms where this criterion can be valuable. First we present an exhaustive method with exponential complexity, and next we give a simple greedy method along with its extension, with linear complexity. Beforehand, we emphasize that these algorithms are based on the following assumptions:

1. the window queries have been ordered according to the Hilbert value of their rectangle centroids (with $O(N \cdot \log N)$ cost).
2. grouping is allowed only to neighbor queries (with respect to Hilbert order).

Later we will generalize to more queries and discuss the pros and cons of such an approach.

4.1 The Exponential Algorithm (Algorithm E)

Consider N unserviced range query requests. For a query q_j, $j=1..N$ there are three alternatives:

1. the query will be executed individually,
2. the query will be combined with its left sibling,
3. the query will be combined with its right sibling.

Therefore, to determine a promising processing schedule, we could consider all possible schedules and select the one with the minimum total execution cost.
Proposition. The number of all possible schedules derived for N range queries under the constraint that each request can be executed either alone or together with its left or right sibling is: $O\left(\left(\frac{1+\sqrt{5}}{2}\right)^{N+1}\right)$. $\square$

It is evident that the execution cost of the algorithm is very high, and therefore unacceptable for practical use in real applications.

4.2 The Linear Algorithm (Algorithm L)

We may reduce the algorithmic complexity by using a simple greedy method. The idea is: given two requests q_1 and q_2, just check if Inequality (5) is satisfied or not. If yes, we will execute the queries as one. If not, we will execute q_1 alone and proceed with q_2 and q_3 until we consider all pending requests.

Algorithm L

[L1] For each $q_i \in S$ calculate the Hilbert values of the window's centroid. Sort the Hilbert values in increasing order to obtain a total order of the query windows.

[L2] Let *pos* denote the current query index. Initialize *pos*=1.

[L3] while ($pos < N$) **do**

   begin

      Test Inequality (5) for query rectangles q_{pos} and q_{pos+1};

      if Inequality (5) is satisfied

      then process the two queries as one **and** set *pos=pos+2*

      else process query q_{pos} **and** set *pos=pos+1*.

   end

   if ($pos==N$) **then** service q_{pos}.

Clearly, the complexity of the algorithm is $O(N \cdot \log N)$, since in step **[L1]** we sort the rectangles. Step **[L3]** takes only $O(N)$, because the queries are scanned only once.

4.3 The Extended Linear Algorithm (Algorithm ExL)

In this subsection we relax the constraint that at most two queries can be executed as one. Algorithm **ExL** derived is an extension of the **L** algorithm, enabling the grouping of more than two window queries.

Consider the queries $q_1, .., q_N$, in increasing order with respect to the Hilbert value of the rectangle centroid. The algorithm tries to pack requests into disjoint sets. We begin with request q_1. Initially the first group G_1 contains only q_1 ($G_1=\{q_1\}$). If the processing of q_1 and q_2 together retrieves less pages than the processing of q_1 plus q_2 (according to Inequality (5)), then $G_1=\{q_1, q_2\}$. If the processing of q_3 and q_2 and q_1 together retrieves less pages than the processing of q_3 plus q_2 plus q_1, then $G_1=\{q_1, q_2, q_3\}$. We continue the same process, until we reach a request q_k such that $EPR(G_1 + q_k) > EPR(G_1) + EPR(q_k)$. When this happens we set $G_1=\{q_1, .., q_{k-1}\}$ and $G_2=\{q_k\}$. Therefore, a second group G_2 is considered. This process is continued until all requests are examined.

Algorithm ExL

[ExL1] For each $q_i \in S$ calculate the Hilbert values of the window's centroid. Sort the Hilbert values in increasing order to obtain a total order of the query windows.

[ExL2] Let *pos* denote the current query index. Initialize *pos*=1. Let *GroupId* denote the current group. Initialize *GroupId*=1.

[ExL3] while ($pos < N$) **do**

   begin

Initialize $EndOfGroup=FALSE$ and $G_{GroupId}=\{q_{pos}\}$;
while (!$EndOfGroup$) **do**
begin
    if ($EPR(G_{GroupId} + q_{pos}) < EPR(G_{GroupId}) + EPR(q_{pos})$)
    then assign q_{pos} to $G_{GroupId}$ and set $pos=pos+1$;
    else set $EndOfGroup=TRUE$ and set $GroupId=GroupId+1$;
    process as one all q_j's $\in G_{GroupId}$;
    end
end
if ($pos==N$) **then** service q_{pos}.

Provided that the query windows have been already sorted with respect to the Hilbert value of their centroid, the time complexity of step [**ExL3**] is linear to the number of requests ($O(N)$).

Finally, another major issue is the separation of the results. After the processing of a multiple range query, we must determine which objects correspond to specific range queries. This operation is CPU-bound and can be performed using computational geometry [12] techniques in order to find the queries that a specific object geometry satisfies.

5 Experimental Results

5.1 Preliminaries

We implemented the R-tree access method with the quadratic split policy, and the algorithms **HS**, **L** and **ExL** in the C programming language under UNIX. The experimentation was performed on DEC 3000 workstation. The page size was set to 2Kbytes. The dataspace dimensions were set to the unit square $[0, 1) \times [0, 1)$ and all datasets were normalized to fall inside the dataspace area. The buffer sizes (in Kbytes) considered in this paper are: 0, 8, 32, 128, 512 and 1024 (i.e. 1 Mbyte). The different datasets used throughout the evaluation of the methods are presented in the next table.

Dataset	Representation of	Object	Population	Source
CP	California places	points	65,252	s2k-ftp.cs.berkeley.edu
CUA	California Urban and Agricultural	rectangles	12,361	s2k-ftp.cs.berkeley.edu
MG	Montgomery County	rectangles	39,323	http://www.census.gov
LB	Long Beach County	rectangles	53,146	http://www.census.gov

Table 2. Datasets used for experimentation.

The major factors that affect the performance of the algorithms are:

- the number of pending window queries,
- the size of the LRU buffer,
- the characteristics of the query windows (i.e. area, perimeter) and
- the characteristics of the dataset (i.e. distribution, coverage, geometry).

Let us investigate the impact of these factors. Figure 3 presents the results for the MG+LB dataset and Figure 4 the results for the CP dataset. Each one of these figures comprises of two parts:

1. The left part ((a) to (c)) presents the cache misses per query when the varying quantities are the LRU buffer size and the number of pending range queries, whereas the query window side is fixed at 0.05.
2. The right part ((d) to (f)) presents the cache misses per query when the varying quantities are the LRU buffer size and the query window side. The number of pending range queries is fixed at 100.

5.2   Interpretation of Results

From Figures 3 and 4 some very interesting observations can be derived. It is easily understood that:

- as the buffer size increases the performance of all methods is improved,
- the more the pending range queries, the more efficient is the derived processing plan,
- as the side of the query window increases, the performance improvement is more significant,
- when the R-tree stores points (CP dataset), the R-tree nodes have (generally) less area and perimeter (in comparison to other datasets) and thus the probability that a page will be referenced by more than one queries decreases. Therefore, the performance improvement of the proposed method in comparison to **FCFS** is less significant (but still present).

By inspecting closer Figures 3 and 4 we derive that:

- The **HS** algorithm, for 0Kbyte buffer has identical performance with the **FCFS** method, since the locality of references is not utilized at all. For LRU buffer sizes ranging between 8Kbytes and 32Kbytes, the performance improvement of **HS**, is around 5% over the **FCFS** method (in some cases reaches 20% for 32Kbytes buffer). However, for large buffer sizes (128Kbytes and above) **HS** is the best choice. In such cases the improvement over the **FCFS** method ranges from 20% to 60%. As stated in a previous, the performance of this algorithm is highly related to the LRU buffer size. The only thing that this algorithm can guarantee, is the locality of references. However, it is not certain that all N requests will be processed without other requests interfering.
- Algorithm **ExL** is the best choice, when no LRU buffer is available. We observe that in cases where the queries cover a large portion of the dataspace (Figures 3f and 4f) **ExL** can achieve up to 80% improvement over **FCFS**. As the buffer size increases, **HS** and **L** are clearly better than **ExL**. This is due to the fact that grouping more than two queries can lead to a large number of unnecessary page accesses.

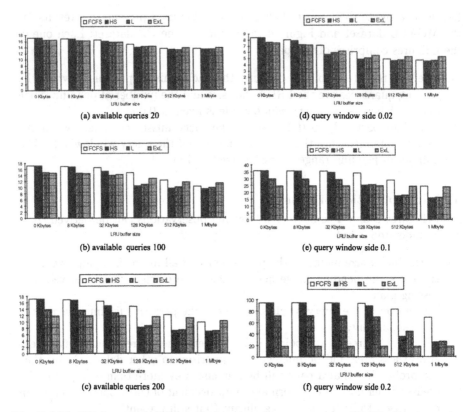

Fig. 3. MG+LB dataset. Left Part: Cache misses per query versus LRU buffer size and number of pending queries (for $q=0.05$). Right Part: Cache misses per query versus LRU buffer size and query window side (for $N=100$).

- Algorithm **L** keeps the balance between algorithms **HS** and **ExL**. For no (or small) LRU buffers, its performance is very close to that of **ExL**, whereas for large LRU buffers, its performance is very close to that of **HS**. In general, **L** achieves a 30% performance improvement over **FCFS**.
- When the LRU buffer size is large (e.g. > 1Mbyte), and the number of pending queries is small (e.g. 20), the performance of **FCFS** method is very close to that of algorithm **L** and slightly better than that of algorithm bf ExL. The reason for this is the number of extra pages fetched by **L** and **ExL**.

6 Conclusions

We proposed a global query optimization technique to improve the performance of a Spatial DBMS when answering multiple range queries. The main result is that a careful preprocessing of the queries can lead to substantial reduction of the number of disk accesses and better cache utilization, in comparison to the **FCFS** method. This goal has been achieved by satisfying two main needs:

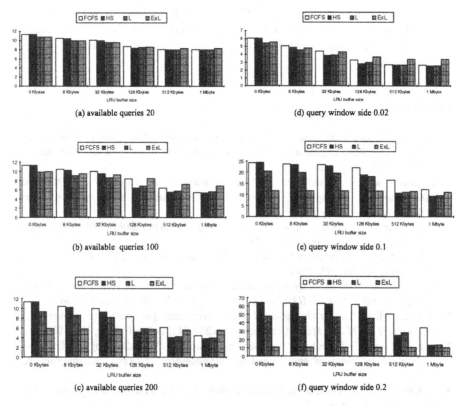

Fig. 4. CP dataset. Left Part: Cache misses per query versus LRU buffer size and number of pending queries (for q=0.05). Right Part: Cache misses per query versus LRU buffer size and query window side. (for N=100).

1. bring *"similar"* query rectangles close to each other, and
2. provide special algorithms to aid the reduction of disk accesses.

To satisfy need 1, we have used the Hilbert space filling curve, and Algorithm **HS** is based only on this sorting according to Hilbert values. To satisfy need 2, we provide three algorithms (**E**, **L** and **ExL**) to combine neighbor (according to Hilbert order) query rectangles. Algorithms **L** and **ExL** are linear and exhibit considerable gain when compared to the conventional **FCFS** approach. We tested our method under different data sets and different LRU buffer sizes. We suggest using algorithm **HS** for large buffers and algorithm **L** in all other cases. Although algorithm **ExL** introduces a substantial improvement in some cases, if the requests represent queries of different users, may impose a large waiting time, as opposed to algorithm **L** which does not introduce much overhead.

Future research may include:

– Application of the method to other R-tree variants and other spatial data structures, modifying accordingly the formula deriving the expected number of disk accesses for a range query (Equation (1)),

- Evaluation of the method when the query distribution follows the object distribution, i.e. each object has the same probability to be retrieved [11],
- Global optimization by considering other more complex spatial queries (e.g. spatial join).

References

1. W. Aref: "Query processing and optimization in spatial databases", Technical Report CS-TR-3097, Department of Computer Science, University of Maryland at College Park, MD, 1993.
2. V. Gaede and O. Guenther: "Multidimensional access methods", *ACM Computer Surveys*, to appear. Address for downloading: http://www.wiwi.hu-berlin.de/gaede/survey.rev.ps.Z.
3. J. Gray and A. Rueter: *Transaction processing - concepts and techniques*, Morgan Kaufmann, San Francisco, CA, 1993.
4. R.H. Gutting: "An introduction to spatial database systems", *The VLDB Journal*, vol.3, no.4, pp.357-399, 1994.
5. A. Guttman: "R-trees: a dynamic index structure for spatial searching", *Proceedings of the 1984 ACM SIGMOD Conference*, pp.47-57, Boston, MA, 1984.
6. H.V. Jagadish: "Linear clustering of objects with multiple attributes", *Proceedings of the 1990 ACM SIGMOD Conference*, pp.332-342, Atlantic City, NJ, 1990.
7. I. Kamel and C. Faloutsos: "On packing R-trees", *Proceedings of the 2nd Conference on Information and Knowledge Management (CIKM)*, Washington DC, 1993.
8. R. Laurini and D. Thompson: *"Fundamentals of spatial information systems"*, Academic Press, London, 1992.
9. V. Ng and T. Kameda: "Concurrent accesses to R-trees", *Proceedings of 3rd International Symposium on Large Spatial Databases (SSD '93)*, pp.142-161, Singapore, 1993.
10. J. Orenstein: "Spatial query processing in an object-oriented database system", *Proceedings of the 1986 ACM SIGMOD Conference*, pp.326-336, Washington DC, 1986.
11. B.U. Pagel, H.W. Six, H. Toben and P. Widmayer: "Towards an analysis of range query performance in spatial data structures", *Proceedings of the 1993 ACM PODS Conference*, pp.214-221, Washington DC, 1993.
12. F.P. Preparata and M.I. Shamos: *Computational geometry: an introduction*, Springer-Verlag, New York, 1985.
13. H. Samet: *The design and analysis of spatial data structures*, Addison-Wesley, Reading, MA, 1990.
14. T. Sellis: "Multiple query optimization", *ACM Transactions on Database Systems*, vol.13, no.1, pp.23-52, 1988.

Optimizing Command Logs by Exploiting Semantic Knowledge

Roland Baumann

Department of Computer Science III
Aachen University of Technology
52056 Aachen, Germany
baumann@i3.informatik.rwth-aachen.de

Abstract. The graph-oriented database management system GRAS is used as a repository in design applications for fine-grained data. It offers an undo / redo mechanism based on command logs. We formalize this mechanism an show how to compute inverse command sequences for undoing the effects of a command. Since command logs tend to become very large, we also present a mechanism to compute the net effects of a command sequence on the fly during normal operation.

1 Introduction

Software systems for design and engineering applications like CAD or CASE deal with highly structured data like VLSI chip layouts or abstract syntax trees. Usually, these applications are also highly interactive, i.e. they respond to user input and immediately reflect the effects of user commands on their display. An important feature of such interactive editing tools is the ability to let the user undo the effects of commands that he or she issued. This helps to experiment with the tools and eases error correction to a great extent.

The structure-oriented database management system GRAS (GRAph Storage) was designed to serve as repository for design applications [5]. It is part of the IPSEN project [7], where it is used as persistent storage for all tools. GRAS' data model are directed, attributed, node and edge labeled graphs. It supports interactive applications by providing a sophisticated undo / redo mechanism [8, 2]. The system stores sequences of graph changing commands in logs and offers checkpoints to mark the states of a graph which need to be reachable by undo and redo. By replaying the logs, undo and redo commands enable applications to reach previous or later checkpoints.

The commands stored in GRAS' logs are on a semantically lower level than the commands offered to the user by an application using GRAS. Nevertheless, such user commands result in a sequence of calls to the GRAS programming interface which can be stored in GRAS' undo / redo logs. When a checkpoint is issued after every action a user performs with the application, GRAS' undo / redo features can be used to directly implement undo / redo of user commands on the stored data. Of course the display of the application has to be adjusted in addition when the underlying data changes due to an undo / redo command.

Undo / redo logs can be stored across session boundaries to enable the user to pick up the next session exactly where he left the previous one. Additionally, GRAS logs are also used to reconstruct versions of graphs from other versions. For these reasons, logs can live an arbitrary long time. Therefore, it is important to store them as space efficient as possible. Besides space efficiency, optimizing logs also reduces execution times during replay. In this paper we present our solution to optimize logs on the fly during normal operation. The logging mechanism of GRAS only logs the commands that contribute to the net effect of a command sequence between two successive checkpoints. In section 2 we introduce the commands which change the state of a GRAS graph and formalize their semantics. Following this, in section 3, we show how the net effect of arbitrary GRAS command sequences can be computed on the fly. In section 4 we take a glance at related work and we conclude the paper with section 5.

2 Logs in GRAS

Before we are able to describe the technique to optimize logs, we have to know the semantics of the operations logged. Since queries do not alter the state of a graph at all, we are only interested in GRAS graph changing commands in the following. To start with, we need a formal model of a GRAS graph and then describe how graph changing commands affect this model.

2.1 GRAS Graphs

GRAS graphs are directed graphs with node and edge labels. Nodes can have an arbitrary number of attributes, which are byte strings of arbitrary length. However, to make this presentation more concise, we disregard attribute operations in this paper. To formalize GRAS graphs, we need the following sets. $\mathcal{N}$ denotes the *set of all node identifiers*, $\mathcal{L}_N$ is the *set of node labels*, and $\mathcal{L}_E$ constitutes the *set of edge labels*.

Definition 1 (Graph). *A GRAS graph G is a tuple (N, E, N_L) with the following meanings: $N \subseteq \mathcal{N}$ is the set of nodes of G; $E \subseteq N \times \mathcal{L}_E \times N$ is the set of edges of G; and $N_L : N \to \mathcal{L}_N$ maps nodes of G to their labels. $\mathcal{G}$ is the set of all GRAS graphs.*

The GRAS application programming interface offers various operations that query and modify the contents of a graph. We define the latter here in terms of the previous definition.

2.2 Graph Changing Commands

GRAS offers commands to modify all components of a graph. These are the basic units of logging in GRAS. We model them as functions that transform graphs.

Definition 2 (Graph changing commands). *Let $G \in \mathcal{G}, G = (N, E, N_L)$. We define the following functions to create and delete nodes and edges and to change the label of a node.*

Create node: $cn : \mathcal{N} \times \mathcal{L}_N \times \mathcal{G} \to \mathcal{G}$ *adds a new node to a graph. Let $n \in \mathcal{N}, l \in \mathcal{L}_N$. If $n \notin N$ then $cn(n, l, G) := (N \cup \{n\}, E, N'_L)$ with $N'_L(n) = l$ for $m = n$ and unchanged otherwise. If $n \in N$, then $cn(n, l, G)$ is not defined.*

Delete node: $dn : \mathcal{N} \times \mathcal{G} \to \mathcal{G}$ *removes a node from a graph. Let $n \in \mathcal{N}$. If $n \in N$, then $dn(n, G) := (N \setminus \{n\}, E', N'_L)$ where $E' = \{(s, l, t) \in E \mid s \neq n \wedge t \neq n\}$ and N'_L is undefined for n and unchanged otherwise. $dn(n, G)$ is undefined if $n \notin N$.*

Change label: $cl : \mathcal{N} \times \mathcal{L}_N \times \mathcal{G} \to \mathcal{G}$. *Change the label of a node in a graph. Let $n \in \mathcal{N}, l \in \mathcal{L}_N$. If $n \in N$ then $cl(n, l, G) := (N, E, N'_L)$ where $N'_L(n) = l$ and $N'_L(m) = N_L(m)$ for all $m \neq n$. $cl(n, l, G)$ is undefined if $n \notin N$.*

Create edge $ce : \mathcal{N} \times \mathcal{L}_E \times \mathcal{N} \times \mathcal{G} \to \mathcal{G}$. *Insert a new edge in a graph. Let $s, t \in \mathcal{N}, l \in \mathcal{L}_E$. If $s, t \in N$ and $(s, l, t) \notin E$ then $ce(s, l, t, G) := (N, E \cup \{(s, l, t)\}, N_L)$. $ce(s, l, t, G)$ is undefined if $s \notin N \vee t \notin N \vee (s, l, t) \in E$.*

Delete edge $de : \mathcal{N} \times \mathcal{L}_E \times \mathcal{N} \times \mathcal{G} \to \mathcal{G}$. *Delete an edge from a graph. Let $s, t \in \mathcal{N}, l \in \mathcal{L}_E$. If $s, t \in N$ and $(s, l, t) \in E$ then $de(s, l, t, G) := (N, E \setminus \{(s, l, t)\}, N_L)$. $de(s, l, t, G)$ is undefined if $s \notin N \vee t \notin N \vee (s, l, t) \notin E$.*

To be able to handle the graph changing commands as transformations between graphs, we view their Curry'd version in the following. So for any $n, s, t \in \mathcal{N}$, $l_N \in \mathcal{L}_N, l_E \in \mathcal{L}_E$ we view $cn(n, l_N), dn(n), ce(s, l_E, t), de(s, l_E, t), cl(n, l_N)$ as partial function from $\mathcal{G}$ into $\mathcal{G}$.

The following example shows how the structure changing commands affect a graph. We start with an empty graph and build up a small list. Nodes are modeled as natural numbers.

Example 1. An application models linked lists as graphs. A list has a node which is anchor to the list and has edges to all members of the list (edge label m). The members of the list are linked by edges with label *next*. The first and last elements in the list are connected to the anchor by *first* and *last* edges, respectively. The list is only accessed by the operations of an abstract data type (ADT), so that a consistent list structure is always guaranteed. The table of Fig. 1 lists five commands executed by a user or an application program on the list ADT in its first column. The corresponding graph changing commands and the resulting graphs are shown in the second and third column, respectively. The last column shows command sequences that undo the effects of the commands in the second column. We explain this later.

For convenience, we refer to the set of all create node commands as *Create-Node*, the set of all delete node commands as *DeleteNode*, and so on. The set $\mathcal{C}$ denotes all graph changing commands. By indexing the sets with a node identifier n, we specify command sets that all have n as one parameter.

For our considerations of GRAS logs, we are only interested in commands and command sequences, which can actually be applied to the graph in questions. If they cannot be applied, they will never be logged, because they are never executed. We call a command c applicable to a graph G, iff $c(G)$ is defined.

Command	Graph Cmds	Graph	Inverse
create	δ_1 =<cn(1,list)>	$G_1 = $ 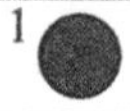	$\overline{\delta_1}$=<dn(1)>
append	δ_2 =<cn(2,elem), ce(1,m,2), ce(1,first,2), ce(1,last,2)>	$G_2 = $ 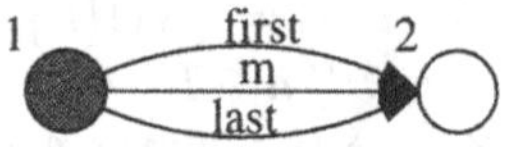	$\overline{\delta_2}$=<de(1,last,2), de(1,first,2). de(1,m,2), dn(2)>
append	δ_3 =<cn(3,elem), ce(1,m,3), de(1,last,2), ce(1,last,3), ce(2,next,3)>	$G_3 = $ 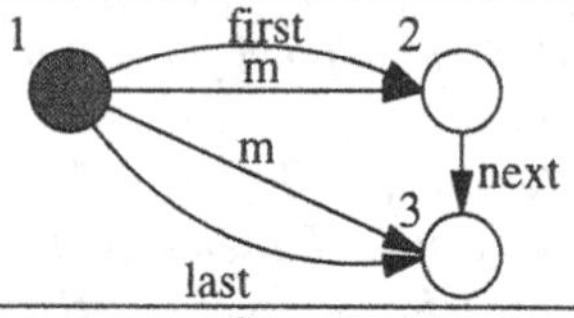	$\overline{\delta_3}$=<de(2,next,3), de(1,last,3), ce(1,last,2), de(1,m,3), dn(3)>
append	δ_4 =<cn(4,elem), ce(1,m,4), de(1,last,3), ce(1,last,4), ce(3,next,4)>	$G_4 = $ 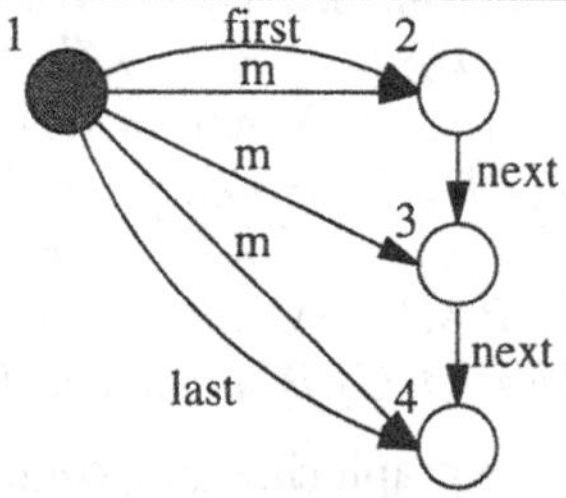	$\overline{\delta_4}$=<de(3,next,4), de(1,last,4), ce(1,last,3), de(1,m,4), dn(4)>
delete first	δ_5 =<dn(2), ce(1,first,3)>	$G_5 = $ 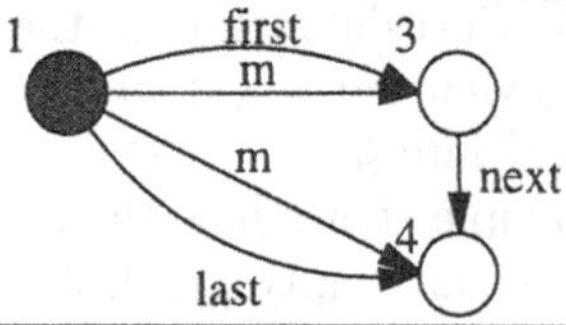	$\overline{\delta_5}$=<de(1,first,3), cn(2,elem), ce(1,first,2), ce(1,m,2), ce(2,next,3)>

Fig. 1. Example of graph commands

2.3 GRAS Logs

We now introduce command sequences and define the inverse of commands and command sequences. The inverse of command sequences are needed to undo the effects of commands and command sequences.

Definition 3. *The set* $\Delta := \{\langle c_1,\ldots,c_n\rangle \mid c_1,\ldots,c_n \in C\}$ *is the* set *of all command sequences.* ε_Δ *is the* empty command sequence. *Let* $\delta = \langle c_1,\ldots,c_n\rangle \in \Delta, G \in \mathcal{G}. \delta$ *is applicable to* $G :\Leftrightarrow \delta = \varepsilon_\Delta$ *or* c_1 *is applicable to* G *and* $\langle c_2,\ldots,c_n\rangle$ *is applicable to* $c_1(G)$.

For convenience, we write $G\langle c_1 \ldots c_n\rangle$ instead of $c_n \circ \ldots \circ c_1(G)$ for the application of a command sequence to a graph G. For the concatenation of two command sequences δ, δ', we simply write $\delta\delta'$.

When a command c is applied to a GRAS graph, we have to log the command itself for later redo but also a command (sequence) that computes the inverse of c for the undo log. The inverse of a command depends not only on the command (arguments) but also on the graph it is applied to. Nevertheless, we speak of the inverse of commands and command sequences and not of inverse of command (sequence) applications. The definition is straight forward, except for delete node command, where it is necessary to log the label and all incident edges of the deleted node.

Definition 4 (Inverse of command sequences). *Let $G \in \mathcal{G}$ with $G = (N, E, N_L)$. We define the inverse function $\mathcal{I} : \mathcal{G} \times \Delta \to \Delta$ for applicable commands as*

1. $\mathcal{I}(G, \varepsilon_\Delta) := \varepsilon_\Delta$.
2. $\mathcal{I}(G, \langle cn(n, l) \rangle) := \langle dn(n) \rangle$.
3. $\mathcal{I}(G, \langle dn(n) \rangle) := \langle cn(n, N_L(n)) \rangle \, CES_n \, CET_n$.

Here, CES_n, and CET_n are command sequences that restore the outgoing and incoming edges, respectively. Formally, this is $CES_n = \langle ce(n, l_e, t) \mid (n, l_e, t) \in E \rangle$ and $CET_n = \langle ce(s, l_e, n) \mid (s, l_e, n) \in E, s \neq n \rangle$. Note: if there are any edges $(n, l, n) \in E$, these will be restored only by the commands in CES_n by convention.

4. $\mathcal{I}(G, \langle cl(n, l) \rangle) := \langle cl(n, N_L(n)) \rangle$.
5. $\mathcal{I}(G, \langle ce(s, l, t) \rangle) := \langle de(s, l, t) \rangle$.
6. $\mathcal{I}(G, \langle de(s, l, t) \rangle) := \langle ce(s, l, t) \rangle$.
7. $\mathcal{I}(G, c\delta) := \mathcal{I}(Gc, \delta)\mathcal{I}(G, c)$.

The last rule of definition 4 states that the inverse of a command sequence stores the inverses of its commands in reverse order. In this way, the inverse of a command sequence δ undoes the effect of the last command of δ first. This is necessary to ensure applicability of the inverse when δ was executed.

Example 2. For the command sequences from Fig. 1, we find inverse command sequences as listed in the last column of table 1. Note that while $\overline{\delta_1}$, $\overline{\delta_2}$, $\overline{\delta_3}$, and $\overline{\delta_4}$ can be computed without knowing the graph, we have to know the edges of node 2 in G_4 to compute $\overline{\delta_5}$.

3 Optimizing GRAS Logs

When we speak of optimizing GRAS logs, we mean optimizing the command sequences associated with each checkpoint in a GRAS log. More precisely, for a command sequence $\delta \in \Delta$, we want to find a sequence δ', such that for each graph $G \in \mathcal{G}$ to which δ is applicable, $G\delta' = G\delta$ holds. In the best case, δ' is the shortest such sequence, i.e. δ' only contains the commands necessary to achieve the net effect of δ.

Even for the small examples of command sequences we have seen so far optimization pays off. Consider e.g. the sequence $\overline{\delta_2}$ from table 1. It was computed as $\mathcal{I}(G_1, \delta_2)$. When applied to G_2, it will first delete some edges leading to node 2 and then delete this node. But deleting node 2 right away would achieve the same effect, because all incident edges of a node are deleted when the node is deleted, anyway. Therefore, the sequence $\langle dn(2) \rangle$ is an optimization for $\overline{\delta_2}$.

In this section, we first describe the optimizations for a command sequence in a declarative way before we describe a model that shows how these optimizations can be computed on the fly.

3.1 Optimizing Command Sequences

We describe the optimizations on command sequences by specifying which operations can be removed from the sequence without changing its effect on any graph. For this purpose, we introduce an equivalence relation on command sequences.

Definition 5. *Two command sequences, δ, $\delta' \in \Delta$ are equivalent, $\delta \equiv \delta'$, if and only if $\forall_{G \in \mathcal{G}} : G\delta = G\delta' \vee \delta, \delta'$ are not applicable to G.*

In the rest of this section, we only consider applicable command sequences, so that the equivalence relation reduces to $G\delta = G\delta'$. We now specify rules that describe situations in which commands can be removed from a command sequence, so that the remaining sequence is equivalent to the original sequence. In the following, let $\delta \in \Delta$ and m be the length of δ. The set W_n shall contain all commands with node n as parameter, that are not create or delete node commands, i.e. $W_n = (C_n \setminus CreateNodes_n) \setminus DeleteNodes_n$. To optimize a command sequence, so that the result has a minimal length, we apply each rule as often as possible in the presented order.

1. Let $n \in \mathcal{N}$ and $i \in \mathbb{N}$ such that the i'th element of δ, denoted by δ_i, is $dn(n)$.
   (a) Every command $c \in W_n$ in the sequence before this delete node command can be removed if no create node command for n lies between c and $dn(n)$: Let $j \in \mathbb{N}$ be the largest number less than i such that $\delta_j = cn(n, l)$ for some $l \in \mathcal{L}_N$. If no such create node command exists, let $j = 0$. Then
   $$\forall_{j<k<i} : \delta_k \in W_n \Rightarrow \delta_1 \cdots \delta_{k-1}\delta_{k+1} \cdots \delta_m \equiv \delta$$
   (b) A pair of create and delete node commands (in this order) can be removed from the sequence, if no commands $c \in C_n$ occur between them: Let $j \in \mathbb{N}$ such that $\delta_j = cn(n, l)$ for some $l \in \mathcal{L}_N$ and $j < i$. Then
   $$(\forall_{j<k<i} : \delta_k \notin C_n) \Rightarrow \delta_1 \cdots \delta_{j-1}\delta_{j+1} \cdots \delta_{i-1}\delta_{i+1} \cdots \delta_m \equiv \delta$$
2. Let $n \in \mathcal{N}$ and $i \in \mathbb{N}$ such that $\delta_i = cl(n, l)$ for some $l \in \mathcal{L}_N$. All change label commands before δ_i can be removed.
   $$\forall_{j<i}\forall_{l \in \mathcal{L}_N} : \delta_j = cl(n, l) \Rightarrow \delta_1 \cdots \delta_{j-1}\delta j + 1 \cdots \delta_m \equiv \delta$$
3. Pairs of matching delete edge and create edge commands can be removed from the sequence. Let $s, t \in \mathcal{N}, l \in \mathcal{L}_E$, and $i, j \in \mathbb{N}$ such that $\delta_i = ce(s, l, t)$ and $\delta_j = de(s, l, t)$. Let further $min = min(i, j)$ and $max = max(i, j)$:
   $$(\forall_{min<k<max} : \delta_k \notin \{dn(s), dn(t), de(s, l, t), ce(s, l, t)\})$$
   $$\Rightarrow \delta_1 \cdots \delta_{min-1}\delta_{min+1} \cdots \delta_{max-1}\delta_{max+1} \cdots \delta_m \equiv \delta$$

After the optimization, the log contains for each node $n \in \mathcal{N}$, at most one delete node command (the first found in the original sequence). If it contains $dn(n)$, this is the first command from C_n in the optimized sequence. The sequence can also contain at most one create node command, either as the first command from C_n in the sequence or after a delete node with no commands from C_n between deletion and creation. This create command corresponds to the last create command for this node in the original sequence. Only after the optional delete and create node commands the optimized sequence might contain commands from W_n. This leads us to the following remark, which is important for optimizing on the fly, because it shows how to order the commands in an optimized sequence.

Remark 1. The regular expression $dn(n)[cn(n,l).W_n^*] \mid [cn(n,l)]W_n^*$ describes the commands for a single node n in an optimized sequence.

3.2 Optimizing on the Fly

The rules we have sketched so far, could directly be used to optimize a given command sequence. We could apply them e.g. every time a checkpoint was issued. However, this would incur a high overhead for the set checkpoint command. Instead, we want to compute the optimized command sequence during normal operation. This might incur a small overhead for all graph changing commands, but takes away the burden from the set checkpoint command. Optimizing on the fly also has the advantage that only the commands of the optimal sequence need be stored, so that less memory is used during logging.

We describe the technique we have used to implement the optimization as a formal model. A command sequence in this model is not simply a series of commands and their parameters, but a structure that can be efficiently queried for the command history. Before we define this structure, we motivate its design with an observation on applicable command sequences.

Since the optimization of command sequences should work for every graph a sequence can be applied to, we cannot exploit our knowledge about the state of a graph when recording commands in a log. Therefore, when recording starts, we have no knowledge about any nodes in the graph. However, we can learn about the state of the graph, or better the state of nodes affected by commands in the log, during recording. We can keep this knowledge for every node and use it to apply the optimizations described above.

Let $G \in \mathcal{G}$ be a GRAS graph. We model the state of a node in form of a finite automaton. For every node $n \in \mathcal{N}$, we start with a state *undefined*, because we do not know whether the node exists in the graph or not. When a command is logged that affects the node, we distinguish three cases:

1. The command is a create node command. Since the command must be applicable to G, we can derive that the node was not in G before the command and that it is afterwards. So the next commands for this node can be deletion or a command from W_n.
2. The command was a delete node command. Then n was in G before the deletion and is not afterwards. The next thing we can expect for this node is a create command.
3. If the command was from W_n, we know that n was in G before and still is there after command execution. Therefore, like in the first case, the next command can be deletion or another from W_n.

Remark 2. The state of each node in a graph follows the state transition diagram in part a) of Fig. 2. The automaton has three states (U = undefined, E = existent,

D = deleted). The three cases described above correspond to the three transitions from state U in the diagram (dn = delete node, cn = create node, and w for a command from W_n) to states E and D.

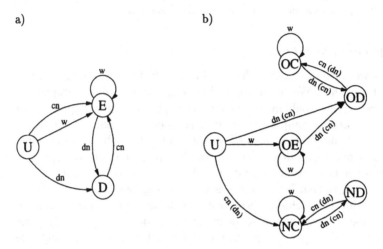

Fig. 2. State transition diagrams for one node in a command sequence

However, this automaton is not sufficient for optimizing on the fly. As we have noted earlier, an optimized sequence contains the first delete node command for node n of the original sequence if the node existed before the commands in the sequence were applied. Therefore, we must keep the information whether a node existed in the original graph or not. We do this by introducing more states for the state transition diagram, leading to the automaton sketched in part b) of Fig. 2. Its states form three groups. The first group contains only the state U=undefined. All states beginning with the letter 'O' mark nodes which existed in the graph when the log started (old nodes, OE=old existent, OD=old deleted, and OC=old created). The two states NC and ND (new created and new deleted) constitute the last group and mark nodes which were not in the graph when the log started. The arc labels of the second automaton are similar to the ones of the first. additionally, the labels in parentheses show the transitions we make in case of a backward command sequence. As can be seen, the states always refer to the graph reached by the commands of the forward command sequence, while the transitions refer to the inverse commands computed during logging.

In the following let $States = \{U, OE, OD, OC, NC, ND\}$ be the set of states of figure 2b).

Definition 6. *An* optimizing command sequence M *is a 3-tuple* $M = (S, L, E)$, *with*

  – $S : \mathcal{N} \to States$ *maps every node to a state of the automaton in Fig. 2b).*

- $L : \mathcal{N} \rightarrow \wp(ChangeLabel_n)$ *maps each node to a set of change label commands.*
- $E \subseteq CreateEdge \cup DeleteEdge$ *contains all relevant edge operations of M.*

$\mathcal{M}$ *is the set of all optimizing command sequences and* $\varepsilon_{\mathcal{M}} = (S_U, L_\emptyset, \emptyset)$ *denotes the empty optimizing command sequence with* $S_U(n) = U$, *and* $L_\emptyset(n) = \emptyset$ *for all* $n \in \mathcal{N}$.

Note that we are not able to determine the order in which commands were logged, once they are stored in an optimizing command sequence. This is not necessary, because we respect the following invariants when logging commands: a) For every node n at most one change label command is stored in $L(n)$. b) For every edge (s, l, t), at most a delete or a create command is logged in E, but not both. Therefore, the commands from L and E are independent from another and can be applied in any order. Albeit important is, that the nodes occurring as parameters in L and E exist when the log is executed. We guarantee this by executing all node deletion and creation commands before any edge commands.

To fill the defined structure with life, we have to define how commands are logged in an optimizing command sequence. Because we want to incrementally compute the net effects of applied commands and since in a backward command sequence commands are logged in reverse order, we must specify two different mechanisms for forward and backward logs. We define the forward logging mechanism first.

Definition 7. *The function* $\mathcal{F} : C \times \mathcal{M} \rightarrow \mathcal{M}$ *logs commands of a forward command sequence in an optimizing command sequence. Let* $M = (S, L, E) \in \mathcal{M}$ *be an optimizing command sequence and* $n \in \mathcal{N}$. *Then* $\mathcal{F}$ *is defined as follows:*

1. $\mathcal{F}(cn(n, l), M) = (S', L', A, E)$ *with* $L'(n) = \{cl(n, l)\}$. *The change label command is only used in this model to store the label of the created node. It will not occur in the resulting command sequence. For this and all following cases, refer to figure 2b) for the value of $S'(n)$.*
2. $\mathcal{F}(dn(n), M) = (S', L', E')$ *where* $L'(n) = \emptyset$, *and* $E' = E' \setminus (CreateEdge_n \cup DeleteEdge_n)$.
3. $\mathcal{F}(cl(n, l), M) = (S', L', E)$ *where* $L'(n) = \{cl(n, l)\}$.
4. $\mathcal{F}(ce(s, l_e, t), M) = (S', L, E')$. *Here, we distinguish two cases for E'. If* $de(s, l_e, t) \in E$ *then* $E' = E \setminus \{de(s, l_e, t)\}$. *If* $de(s, l_e, t) \notin E$ *then* $E' = E \cup \{ce(s, l_e, t)\}$.
5. $\mathcal{F}(de(s, l_e, t), M) = (S', L, E')$. *In analogy to the create edge command, we define* $E' = E \setminus \{ce(s, l_e, t)\}$ *if* $de(s, l_e, t) \in E$ *and* $E' = E \cup \{de(s, l_e, t)\}$ *otherwise.*

The main difference between and optimizing forward and backward command sequence is this: Since the commands in a backward sequence are executed in reverse order as they were logged, we "know the future" when recording the commands. For example, when a delete node command is logged for node n, we know that we do not need to log any other commands for this node thereafter, because it will be deleted when the log is executed.

Definition 8. *The function* $\mathcal{B} : \mathcal{C} \times \mathcal{M} \rightarrow \mathcal{M}$ *logs commands of a backward command sequence in an optimizing command sequence. Let* $M = (S, L, A, E) \in \mathcal{M}$ *be an optimizing command sequence and* $n \in \mathcal{N}$*. Then* $\mathcal{B}$ *is defined as follows:*

1. $\mathcal{B}(cn(n, l), M) = (S', L', E)$*. If* $L(n) = \emptyset$ *then* $L'(n) = \{cl(n, l)\}$*, otherwise* $L'(n) = L(n)$*. We only need to log the label of the first create node or change label command, because this will be the one taking effect when the log is applied later. For this and all following cases, refer to the labels in parentheses of the state transitions of figure 2b) for the value of* $S'(n)$*.*

2. $\mathcal{B}(dn(n), M) = (S', L, E)$*. We do not change any values of* L *and* E*. If any commands for* n *are logged,* $S(n)$ *must be one of* $\{OD, ND\}$ *and we know that a create node command was logged for this node already. The commands logged so far will take effect after the delete node, and are therefore kept in the log.*

3. $\mathcal{B}(cl(n, l), M)$*. Like for all remaining cases, the result of* $\mathcal{B}$ *here is* M *if* $S(n) \in \{OC, NC\}$*, since in that case, a delete node command already occurred and all further commands affecting* n *can be ignored. Otherwise, it is* (S', L', E) *where* $L'(n) = L(n)$ *if* $L(n) \neq \emptyset$ *and* $L'(n) = \{cl(n, l)\}$ *if* $L(n) = \emptyset$*.*

4. $\mathcal{B}(ce(s, l_e, t), M)$ *the same as* $\mathcal{F}(ce(s, l_e, t))$ *except that we only need to log, if* $S(s) \notin \{OC, NC\}$ *and* $S(t) \notin \{OC, NC\}$*.*

5. $\mathcal{B}(de(s, l_e, t), M)$ *like above.*

Now that we have specified how commands are logged in an optimizing command sequence, we must define in which order the commands in such a sequence are executed. We obtain the order from the state a node has reached in the automaton of figure 2b. In case of a forward command sequence, we follow the transitions from U to the state reached. For a backward command sequence, we start from the state reached and traverse the transitions in reverse direction.

Definition 9. *The functions* $\Delta_{\mathcal{F}}, \Delta_{\mathcal{B}} : \mathcal{M} \rightarrow \Delta$ *map the commands of an optimizing command sequence to a command sequence for forward and backward logging, respectively. For simplicity, we write* $\langle X \rangle$ *for the command sequence containing all commands from set* X *in an arbitrary order.*

Let $M = (S, L, E) \in \mathcal{M}$ *be an optimizing command sequence. To execute the commands of* M *as a forward or backward command sequence, let for each node* $n \in \mathcal{N}$ δ_n *be defined according to Fig. 3. Then* $\Delta_{\mathcal{F}}(M)$ *is the concatenation of all* δ_n *from the second column followed by the commands in* E*:* $\Delta_{\mathcal{F}}(M) := (\Pi_{n \in \mathcal{N}} \delta_n).\langle E \rangle$*. The same applies to* $\Delta_{\mathcal{B}}(M)$ *with the third column of Fig. 3.*

Our implementation of command log optimization closely resembles the formal model presented. For every node occurring as parameter in a command log, we keep information about change label (and also attribute modification) commands in a hash table. Likewise, we keep all edge commands in a table that can be efficiently accessed by source and target node identifiers of a command. The structures are kept in main memory until a checkpoint is issued. Then they are written to stable storage as a sequence as described by the functions $\Delta_{\mathcal{F}}$ and $\Delta_{\mathcal{B}}$.

$S(n)$	δ_n for $\Delta_{\mathcal{F}}$	δ_n for $\Delta_{\mathcal{B}}$
U	ε_Δ	ε_Δ
OE	$\langle L(n) \rangle$	$\langle L(n) \rangle$
OC	$\langle dn(n) \rangle$	$\langle cn(n,l) \rangle$ with $\{cl(n,l)\} = L(n)$
OD	$\langle dn(n)\, cn(n,l) \rangle$ with $\{cl(n,l)\} = L(n)$	$\langle dn(n)\, cn(n,l) \rangle$ with $\{cl(n,l)\} = L(n)$
NC	$\langle cn(n,l) \rangle$ with $\{cl(n,l)\} = L(n)$	$\langle dn(n) \rangle$
ND	ε_Δ	ε_Δ

Fig. 3. Commands for node n from an optimizing command sequence

4 Related Work

All papers dealing with log optimization have their motivation in common. In all cases, optimizing logs reduces both storage space and execution time of logs. In [4] the authors describe how to optimize archive logs by scanning a log sequentially backwards. During the scan, they store information about which records were already written in a bit map. In this way, only the last write for each record is kept in the optimized log. This technique is explicitly designed for off-line operation and therefore not suited for our purposes. However, we also use a bit map to mark the parts of an attribute that were already modified in a backward log (though this is not described in this paper).

Blaustein and Kaufmann [1] use logs to reintegrate the databases replicated at different sites after a communication failure. They merge the two logs recorded at each site and aim to delete redundant operations from the result. Like in our approach, the operations on a database must belong to a known class of transactions with specified semantics. By modeling the dependencies between transactions with a graph they use graph rewriting rules to remove redundant transactions. In this approach, the optimizations are done when two logs are merged, while redundant operations are not considered during normal operation.

Like in replicated databases, disconnected file systems need to reintegrate the effects of operations performed on a system which was working autonomously for some time. Like in GRAS, the operations which modify a file system are known beforehand and their effects can be computed from their parameters and the state of the file system. In [3] Huston and Honeyman use peephole optimization known from compiler construction to find redundant operations in a log. The rules they use are very similar to the rules described in subsection 3.1. Since this is a declarative approach, there is no way to perform these optimizations during normal operation, Instead, they trigger the optimizer when necessary, e.g. when log space shortens.

Very close to our approach is the work on log optimization in the context of the distributed file system Coda [6]. The optimizations are similar to the ones in GRAS and are computed during normal operation. The logs are held in separate command sequences for each file identifier, so that they can be efficiently searched and accessed. Different to our approach is that the state of a file (existent, not existent) is not explicitly modeled but has to be inferred each time an operation is logged. As there is no undo in a file system, there also is no need to compute and optimize the inverse of command sequences there.

5 Conclusion

We have presented our work on log optimization in the graph-oriented DBMS GRAS. Mechanism for both, forward and backward log optimization were introduced. The mechanisms work on a common data structure and compute the net effect of command sequences on the fly. The technique described is already implemented and successfully used in GRAS. Still missing is an evaluation of our approach by comparing the length of optimized and not optimized command logs for the tools using GRAS. However, the effects of optimization on the runtime of these tools are neglectible.

The described mechanisms rely on the fact that GRAS offers only a few types of commands to modify a graph. This is in contrast to object-oriented database management systems, were objects can be modified through their methods in a way the database system does not know in advance but that are specified by the application logic. It would be possible, however, to translate the operations on objects, their attributes and relations specified in terms of a programming language to operations on nodes, node attributes and edges. This lead to a language independent kernel for an object-oriented DBMS and enabled one to use techniques like described in this paper.

References

[1] Barbara T. Blaustein and Charles W. Kaufman. Updating replicated data during communications failures. In Alain Pirotte and Yannis Vassiliou, editors, *11th International Conference on Very Large Data Bases*, pages 49–58, Stockholm, Sweden, August 1985. Morgan Kaufmann.

[2] Reiner Gombert. Extensions to GRAS user-recovery. Master's thesis, RWTH Aachen, Department of Computer Science III, 1995.

[3] L. B. Huston and P. Honeyman. Peephole log optimization. Technical Report 95-3, Center for Information Technology Integration, Univ. of Michigan, January 1995.

[4] John Kaunitz and Louis van Ekert. Audit trail compaction for database recovery. *Communications of the ACM*, 27(7):678–683, July 1984.

[5] Norbert Kiesel, Andreas Schürr, and Bernhard Westfechtel. GRAS, a graph-oriented (software) engeneering database system. *Information Systems*, 20(1):21–51, 1995.

[6] James Jay Kistler. *Disconnected operation in a distributed file system*, volume 1002 of *LNCS*. Springer-Verlag Inc., 1995.

[7] M. Nagl, editor. *Building Tighthly Integrated Software Development Environments – The IPSEN Approach*, volume 1170 of *LNCS*. Springer-Verlag, 1996.

[8] Bernhard Westfechtel. Extension of a graph storage for software documents with primitives for undo/redo and revision control. Aachener Informatik-Berichte 89-8, RWTH Aachen, Lehrstuhl für Informatik III, 1989.

A Distributed Algorithm for Global Query Optimization in Multidatabase Systems

Silvio Salza[1], Giovanni Barone[1], and Tadeusz Morzy[2]

[1] Università di Roma "La Sapienza", Dipartimento di Informatica e Sistemistica,
via Salaria 113, I-00198 Roma, Italy
{salza,barone}@dis.uniroma1.it
[2] Technical University of Poznań, Institute of Computing Sciences,
Ul. Piotrowo 3A, 60-965 Poznań, Poland
morzy@put.poznan.pl

Abstract. In multidatabase systems the heterogeneity and the autonomy of the sites preclude the applicability of the classical query optimization algorithms used in distributed database systems, and therefore new approaches have to be investigated. In this paper we propose a distributed optimization algorithm that makes very general assumptions on the cost function, and on the degree of autonomy of the federated sites. The algorithm is based on a cooperative approach where cost of a query execution plan is evaluated as the composition of the cost estimates produced by the local sites where each part of the computation has to be performed. During the optimization process larger and larger partial execution plans are considered, and the the relative cost estimates are exchanged between the sites. Duplicated and unnecessary computation is avoided by discarding as soon as possible partial plans that are dominated by an equivalent one. The paper substantially extends the results of a previous paper, where we first introduced the idea of cooperative optimization, by removing major restrictions on the query model, and by considering not only sequential execution plans but also parallel ones.

1 Introduction

A multidatabase system (MDBS) integrates information from heterogeneous preexisting database systems, called component local database systems (LDBS), to support global applications accessing data at more than one LDBS. A key feature of MDBSs is the local autonomy that each LDBS retains to manage its own data and serve its existing applications.

A user can issue a global query on an MDBS to retrieve data from several local databases. Due to location transparency the user does not need to know where the data is stored and how the result is processed. The MDBS hides not only differences in user interfaces and data models, but also optimization and execution details. How to efficiently process a global query is the task of *Multidatabase Query Optimization (MQO)*. Like in traditional Distributed Database Systems (DDBS), the MDBS has to select the execution plan with minimum estimated processing and transmission cost. Although the basic query optimization paradigm remains unchanged, in MDBSs the optimization process becomes far more complex than in homogeneous DDBSs. This is due to several reasons. First, because of the autonomy local cost information needed for global query optimization (e.g local cost formulas) typically is not available to the MDBS. Second, the MDBS has neither direct control over queries executed at LDBS, nor direct access to their internal data structures. Consequently, the classical algorithms proposed for global query optimization in traditional homogeneous distributed database systems are not appropriate for MDBS.

The problem has recently attracted a number of contributions [1–3, 5–10, 12, 13]. Most of this work has concentrated on developing new techniques to derive approximates cost models for autonomous LDBSs. In [2], Du et al. have proposed a *calibration method* to deduce the necessary local information. The idea is to use a synthetically created database, and to run a set of queries against this database, to deduce the coefficients in cost formulas for the underlying LDBS. However, sometimes it may not be possible (or not allowed) to create the calibrating database at some local sites. Another way to deduce the necessary local information, based on a query sampling method, has been presented in [12, 13]. This method consists in grouping all possible queries on each LDBS into classes, and running a sample query workload for each class. The costs of sample queries are then used to derive a general cost formula for the queries in the query class by multiple regression. However, the method has some shortcomings as well, since the estimation process heavily depends on the system contention and it may be difficult (or not allowed) to run all types of sample of queries necessary to correctly deduce cost formulas.

In [6, 7] the architecture of a multidatabase query optimizer and the problems arising from the heterogeneity and local autonomy of component LDBS are presented and discussed. In [5], Lee et al. have considered the MQO problem for replicated MDBS. In [3] the problem of reducing multidatabase query response time by tree balancing has been considered. The authors propose the two-phase optimization strategy that first produces a left deep join tree query execution plan, and then, the plan is improved with respect to response time using tree transformations. Finally an interesting algorithm has been presented in [1], to modify a query execution plan on-the-fly in response to unexpected delays that can arise due to communication problems in obtaining partial results.

In contrast to the above methods, focusing on techniques of cost estimation of local query processing, we have introduced in a previous paper [10] an innovative approach to multidatabase query optimization based on the cooperation of among the LDBSs in the evaluation of the execution cost of a global query execution plan. The main idea behind this approach is to delegate the evaluation of the processing cost of each part of the execution plan to the LDBS where the computation would be performed. However, the algorithm presented in [10] has several major limitations. First, global queries must be represented by connected planar graphs where arcs represent binary join conditions among sites. Therefore join conditions involving more than two sites are not allowed. Second, the search space is restricted to strictly sequential execution plans, thus not considering parallel (bushy) plans, and so preventing to reach the optimal solution when the goal is minimizing query response time. Moreover, the algorithm does not consider plans with cartesian products. Third, the optimization process is synchronous, in the sense that each step of the algorithm may begin only after all sites have completed the previous step of the computation.

In this paper we present a new and more general decentralized and distributed optimization algorithm that substantially extends our previous results. The algorithm is based on the same idea of delegating the evaluation of the execution cost of the elementary steps to the LDBSs where the computation is performed, but refers to a much more general query execution model in which the query structure is represented by a hypergraph whose hyperarcs represent join conditions involving any number of sites. Moreover the search space has been extended to consider parallel query execution plans as well as plans with cartesian products. Finally, the structure of the distributed computation is more flexible since each site, during the optimization process, performs its own computation asynchronously, being triggered only by the arrival of the partial results it needs from the other sites. The computational complexity of the algorithm is also analyzed, which, though exponential in the general case, becomes polynomial in the number of sites in the interesting case of linear queries.

The rest of the paper is organized as follows. Section 2 describes the query execution model and the decomposition of global queries. Section 3 discusses the execution model and the structure of the global query execution plans. In Section 4 the global query optimization problem is formulated, and some special properties of the cost function are discussed. The distributed cooperative query optimization algorithm is then presented in Section 5. Finally Section 6 summarizes the conclusions.

2 The Query Execution Model

The MDBS model used here is basically that of [10] and repeated only for the sake of completeness. A MDBS is a collection of sites $S = \{S_1, \ldots S_n\}$ with component local database systems $LDBS_1, \ldots, LDBS_n$, autonomous and possibly heterogeneous [11]. Each LDBS may have its own data model and a local database schema managed by the local database management system. The portion of the local database schema available at the MDBS level is called an *export schema*. Export schemas of LDBSs are imported and integrated into a *federated schema*. During the integration process, possible data and structural inconsistencies are resolved [4]. Without any loss of generality, we assume in the remainder of the paper that the export schema of each LDBS coincides with its component schema, and that all the sites have the same federated schema. Although we do not make any particular assumption on local data models, we assume that the global data model, and hence all the export schemas and the federated schema, are relational.

All the sites are connected by a network about which we do not make any special assumption, other than that all sites are, either directly or indirectly, connected to each other, and that each component LDBS may determine at any time the transmission cost of a message to any other site.

Due to autonomy of LDBSs, there is a clear distinction in an MDBS between *local queries* and *global queries*. A local query is a query on the local schema that accesses only data controlled by a single LDBS. It is locally submitted to and executed by the LDBS, without the control of the MDBS. A global query is a query on the federated schema that accesses data controlled by more than one LDBS. It is submitted to the MDBS that coordinates its execution by interacting with the LDBS. For sake of simplicity, we restrict ourselves to considering *global SPJ queries*, i.e. with select, join and project operations only. This is indeed a quite general class of queries, since more complex queries that include unions are usually decomposed during the optimization process into a set of SPJ queries that are optimized independently. Moreover, we assume for simplicity that export schemas of LDBS do not contain replicated data.

In evaluating a global query it may be necessary to perform local computations in several LDBSs, and then exchange intermediate results among them to perform global joins across local databases, i. e. between relations from different export schemas. Without any specific assumption on the local data models and without violating the local autonomy, we assume that each participating LDBS can perform at the MDBS level a *federated-join* operation, that consists in joining a local intermediate result and an *imported relation*, i.e. the result of a partial subquery imported from another site.

According to our execution model a global query Q is decomposed into a set of *local subqueries* Q_i (one for each site S_i involved in the query), that can be directly evaluated by local DBMS. All conditions that involve only attributes of the same LDBS are pushed into local subqueries. Local subqueries are connected by a set of *global join* conditions, that can be enforced at the global level through the execution of federated join operations.

The decomposition of the global query can be performed by pushing local select and join conditions into local subqueries, whenever possible, and incorporating the remaining conditions into federated joins [10]. Each local subquery incorporates a projection which eliminates all attributes which are neither in the final result nor involved in some global join; the latter attributes will be eventually eliminated later, after performing the corresponding joins. Without any loss of generality we will actually disregard the projections, by simply assuming that every attribute not in the final result is eliminated as soon as possible during the global query evaluation process.

The global structure of a query Q can then be represented in by a *query hypergraph* $\mathcal{H}_Q = \langle \mathcal{N}_Q, \mathcal{E}_Q \rangle$ where the nodes $S_i \in \mathcal{N}_Q$ represent the sites involved in the query, and the hyperedges $E_i \in \mathcal{E}_Q$ represent the global conditions. Each hyperedge $E_i = \{S_{i_1}, \ldots, S_{i_k}\}$ is actually the subset of all the sites that have at least one attribute involved in a given global join condition. Note that more

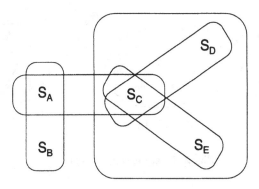

Fig. 1. Query hypergraph

than one condition may correspond to the same hyperedge. The hypergraph of a sample query, involving five sites S_A, S_B, S_C, S_D, S_E, is represented in Figure 1.

Without any substantial loss of generality we restrict to the case of *connected global queries*, where the hypergraph is connected, i.e. each node belongs to at least one hyperedge, and for any two nodes there is a chain of hyperedges connecting them. It is in fact quite evident that a *not connected* global query can always be decomposed into a set of subqueries that can be optimized independently, without precluding the global optimal solution.

3 Query Execution Plans

As pointed out above, in our execution model the evaluation of a global query is a two-level process, which consists first in evaluating in each site the local subquery, and then in connecting the results with a set of federated-join operations. Formally, at the global level, the execution process is specified by a *Query Execution Plan (QEP)* that defines a partial order in the execution of the federated-join operations. A QEP can be represented as a binary tree with leaves corresponding to the local subqueries, and internal nodes representing federated-join operations between intermediate results, with the convention that the operation is performed in the site where the operand corresponding to the left subtree has been computed. Each subtree of a QEP is called a *Partial Query Execution Plan (PQEP)* and represents the evaluation of an intermediate result, i.e. a subquery of the given query. For each PQEP $\mathcal{P}$ we define the set of sites $R(\mathcal{P})$ corresponding to the leaves of $\mathcal{P}$, and we denote the corresponding subquery as $Q(R(\mathcal{P}))$.

Each internal node of a QEP represents a PQEP $\mathcal{P} = \mathcal{P}_l \oplus \mathcal{P}_r$ which is the *composition*, i.e. the federated-join between the two intermediate results corresponding to its left and right subtrees $\mathcal{P}_l$ and $\mathcal{P}_r$. The root of $\mathcal{P}$ has an *associated set* of join conditions that are enforced during the execution of the corresponding federated-join. These are all the global conditions that could not be enforced earlier in the computation.

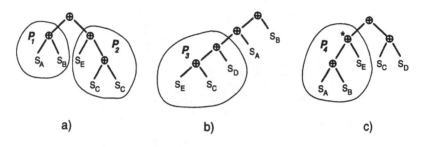

Fig. 2. Query execution plans

If an internal node in a PQEP has an empty set of associated conditions, that means that the corresponding federated join degenerates to a cartesian product. But it is quite evident that for a global query there may be no QEP without-global cartesian products. Therefore it is not possible, in general, to restrict, as usually done in query optimization, to execution plans without cartesian products. Nevertheless, we decide to avoid *unnecessary* cartesian products, i.e. to accept them only if the global query has no QEP without cartesian products.

More formally we say that a PQEP $\mathcal{P}$ is *valid* if one of the two following conditions hold:

i) the PQEP is part of a QEP with no cartesian products;
ii) there is no QEP for the given query without cartesian products, and for each federated-join in $\mathcal{P}$, say $\mathcal{P}_x = \mathcal{P}_l \oplus \mathcal{P}_r$, there is at least one hyperedge E_i connecting $R(\mathcal{P}_l)$ and $R(\mathcal{P}_r)$, i.e $E_i \cap R(\mathcal{P}_l) \neq \emptyset$ and $E_i \cap R(\mathcal{P}_r) \neq \emptyset$.

Accordingly we say that a subquery is valid if there is at least a valid PQEP for it.

For every valid subquery, several valid PQEPs exist in general. We shall call them *comparable*, since they compute the same subquery and, as we will see in the following sections, must be compared in the optimization process in order to select the one with the lowest cost. On the other hand we say that two PQEPs $\mathcal{P}_l$ and $\mathcal{P}_r$ are *composable* if it is possible to compose them to form a valid PQEP $\mathcal{P} = \mathcal{P}_l \oplus \mathcal{P}_r$. The corresponding subqueries $Q(R(\mathcal{P}_l))$ and $Q(R(\mathcal{P}_r))$ are said to be *composable* as well. Moreover given a valid subquery Q, we say that Q is *computable* in a site S_i, if there is at least a valid PQEP for Q with the last federated join performed in S_i, and that Q is *usable* in a site S_i if there is some subquery Q' computable in S_i that is composable with Q. Finally, given a subquery Q we say that every site $S_p \in R(Q)$ is a *producer* for Q, and that a site $S_c \notin R(Q)$ is a *consumer* for Q if Q is usable in S_c.

Three different QEPs for the global query of Figure 1, are represented in Figure 2. According to our definitions, plans a) and b) are valid QEPs, but plan c) is not because the federated-join marked by * degenerates into a cartesian product, and there is at least one valid QEP for the given query. The subtrees $\mathcal{P}_1$, $\mathcal{P}_2$, $\mathcal{P}_3$ correspond to valid PQEPs, as part of valid QEPs, and $\mathcal{P}_4$ is invalid since it cannot be part of any valid QEP. $\mathcal{P}_2$, $\mathcal{P}_3$ are also comparable, since they compute the same subquery $Q(S_C, S_D, S_E)$, that is therefore a valid subquery. Moreover $\mathcal{P}_1$, $\mathcal{P}_2$ are composable, and so are the corresponding subqueries $Q(S_A, S_B)$ and $Q(S_C, S_D, S_E)$. Subquery $Q(S_A, S_B)$ is usable in S_C, S_D and S_E, since it is composable with valid subqueries $Q(S_C)$, $Q(S_C, S_D)$ and $Q(S_C, S_E)$ which are computable respectively in these sites. We may also say that S_A and S_B are producers for $Q(S_A, S_B)$ and that S_C, S_D and S_E are consumers for that subquery.

4 Global Query Optimization

According to the query execution model discussed in the previous section, we consider the decomposition of the global query into local subqueries as a preliminary step, and then restrict the optimization problem to the selection of the best QEP, i.e. the best partial ordering of the federated-join operations. We therefore make a clear distinction between two optimization levels:

- *global optimization*: selecting the optimal *global* execution plan;
- *local optimization*: selecting the best *local* execution plans, i.e. the best way to perform each federated-join in the global QEP in the local site where it must be executed.

The problem arises since the two levels are strictly interconnected, and, because of the autonomy of the sites, the local optimization part can only be performed locally. The same kind of stratification is in the cost function, since no site has a complete information on other component LDBSs (database profiles, access methods, local cost functions, etc). Therefore, no single site can evaluate (or estimate) the total cost of a QEP. On the other hand, each site can solve its own local optimization problem and evaluate the cost of the federated-join operations it has to perform, and the cost of sending the results to neighbor sites, provided that a suitable information on the extensional characteristics of the imported relations is supplied to it.

This means that the total execution cost of a QEP must be computed *incrementally* through the *cooperation* of all the sites involved. Each site evaluates the cost of its part of the computation and the characteristics of the result, and eventually sends this information to the sites that may use it in further computation. Due to the (presumably) small number of LDBSs in an MDBS, and therefore of sites involved in the query, it makes sense to consider an exhaustive approach, i.e. taking into account all the valid QEP and computing the exact optimum.

Given a PQEP $\mathcal{P}$ and a site $m \notin R(\mathcal{P})$ in the MDBS, the cost function $C(m, \mathcal{P})$ gives the total cost of evaluating, in the order specified by $\mathcal{P}$, the partial query associated to it, and of sending the result to node m, that may utilize it as an operand for a further federated-join operation. Moreover given two comparable PQEP $\mathcal{P}_1$ and $\mathcal{P}_2$ and a site $m \notin R(\mathcal{P}_1) \cup R(\mathcal{P}_2)$, we say that $\mathcal{P}_1$ *dominates* $\mathcal{P}_2$ in the site m if $C(m, \mathcal{P}_1) < C(m, \mathcal{P}_2)$.

During the optimization procedure, that we shall discuss in the next section, the cost function allows to compare any two comparable PQEPs (i.e. that compute the same subquery) in order to select the one with the lower cost and possibly disregard the other one in evaluating the cost of larger PQEPs.

According to the incremental structure of our query execution model, and without any substantial loss of generality, we may assume for the cost function the following incremental structure:

$$C(m, \mathcal{P}_i) = F_i(m, \mathcal{P}_i, \emptyset)$$
$$C(m, \mathcal{P}_i \oplus \mathcal{P}) = C(i, \mathcal{P}_i) + C(i, \mathcal{P}) + F_i(m, \mathcal{P}_i, \mathcal{P})$$

where the first equation is for the case of a local subquery, and $F_i(m, \mathcal{P}_i, \mathcal{P})$ represents the cost of computing in site S_i the federated-join between a local intermediate result specified by $\mathcal{P}_i$, and the imported relation specified by $\mathcal{P}$, plus the transmission cost, i.e. the cost of sending the result to the destination site m. Note that, under very general assumptions, for any two sites the transmission cost depends only on the subquery and not on the PQEP.

It is easy to prove that any cost function with the incremental structure defined above has the very interesting property that, if a PQEP $\mathcal{P}'_1$ dominates another PQEP $\mathcal{P}'_2$ *in a given site i*, then replacing $\mathcal{P}'_1$ with $\mathcal{P}'_2$ in any PQEP computed in i, would not improve its execution cost. This property, that we shall call *composition consistency*, allows to prune the search space during the optimization process, by discarding a PQEP any time a comparable one is found to have a better cost. This is actually a natural consequence of the structure of the execution model, and of the incremental way in which the computation is performed, and all the cost functions we may reasonably think about, involving the sum of local execution cost and transmission cost, are indeed composition consistent.

Note that the *incremental* cost computed by F_i only depends on information *local* to site i, and on *extensional parameters* (i.e. relation and attribute cardinality etc.) of the intermediate result defined by $\mathcal{P}$.

5   The Cooperative Optimization Algorithm

Let us consider a global query $\mathcal{Q}$, with query hypergraph $\mathcal{H}_Q = \langle \mathcal{N}_Q, \mathcal{E}_Q \rangle$ and let us assume that all the n sites in the multidatabase are involved in the query, i.e. there is a node in $\mathcal{H}_Q$ for every site in the MDBS.

The distributed optimization algorithm is based on the incremental structure of the PQEPs, that are built through composition of other PQEPs, and on the cooperation between the different sites (according to their *consumer producer* roles) in evaluating the cost of PQEPs, and finally in selecting an optimal QEP. More specifically, referring to the definitions given in Section 3, each site has the responsibility of selecting the best PQEP for each subquery Q for which it is a *producer*, i.e that is *computable* in that site, and sending the corresponding cost estimate to all the of the other sites that are *consumers* of Q, i.e. where

Q is *usable*. These cost estimates can then be used by each site to evaluate the cost of a larger PQEP. Since it is assumed that the cost function is composition consistent, this guarantees, as we shall see later, that only a lowest cost PQEP for a given subquery in a given site should be considered for the computation of further PQEPs.

The computation that takes place in each site S_i during the distributed optimization process is represented by the *computational graph* of the site. The graph has a node for each valid subquery Q computable in the site and a directed edge between any two nodes Q and Q' such that there exists a valid subquery Q'' composable with Q such that the result of their composition is Q'. In other terms each node of the graph corresponds to a subquery *produced* in the given site, and each edge corresponds to a subquery *consumed* in the site. Note that the computational graph is a DAG with a source node representing the local subquery of site S_i and a sink node representing the global query.

More formally given a site S_i and a subquery Q for which S_i is a producer, there are in general several valid PQEPs for Q with the last join performed in S_i. We denote with $O_{S_i}(Q)$ the *local optimum* for Q in S_i, i.e. the PQEP with the lowest cost among the ones with the last federated join performed in S_i. Similarly, given a subquery Q for which S_i is a consumer we denote with $O_{S_i}^*(Q)$ the *global optimum* for Q in S_i, i.e. the PQEP that delivers the result of Q in S_i with the lowest cost.

The main idea in the algorithm is to get to the optimal QEP by incrementally computing local and global optima for larger and larger subqueries with a bottom-up strategy. Actually the algorithm restricts to considering only a subset of possible PQEP for each subquery Q, which may preclude from getting to the actual optima. Therefore we use in the following description the symbols $\Omega_{S_i}(Q)$ and $\Omega_{S_i}^*(Q)$ instead of $O_{S_i}(Q)$ and $O_{S_i}^*$ for local and global 'optima' computed by the algorithm. The computation can be sketched as follows:

- Each site S_i computes the optimal execution plan for its local subquery $\Omega_{S_i}(Q_i)$ and the corresponding cost $C(m, \Omega_{S_i}(Q_i))$ and estimates of the extensional parameters and sends them to each consumer site m ;
- for each subquery Q_c for which a given site S_i is *consumer*, i.e. corresponding to some (possibly several) edges in its computational graph, the site waits for the PQEP cost and parameter estimates from all the producers of that subquery; then selects $\Omega_{S_i}^*(Q_c)$ as the one with the lowest cost;
- for each pair of subqueries Q and Q' for which a given site S_i is *producer*, and with the corresponding nodes inthe computational graph connected by an edge corresponding to the subquery Q'', when $\Omega_{S_i}(Q)$ and $\Omega_{S_i}^*(Q'')$ have been computed, then the cost of the PQEP $\Omega_{S_i}(Q) \oplus \Omega_{S_i}^*(Q)$ is evaluated, and we say that the edge has been *solved*;
- for each subquery Q_p for which a given site S_i is *producer*, i.e. corresponding to a node in its computational graph, when all the edges entering Q_p have been solved then $\Omega_{S_i}(Q_p)$ is computed as the PQEP with least cost for Q_p among all the ones computed for the entering edges;

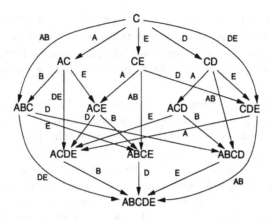

Fig. 3. The computational graph

- when $\Omega_{S_i}(Q_p)$ has been computed for a subquery Q_p its cost $C(m, \Omega_{S_i}(Q_p))$ and the corresponding parameter estimates are sent to each site m which is a consumer for Q_p;
- when $\Omega_{S_i}(Q)$ for the global query in each site is computed, the corresponding cost estimate is sent to all other sites, thus allowing the selection of the one with the lowest cost among them.

The optimality of the algorithm can be proved by showing that $\Omega_{S_i}(Q)$ and $\Omega_{S_i}^*(Q)$ as computed by the algorithm are actually the local and global optima and therefore that discarding dominated PQEPs does not prevent the generation of an optimal QEP. This can be proved by induction on the size of the query, i.e. in the number of the sites involved. The proof is omitted because of space limitations.

An example of computational graph is shown in Figure 3, where the computational graph of site S_C and the query with hypergraph in Figure 1 is depicted. To make the picture more readable we use a short notation for the subqueries, just denoting them with the indices of the sites involved. For instance subquery $Q(S_A, S_C, S_E)$ is denoted by ACE.

¿From a practical point of view, the most interesting feature of the distributed algorithm is that it is totally decentralized and *asynchronous*, in the sense that the computation in each site proceeds autonomously and it is simply triggered by the arrival of the intermediate results from the other sites. The algorithm is organized in such a way that dominated PQEPs are discarded by the consumer site to which they have been sent while computing the global optimum. Therefore each consumer site uses for further computations only the best from any set of comparable PQEPs. Similarly, each producer site discards all dominated PQEPs while computing a local optimum.

The number of PQEPs evaluated by the algorithm, and therefore its complexity heavily depends on the topology of the query graph. In the worst case, i.e. when the query hypergraph has at least one hyperedge for each pair of nodes, the complexity is exponential in the number n of sites involved in the query. To prove this, consider that the number of subqueries of length k that are computable in a given site is $\binom{n-1}{k-1}$, and the number of subqueries composable with each of them is $\sum_{i=1}^{n-k}\binom{n-k}{i}$. Therefore the number of plans evaluated in each site is:

$$\sum_{k=1}^{n-1}\binom{n-1}{k-1}\sum_{i=1}^{n-k}\binom{n-k}{i} = O(3^n)$$

The number of messages sent during the optimization process also depends on the topology of the query graph. In the case of a fully connected query graph the number of messages is $O(n2^n)$. This can be proved by considering that for $k = 1 \ldots n-1$ each PQEP of length k generated by the algorithm is sent to all the remaining $n-k$ sites not included in the PQEP, and since in the last step each candidate QEP is sent to $n-1$ sites, the total number of messages is:

$$\sum_{k=1}^{n-1}\binom{n-1}{k-1}(n-k) = O(n2^n)$$

The fully connected graph that we consider as the worst case, is however a very unlikely one. In practical cases the hypergraph has a far simpler structure and the complexity dramatically decreases. In particular for linear queries it can be shown that the complexity becomes polynomial.

6 Conclusions

In this paper we propose a parallel and distributed algorithm for global query optimization in heterogeneous federated database systems. The algorithm makes very general assumptions on the cost function, and on the degree of autonomy of the federated sites. More precisely we assume that local cost functions and database statistics are not available at the multidatabase level, but that every site is willing to cooperate with the others in providing cost estimates of local computations.

The main idea is that, even with the broader assumptions on the autonomy of the sites, the cost of each execution plan to be compared during the optimization process can be evaluated by composing local cost estimates by the sites where each part of the computation would be performed. All sites therefore cooperate, but each one acts autonomously, according to its own *computational graph*. Its computation proceeds asynchronously, being simply triggered by the arrival of the intermediate results from the other sites. Duplicated and unnecessary computation is avoided by discarding as soon as possible all the partial execution plans that are dominated by some equivalent one.

The cooperative approach to global query optimization was originally introduced in a previous paper of ours [10], but referring to a rather limited query execution model, that allowed only strictly sequential plans, and set several limitations on the global query structure. This paper extends the previous results in several ways. First we consider a far more general query model, with join conditions involving any number of sites. Moreover we extend the execution model to parallel query execution plans, and we consider also plans with cartesian products. Finally the class of *composition-consistent* cost functions for which the optimality of the algorithm is proved is general enough to include both the total execution cost and the query response time.

References

1. Amsaleg, L., Franklin, M. J., Tomasic, A., Urhan, T., *Scrambling Query Plans to Cope With Unexpected Delays*, Proc. of the 4th Int. Conf. on Parallel and Distributed Information Systems, Miami Beach (Florida), 1996, IEEE Computer Society Press, p. 208-219.
2. Du, W, et al., *Query optimization in heterogeneous DBMS*, Proc. of the 18th VLDB Conference, Vancouver, 1992, pp. 277-291,
3. Du, W., Shan, M.-C., and Dayal, U., *Reducing multidatabase query response time by tree balancing*, Proc. of ACM-SIGMOD Int. Conf. On Management of Data, San Jose, USA, 1995, pp. 293-303.
4. Kim, W., Choi, I., Gala, S., and Scheevel, M., *On resolving schematic heterogeneity in multidatabase systems*, in *Modern Database Systems* [ed. W. Kim], Addison-Wesley Pub. Co., 1995, pp. 521-550.
5. Lee, C., Chen, C-J., and Lu, H., *An aspect of query optimization in multidatabase systems*, SIGMOD Record, vol. 24, No. 3, 1995, pp. 28-33.
6. Lu, W, et al., *On global query optimization in multidatabase systems*, Proc. of 2nd Int. Workshop on Research Issues on Data Eng., Tempe, 1992, pp. 217-227,
7. Lu, W, et al., *Multidatabase query optimization: issues and solutions*, Proc. of 3rd Int. Workshop on Research Issues on Data Eng., Vienna, 1993, pp. 137-143,
8. Meng, W., and Yu, C., *Query optimization in multidatabase systems*, in *Modern Database Systems* [ed. W. Kim], Addison-Wesley Pub. Co., 1995, pp. 551-572.
9. F. Ozcan, F., Nural, S., Koksal, P., Evrendilek, C., Dogac, A., *Dynamic query optimization in multidatabases*, Bulletin of the TC on Data Engineering, vol. 20, No. 3, September 1997, p. 38 - 45
10. Salza, S., Barone, G., and Morzy, T., *Distributed query optimization in loosely coupled multidatabase systems*, Proc. of 5th Int. Conf. on Database Theory, Prague, 1995, pp. 40-53.
11. Sheth, A., Larson, J., *Federated database systems for managing distributed, heterogeneous, and autonomous databases*, ACM Computing Surveys, 22, 1990, pp. 183-236.
12. Zhu, Q, Larson, P-A, *A query sampling method for estimating local cost parameters in a multidatabase system*, Proc. of 10th Int. Conf. on Data Eng., Houston, 1994, pp. 144-153.
13. Zhu, Q, Larson, P-A, *Building Regression Cost Models for Multidatabase Systems*, Proc. of the 4th Int. Conf. on Parallel and Distributed Information Systems, Miami Beach (Florida), 1996, IEEE Computer Society Press, p. 220-231.

Transaction Management in Databases Supporting Collaborative Applications

Waldemar Wieczerzycki

Department of Information Technology
University of Economics at Poznań
Mansfelda 4, 60-854 Poznań, Poland
e-mail: wiecz@kti.ae.poznan.pl.

Abstract. In the paper a particular approach to transaction management in databases supporting collaborative applications is proposed. It is based on a new transaction model which allows practically unrestricted collaboration among members of the same team. The basic assumption of this model is that collaborating users try to solve their access conflicts on a higher level than the level of a database management system. Users are not mutually isolated, as it happens in classical databases. They can freely negotiate, presenting their intentions concerning future work. The proposed approach was verified in *Agora* prototype which is a Web-based conferencing system, offering conference participants a flexible tool for collaborative document writing. *Agora* is implemented on the top of Oracle RDBMS.

1 Introduction

In the last few years, the functionality and applicability of systems for supporting group work has expanded, leading to their growing application to organizational, information, design, communication, and cooperation processes. As a result, there are many prototype systems supporting collaborative work developed up till now [2], [4], [7], [10], [12], [19]. There are also some commercial products addressed to support enterprises in their business processes. A common feature of the majority of this systems is that they require functions and mechanisms naturally available in database management systems, e.g. data persistency, access authorization, concurrency control, consistency checking and assuring, data recovery after failures, etc. Notice, however, that these functions are generally implemented in collaborative systems from scratch, without any reference to the database technology. Some systems provide gateways to classical databases, however these databases are autonomous and external to them, thus database access is organized in a conventional manner.

Since the theory and technology of classical databases is very mature, commonly accepted and verified over many years, the following question naturally arises: can we apply this technology in collaborative systems, instead of re-implementing database functions from scratch and embedding them in collaborative systems? In other words:

can we develop collaborative systems as database applications, thus probably saving time normally spent on re-implementation of selected database functions? As usually, we can obviously try, but there is one substantial drawback we have to take into account. Almost every commercial database management system provides classical *ACID* transactions [11], which are atomic, consistent, durable, and, what is the most important, which work in isolation. The last property is the most painful, if we consider requirements of collaborative systems.

In such situation, in order to develop collaborative database applications, we have to extend database technology. There are two possible directions. The first one consists in avoiding the concept of transaction and transaction management mechanisms. Non-transactional databases, however, are generally unsafe, and it is very difficult to preserve the consistency of information stored in them. The second direction aims to avoid ACID transactions, and propose new transaction models which are more oriented for advanced database applications, especially for collaborative applications, thus preserving all advantages of transactional systems.

There are many advanced transaction models proposed in the literature [5]. Two early non-traditional models are: nested transactions and Sagas. *Nested transactions* [14] support modularity, failure handling and intra-transaction parallelism. They are very important in the development of other, more advanced models (e.g. ACTA model [3]), because they introduce the idea of structuring a transaction into a tree (or hierarchy) of subtransactions and non-vital subtransactions. *Sagas* [9], based on the compensating transactions, consist of a set of subtransactions. They relax the property of isolation by allowing a saga to reveal its partial results to other transactions before it is complete. Sagas are useful only when subtransactions are relatively independent (because of consistency problems) and each subtransaction can be successfully compensated.

There are some advanced transaction models which are addressed to distributed databases and multidatabases. *DOM transactions* [1] extend the concept of nested transactions proposing, so called, closed nested subtransactions, open nested subtransactions, and combinations of the two. *Flex* transaction model [6] allows the user to specify a set of functionally equivalent subtransactions, each of which when completed will accomplish a particular task. This model also allows the specification of dependencies on the subtransactions. *Polytransactions* [18] facilitate the support of interdependent data in multidatabase environments. Interdependent data is defined to be two or more data items stored in different databases that are related to each other through an integrity constraint.

Finally, there are transaction models supporting cooperation between transactions. The most general approach proposes the *cooperative transaction hierarchy* [16] which allows to associate transactions encompassed by a transaction group with individual designers. The notion of correctness defined by serializability is substituted by the notion of user-defined serializability. Because isolation between transactions is not required, the transaction hierarchies allow cooperation between transactions and also help to alleviate the problems caused by long-lived transactions. Other transaction models from this group are not so general, since they are addressed to particular application domains. *Cooperative SEE transactions* [13] were developed for software engineering environments. *ConTract* model [17] is mainly addressed to office automation, CAD and manufacturing control. *S-transactions* [8] support cooperation in the international banking system. A particular transaction model was also proposed for open distributed publication environment [15].

Taking into account the needs of generally understood collaborative work, *cooperative transaction hierarchies* [16] are very promising, since transactions form the same group are not isolated mutually and can correspond to different, though somehow related tasks. Notice, that this approach, similarly to all the other approaches mentioned above, uses a tree-structured transaction model.

An attempt to apply hierarchical transactions to databases has some disadvantages. Contrarily to flat transactions, hierarchical transactions require sophisticated transaction management methods and, as a consequence, additional system overhead which reduces its performance. Moreover, hierarchical transactions are still not sufficient, considering expectations of collaborating users, since in many situations the transaction correctness criterion restricts wide cooperation. Finally, they are not so reliable as flat transactions, since in practice commercial databases use the latter ones.

In this paper we propose a solution of problems mentioned above by the use of flat transactions, in which, in comparison to classical ACID transactions, the isolation property is relaxed. Briefly, it can be achieved by assigning the entire group of collaborating users to the same transaction, still preserving, however, the identity of individuals. The proposed transaction model is inspired by the natural perception, that a team of intensively cooperating users can be considered as a single virtual user, who has more than one brain trying to achieve the assumed goal, and more than two hands operating on keyboards.

We feel that the proposed transaction model has many advantages. First of all, it is very straightforward and not complex, thus the management of transactions of this type does not cause substantial problems. Second, the proposed transaction model allows practically unrestricted collaboration among members of the same team. As a consequence, it fulfills their requirements and simplifies their work. Third, since the users of the same team preserve their identity, the database management system can efficiently support users' awareness and notification, which are two very important functions of every collaborative system. Finally, the proposed model is very close to the classical ACID transaction model. As we have mentioned before, it makes the model more reliable and easy to implement, since classical ACID transactions dominate at the commercial database market.

It is worth to emphasize that both the transaction model and transaction management mechanisms have been elaborated parallel to the development of the prototype collaborative system, called *Agora*. Thus, the proposed approach is not purely theoretical, but instead, it reflects the problems and solutions which occurred during the implementation of *Agora*.

The paper is structured in the following way. In Section 2 basic concepts of the approach are introduced and the multiuser transaction model is presented. In Section 3 *Agora* prototype is briefly presented and selected implementation issues concerning multiuser transactions are discussed. Section 4 concludes the paper.

2 Transaction Model

2.1 Basic Concepts

Before we introduce multiuser transactions, we have to define some basic concepts. A single database can be accessed in practice by an arbitrary number of users who work independently, or collaborate with other users being members of the same working group. Depending on whether users collaborate or not, and how tight is their collaboration, we distinguish two levels of users grouping: conferences and teams. A *conference* C_i groups users who aim to achieve the common goal, e.g. to write a co-authored book, design a new version of an electronic chip. Users belonging to the same conference can communicate with each other and be informed about progress of common work by the use of typical conferencing tools, like message exchange, negotiation, etc. Conferences are logically independent, i.e. a user working in the scope of a single conference is not influenced by work being done in other conferences. It is possible for a single user to participate simultaneously in many conferences through different windows of collaborative application, thus the intersection between two conferences need not be empty. In this case, however, actions performed in one conference are logically independent from actions performed in other conferences. There is one pre-defined (default) conference C_d which groups all the users of a database. Pre-defined conference C_d differs form other conferences C_i, because its attendees need not collaborate. In other words, if a user U_i does not belong to any conference C_i, except C_d (in which he is included by default), he is independent from all other users.

Users belonging to the same conference can collaborate tightly or loosely, depending on whether they perform the same common task, or they just aim to achieve the same final goal, respectively. Tightly collaborating users are grouped into the same team T_i. Thus, a *team* is a subset of a corresponding conference, with the restriction that a single user U_i belongs in the scope of a single conference exactly to one team, in particular, to a single-user team. Of course, if he is involved in many conferences, say n, then he belongs to n teams.

To illustrate the concepts introduced so far, let us consider the example given in Fig. 1. The default conference C_d groups all the database users. There are two non-default conferences: C_1 and C_2. Users attending conference C_1, namely: U_2, U_3, U_4 and U_5, work on the same conference paper, while users attending C_2 prepare a business contract. Users U_2 and U_3 belong to the same team t_{11}, since they cooperatively work on three first chapters of the paper, while users U_4 and U_5 belong to team t_{12}, which works on the reference list of this paper. In the case of conference C_2, users U_5 and U_6 belong to team t_{21} which works on formal aspects of the contract, while a single-user team t_{22}, composed of U_7, works on financial details of the same contract. Notice two particular users: U_5 and U_1. User U_5 works simultaneously in the scope of two different conferences, while user U_1 works independently of other users, writing a letter to his girl-friend.

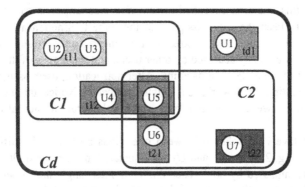

Fig. 1. Conferences and teams

2.2 Multiuser Transactions

A *multiuser transaction* is a flat, ordered set of database operations performed by users of the same team, which is atomic, consistent and durable. In other words, a multiuser transaction is the only unit of communication between a virtual user representing members of a single team, and the database management system. In the example shown in Fig. 1, five multiuser transactions are executed in DBMS, which correspond to the following teams: t_{11}, t_{12}, t_{21}, t_{22} and t_{d1}.

Formally, a multiuser transaction is defined as a triple:
$$MT = (Tid, Cid, tid),$$
where *Tid* is a transaction identifier, *Cid* is an identifier of the encompassing conference, and *tid* is an identifier of the team to which *MT* is assigned.

Two multiuser transactions from two different conferences behave in the classical way, which means that they work in mutual isolation, and they are serialized by database management system. In case of access conflicts, resulting from attempts to operate on the same data item in incompatible mode, one of transactions is suspended or aborted, depending on the concurrency control policy. The same concerns two multiuser transactions which belong only to default conference C_d.

Two multiuser transactions from the same conference behave in a non-classical way, which means that the isolation property is partially relaxed for them. In case of access conflicts, so called *negotiation mechanism* is triggered by DBMS, which informs users assigned to both transactions about the conflict, giving them details concerning operations which have caused it. Then, using conferencing mechanisms provided by the system, users can consult their intended operations and negotiate on how to resolve their mutual problem. If they succeed, transactions can be continued, otherwise classical mechanisms have to be applied.

A particular mechanisms is used in case of operations of the same multiuser transaction, if they are performed by different users, and they are conflicting in a classical meaning. There is no isolation between operations of different users, however in this situation so called *notification mechanism* is triggered by DBMS, which aims to keep the users assigned to the same transaction aware of operations done by other users. We have to stress that it concerns only the situation when a user accesses data previously accessed by other users, and the modes of those two accesses are incompatible in a classical meaning. After notification, users assigned to the same transaction continue their work, as if nothing happened. Notice, that in case of users of the same team, we assume not only strict collaboration, but also deep mutual confidence.

Different levels of isolation between operations performed by different users are illustrated in Fig. 2. Users U_1 and U_2 are associated to the same multiuser transaction, which is encompassed by conference C_1. They intermingle their operations, but they both see all the operations performed from the beginning of the transaction. They are totally isolated from users U_3 and U_4, whose transactions are encompassed by conference C_2. Users U_3 and U_4 are partially isolated, because they belong to different teams: t_{21} and t_{22}, respectively. U_3 does not see operations of U_4, except the one which causes a conflict. In case of U_4 the situation is symmetric. This can help in solving access conflict in the near future by mutual negotiations.

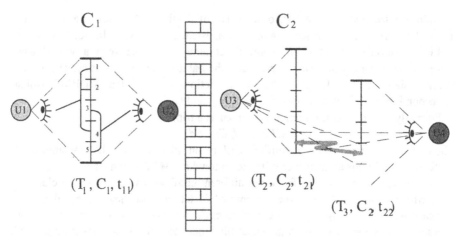

Fig. 2. Different levels of isolation

2.3 Operations on Multiuser Transactions

Every multiuser transaction is started implicitly by *initialize(T$_i$)* operation, which is performed automatically by the system on the very beginning of a team session, after the first database operation is requested by one of team members. This team member is called a *transaction leader*. *initialize(T$_i$)* is also triggered automatically, directly after one of team members performs explicit *commit(T$_i$)* operation, or implicit *auto-commit(T$_i$)* database operation. All consecutive transactions of the same team are executed in a serial order.

After a multiuser transaction is initialized by the transaction leader, other team members can enter it at any moment of the transaction execution, by the use of explicit *connect(T_i)* operation, which is performed in asynchronous manner. Once connected to the transaction, any member of a team can perform *disconnect(T_i)* operation, providing there is still at least one user assigned to this transaction. *disconnect(T_i)* operation brakes the link between transaction T_i and the user, who can next:

1. close his session,
2. suspend his operations for a particular time moment and re-connect to the same transaction later,
3. wait until transaction commits and connect to the next multiuser transaction of the same team,
4. continue to work with different team in the scope of another multiuser transaction, providing he belongs to more than one team.

In cases: 1, 2 and 4, *disconnect(T_i)* operation plays the role of *sub-commit* operation, which means that the respective user intends to commit his own operations, and leaves the final decision whether to commit or not the multiuser transaction to his colleagues, to whom he trusts.

Operations introduced up till now concern a single multiuser transaction. Next two operations: *merge(T_i)* and *split()* are special, since they concern two transactions. *Transaction T_j* can merge into transaction T_i by the use of *merge(T_i)* operation, providing the members of a team assigned to T_i allow for it. After this operation, transaction T_j is logically removed from the system, i.e. operation *abort(T_j)* is automatically triggered by the DBMS, and all T_j operations are logically re-done by transaction T_i. These actions are only logical, since in fact operations of T_j are just added to the list of T_i operations, and T_i continues its execution, however, the number of users assigned to it is now increased. It means, that until the end of T_i execution, the team assigned previously to T_j is merged into the team assigned to T_i. Of course, *merge(T_i)* operation is only allowed in the scope of the same conference. *merge(T_i)* can be useful when an access conflict between two teams of the same conference arises.

To practically illustrate *merge* operation, consider two teams t_{11} and t_{12} working on the same journal paper, in the scope of the same conference C_1. For a long time both teams work independently on two different chapters of the paper. When chapters are almost ready, both teams try to introduce mutual references between these chapters, and check the consistency of a common work. First attempt causes access conflict which can be avoided by *merge* operation.

Similarly to *merge* operation, *split()* operation can be used in order to avoid access conflicts. *split()* operation causes that a single multiuser transaction T_i is split into two transactions: T_i and T_j. After *split()* operation, a subset of team members, originally assigned to T_i, is re-assigned to newly created transaction T_j. Also all operations performed by re-assigned users are logically removed from transaction T_i and redone in transaction T_j directly after its creation.

Contrarily to *merge* operation which is always feasible, providing members of the other team allow it, *split* operation can be done only in particular contexts. Speaking very briefly, a transaction can be split if two sub-teams, which intend to separate their further actions, have operated on disjoint subsets of data, before *split* operation is requested. If the intersection between the data accessed is not empty, *split* operation is still possible, providing the data have been accessed by the two sub-teams in a compatible mode (in a classical meaning).

There is one more constraint concerning *split* operation. The resulting two transactions are related to each other in such a way that they can be either both committed or aborted. It is not possible to abort one of them and commit the other, since in this case the atomicity property of the original transaction (i.e. the transaction before *split* operation was requested) would be violated.

Finally, there are two typical operations on transactions: *commit* and *abort* which are performed in the classical manner.

All the operations presented above are illustrated in Fig. 3. Fig. 3a) shows *initialize, connect, disconnect* and *commit* operations, Fig. 3b) shows *merge* operation, while Fig. 3c) shows *split* and *abort* operations.

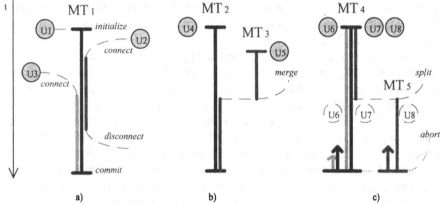

Fig. 3. Operations on multiuser transactions

3 Prototype Collaborative Database Application

Most of the concepts introduced in previous section have been implemented in *Agora* prototype system. *Agora* is composed of two functional parts. The first one is a virtual conference tool, and the second one is a support for collaborative document writing. *Agora* provides negotiators (i.e. conference participants) with an arbitrary number of conferences and arbitrary number of collaboratively written versionable documents, with the restriction that only one document can be associated with a single conference. All negotiators discuss and present their positions by exchanging electronic messages. Each negotiator of a conference sees all the messages exchanged. A negotiator can be involved in several negotiations simultaneously, i.e. he can virtually attend different conferences. Negotiations in different conferences may concern different topics, different aspects of the same topic, or the same topic discussed by different partners.

The part of *Agora* devoted to support collaborative writing is required to prepare a final document, which is a result of negotiations. This common document is seen and accessible to all the negotiators. When a negotiator writes or modifies a paragraph of the document and commits changes, it becomes instantaneously visible to other negotiators. Next, any negotiator can modify this paragraph. *Agora* provides versioning mechanisms which additionally facilitate collaborative writing.

Agora has been implemented in Java language and connected to the Oracle database management system through Java Database Connectivity interface (JDBC) to provide persistency of both documents and negotiation history. The use of Java and JDBC provides *Agora* with platform independence, concerning hardware, operating systems and database management system.

In the following subsections we first briefly present basic functions of Agora system which concern negotiation and collaborative writing. Next, we discuss some implementation issues.

3.1 Negotiation Support

Negotiations are supported by *Agora* through the concept of conferences. A conference is a virtual place where distributed negotiators meet together through *WWW* and conduct negotiations by exchanging electronic messages. The aim of negotiations is to collaboratively prepare an electronic document. A way of its preparation is described in the next subsection. A conference is created by *Agora administrator* on demand of a *conference leader*. He is responsible for allocation of negotiators to his conference. A negotiator may be any *Agora* user, i.e., a person who is registered in the *Agora* database of users by the *Agora* administrator.

A message exchanged during negotiations appears at the respective conference and is readable to all the negotiators. It contains: the name of the negotiator who has sent it, the date of issue, a subject which summarizes message content, the text of the message, and optionally a list of attachments that can be read by the use of tools such as text editors, spreadsheets, browsers, etc.

During the negotiations, their course is permanently available through scrolling up and down the conference page, so a negotiator can come back to any position from the past. After the negotiations, their history is stored in the *Agora* database for 30 days. It is then available to all the negotiators. Before this deadline, the negotiation leader can archive negotiation history, thus making it permanent in the *Agora* database.

3.2 Collaborative Document Writing

The general aim of negotiations is preparation of an electronic document, e.g. a journal paper, a marketing leaflet, a technical documentation, a business contract, etc. *Agora* provides negotiators with an integrated tool for collaborative development of this document, which works according to the transaction model presented in Section 2.

A document is defined as a linear set of *paragraphs*. A paragraph is an item terminated by *New-line* character, e.g. a sentence, a header, a title, a mathematical formula or a figure. Although the structure of a document is flat and linear, it is visualized with respect to the hierarchy of its headers in order to facilitate navigation through it (cf. Fig. 4).

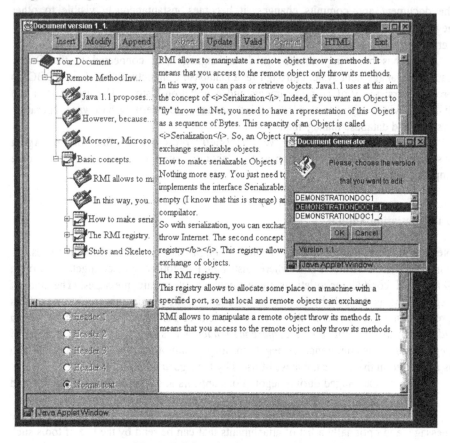

Fig. 4. Collaborative document writing

Collaborative writing is performed as follows. *Agora* keeps all the documents in a database at the server. Each document may exist in several versions which are identified. A copy of a document version maintained at the server is called *global*. If a negotiator wants to read or edit a version of a document, *Agora* prepares a local copy for him. A negotiator can: modify a paragraph, in particular remove it, append/insert a new paragraph, validate changes made to a paragraph in a local copy of a document version, commit changes to the global copy of a document version, abort changes done, or refresh copy to re-read the global copy of the document version concerned.

3.3 Implementation Issues

Agora architecture is client-server. Both clients and the server are implemented as *Java* objects which communicate by *Remote Method Invocation (RMI)*. The *Agora* server is connected to a database management system by *Java-Database Connectivity (JDBC)* interface.

Concurrency control mechanisms provided by Oracle DBMS are overridden in *Agora* Server, what is necessary to validate the concept of multiuser transactions and new concurrency control mechanisms proposed in this paper.

Every document version is stored in one database table, thus if a document is available in *n* versions, then *n* tables have to be created. The first version of a document is entirely represented in a respective table, while in case of derived document versions only differences in comparison to the parent document version are represented, i.e. paragraphs explicitly modified in the child document version. This aims to avoid redundancy which can be really painful in case of documents having many slightly different versions.

Every paragraph of a document version is stored in a single raw of a corresponding table, which is composed of a paragraph content and its layout attributes. Paragraph content is modeled by a single attribute of *long raw* type. It means that a paragraph can contain not only pure text but also multimedia data (pictures, sounds, etc.). Layout attributes contain typical information about the way a paragraph is visualized to the users, e.g. color, font, size, indent.

4. Conclusion

A particular approach to transaction management in databases supporting collaborative applications has been proposed. It is based on a new transaction model which is very straightforward and natural, on one hand, and allows practically unrestricted collaboration among members of the same team, on the other hand. The basic assumption of this model is that collaborating users try to solve their access conflicts on a higher level than the level of a database management system, as it happens classically. The DBMS presents to the users available information on access conflicts. Then the users can negotiate, presenting their intentions concerning future work, and choose one of proposed transaction management mechanisms which aim at conflict avoidance. During collaborative work, DBMS supports users' awareness and notification, which are two very important functions of every cooperative system

The proposed approach was verified in *Agora* prototype which is a Web-based conferencing system, offering conference participants a flexible tool for collaborative document writing. It is worth to emphasize that *Agora* is implemented on the top of a conventional and commercial database system, i.e. Oracle RDBMS, instead of another prototype specifically designed to support object versioning mechanisms. It makes the achieved results more reliable.

References

1. Buchmann A., Ozsu M.T., Hornick M., Georgakopoulos D.: A Transaction Model for Active Distributed Object Systems, in: Elmagarmid A. (ed.), Advanced Transaction Models, Morgan Kaufmann, 1992
2. Crowley, T., P. Milazzo, E. Baker, H. Forsdick, and R. Tomlinson.: MMConf: An Infrastructure for Building Shared Multimedia Applications, Proc. of ACM Conference on Computer Supported Cooperative Work, October 1990, pp. 329-342.
3. Chrysanthis P.K., Ramamtitham K.: Acta - A framework for specifying and reasoning about transaction structure and behavior, Proc. of ACM-SIGMOD Int. Conference on Management of Data, 1990.
4. Ellis, C.A, Gibbs S.J. and Rein G.L.: Groupware: Some Issues and Experiences, CACM 34:1 (January 1991), pp.38-58.
5. Elmagarmid A. (ed.): Database Transaction Models, Morgan Kaufmann, 1992.
6. Elamagarmid A., Leu Y., Litwin W., Rusinkiewicz M.: A Multidatabase Transaction Model for Interbase, Proc. of VLDB Conf., Brisbane, 1990.
7. Ensor, J.R., S.R. Ahuja, D.N. Horn, and S.E. Lucco.: The Rapport Multimedia Conferencing System: A Software Overview, Proceedings of the 2nd IEEE Conference on Computer Workstations, March 1988, pp. 52-58.
8. Eliassen F., Veijalainen J., Tirri H.: Aspects of transaction modeling for interoperable information systems, in: Interim Report of the COST 11ter Project, 1988.
9. Garcia-Molina H, Salem K.: Sagas, Proc. of the ACM Conf. on Management of Data, 1987.
10. Garfinkel, D., B. Welti, and T. Yip.: HP Shared X: A Tool for Real-Time Collaboration, Hewlett-Packard Journal, April 1994, pp. 23-24.
11. Gray J.: Notes on Database Operating Systems, Operating Systems: An Advanced Course, Springer-Verlag, 1978.
12. Hill, R., T. Brinck, S. Rohall, J. Patterson, and W. Wilner.: The Rendezvous Architecture and Language for Constructing Multiuser Applications, ACM Transactions on Computer Human Interaction 1:2 (June 1994).
13. Heiler S., Haradhvala S., Zdonik S., Blaustein B., Rosenthal A.: A flexible framework for transaction management in engineering environments, in: Elmagarmid A. (ed.), Database Transaction Models, Morgan Kaufmann, 1992.
14. Moss J. E.: Nested Transactions: An Approach to Reliable Distributed Computing, The MIT Press, 1985.
15. Muth P., Rakow T.C., Klas W., Neuhold E.J.: A transaction model for an open publication environment, IEEE Data Engineering Bulletin, 14(1), 1991.
16. Nodine M., Zdonik S.: Cooperative transaction hierarchies: A transaction model to support design applications, Proc. fo VLDB Conf., 1984.
17. Reuter A.: Contract: A means for extending control beyond transaction boundaries, Proc. of 2nd Workshop on High Performance Transaction Systems, 1989.
18. Rusinkiewicz M., Sheth A.: Polytransactions for managing interdependent data, IEEE Data Engineering Bulletin, 14(1), 1991.
19. Stefik, M., G. Foster, D.G. Bobrow, K. Kahn, S. Lanning, and L. Suchman.: Beyond the Chalkboard: Computer Support for Collaboration and Problem Solving in Meetings, CACM 30:1 (January 1987), pp. 32-47.

Object-Oriented Design of a Flexible Workflow Management System

Mathias Weske

Lehrstuhl für Informatik, Universität Münster
Steinfurter Straße 107, D-48149 Münster, Germany
weske@helios.uni-muenster.de

Abstract. Workflow management systems aim at controlling the execution of complex application processes in distributed environments. Workflow management currently moves from modeling and executing mostly static structured workflows to supporting flexible workflows, which are typically executed in distributed and heterogeneous environments. This paper discusses the use of distributed object technology to built a flexible workflow management system. In particular, based on a detailed object-oriented object model, we discuss the dynamic behavior of workflow instances, and we show how flexibility requirements have influenced our design.

Keywords: workflow management system design, object modeling, flexible workflow management, distributed workflow executions

1 Introduction

Workflow management has gained increasing attention recently as a core technology to foster information system development in dynamically changing and distributed environments [6, 13, 22]. While the first generation of workflow management systems (WFMS) were developed to control the execution of business applications with fairly static structures to be executed in homogeneous environments, recently the need for enhanced flexibility and the integration of applications in heterogeneous environments emerged [24, 19]. In this paper we look into these issues. In a first step, an object model of a workflow management system is developed, which identifies workflow relevant objects and their relationships. In a second step, we show how the design decisions as specified in the object model support flexibility, namely by permitting dynamic modifications of running workflow instances.

The work presented in this paper is influenced by the OMG's (Object Management Group) quest for the specification of a Workflow Facility [17]. In recent years, the OMG has led the development of the CORBA (Common Object Request Broker Architecture) standard for distributed object computing; while the specification of basic CORBA Common Object Services (COS) [16, 23] can be considered completed, the focus recently has turned to the specification of higher-level and domain-specific concepts, known as CORBA Facilities. In this context, the CORBA Workflow Facility currently is in the process of specification. A number of proposals by major workflow system vendors were submitted [1, 15, 9, 4], most of which expose considerable deficiencies in object modeling and in showing how existing CORBA COS can be used to implement the respective systems [21]. As opposed to these proposals, our approach to object oriented modeling and development of a flexible workflow management system is not restricted by existing products which we want to adapt to an upcoming standard; we are currently implementing the system whose design is presented in this paper using the Orbix [11] object request broker implementation.

The paper is organized as follows: Section 2 introduces preliminaries on workflow management and workflow modeling and execution. Section 3 proposes an object model of a flexible workflow management system. In Section 4 we describe the dynamic behavior of workflow instances; Section 5 discusses flexibility issues by showing how the emerging requirements on enhanced flexibility of workflow management systems has influenced the design decisions. A section on related work and a summary conclude this contribution.

2 Preliminaries

Workflow management deals with modeling and controlling the execution of application processes in given organizational and technical environments. To control the execution of a workflow instance, a workflow management system requires a computerized representation of the respective business process. These representations are known as workflow models, which are expressed in workflow languages [26]. To cope with the problem complexity in workflow applications, workflow languages usually support some form of hierarchical specification. In graph-based workflow languages [13], for instance, workflow models are specified as enhanced directed graphs (workflow model graphs), in which nodes represent activities and edges represent constraints between activities, e.g., control flow dependencies and data flow dependencies. A node of a workflow model graph can represent either an atomic workflow (in which case an application program is specified, which implements the workflow) or a complex workflow, which is refined by another workflow model graph. This specifies a tree-like structure of complex workflow models, where the root node (toplevel workflow) represents the application, the inner nodes represent other complex workflow models, and the leaf nodes represent atomic workflows, which are implemented by application programs.

Depending on the workflow language and on the workflow management system used, several dimensions are covered; these dimensions are also known as workflow aspects [12]. The functional aspect specifies what has to be done within a workflow; the operational aspects determines how it is done, i.e., which techniques and tools are used to perform activities. The behavioral aspect defines when and under which conditions a workflow is executed. The informational aspect specifies the data objects which are being manipulated during workflow executions and the flow of data between workflow activities. The organizational aspect describes the roles and personnel which are involved in workflow executions. Workflow languages allow the specification of workflow models, such that the workflow aspects are defined independently. This approach allows to concentrate on specific aspects separately when modeling workflows.

3   Object Model

A concise object model is an important requirement for the development of complex software systems. This section discusses a logical object model of a workflow management system, which centers around workflow-related entities and their relationships from a logical point of view without prescribing implementation details. These aspects are covered by a design object model, which is described in [25].

The central class of the object model is the Workflow class, which appears in the center of the object model in Figure 1, showing the object model in UML notation [18]. The Workflow class contains workflow objects which are partitioned into workflow model objects (or workflow models) and workflow instance objects (or workflow instances). By representing by a single class workflow models and workflow instances, redundancy is omitted, and the border between a workflow's built time and its run time (as typically found in today's commercial WFMS [8]) is broken, which is important when it comes to supporting flexibility properties, which will be discussed below.

Each workflow instance is instantiated using a workflow model. The relationship between workflow instances and workflow models is represented by the instance-of relationship. Workflows can be either complex or atomic, and atomic workflows are either manual or automatic, leading to the generalization hierarchy shown in Figure 1. Workflows can be related to each other in hierarchical fashion, representing the functional decomposition of the application process, hence the functional aspect, as discussed in the previous section. Each application process is typically represented by a complex workflow, which consists of a number of sub-workflows. Sub-workflows of a given complex workflow can be related to each other by control flow and data flow. The WF-SubWF Relationship determines for each complex workflow its constituent (sub-)workflows. Notice that each workflow model can be re-used in multiple complex workflows, i.e., it can occur as a sub-workflow in different complex workflows. This concept to re-use workflow models is represented in the object model as follows. For each occurrence of a workflow in a complex workflow, one object in the WF-SubWF Relationship class is created. Since the control flow and data flow constraints can (and often will) vary in different occurrences of a given workflow, control flow and data flow constraints are defined based on WF-SubWF Relationship objects rather than on workflow objects.

To explain the object model in more detail, we use an example, which is shown in Figure 2. In part (a) of that figure, a set of workflow models are con-

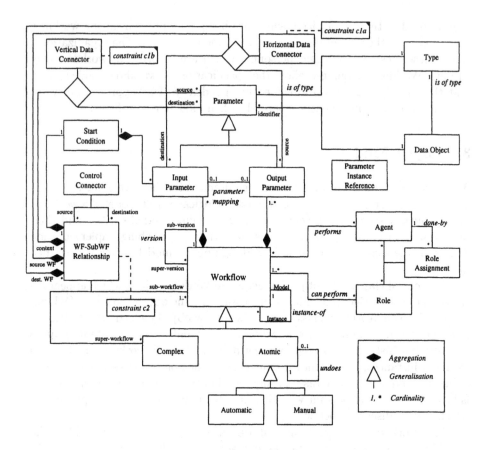

Fig. 1. Object Model

nected to each other by WF-SubWF Relationships (represented by dotted lines) and control flow constraints (represented by solid arcs). The hierarchical structure of the complex workflow is represented by distinct WF-SubWF Relationship objects $o_1 = (1, 2), o_2 = (1, 4), o_3 = (1, 3), o_4 = (1, 2), o_5 = (4, 2), o_6 = (4, 3)$. Notice that workflow model 2 appears twice in complex workflow 1 (represented by WF-SubWF Relationship objects o_1 and o_4) and once as a sub-workflow of complex workflow 4 (represented by o_5). The control connectors shown are represented by Control Connector objects $(o_1, o_2), (o_2, o_3), (o_3, o_4), (o_5, o_6)$, where (s, t) specifies a control connector with source s and target t. Notice that a control connector connects two objects of the WF-SubWF Relationship class rather than two objects of the Workflow class. As explained above, this allows to define different control connectors for different occurrences of a given sub-workflow. In fact, workflow 2 is involved in two control connectors: Control flow $2 \rightarrow 4$ is represented by Control Connector object (o_1, o_2), while $3 \rightarrow 2$ is represented by (o_3, o_4).

Each workflow has a set of input parameters and a set of output parameters, specified in the object model by the Input Parameter class and the Output

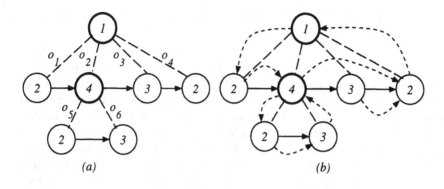

Fig. 2. Complex Workflow Model with Control Flow (a) and Data Flow (b).

Parameter class, resp., which are sub-classes of the Parameter class. Data flow can be vertical or horizontal. Vertical data flow corresponds to data flow from a complex workflow to one or more of its sub-workflows (or vice versa), while horizontal data flow connects (parameters of) sub-workflows of a given complex workflow. Hence, the informational aspect is covered by the parameter classes and the Data Connector class; application data is maintained in the Data Object class, and Type class maintains information on the data types of data objects.

In our object model, vertical data flow is represented by the Vertical Data Connector relation between two parameter objects (source parameter, destination parameter) and one WF-SubWF Relationship object. Notice that a single object of the WF-SubWF Relationship class suffices, since it defines the connection between a complex workflow and one of its sub-workflows, i.e., a single WF-SubWF Relationship object represents both workflow objects involved in a vertical data flow. Vertical data flow either connects two input parameters (vertical data flow direction "down") or two output parameters (direction "up"). Horizontal data flow relates two WF-SubWF Relationship objects, one Input Parameter object and one Output Parameter object.

In Figure 2(b), the sample workflow model is enhanced with data flow (represented by dotted arrows; for better readability, data connectors are drawn between workflow models rather than between parameters of workflow models). In the example, complex workflow 1 passes data to the leftmost instance of sub-workflow 2, and it receives data from the second instance of sub-workflow 2. The leftmost instance of sub-workflow 2 is represented by WF-SubWF Relationship object o_1, while the rightmost occurrence is represented by object o_4, as shown in Figure 2(a). The data flow from 1 to the leftmost occurrence of sub-workflow 2 – assuming input parameter ip_1 of workflow object 1 is connected to input parameter ip_2 of sub-workflow 2 – is represented by Vertical Data Connector object (ip_1, ip_2, o_1), such that ip_1 is the source parameter, ip_2 is the destination parameter, and o_1 is the WF-SubWF Relationship object. The second example of vertical data flow is given by (op_2, op_1, o_4), assuming that op_2 and op_1 are the output parameters of the rightmost occurrence of workflow 2 and of workflow 1, resp.

Horizontal data flow is specified by a triple of the form (Output Parameter object, Input Parameter object, pair of WF-SubWF Relationship objects). An example of horizontal data flow connects workflow models 2 and 4 in complex workflow model 1, which is represented by $(op_2, ip_4, (o_1, o_2))$, assuming that op_2 is an output parameter of workflow model 2 and ip_4 is an input parameter of workflow model 4. Notice that parameter op_2 participates in different data flows. Hence, for each occurrence of a workflow model in a complex workflow model, new data flow constraints can be defined, supporting the modular design and reusability of workflow models. The other horizontal data flows are represented by $(op_4, ip_2, (o_2, o_4))$, $(op_3, ip_2, (o_3, o_4))$, $(op_2, ip_3, (o_5, o_6))$.

For each workflow object a start condition specifies if and when the workflow object can be started during a particular workflow execution. This condition may use the value of any input parameter and information on the termination of other workflows. Control flow is implemented by a special form of data flow, which is called control flow relevant data flow; it works as follows:

Assume there is a data flow $i \to j$ between workflow models i and j, defining the sequential execution of the two workflows. Then on the termination of workflow i a control flow relevant data flow is generated by i. The respective parameter is then passed to j. This information is used by j's start condition as follows. Each start condition is composed of two parts, the first one of which consists of a list of control flow relevant input parameters; the second part is based on traditional data flow. (An example of the latter is "start the workflow if the value stored in input parameter ip_j is less than x".) Control flow is implemented by the flow of data values "not-signaled", "true-signaled" and "false-signaled". Start conditions can be evaluated only if the control flow relevant input connectors are either "true-signaled" or "false-signaled", i.e., workflow instances cannot be started until predecessor workflow instances have terminated ("true-signaled"), or until the system determines that they will not be executed ("false-signaled") due to skipping activities or dead-path-elimination [13].

We remark that the behavioral aspect is covered by control connectors as specified in the control connector class and by start conditions. Notice that by allowing each workflow model to have different start conditions in different complex workflows, flexible composition of complex workflow models from existing workflow models is supported. The organizational aspect is specified in the Role class, which maintains information on the roles and – using the relationship to the agent class – the persons in the organization which are skilled and ready to perform the activity. The operational aspect is defined in the atomic workflow class; this class holds for each atomic workflow an application program which is executed to perform the atomic workflow.

Workflow instance objects are created using workflow model objects. We now discuss a workflow instance created using workflow model 1, as shown in Figure 2. The workflow instance is depicted in Figure 3(a). For each occurrence of a workflow model, a new workflow instance object is created. For example, a

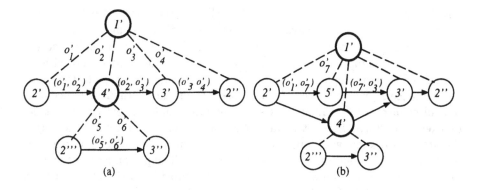

Fig. 3. Complex (a) and Dynamically Modified Workflow Instance (b)

workflow instance object $1'$ is created using workflow model 1. Workflow model object 2 appears three times in the example; hence, three workflow instance objects are created during the execution of complex workflow $1'$, referred to by $2', 2''$, and $2'''$, resp. Besides the workflow instance objects, instance-objects of other classes are also created, for instance in the WF-SubWF Relationship class. While objects o_1 through o_6 of that class represent the relationships between workflow model objects, new objects of the WF-SubWF Relationship class are created to reflect the relationships between specific workflow instance objects. In the example, objects o_1' through o_6' of the WF-SubWF Relationship class are created during the execution of complex workflow instance $1'$, such that $o_1' = (1', 2'), o_2' = (1', 4'), o_3' = (1', 3'), o_4' = (1', 2''), o_5' = (4', 2'''), o_6' = (4', 3'')$. It also applies for data connectors: For each data connector object connecting workflow model objects, a new data connector object is created, which represents the data flow between workflow instances (Due to better readability, data flow instance objects are not shown in Fig. 3.). We remark that the Parameter Instance Reference class specifies the link between parameters and data objects, which are maintained in the Data Object class.

4 Modeling Dynamic Behavior

After discussing how workflow models and workflow instances are represented in our object model, we now describe how workflow instances are executed. This description is based on the sample workflow instance $1'$, as shown in Figure 3(a). The toplevel workflow instance is created following an external event which triggers the start of a business process, e.g., a customer order arrives in a company. The creation of workflow instance $1'$ is followed by the creation of its immediate sub-workflow instance objects $2', 4', 3', 2''$. At this point, the sub-workflows of complex workflow instance $4'$ are not yet created. Creating workflow instances as they are needed ('on the fly') presents a nice way to reduce overhead (in some workflow instances, certain paths may not be executed and, consequently, certain workflow sub-trees may not be needed) and to react in a flexible manner to changes in the workflow environment, as will be discussed in Section 5.

Workflows are executed in a distributed fashion. In our example, the execution of the complex workflow instance 1′ is done distributed and without centralized control: Toplevel workflow instance 1′ sends a message to the workflow instance 2′, which is the only sub-workflow instance without any incoming control connector. 2′ evaluates its start condition and if it evaluates to true, its execution starts. Since it is an atomic workflow, a work item representing the atomic workflow will appear on the work item list of the person which is selected by role resolution to perform this activity. The person selects the work item, and the application program is started and provided with data, as defined by the vertical data flow from the toplevel workflow to 2′. When the person completes the activity, the workflow instance 2′ is notified. It sends a message to 4′, etc. Finally, the toplevel workflow instance is notified about the completion of its sub-workflows, completing the toplevel workflow.

Notice that there is no centralized workflow engine controlling the execution of the complex workflow. In contrast, each complex workflow instance instantiates its immediate sub-workflows. The sub-workflows are not controlled by the complex workflow; workflows objects communicate by sending and receiving messages, which is a natural way of describing communication in object oriented systems. This approach is very appropriate in workflow environments, since these are inherently distributed, such that centralized solutions will suffer from the central workflow engine being the bottleneck of the system or a single point of failure.

5 Flexibility Issues

Recently the need for enhanced flexibility of workflow management system has emerged in the context of workflow applications in the natural sciences [10, 14, 24, 7], in engineering, and in advanced business applications [5, 19]. We now show how flexibility requirements have shaped the object modeling and state modeling as presented above. While important flexibility operations can be classified in dynamic modification operations and user intervention operations [27], this paper concentrates on dynamic changes of workflow instances, using our example.

Again consider the workflow instance shown in Figure 3(a). Assume while executing 2′, the user (or the workflow administrator) wants to perform a dynamic change by inserting another workflow instance based on an atomic workflow model 5, to be executed concurrently with workflow instance 4′. A sample reason for this situation is that the user requires additional information, for which no activity has been defined in the workflow model. In this case, the user may want to include another sub-workflow which gets hold of the information by, e.g., accessing a database. If the information is required to execute workflow instance 3′ and the inserted workflow instance is independent from the workflow instance 4′ then the two can be performed concurrently. This dynamic change results in the workflow instance shown in Figure 3(b). From a system's perspective, the dynamic change is reflected by (i) creating a workflow instance 5' using a predefined workflow model 5, (ii) creating a new WF-SubWF Relationship object $o'_7 = (1', 5')$, (iii) creating control flow objects $(o'_1, o'_7), (o'_7, o'_3)$ to reflect the control flows $2' \to 5'$ and $5' \to 3'$, resp., and (iv) creating the respective data flow connectors. We remark that these operations can be executed while the workflow runs. However, in order to make sure that the parts which are changed by a dynamic modification are not started early in the course of the workflow execution, workflow instances $3'$ and $4''$ can be suspended temporarily. After the dynamic change operations are completed, workflow instance $2'$ sends messages to workflow instance $4'$ and to (the newly inserted) workflow instance $5'$. When both are completed, the execution of the toplevel workflow can continue with sub-workflows $3'$ and $2''$.

If changes to the data flow occur during dynamic change operations, additional steps have to be carried out. Assume in our example there is a data flow from workflow instance $2'$ to the inserted workflow instance $5'$. This is reflected by creating a horizontal data flow object $(op'_2, ip'_5, (o'_1, o'_7))$. After $2'$ terminates, the data in op'_2 is passed to ip'_5 to implement the defined data flow. Assume there is a data flow defined from $5'$ to $3'$. This data flow can be represented by a horizontal data flow object $(op'_5, ip'_3, (o'_7, o'_3))$. Adding this data flow constraint requires workflow instance $3'$ to be updated to make use of this data flow.

Notice that this section discusses dynamic changes from a system's perspective, especially focused around how the insertion of a sub-workflow can be performed and which objects are involved. There are additional issues related to dynamic changes, ranging from correctness criteria of dynamic change operations to authorization management (who is allowed to perform dynamic change operations on which workflow instances) and user interface requirements; these questions are topics of ongoing research.

6 Related Work

Important topics in recent workflow research include enhancing the flexibility of workflow management systems [7, 19, 27, 5] and object-oriented approaches [20, 2] to the development of workflow management systems, especially in the context of the specification of the OMG Workflow Facility [17], which is currently underway.

A number of submissions to the Request for Proposals of the OMG Workflow Facility were received, which were submitted by major workflow vendors [15, 1, 4, 9]. Generally speaking, these submissions are based on the designs of the workflow management systems already developed by the submitting companies. These systems were developed using mostly traditional techniques, like relational databases, a centralized workflow engine and a number of workflow clients accessing the centralized engine using a client/server approach. Since a CORBA-based re-implementation of their systems is not an option for most workflow vendors, the specifications as described in the submissions are tailored more towards the running systems than towards object modeling techniques, which may be a reason for the deficiencies of the submissions, as far as object modeling and embedding of the Workflow Facility in the CORBA Common Object Service [16] context is concerned. A detailed critique of the initial submissions is given in [21].

The Meteor$_2$ project [20] at the University of Georgia allows the definition of workflow models and the automatic generation of workflow code from workflow models which then is executed in a distributed environment using CORBA infrastructure. While the approach allows the distributed execution of workflows, flexibility issues are not considered in that project. In fact, adding flexibility operations like changing the control flow or adding new activities to workflow instances may be complicated by the fact that workflow code is already distributed throughout a distributed system and running.

In terms of flexibility issues in workflow management, the ADEPT framework and the FUNSOFT approach are discussed now. In the ADEPT framework, workflow models are defined by symmetric graphs with specific workflow relevant nodes [19]. Branching is modeled by AND split, OR split, XOR split nodes, which are followed by the respective join nodes. Based on this framework, a set of change operations are specified to allow controlled dynamic changes of workflow instances by users. For instance, adding an activity to a workflow instance involves embedding the added activity into the workflow model and performing a number of operations on the resulting workflow graph to make sure the structure of the graph is consistent with the symmetric structure of workflow model graphs as specified in the ADEPT framework. While ADEPT presents a mathematically founded framework for flexible workflow management, design considerations of a workflow management system providing this functionality are not yet described. In the FUNSOFT approach to modeling and executing workflows, workflow models are specified by FUNSOFT nets, a variant of higher Petri nets geared towards workflow management. Flexibility is achieved by allowing sub-nets to be defined while the workflow runs, achieved by a technique called late modeling. The FUNSOFT net explicitly contains black boxes, i.e., sub-nets which have to be defined during runtime of the workflow [7]. This form of flexibility is rather limited since the position to be specified during runtime has to be known in advance. Dynamic changes due to unanticipated situations in the execution environment of the workflow cannot be handled by that approach. The functionality discussed in [7] is implemented in the CORMAN prototype.

7 Conclusions

As was shown in this paper, there are other good reasons for using distributed object technology to develop a workflow management system. First of all, the development of complex software systems in general may benefit from distributed object technology, especially in distributed environments. In addition, workflow-specific properties arise. In particular, using standardized interfaces of workflow services can provide (i) integration of existing domain-specific tools to be used in workflow executions, (ii) interoperability between different workflow management systems. Furthermore, (iii) data flow can be implemented by passing object references between workflow activities, which will become even more important when implementations of the CORBA Business Object Facility [3] will be available.

This paper discusses an object model to design a flexible, distributed workflow management system based on object technology. Its key features are a strict object-oriented approach, the modeling of workflow models and workflow instances in a single class and providing a high degree of flexibility in re-using workflow models. For further information on a design object model and on additional flexibility issues, the reader is referred to [25]. Based on the material presented in this paper, we are currently implementing a prototype of a flexible workflow management system using the Orbix [11] Object Request Broker.

As discussed in the section on flexibility, other important issues in flexible workflow management are in the center of ongoing work and will be the topic of future work as well, for instance correctness criteria of dynamic change operations, authorization management and issues in user interface design. We believe that the object model presented in this paper will provide an adequate basis for these research and development activities.

Acknowledgment: The author appreciates the work of colleagues and students involved in the WASA project at the University of Münster.

References

1. CoCreate Software, et al. *jFlow. Submission to Request for Proposals OMG Workflow Facility*, 1997. OMG Document bom/97-08-05, 1997. (available from www.omg.org)
2. Dogac, A., Gokkoca, E., Arpinar, S., Koksal, P., Cingil, I., Arpinar, B., Tatbul, N., Karagoz, P. Halici, U., Altinel, M.: *Design and Implementation of a Distributed Workflow Management System: METUFlow.* NATO ASI Workshop, Istanbul, August 12–21, 1997. To appear in Springer ASI NATO Series
3. Data Access Technologies, Inc., et al. *Combined Business Object Facility Proposal.* OMG Business Object Domain Task Force BODTF-RFP 1 Submission. OMG Document bom/97-11-09, 1997.
4. Electronic Data Systems Corporationate Software. *Submission to Request for Proposals OMG Workflow Facility*, 1997. OMG Document bom/97-08-06, 1997. (available from www.omg.org)
5. C. Ellis, K. Keddara, G. Rozenberg. *Dynamic Change Within Workflow Systems.* In Proc. Conference on Organizational Computing Systems (COOCS), Milpitas, CA 1995, 10–22.
6. D. Georgakopoulos, M. Hornick, A. Sheth. *An Overview of Workflow Management: From Process Modeling to Workflow Automation Infrastructure.* Distributed and Parallel Databases, 3:119–153, 1995.
7. J. Hagemeyer, T. Herrmann, K. Just-Hahn, R. Striemer. *Flexibility in Workflow Management Systems (in German).* Software-Ergonomie '97, 179–190, Dresden, March 1997.
8. IBM. *IBM FlowMark: Modeling Workflow, Version 2 Release 2.* Publ. No SH-19-8241-01, 1996.
9. Intelligent Systems Technology Inc. *Submission to Request for Proposals OMG Workflow Facility*, 1997. OMG Document bom/97-08-07, 1997. (available from www.omg.org)

10. Y. Ioannidis (ed.). *Special Issue on Scientific Databases*. Data Engineering Bulletin 16 (1) 1993.

11. Iona. *Programming Guide Orbix 2*. Iona Technologies PLC, March 1997

12. Jablonski, S., Bußler, C.: *Workflow-Management: Modeling Concepts, Architecture and Implementation* International Thomson Computer Press, 1996

13. F. Leymann, W. Altenhuber. *Managing Business Processes as an Information Resource*. IBM Systems Journal 33, 1994, 326–347.

14. C.B. Medeiros, G. Vossen, and M. Weske. *WASA: A workflow-based architecture to support scientific database applications (Extended Abstract)*. In *Proc. 6th DEXA Conference*, London, Springer LNCS 978, 574–583, 1995.

15. Northern Telecom. *Submission to Request for Proposals OMG Workflow Facility*. OMG Document bom/97-08-04, 1997. (available from www.omg.org)

16. OMG. *CorbaServices: Common Object Services Specification*. (available from www.omg.org)

17. OMG: *Workflow Management Facility: Request for Proposals*. OMG Document cf/97-05-06, 1997 (available from www.omg.org)

18. Rational Software et al. *Unified Modeling Language – UML Notation Guide. Version 1.1*, September 1997. (available from www.rational.com/uml)

19. M. Reichert, P. Dadam. *Supporting Dynamic Changes of Workflows Without Loosing Control*. To appear: Journal of Intelligent Information Systems, Special Issue on Workflow and Process Management, Vol. 10, No. 2, 1998.

20. Sheth, A., Kochut, K.J.: *Workflow Applications to Research Agenda: Scalable and Dynamic Work Coordination and Collaboration Systems*. NATO ASI Workshop, Istanbul, August 12–21, 1997. To appear in Springer ASI NATO Series

21. W. Schulze. *Evaluation of the Submissions to the Workflow Management Facility RFP*. OMG Document bom/97-09-02, 1997.

22. A. Sheth, D. Georgakopoulos, S.M.M. Joosten, M. Rusinkiewicz, W. Scacchi, J. Wileden and A. Wolf. *Report from the NSF Workshop on Workflow and Process Automation in Information Systems*. Technical Report UGA-CS-TR-96-003 University of Georgia, Athens, GA, 1996.

23. J. Siegel. *Corba – Fundamentals and Programming*. John Wiley, 1996.

24. G. Vossen, M. Weske. *The WASA Approach to Workflow Management for Scientific Applications*. NATO ASI Workshop, Istanbul, August 12-21, 1997. To appear in: Springer ASI NATO Series.

25. M. Weske, D. Kuropka, J. Hündling, H. Schuschel. *Design of a Flexible Workflow Management System for Corba Architectures. (in German)* Technical Report Angewandte Mathematik und Informatik 18/97-I, Universität Münster, 1997.

26. M. Weske, G. Vossen. *Workflow Languages*. To appear in: P. Bernus, K. Mertins, G. Schmidt (Editors): Handbook on Architectures of Information Systems, Springer, 1998.

27. M. Weske. *Flexible Modeling and Execution of Workflow Activities*. In Proceedings of 31st Hawai'i International Conference on System Sciences, Software Technology Track (Vol VII), 713-722. IEEE Computer Society Press, 1998.

Extending Transaction Closures by N-ary Termination Dependencies

Kerstin Schwarz, Can Türker, and Gunter Saake

Otto-von-Guericke-Universität Magdeburg
Institut für Technische und Betriebliche Informationssysteme
Postfach 4120, D–39016 Magdeburg, Germany
{schwarz|tuerker|saake}@iti.cs.uni-magdeburg.de

Abstract. Transaction dependencies have been recognized as a valuable
method in describing restrictions on the executions of sets of transactions. A transaction closure is a generalized transaction structure consisting of a set of related transactions which are connected by special dependencies. Traditionally, relationships between transactions are formulated
by *binary* dependencies. However, there are applications scenarios where
dependencies must be specified among more than two transactions. Since
n-ary dependencies cannot be expressed by binary dependencies, appropriate extensions are required. In this paper, we extend the concept of
transaction closure by *ternary* termination dependencies. We show how
n-ary termination dependencies can be expressed by binary and ternary
termination dependencies. As a result, we present rules for reasoning
about the combination of these termination dependencies.

1 Introduction

The concept of transaction closure [10] provides a uniform framework for describing advanced transactions and activities. A transaction closure consists of a
set of related transactions which are connected by dependencies. By using special
dependencies we are able to model classical nested transactions as well as activities where a transaction may survive the termination of its parent transaction.
This is needed for example in models for long-during activities [4, 9], workflows
[6], or transactions in active databases [7, 2]. The concept of transaction closure
enables us to model such advanced applications in a modular way.

Transaction dependencies have been recognized as a valuable method in describing certain restrictions on the executions of sets of transactions [1, 12]. In [11]
we have introduced different kinds of binary dependencies. We distinguished between termination, object visibility, and execution dependencies. However, there
are application scenarios which cannot be modeled by only binary dependencies. This is due to the fact that in general *n-ary* dependencies which describe
relationships among more than two transactions cannot be expressed by a set

This research was partly supported by the German State Sachsen-Anhalt under FKZ
1987A/0025 and 1987/2527R.

132

of binary dependencies. For instance, the fact that a transaction t_i has to be aborted in case two other transactions t_j and t_k abort can only be expressed by a ternary dependency.

In this paper, we concentrate on termination dependencies and extend our framework by n-ary termination dependencies. First, we investigate n-ary relationships among transactions and define a set of *ternary* dependencies. We show that each kind of n-ary dependency can be expressed by a combination of binary and ternary dependencies. Since ternary dependencies may be influenced by other ternary or binary dependencies defined on the same (sub)set of transactions, we have to analyze the connection between binary and ternary dependencies. Some of these dependency combinations are valid and reasonable; others are incompatible in the sense that the ternary dependency is relaxed by the binary dependencies. As a result, we derive rules for reasoning about the combination of two dependencies. Using these rules we are able to state how two or more transactions are interrelated.

The paper is organized as follows: Sect. 2 provides the basic notions whereas Sect. 3 introduces ternary termination dependencies. In Sect. 4, we show how n-ary termination dependencies can be expressed by binary and ternary dependencies. In Sect. 5, the ternary dependencies among three transactions are combined with binary termination dependencies between pairs of the corresponding transactions. An example scenario of a transaction closure containing binary and ternary dependencies is considered in Sect. 6.

2 Foundations

Traditionally, a *transaction* is an execution unit consisting of a set of database operations. A transaction t_i is started by invoking the primitive *begin* (b_{t_i}) and is terminated by either *commit* (c_{t_i}) or *abort* (a_{t_i}). These primitives are termed as *significant events* [3]. A transaction invokes operations, termed as *object events*, to access and manipulate the state of database objects. A *history* of a concurrent execution of a set of transactions T comprises all events associated with the transactions in T and indicates the (partial) order in which these events occur. The complete history contains only terminated transactions and is denoted as H, the current (incomplete) history is termed as H_{ct}.

A set of transactions with dependencies among them can be considered as *transaction closure* [10, 11]. The concept of transaction closure is a generalization of the well-known concept of nested transactions [8]. Each transaction closure consist of a set of transactions. Exactly one of these transactions is denoted as root transaction. A root transaction is a transaction which has no parent. Each non-root transaction has exactly one parent and its initiation must follow the initiation of the parent. Each transaction closure is acyclic. The effects of transactions on other transactions are described by dependencies which are constraints on possible histories. We distinguish between *termination, object visibility,* and *execution dependencies.*

Constraints on the occurrence of the significant termination events commit and abort leads to different termination dependencies. In case of two transactions t_i and t_j there are four possible combinations of termination events:

(1) both transactions abort (a_{t_i}, a_{t_j}),
(2/3) one transaction commits whereas the other one aborts $(a_{t_i}, c_{t_j})/(c_{t_i}, a_{t_j})$,
(4) both transactions commit (c_{t_i}, c_{t_j}).

These termination event combinations may be valid in any order (denoted by ✓) or are not valid (denoted by —). As depicted in Table 1, we identify five dependencies as reasonable according to real-world application semantics. The termination dependency between t_i and t_j is called *vital-dependent*, denoted as $vital\_dep(t_i, t_j)$, if the transactions are *abort-dependent* on each other. That is, the abort of transaction t_i leads to the abort of t_j and vice versa. Thus, either the transactions commit together or both abort. The vital-dependent dependency is (as the name suggests) a combination of the dependencies *vital* and *dependent*. The *vital* dependency between two transactions t_i and t_j, denoted as $vital(t_i, t_j)$, concerns the case where the abort of transaction t_i leads to the abort of t_j. In contrast, a *dependent* transaction t_j has to abort if t_i aborts. This fact is defined as $dep(t_i, t_j)$. Two transactions are called *exclusive* dependent on each other, denoted as $exc(t_i, t_j)$, if only one of the transactions is allowed to finish successfully. Our fifth dependency concerns the case where each combination of transaction termination events is valid. Therefore, the involved transactions t_i and t_j are called *independent*, denoted as $indep(t_i, t_j)$. For a formal definition of the termination dependencies and more detail information see [11].

t_i	t_j	$vital\_dep(t_i, t_j)$	$vital(t_i, t_j)$	$dep(t_i, t_j)$	$exc(t_i, t_j)$	$indep(t_i, t_j)$
a_{t_i}	a_{t_j}	✓	✓	✓	✓	✓
a_{t_i}	c_{t_j}	—	—	✓	✓	✓
c_{t_i}	a_{t_j}	—	✓	—	✓	✓
c_{t_i}	c_{t_j}	✓	✓	✓	—	✓

Table 1. Termination Dependencies between two Transactions t_i and t_j

3 Ternary Termination Dependencies

Relations between activities refer to dependencies between transactions of a transaction closures. In [11] we defined different binary transaction termination dependencies such as *vital, dependent, vital-dependent, exclusive,* and *independent*. Obviously, we cannot express all possible kinds of relations among transactions using only binary dependencies as illustrated by the following example.

Example 1. Assume, we want to book a room in one of the hotels Hilton and Maritim, respectively, and hire a car. Booking a room in the Hilton hotel is realized by transaction t_i and in the Maritim hotel by transaction t_j. Hiring a car is represented by transaction t_k. In case we cannot book a room in one of the hotels (both t_i and t_j abort), we do not need to hire a car (abort of t_k).

An attempt to model this situation by binary dependencies may be first to cancel the hiring of the car in case a room in the Hilton hotel is not available and second to cancel the hiring of the car if we cannot book a room in the Maritim hotel. This is equivalent to the dependencies $vital(t_i, t_k)$ and $vital(t_j, t_k)$. However, this specification would lead to an abortion of the car hiring (transaction t_k) in case either t_i or t_j aborts (which means that one room cannot be booked). Consequently, a car can only be rent in case a room in both hotels is booked. This contradicts the intended semantics of the example scenario. □

Thus, statements such as *"if both transactions t_i and t_j aborts, then transaction t_k has to abort, too"* corresponds to the following formulas[1] which cannot be expressed by binary dependencies:

$$((a_{t_i} \wedge a_{t_j}) \Rightarrow a_{t_k}) \equiv (a_{t_i} \Rightarrow (a_{t_j} \Rightarrow a_{t_k})) \tag{1}$$

Therefore, we have to extend our framework by ternary termination dependencies. Formula (1) forces the abort of transaction t_k in case both transactions t_i and t_j abort. However, the abort of t_k may also be the consequence of the commit of one the transactions t_i and t_j. We define the following ternary dependencies:

Definition 1 (Vital). *The predicate $vital(t_i, t_j, t_k)$ is true if and only if transaction t_k has to abort in case both transactions t_i and t_j abort:*

$$vital(t_i, t_j, t_k) :\Leftrightarrow (a_{t_i} \wedge a_{t_j}) \Rightarrow a_{t_k}$$

Definition 2 (Dependent). *The predicate $dep(t_i, t_j, t_k)$ is true if and only if transaction t_k has to abort in case transaction t_i commits and transaction t_j aborts:*

$$dep(t_i, t_j, t_k) :\Leftrightarrow (c_{t_i} \wedge a_{t_j}) \Rightarrow a_{t_k}$$

Definition 3 (Exclusive). *The predicate $exc(t_i, t_j, t_k)$ is true if and only if transaction t_k has to abort in case both transactions t_i and t_j commit:*

$$exc(t_i, t_j, t_k) :\Leftrightarrow (c_{t_i} \wedge c_{t_j}) \Rightarrow a_{t_k}$$

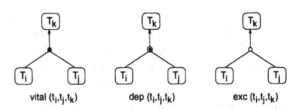

vital (t_i, t_j, t_k) dep (t_i, t_j, t_k) exc (t_i, t_j, t_k)

---

[1] For improving the readability we simplify the predicate $(a_{t_i} \in H)$ to (a_{t_i}). This is also done for the other transactions and termination events.

Table 2 illustrates the termination events of the transactions t_i, t_j, and t_k. The dependencies introduced so far disallow exactly one termination event combination. Ternary vital dependencies disallow the cases where two transactions abort and one commits, e.g. $vital(t_i, t_j, t_k)$ disallows that t_i and t_j abort whereas t_k commits. Ternary dependent transactions disallow a case where two transactions commit and one aborts. In contrast, ternary exclusive dependencies disallow the case where all related transactions commit.

Theorem 1. *The following relationships immediately follows from the Definitions 1 to 3 (Therefore, we omit the (trivial) proofs):*

$$vital(t_i, t_j, t_k) \equiv vital(t_j, t_i, t_k) \qquad (2)$$

$$dep(t_i, t_j, t_k) \equiv dep(t_k, t_j, t_i) \qquad (3)$$

$$exc(t_i, t_j, t_k) \equiv exc(t_i, t_k, t_j) \equiv exc(t_k, t_i, t_j) \qquad (4)$$

A binary dependency between t_i and t_j either disallows no ($indep(t_i, t_j)$), two or four ($vital\_dep(t_i, t_j)$) termination event combinations among three transactions t_i, t_j, and t_k. In contrast, an arbitrary termination event combination can be disallowed using the introduced ternary dependencies. Thus, this set of ternary dependencies is minimal. All other kinds of dependencies among three transactions can be expressed by combinations of ternary and binary dependencies.

	a_{t_i} a_{t_j} a_{t_k}	a_{t_i} a_{t_j} c_{t_k}	a_{t_i} c_{t_j} a_{t_k}	a_{t_i} c_{t_j} c_{t_k}	c_{t_i} a_{t_j} a_{t_k}	c_{t_i} a_{t_j} c_{t_k}	c_{t_i} c_{t_j} a_{t_k}	c_{t_i} c_{t_j} c_{t_k}
$vital(t_i, t_j, t_k)$	✓	—	✓	✓	✓	✓	✓	✓
$vital(t_i, t_k, t_j)$	✓	✓	—	✓	✓	✓	✓	✓
$vital(t_k, t_j, t_i)$	✓	✓	✓	✓	—	✓	✓	✓
$dep(t_i, t_j, t_k)$	✓	✓	✓	✓	✓	—	✓	✓
$dep(t_j, t_i, t_k)$	✓	✓	✓	—	✓	✓	✓	✓
$dep(t_i, t_k, t_j)$	✓	✓	✓	✓	✓	✓	—	✓
$exc(t_i, t_j, t_k)$	✓	✓	✓	✓	✓	✓	✓	—

Table 2. Termination Event Combinations of Ternary Termination Dependencies

4 N-ary Termination Dependencies

Additionally to binary and ternary dependencies, there may be relationships among more than three transactions. Such n-ary dependencies can be expressed by binary and ternary dependencies. This is done by decomposing an n-ary dependency into a set of binary and ternary dependencies which are connected by so-called dummy-transactions. For example, the 5-ary dependency

$$vital(t_i, t_j, t_k, t_l, t_m) \Leftrightarrow ((a_{t_i} \wedge a_{t_j} \wedge a_{t_k} \wedge a_{t_l}) \Rightarrow a_{t_m})$$

can be expressed by the following ternary dependencies including the dummy transactions t_a and t_b:

$$(a_{t_i} \wedge a_{t_j}) \Leftrightarrow a_{t_a}$$
$$(a_{t_k} \wedge a_{t_l}) \Leftrightarrow a_{t_b}$$
$$(a_{t_a} \wedge a_{t_b}) \Rightarrow a_{t_m}$$

An equivalence expression can be transformed into a conjunction of binary and ternary dependencies as follows:

$$((a_{t_i} \wedge a_{t_j}) \Leftrightarrow a_{t_a}) \equiv ((a_{t_i} \wedge a_{t_j}) \Rightarrow a_{t_a}) \wedge (a_{t_a} \Rightarrow (a_{t_i} \wedge a_{t_j})))$$
$$\equiv (\underbrace{(a_{t_i} \wedge a_{t_j}) \Rightarrow a_{t_a}}_{vital(t_i,t_j,t_a)}) \wedge (\underbrace{a_{t_a} \Rightarrow a_{t_i}}_{vital(t_a,t_i)}) \wedge (\underbrace{a_{t_a} \Rightarrow a_{t_j}}_{vital(t_a,t_j)}))$$

Analogously, the second equivalence is transformed into a set of binary and ternary dependencies among the transactions t_k, t_l, and t_b:

$$((a_{t_k} \wedge a_{t_l}) \Leftrightarrow a_{t_b}) \equiv ((a_{t_k} \wedge a_{t_l}) \Rightarrow a_{t_b}) \wedge (a_{t_b} \Rightarrow (a_{t_k} \wedge a_{t_l})))$$
$$\equiv (\underbrace{(a_{t_k} \wedge a_{t_l}) \Rightarrow a_{t_b}}_{vital(t_k,t_l,t_b)}) \wedge (\underbrace{a_{t_b} \Rightarrow a_{t_k}}_{vital(t_b,t_k)}) \wedge (\underbrace{a_{t_b} \Rightarrow a_{t_l}}_{vital(t_b,t_l)}))$$

In summary, the 5-ary dependency and its equivalent representation with only ternary and binary dependencies is illustrated below. A binary dependency like $vital(t_a, t_i)$ is represented by an arrow from t_a to t_i:

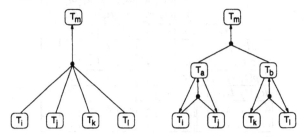

The method of decomposition can also be used for ternary dependent and exclusive dependencies. Rules for reasoning about the transitive relationship between two arbitrary transactions of a transaction closure can be generated considering the introduced termination dependencies. In case of n-ary dependencies, we have to consider the combination and transitive relation of each type of n-ary dependency. However, this is too complex. N-ary dependencies are easier to handle when they are mapped onto binary and ternary dependencies.

The following example illustrates the decomposition of a 4-ary dependency which contains a disjunction of events on the right-hand side of the implication:

$$((a_{t_i} \wedge a_{t_j}) \Rightarrow (a_{t_m} \vee a_{t_n})) \equiv (c_{t_i} \vee c_{t_j} \vee a_{t_m} \vee a_{t_n}) \equiv (\underbrace{(a_{t_i} \wedge a_{t_j} \wedge c_{t_m}) \Rightarrow a_{t_n}}_{vital(t_i,t_j,t_k,t_m)})$$

The resulting expression $((a_{t_i} \wedge a_{t_j} \wedge c_{t_m}) \Rightarrow a_{t_n})$ can be decomposed to a ternary dependency involving the dummy transaction t_a:

$$(a_{t_i} \wedge a_{t_j}) \Leftrightarrow a_{t_a}$$
$$(a_{t_a} \wedge c_{t_m}) \Rightarrow a_{t_n}$$

Using the method described above, each n-ary dependency can be decomposed into a set of binary and ternary dependencies with dummy transactions.

5 Combining Binary and Ternary Dependencies

In this section, we consider ternary termination dependencies among the transactions t_i, t_j, and t_k in combination with binary dependencies between each related transaction pair. We start with the ternary vital dependency. As depicted below, the ternary dependency among transactions t_i, t_j, and t_k is $vital(t_i, t_j, t_k)$, the transactions t_i and t_k are related over the dependency $X(t_i, t_k)$, t_k and t_j over dependency $Y(t_k, t_j)$, and t_i and t_j over dependency $Z(t_i, t_j)$:

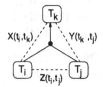

The binary termination dependencies are graphically represented as follows:

$$vital(t_i, t_j) \text{ corresponds to } t_i \longrightarrow t_j$$
$$dep(t_i, t_j) \text{ corresponds to } t_i \longleftarrow t_j$$
$$vital\_dep(t_i, t_j) \text{ corresponds to } t_i \longleftrightarrow t_j$$
$$exc(t_i, t_j) \text{ corresponds to } t_i \longleftrightarrow\!\!\!\!/\;\; t_j$$
$$indep(t_i, t_j) \text{ corresponds to } t_i \longrightarrow\!\!\!\!\!\!- t_j$$

5.1 Considering Dependency $Z(t_i, t_j)$

We start with the discussion of the dependency $Z(t_i, t_j)$ in combination with the ternary vital dependency $vital(t_i, t_j, t_k)$. We show that there are dependency combinations where the ternary dependency can be substituted by a binary dependency without changing the effect of the dependency combination. The dependency $Z(t_i, t_j)$ can be one of the five termination dependencies:

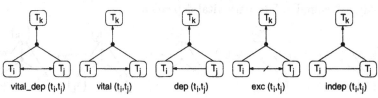

1. vital_dep(t_i, t_j) ∧ vital(t_i, t_j, t_k): The ternary dependency $vital(t_i, t_j, t_k)$ states that t_k has to abort if both t_i and t_j abort. Due to $vital\_dep(t_i, t_j)$, both transactions t_i and t_j abort if either t_i or t_j aborts. For expressing such a relationship among three transactions we do not need a ternary dependency:

$$\underbrace{(a_{t_i} \Rightarrow a_{t_j} \wedge a_{t_j} \Rightarrow a_{t_i})}_{vital\_dep(t_i, t_j)} \wedge \underbrace{((a_{t_i} \wedge a_{t_j}) \Rightarrow a_{t_k})}_{vital(t_i, t_j, t_k)} \equiv \underbrace{(a_{t_i} \Rightarrow a_{t_j} \wedge a_{t_j} \Rightarrow a_{t_i})}_{vital\_dep(t_i, t_j)} \wedge \underbrace{(a_{t_i} \Rightarrow a_{t_k})}_{vital(t_i, t_k)}$$

An alternative to force t_k's abort is to extend $vital\_dep(t_i, t_j)$ by $dep(t_k, t_j)$.

2. vital(t_i, t_j) ∧ vital(t_i, t_j, t_k): The ternary dependency $vital(t_i, t_j, t_k)$ requires the abortion of transaction t_k if both transactions t_i and t_j abort; $vital(t_i, t_j)$ forces transaction t_k to abort if t_i aborts. As in the case before, the same situation can be modelled without the ternary dependency, for instance, as follows:

$$\underbrace{(a_{t_i} \Rightarrow a_{t_j})}_{vital(t_i, t_j)} \wedge \underbrace{((a_{t_i} \wedge a_{t_j}) \Rightarrow a_{t_k})}_{vital(t_i, t_j, t_k)} \equiv \underbrace{(a_{t_i} \Rightarrow a_{t_j})}_{vital(t_i, t_j)} \wedge \underbrace{(a_{t_i} \Rightarrow a_{t_k})}_{vital(t_i, t_k)}$$

3. dep(t_i, t_j) ∧ vital(t_i, t_j, t_k): Since $vital(t_i, t_j) \equiv dep(t_j, t_i)$ holds [11], the result is similar to the previous case. The only difference is that here transaction t_j (instead of t_i) force the abortion of the other transactions.

4. exc(t_i, t_j) ∧ vital(t_i, t_j, t_k): Due to the $exc(t_i, t_j)$, one of the transactions t_i and t_j has to abort in case the other one commits. The ternary vital dependency cause the abortion of transaction t_k, if both t_i and t_j abort. In this case, we cannot express such as relationship by binary dependencies. For instance, the transactions t_i and t_j book a room in different hotels whereas transaction t_k prints the invoice. In case one room is booked, the other booking transaction has to be canceled. This is modeled by the exclusive dependency. On the other hand, if we cannot book a room in any hotel, then the whole transaction closure has to be canceled. This is specified by the ternary vital dependency.

5. indep(t_i, t_j) ∧ vital(t_i, t_j, t_k): Independent transactions have no influence on each other. A ternary vital dependency is an additional restriction on the execution of the corresponding transactions.

5.2 Considering the Dependencies X(t_i, t_k) and Y(t_k, t_j)

The dependency $vital(t_i, t_j, t_k)$ disallows the case where transaction t_k commits and the transactions t_i and t_j abort. In the sequel, we consider how far the dependencies $X(t_i, t_k)$ and $Y(t_k, t_j)$ already avoid this case. So, we do not need to specify a "redundant" ternary vital dependency.

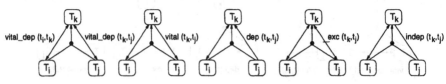

1. vital-dependent: As depicted above, the ternary vital dependency is already fulfilled if one of the dependencies $X(t_i, t_k)$ and $Y(t_k, t_j)$ is vital-dependent. That is, the termination event combination $(a_{t_i}, c_{t_k}, a_{t_j})$ is already disallowed. The abortion of t_i or t_j leads to the abortion of t_k in case of $vital\_dep(t_i, t_k)$ and $vital\_dep(t_k, t_j)$, respectively. In this case, transaction t_k cannot commit. Thus, the dependency $vital(t_i, t_j, t_k)$ does not put further constraints on the termination events of the related transactions.

2. vital/dependent: The termination event combination $(a_{t_i}, c_{t_k}, a_{t_j})$ is already disallowed by the dependencies $vital(t_i, t_k)$ and $dep(t_k, t_j)$. In contrast, the dependencies $vital(t_k, t_i)$ and $dep(t_j, t_k)$ specify that the transactions t_i and t_j, respectively, are aborted in case t_k aborts. In these cases, the ternary vital dependency is a further constraint on the execution of the related transactions.

3. exclusive/independent: Exclusive dependencies for $X(t_i, t_k)$ and $Y(t_k, t_j)$ cannot avoid the case in which transaction t_k commits and the other transactions abort. Therefore, in this case we need the ternary dependency to force t_k's abort in case of the abort of both t_i and t_j. The same is valid for independent transactions which do not influence each other.

5.3 Combining the Dependencies $X(t_i, t_k)$, $Y(t_k, t_j)$, and $Z(t_i, t_j)$

Up to now, we investigated the dependencies $X(t_i, t_k)$, $Y(t_k, t_j)$, and $Z(t_i, t_j)$ in combination with the ternary vital dependency. As a result we obtained the following dependencies which can be (reasonable) combined with $vital(t_i, t_j, t_k)$:

$$X(t_i, t_k) : indep(t_i, t_k), exc(t_i, t_k), dep(t_i, t_k) \tag{5}$$

$$Y(t_k, t_j) : indep(t_k, t_j), exc(t_k, t_j), vital(t_k, t_j) \tag{6}$$

$$Z(t_i, t_j) : indep(t_i, t_j), exc(t_i, t_j) \tag{7}$$

Due to space restrictions, we summarize the valid dependency combinations for $dep(t_i, t_j, t_k)$ and $exc(t_i, t_j, t_k)$ and only discuss some interesting cases.

The dependency $dep(t_i, t_j, t_k)$ forces the abort of t_k in case t_i commits and t_j aborts. If dependency $Z(t_i, t_j)$ is $vital\_dep(t_i, t_j)$ or $dep(t_i, t_j)$, then the case that t_i commits and t_j aborts cannot occur. The dependencies $vital\_dep(t_i, t_k)$ and $dep(t_i, t_k)$ require t_i's abort in case t_k abort. This contradicts $dep(t_i, t_j, t_k)$. Additionally, the combinations of $dep(t_i, t_j, t_k)$ with $vital(t_i, t_k)$, $exc(t_k, t_j)$, and $exc(t_i, t_j)$ can also be expressed by only binary dependencies. The dependencies $exc(t_i, t_k)$, $vital\_dep(t_k, t_j)$ and $dep(t_k, t_j)$, on the other hand, makes the dependency $dep(t_i, t_j, t_k)$ superfluous. Here, only the commit of t_i and the abort of t_j, respectively, leads to an abort of t_k. The following binary dependencies can be combined with $dep(t_i, t_j, t_k)$:

$$X(t_i, t_k) : indep(t_i, t_k) \tag{8}$$

$$Y(t_k, t_j) : indep(t_k, t_j), vital(t_k, t_j) \tag{9}$$

$$Z(t_i, t_j) : indep(t_i, t_j), vital(t_i, t_j) \tag{10}$$

Due to dependency $exc(t_i, t_j, t_k)$, transaction t_k aborts in case both transactions t_i and t_j commit. Since a binary exclusive dependency between the related transactions already disallows that all transactions t_i, t_j, and t_k commit, the ternary dependency $exc(t_i, t_j, t_k)$ is superfluous. The following dependencies can be combined with $exc(t_i, t_j, t_k)$ without relaxing the latter dependency:

$$X(t_i, t_k) : indep(t_i, t_k), \; vital(t_i, t_k) \tag{11}$$
$$Y(t_k, t_j) : indep(t_k, t_j) \tag{12}$$
$$Z(t_i, t_j) : indep(t_i, t_j) \tag{13}$$

The combination of $exc(t_i, t_j, t_k)$ with the remaining binary dependencies can be expressed by only binary dependencies.

6 Example Transaction Closure

The following example is intended to clarify the application of transaction closures containing ternary termination dependencies. Especially, we show the combination of the ternary and binary termination dependencies in such a transaction closure. The transaction closure in our example can be considered as a workflow with special dependencies among the related transactions.

Example 2. A commonly used example is a travel planning activity. In our example this activity consists of reserving a flight, booking a room in the Hilton hotel including a diving course or booking a room in the Maritim hotel including a car rental. We model this activity as a transaction closure with the transactions t_2, t_3, t_4, t_5, t_6, and the coordinating root transaction t_1. Transaction t_2 represents the flight reservation which is essential for the trip. Moreover, a room in the Hilton hotel (t_3) or in the Maritim hotel (t_4) may be booked. The diving course (t_5) is directly connected with a room in the Hilton hotel. Additionally, we try to rent a car (t_6) which is a condition for staying at the Maritim hotel.

One possibility to model this scenario is as follows. The transactions t_2, t_3, and t_4 are child transactions of the root transaction t_1 and are connected to transaction t_1 by the following binary termination dependencies:

$$vital\_dep(t_1, t_2) \land vital(t_1, t_3) \land vital(t_1, t_4)$$

Transaction t_3 is vital for t_5 whereas transaction t_6 is vital-dependent on t_4:

$$vital(t_3, t_5) \land vital\_dep(t_4, t_6)$$

The travel planning activity has to be canceled if there is no room available in the hotels. Furthermore, there is the restriction that we only need a room in one of the hotels. These facts are expressed by the following dependencies:

$$vital(t_3, t_4, t_1) \land exc(t_3, t_5, t_4) \land exc(t_3, t_4)$$

Our example transaction closure is graphically illustrated as follows:

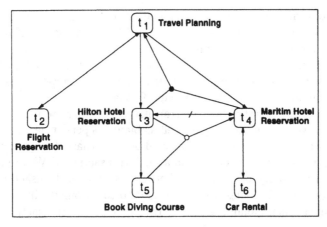

From our dependency definitions and the rules (5)–(13) we can now derive whether the specified ternary dependencies can be simplified to binary dependencies or not. We start with the ternary dependency $vital(t_3, t_4, t_1)$ and the corresponding transactions t_3, t_4, and t_1. The following dependencies are specified for $X(t_3, t_1)$, $Y(t_1, t_4)$, and $Z(t_3, t_4)$ (Here, we used the rule: $vital(t_i, t_j) \equiv dep(t_j, t_i)$):

$$dep(t_3, t_1) \wedge vital(t_1, t_4) \wedge exc(t_3, t_4)$$

Considering the rules (5)–(7) these dependencies are reasonable for $X(t_3, t_1)$, $Y(t_1, t_4)$, and $Z(t_3, t_4)$ in combination with $vital(t_3, t_4, t_1)$.

The ternary dependency $exc(t_3, t_5, t_4)$ has to be considered in combination with the dependencies $X(t_3, t_4)$, $Y(t_4, t_5)$, and $Z(t_3, t_5)$. If there is no dependency explicitly defined on these transaction pairs, we assume that the corresponding transactions are independent:

$$exc(t_3, t_4) \wedge indep(t_4, t_5) \wedge vital(t_3, t_5)$$

According to rule (11) the ternary dependency $exc(t_3, t_5, t_4)$ can be simplified when it is considered together with the dependency $exc(t_3, t_4)$. In this case, transaction t_4 aborts if transaction t_3 commits. However, the ternary exclusive dependency specifies that both transactions t_3 and t_5 have to commit to force the abort of t_4. Here, we have to decide whether $exc(t_3, t_4)$ or $exc(t_3, t_5, t_4)$ better fits the application semantics. In this example, the binary dependency is essential because only one of the room booking transactions should finish successfully. The diving course is only booked in addition to the room in the Hilton hotel. In consequence, the ternary exclusive dependency can be removed.   □

Different ternary and binary termination dependencies allows the transaction designer to specify complex applications. Example 2 showed that we are able to reason about the dependencies of a transaction closure definition.

7 Conclusions and Outlook

Transaction closures are collections of transactions where the connection between the transactions is specified by special dependencies. In this paper, we extended the framework by ternary termination dependencies. The fact that n-ary termination dependencies can be expressed by combinations of binary and ternary dependencies make the problem of reasoning about the correctness of dependency combinations much more simple. In this context, we analyzed the relationship between ternary and binary dependencies. As a result, we stress out that some combinations are invalid or superfluous.

Currently we are investigating the transitivity of ternary termination dependencies. Here, we consider ternary as well as binary dependencies. For example, three transactions t_i, t_j and t_k are connected over a ternary dependency and one of them, e.g. t_i, is binary dependent on a forth transaction t_l. We are interested in the transitive binary dependencies between t_l and the transactions t_j and t_k. Our goal is to derive rules which can be used to automatically compute the transitive dependencies among arbitrary transactions of a transaction closure.

References

1. P. C. Attie, M. P. Singh, E. A. Emerson, A. Sheth, M. Rusinkiewicz. Scheduling Workflows by Enforcing Intertask Dependencies. *Distributed Systems Engineering*, 3(4):222–238, 1996.
2. A. Buchmann, M. T. Özsu, M. Hornick, D. Georgakopoulos, F. Manola. A Transaction Model for Active Distributed Object Systems. In [6], pp. 123–151.
3. P. K. Chrysanthis, K. Ramamritham. Synthesis of Extended Transaction Models Using ACTA. *ACM Transaction on Database Systems*, 19(3):450–491, 1994.
4. U. Dayal, M. Hsu, R. Ladin. A Transaction Model for Long-Running Activities. In G. M. Lohmann, A. Sernadas, R. Camps (eds.), *Proc. VLDB'91*, pp. 113–122. Morgan Kaufmann, 1991.
5. A. K. Elmagarmid (ed.). *Database Transaction Models For Advanced Applications*. Morgan Kaufmann, 1992.
6. D. Georgakopoulos, M. Hornick, A. Sheth. An Overview of Workflow Management: From Process Modeling to Workflow Automation Infrastructure. *Distributed and Parallel Databases*, 3(2):119–153, 1995.
7. M. Hsu, R. Ladin, D. R. McCarthy. An Execution Model For Active Data Base Management Systems. In C. Beeri, J. W. Schmidt, U. Dayal (eds.), *Proc. 3rd Int. Conf. on Data and Knowledge Bases: Improving Usability and Responsiveness, 1988*, pp. 171–179, Morgan Kaufmann, 1988.
8. J. E. B. Moss. *Nested Transactions: An Approach to Reliable Distributed Computing*. MIT Press, Cambridge, MA, 1985.
9. M. Rusinkiewicz, W. Klas, T. Tesch, J. Wäsch, P. Muth. Towards a Cooperative Transaction Model — The Cooperative Activity Model. In U. Dayal, P. M. D. Gray, S. Nishio (eds.), *Proc. VLDB'95*, pp. 194–205, Morgan Kaufmann, 1995.
10. K. Schwarz, C. Türker, G. Saake. Analyzing and Formalizing Dependencies in Generalized Transaction Structures. In *Proc. Int. Workshop on Issues and Applications of Database Technology, IADT'98*, 1998.
11. K. Schwarz, C. Türker, G. Saake. Transitive Dependencies in Transaction Closures. In *Proc. Int. Database Engineering and Applications Symposium, IDEAS'98*, 1998.
12. J. Tang, J. Veijalainen. Enforcing Inter-task Dependencies in Transactional Workflows. In S. Laufmann, S. Spaccapietra, T. Yokoi (eds.), *Proc. 3rd Int. Conf. on Cooperative Information Systems, CoopIS'95*, pp. 72–86, 1995.

Distributed Information Systems
(Extended Abstract)

Ralf Kramer, Peter C. Lockemann

Forschungszentrum Informatik (FZI)
Haid–und–Neu–Str. 10-14, D–76131 Karlsruhe, Germany;
{kramer, lockemann}@fzi.de; http://www.fzi.de/dbs/dbs.html

1 Introduction and Background

FZI is a non-profit research center dedicated to the transfer of new research results to the practice. With currently 9 scientists the database research group focuses on different aspects of data intensive, distributed information systems in several application areas [8].

2 Research Areas

2.1 Web-Based Catalogue Systems

Information systems such as the Web and Digital Libraries contain more data than ever before, are globally distributed, are easy to use and, therefore, become accessible to huge, heterogeneous user groups. The enormously large amount of heterogeneous information requires powerful tools for highly selective information retrieval. Catalogue systems allow to find relevant information and to get a first description of this information in order to find out whether or not it is useful to answer a specific question. They are thus essential ingredients for large scale distributed information systems.

FZI explores associated issues in real world case studies in the area of federated environmental information systems. Two Web-based environmental catalogue systems, the German/Austrian WWW-UDK [6] and the European Web-CDS [1], currently provide a testbed to evaluate database access strategies for the Web with special focus on Java-based approaches and to study interoperability among catalogue systems, their components, and among catalogue systems and underlying information systems. The Web version of the environmental data catalogue UDK is based on the classical HTTP and CGI approach, but takes advantage of Java Applets for dedicated tasks such as complex navigations and data updates. WWW-UDK provides on-line access to underlying data sources (e.g., legal and geographic information systems). Under a contract to the European Environment Agency, Web access to the European Catalogue of Data Source (CDS) is being developed. Several interoperable components for search and retrieval, updates, geographic search, and the general thesaurus module GenThes, which uses the General European Multilingual Environmental Thesaurus GEMET, employ Java either at the server site (Servlets) or at the client site (Applets).

2.2 Thesaurus Federations

Catalogue systems require distinct components that support heterogeneous user groups with diverse terminologies and languages. Thesauri are a suitable starting point. However, multilingual and multi-subject information systems as well as the different user groups require more than the traditional single-language, narrow-focus thesauri. Thesaurus federations [5, 9], a loose compound of distributed, multi- or monolingual thesauri, provide a more extensive and more selective vocabulary, that goes beyond the concepts of multi-thesaurus systems.

The component thesauri of a thesaurus federation retain their autonomy. A federation consists of all terms and relations of the member thesauri. It contains knowledge about relations between terms from different thesauri (inter-thesaurus relations). As a result, the federation provides an integrated view of the overall vocabulary. The framework of thesaurus federations addresses the integration on a technical level (distribution across heterogeneous platforms), a schema level (heterogeneous data models, schema mapping), and an instance level (find, classify, and establish inter-thesaurus relations). A certain resilience to unavoidable inconsistencies must be provided by systems features if one accepts, as one should do, the autonomy of the component thesauri.

We have developed a mediator-/wrapper-based federation architecture together with a prototype which demonstrates the usefulness of the approach for indexing and retrieval. To improve the semi-automatic generation of inter-thesaurus relations we currently work on a promising combination of graph-based and linguistic methods.

2.3 Integration of Host-Based Systems

Distributed object-oriented environments are the architecture for supporting today's highly flexible business processes. Often, however, existing host-based systems become a barrier to changing business processes. Nonetheless, a way must be found to integrate them into the new environments in order to preserve the earlier large investments for them. Our research activities focus on the crucial aspect of overcoming the semantic heterogeneity of the old and new systems that have to cooperate. The basic strategy that prepares existing information systems for cooperation is object-oriented reverse engineering, a data-driven approach that supports the deduction of semantic information from legacy systems and that takes into account all available information, including databases, programs, documentation, and experts' experiences.

We follow an approach [2, 3] that derives, during the process of information gathering, an object-oriented model of the legacy systems. The result can be used in two ways. First, it forms the basis for defining and implementing the cooperation between systems components by providing an object-oriented interface to the legacy system. Second, it increases the level of abstraction in such a way that old and new systems can be compared. The two uses are related. Co-operation can only be achieved if the functions and processes of corresponding entities are similar or complementary. If no semantically homogeneous interpretation can be found, a co-operation is not feasible.

2.4 Component-Based Workflow Architectures

We expect that the potential of distributed information systems can only be fully exploited if system components are able to cooperate. One area where this becomes ever more apparent are business processes. Business and workflow support is an increasingly important means for enterprises to maintain and enhance their competitiveness. Our CompFlow approach [11, 10] is a generic architecture for the support of workflows. Its basic characteristic is its strict separation of aspects. CompFlow uses aspect-oriented components to execute workflows in a fully distributed manner, avoiding the bottlenecks created by a centralized workflow engine. Starting from a workflow model, sets of components supporting the different aspects of a workflow such as control flow, data flow etc. are combined via a so-called component weaver. The genericity of our approach offers several advantages. CompFlow can easily be applied to component-based frameworks such as ActiveX/DCOM, Enterprise JavaBeans or CORBA. It is easy to exchange components and thereby to reflect workflow changes. CompFlow makes it particular easy to adapt workflows to business process changes by providing an incremental transformation from the business process to the workflow model.

2.5 Configurable Event-Triggered Services

Cooperation must be based on the possibility of spontaneous, and hence, asynchronous communication. Such communication can be based on the notion of event and event processing. Event processing is particular challenging in today's distributed, heterogeneous information systems. For technical integration and access to heterogeneous sources, we rely on CORBA for servers combined with Web technology for clients. We augment this technology by active functionality, as known from Active Database Systems ECA rules [12, 4]. Our main objective is to add value in terms of functionality, robustness, and flexibility to the basic CORBA event service. Our testbed is a novel architecture and prototype implementation, C2offein, a service set contributing Active DBMS-style active functionality to CORBA-based, distributed and heterogeneous systems. Since different applications need different kinds of active functionality, C2offein is widely configurable in its overall functionality, ranging from an event monitoring service up to full distributed ECA rule processing. We claim that our approach is superior compared to monolithic approaches like those traditionally used, e.g., in Active DBMS, in its flexibility and "smartness".

3 Outlook

We believe that further technical challenges lie in large-scale applications such as electronic commerce and interoperable and cooperative catalogue systems. For example, electronic payment is one part of e-commerce that has a growing impact on, e.g., catalogue systems on the Web. As there is a whole variety of catalogue systems even in distinctive application areas, interoperability among catalogue systems [7] is of increasing importance. Consequently, we extend our current activities into these areas. We focus on catalogue interoperability in an EU-funded project *European Environmental Information Services*. In this context we also address the issues of quality of services in distributed information systems. E-commerce is an example of cooperative distributed information systems. Such systems offer the potential for new services that add value by combining several individual services into complete solutions for customer problems. Consequently, we plan to extend a regional pilot system for e-commerce in the direction of compound services, and to develop suitable technology for it.

References

1. W. Kazakos, R. Kramer, R. Nikolai, and C. Rolker. WebCDS – A Java-based Catalogue System for European Environment Data. In *Proc. Intl. WS on Issues and Applications of Database Technology*, Berlin, Germany, July 1998.
2. U. Kölsch and J. Laschewski. Objectifying legacy application systems using a specification language framework. In *Proc. of the ICSE-19 Workshop Migration Strategies for Legacy Systems*, pages 1–6, Boston, USA, May 1997.
3. U. Kölsch and M. Wallrath. A process model for controlling and performing re-engineering tasks. In *Proc. 1st Euromicro Conference on Software Maintenance and Reengineering*, pages 20–23, Berlin, Germany, March 1997. IEEE CS Press.
4. A. Koschel and P. C. Lockemann. Distributed Events in Active Database Systems - Letting the Genie out of the Bottle. *Journal of Data and Knowledge Engineering (DKE) - Special Issue*, 25:11–28, March 1998.
5. R. Kramer, R. Nikolai, and C. Habeck. Thesaurus federations: Loosely integrated thesauri for document retrieval in networks based on internet technologies. *International Journal On Digital Library* , 1(2):122–129, September 1997.
6. R. Kramer, R. Nikolai, A. Koschel, C. Rolker, P. C. Lockemann, A. Keitel, R. Legat, and K. Zirm. WWW-UDK: A Web-based Environmental Metainformation System. *ACM SIGMOD Record*, 26(1), March 1997, http://www.cs.umd.edu/areas/db/record/issues/9703/index.html.
7. R. Kramer, R. Nikolai, C. Rolker, S. Bjarnason, and S. Jensen. Interoperability Issues of the European Catalogue of Data Sources (CDS). In *Proceedings of the 2nd IEEE Metadata Conference*, page http://computer.org/conferen/proceed/meta97/papers/rkramer/rkramer.html, Silver Spring, USA, September 1997.
8. P. C. Lockemann, U. Kölsch, A. Koschel, R. Kramer, R. Nikolai, M. Wallrath, and H.-D. Walter. The Network as a Global Database: Challenges of Interoperability, Proactivity, Interactiveness, Legacy. In M. Jarke et al, eds, *Proc. 23rd VLDB*, pages 567–574, Athens, Greece, August 1997.
9. R. Nikolai, A. Traupe, and R. Kramer. Thesaurus Federations: A Framework for the Flexible Integration of Heterogeneous, Autonomous Thesauri. In *Proc. Conference on Research and Technology Advances in Digital Libraries (ADL'98)*, pages 46–55, Santa Barbara, USA, April 1998.
10. U. Assmann R. Schmidt. Extending Aspect-Oriented Programming in Order to Flexibly Support Workflows . In *Proceedings of the ICSE98 AOP Workshop*, pages 41–46, April 1998.
11. R. Schmidt and U. Assmann. CompFlow: A Component-based and Aspect-separated Architecture for Workflow Support. In *Proceedings of the EDBT98 Workflow Management Workshop*, to appear, March 1998.
12. G. von Bültzingsloewen, A. Koschel, and R. Kramer. Active Information Delivery in a CORBA-based Distributed Information System. In K. Aberer and A. Helal, eds., *Proc. 1st IFCIS International Conf. on Cooperative IS (CoopIS'96)*, pages 218–227, Brussels, Belgium, June 1996. IEEE CS Press.

Integrated Web - Database Applications for Electronic Business (Extended Abstract)

Wojciech Cellary

Department of Information Technology
The Poznań University of Economics
Mansfelda 4, 60-965 Poznań, Poland
cellary@kti.ae.poznan.pl; http://www.kti.ae.poznan.pl

1 Introduction

In this paper we present two ongoing research projects realized in the Department of Information Technology, University of Economics at Poznań. From the technical point of view, these projects are based on integration of Web technology with database technology. From the application point of view, they concern electronic business, in particular business-to-business electronic commerce.

2 Agora – A Negotiation Tool

Recent explosion of World-Wide Web and related technologies changes significantly the way business is made. Electronic business and commerce may be classified as *business-to-customer* and *business-to-business*. Currently most applications concern business-to-business electronic commerce, which relates partners who knows each other and mutually trust. An important part of their activity is negotiating contracts. In the project considered we develop a system, called *Agora*, which supports business-to-business negotiations through the Web, aiming at concluding a business contract [3, 4]. The *Agora* roots are related to *Computer Supported Collaborative Work*. *Agora* is composed of two strictly interacting functional components. The first component is the *virtual negotiation table*. The second one is the tool for collaboratively writing documents. *Agora* provides negotiators with an arbitrary number of virtual tables. All negotiators around the table discuss and present their positions by exchanging electronic messages. A negotiator can be involved in several negotiations simultaneously, i.e., a negotiator can virtually sit at different tables.

The part of *Agora* devoted to support collaborative document writing is required to prepare a final contract, which is a result of negotiations. The contract is a common document seen and accessible to all the negotiators. When a negotiator writes or modifies a paragraph of the contract and commits the changes, then it becomes instantaneously visible to other negotiators. Next, any negotiator can modify this paragraph. *Agora* provides versioning mechanisms, which additionally facilitate collaborative writing. Revisions and variants of the document are stored in the system, which can be useful in the case of unsatisfactory results of document evolution, when a rollback operation is required.

The key problem of *Agora* is a transaction model. Classical flat, ACID transactions are not appropriate for collaborative work. Hierarchical transactions require sophisticated management methods. Moreover, hierarchical transactions are still not sufficient, considering expectations of collaborating users, since in many situations the transaction correctness criterion restricts wide cooperation. In *Agora* flat transactions are used, in which the isolation property is relaxed [6–9]. It is achieved by assigning the entire group of collaborating users to the same transaction, still preserving, however, the identity of individuals. The proposed transaction model is inspired by the natural perception, that a team of intensively cooperating users can be considered as a single virtual user, who has more than one brain trying to achieve the assumed goal, and more than two hands operating on keyboards.

The proposed transaction model has many advantages. First it is very straightforward, which simplifies transaction management. Second, it allows practically unrestricted collaboration among members of the same team. Third, since the users of the same team preserve their identity, the DBMS can efficiently support users' awareness and notification. Finally, the proposed model may be easily implement by the use of commercially available DBMSs.

3 WebWisdom – A Distant Teaching Tool

Public, mass education becomes nowadays one of the important issues, not only for schools and universities, but also for companies and their continuous education programs. The education process should be as cheap as possible, as effective as possible, and as fast as possible. As it is widely known, with standard teaching techniques it is not possible to teach a large group of people effectively, fast and cheap. Moreover, as teaching material evolves, the teachers must continuously learn a lot.

A solution to this problem can be distance teaching, by the use of Internet and its modern technologies. To this end, on one hand effective synchronous network transmission and end-user graphical user interfaces must be provided. On the other hand, as the teaching material keeps growing, becomes more and more complicated and user interfaces become more multimedia oriented, a key issue of a distance teaching system becomes a data repository. Such repository must guarantee efficient storage of various types of data, multi-user access for authoring and retrieval, possibility to define user access privileges, ease of preparation of new courses, which employ old and new educational material.

To solve these problems we develop a system called *WebWisdom* in a common project with the Northeast Parallel Architecture Center at the Syracuse University, Syracuse, USA. In *WebWisdom* teaching material in the repository is divided into presentations. A presentation is an ordered set of foils followed by a description. There are two kinds of descriptions: a global one - for all the foils in a presentation and a local one - separately for each foil. A foil can be: an image, an unformatted or formatted text, a program (e.g., an applet), or any media data presentable by a browser. The key characteristics of *Web Wisdom* are the following:

- use of a database as a repository for presentations,
- importing presentations prepared by any presentation-editing tool,
- use of sets of images and/or texts prepared by any image- or text-processing tool (scanned pictures, formatted texts, text&graphics documents, HTML documents),
- use of programs written in any programming language, Java applets, inter-active examples, etc.,
- consistent and unified presentation storage, regardless of the type of a pre-sentation, its structure, editing tool, etc.,
- presentation meta-data storage (author name, creation date, keywords, ab-stract, modification history, use history, formatting and presentation at-tributes, etc.),
- storage of additional information for presentations: add-ons and sounds,
- copying, moving, editing, renaming, and deleting presentations,
- composing presentation on the base of other presentations or their parts,
- managing sets of presentations by a hierarchy of folders called *foilworlds*,
- managing users and user privileges,
- enabling different methods of displaying presentations by the use of tem-plates,
- displaying presentations locally and remotely (by the use of Internet) in a form described by a given template,

Web Wisdom with customizable and extensible Web-based presentation tools and uniform educational data repository supporting both data abd meta-data describing them, gives a thorough and convenient platform for implementing synchronous and asynchronous Web-based teaching systems.

References

[1] Beca, L., G. Cheng, G. C. Fox, T. Jurga, K. Olszewski, M. Podgorny and K. Wal-czak: Web Technologies for Collaborative Visualization and Simulation, 8th SIAM Conference on Parallel Processing, Minneapolis, USA, March 14-17, 1997

[2] Beca, L., G. Cheng, G. C. Fox, T. Jurga, K. Olszewski, M. Podgorny, P. Sokolowski, and K. Walczak: Java Enabling Collaborative Education HealthCare and Comput-ing, Concurrency: Practice and Experience, Vol. 9, 1997

[3] Cellary, W., K. Walczak and W. Wieczerzycki: Database Support for Intranet Based Business Process Re-engineering, Informatica - An International Journal of Com-puting and Informatics, Slovenian Society of Informatics, Ljubljana, Slovenia, Vol. 22, 1998

[4] Cellary, W., W. Picard and W. Wieczerzycki: Web-Based Business-to-Business Negotiation Support, International Conference on Trends in Electronic Commerce TrEC'98, Hamburg (Germany) 1998.

[5] Podgorny, M., K. Walczak, D. Warner and G. C. Fox: Internet Groupware Technologies - Past, Present, and Future, International Conference on Business Information Systems BIS'98, Poznan (Poland), April, 1998

[6] Wieczerzycki, W.: Advanced Transaction Management Mechanisms for Document Databases, 3rd World Conf. on Integrated Design and Process Technology - IDPT'98, Berlin, Germany.

[7] Wieczerzycki, W.: Database and Transaction Model for Dynamic and Cooperative Workflows, Journal of Computing and Information Technology - CIT, Zagreb, Croatia, 1998.

[8] Wieczerzycki, W.: Multiuser Transactions for Collaborative Database Applications, 9th International Conference on Database and Expert Systems Applications - DEXA'98, Vienna, 1998.

[9] Wieczerzycki W.: Transaction Management in Databases Supporting Collaborative Applications, Second East-European Symposium on Advances in Databases and Information Systems - ADBIS'98, Poznan, 1998.

Term Weighting in Query-Based Document Clustering
(Extended Abstract)

Kai Korpimies and Esko Ukkonen

Department of Computer Science, PO BOX 26 FIN-00014 University of Helsinki, Finland.
Kai.Korpimies@cs.helsinki.fi
Esko.Ukkonen@cs.helsinki.fi

Abstract. Search agents in the World-Wide Web are able to find documents which match user-submitted queries. As the number of matching documents returned by the agent is often very large, it would be easier for the user to browse through clusters rather than individual documents when searching for the documents which really satisfy his information needs. In this paper we introduce a new approach to term weighting for the document similarity measures needed in clustering. The approach is based on term occurrence frequencies within the set of documents which match an initial query. We suggest that this approach might perhaps be useful in noise reduction in the very rich and heterogenous environment of the Web.

1 Background

As more and more information becomes available in the World-Wide Web, there's a growing need for navigational tools. Search agents are likely to benefit from clustering: documents, which match an initial query submitted by a user are grouped according to their similarities, after which the user is allowed to redirect his query by browsing through the clusters and choosing the relevant ones. Examples of such combinations of querying and browsing include the *Scatter/Gather* approach described in [1] and the WWW-related experiments in [4].

All kinds of clustering requires in addition to a clustering algorithm some kind of a measure with which the similarities of objects (or distances between them) can be estimated. In document clustering, similarities are usually measured by analyzing term co-occurrences in the documents: basically, documents which share many terms are considered similar (see e.g. [3]).

2 Contextual Term Weighting

Not all terms are as important when document similarities are measured. If a term is frequent in the collection of documents, it can be given relatively small weight because it isn't likely to point out the differences between documents well enough. Term occurrence frequency in a collection is often seen as the number of documents with the term in question; this is called the term's *document frequency* or *df* for short, while *idf* refers to the *inverse document frequency*. The greater the *idf* value a term has, the more weight it should have within the similarity measure. This approach has been very widely used (see e.g. [3] and [1]).

Terms tend to have very different co-occurrence frequencies in different contexts (here contexts are seen as subsets of the document collection). We argue that if a subset *R* of documents, defined through query-document matching, is to be clustered, (as in [1] and [4]), special importance should be given to term occurrence frequencies within this set *R*. In specific, terms which are frequent in *R* should be given only small weights. As an example, if the initial query is *"acid rain"*, locally frequent terms like *"pollution"* or *"environment"* could well be excluded from the analysis or given only a very small weight: it doesn't tell much about the differences between any two documents if these terms are found in them or not, providing that the two documents satisfy the query. However, if we rely only on the collection-wide *idf*-weighting, the two terms would not be given particularly small weights if they aren't very frequent in the collection as a whole. On the other hand, it might perhaps be useful also to give less weight to terms which are *too* infrequent in *R*.

Term occurrence frequencies local to queries have previously been studied in [2]: the purpose was to find the documents which would give broad overview descriptions of the search topic expressed in a query.

3 Preliminary Experimental Results

We used *clustering potential* as the measure for the effectiveness of a term weighting scheme in clustering. To define the clustering potential we need a set *S* of documents, a division of *S* into *C* subsets (which will also be called clusters here) $S_1, \ldots, S_c$ and a document similarity measure $sim(D_i, D_j)$ (we used the *Cosine coefficient*, see e.g. [3]) which employs a term weighting scheme *tw*. Let $csim(tw)$ be the average of similarities between every possible pair of documents (D_k, D_l) in *S* for which it holds that D_k and D_l are in the same cluster. If $csim'(tw)$ is the average similarity between each possible pair of documents in *S*, the clustering potential of a term weighting scheme can be defined as in Definition 1.

Definition 1. (clustering potential of a term weighting scheme)

$$clpot(tw) = \frac{csim(tw)}{csim'(tw)} \tag{1}$$

We began by submitting an initial query *Q: "acid rain"* for a search agent in the World-Wide Web. From the retrieved documents, we subjectively identified a small number of examples falling clearly into the following three categories: the causes of acid rain, the effects of acid rain and the remedies or methods for controlling acid rain. After this, we calculated the clustering potential according to Definition 1 for two term weighting schemes: *cidf* defined in Definition 2 and the standard *idf* (see Sect.2). All values w_{ij} and $rel(Q, D_i)$ were binary in our experiments.

Definition 2. (Contextual inverted document frequency)

$$cidf(Q, t_j) = \frac{1}{\sum_{i=1}^{n} w_{ij} * rel(Q, D_i)} \tag{2}$$

Where w_{ij} stands for the weight of term t_j in document D_i, n is the number of documents in the collection and $rel(Q, D_i)$ indicates the degree to which document D_i matches query Q.

When the two weighting schemes were used separate of each other, the *cidf*-weighting provided an improvement of 18 % compared with *idf*-weighting and an improvement of 34 % when compared with the situation where all terms had equal weights. The clustering potential was improved when the two weighting schemes were combined through the use of thresholds values: as 70 % of terms were excluded from similarity measurements based on low *idf*-values, the clustering potential of the *cidf*-weighting scheme was improved with further 30 %.

4 Conclusions and Further Research

We have suggested that if the starting point for clustering is a query, the similarity measures used in document clustering could benefit from term weighting based on the occurrence frequencies of the terms in those documents which match the query in question. The preliminary results are encouraging but proper large-scale experiments would still be required: the results depend among other things on the given clustering, the similarity measure used and the set of documents which match the original query. Also, the use of *minimum* thresholds for term frequencies should be studied.

References

1. M. A. Hearst & J. O. Pedersen: "Reexamining the Cluster Hypothesis: Scatter/Gather on Retrieval Results". In Proc. of the 19th Annual International ACM SIGIR Conference on Research and Development in Information Retrieval. Zurich, Switzerland 1996.
2. K. Korpimies & E. Ukkonen: "Searching for General Documents". In Proc. of the International Conference on Flexible Query Answering Systems (FQAS'98). Lecture Notes in Artificial Intelligence, Springer 1998.
3. Gerald Salton: "Automatic text processing: the transformation, analysis, and retrieval of information by computer". Addison-Wesley, Reading, MA, 1989.
4. O. Zamir, O. Etzioni, O. Madani & R. M. Karp: "Fast and Intuitive Clustering of Web Documents". In Proc. the Third International Conference on Knowledge Discovery and Data Mining. Newport Beach, CA, 1997.

Discovery of Object-Oriented Schema and Schema Conflicts (Extended Abstract)

Hele-Mai Haav and Mihhail Matskin

Institute of Cybernetics, Akadeemia tee 21, EE0026 Tallinn, Estonia
Norwegian University of Science and Technology, N-7034 Trondheim, Norway
helemai@cs.ioc.ee,misha@idi.ntnu.no

Abstract. In this paper, we propose an approach and a general schema of algorithms for automatic detection of conflicts between schema and underlying object base. Our approach is distinguishable by first discovering schema from given set of objects and then comparing it to the existing schema for discovery of schema conflicts. The approach is based on the comparison of the two inheritance lattices: one constructed on the basis of class library and another discovered from object base using one of the general conceptual classification methods.

1 Introduction

Occurrence of different schema conflicts and inadequate representation of object base by given schema become to be problems within evolving object-oriented or object- relational database environment. One of the solutions can be automatic discovery of object-oriented (OO) schema and schema conflicts.

Our proposal involves two components: automatic discovery of OO schema from object base and detection of schema conflicts to ensure conformance between class lattice (schema) and underlying object base.

This approach differs from dynamic schema evolution approaches [4] which do not pay attention to the situations, where change to object system is initiated by changes to object base. In contrast, we consider both directions of changes: from schema to object base, and from object base to schema.

For discovery of schema from given set of objects, we use one of the general conceptual classification methods: the Galois approach [2, 3]. The discovered schema is then compared to the existing schema for detecting, and to some extent recovering schema conflicts. General framework of algorithms for discovery of schema conflicts is the main contribution of this work.

In this abstract we show how a class lattice is discovered from a given set of objects, and how automatically find schema conflicts and ensure conformance of the schema and object base.

2 Discovery of OO schema as construction of a class lattice

Discovery of a class lattice from a given set of objects can be formalised as a classification problem within a context (O, C, R), where O denotes a set of objects (instances), C is a set of names of class descriptions from what objects obtain properties (state variables and methods), and R is a binary relationship "belong-to" between these two sets which indicates for each object-class definition pair whether the properties defined by the class description apply to the object or not i.e. whether the object belongs to the class or not.

We denote objects by their identity (Oid) and class descriptions by their names. Let O be a finite set of object identifiers and C be a finite set of class names representing corresponding classes. Let R be a binary relationship on $O \times C$ representing that an object belongs to any one of the classes from C. For $o \in O$ and $c \in C$ we note R(o, c)=1 if oRc and R(o, c)=0 if o¬Rc. Such a relationship can be represented by the Boolean matrix. We assume an extended OODM formally defined as a Galois lattice of a binary relationship R on $O \times C$, where O is a set of objects (Oid-s) and C is a set of classes to which objects belong. Every element of this object model is a pair (X,Y) where X is a subset of O and Y is an arbitrary part of C.

Thus, our object model connects both class lattice defined as a partial order of class definitions and object lattice defined as an inclusion order of instances of class definitions into one lattice by means of a Galois connection (f, g) [2].

On the basis of such a model we can easily see (compute) what objects share what classes together with their properties defined by corresponding class descriptions. We can also derive inheritance class lattice from the full object model.

The inheritance class lattice constructed from the given binary relationship R corresponds to the OO schema. The process of construction of the lattice can be seen as a schema discovery process. As we are always able to construct inheritance lattice from the given relationship R, then in principle, we need to discover the matrix representing the binary relationship R on $O \times C$.

For the purpose of discovery of schema conflicts, we need to obtain also binary relationship R1 on $O1 \times C$, where C is a set of class names, O1 is a set of abstract names of potential objects which may belong to a corresponding classes from C. On the basis of R1, we can construct inheritance lattice of a class library.

In order to ensure that the two matrices representing binary relationships R and R1 become comparable, we reduce the matrix representing the relationship R to show only non equal rows, which means that we glue equal rows to form one row indicating that a set of objects has all the same values of "belong-to" relationship R. We can also denote this set of objects by some name, if necessary. We do not foresee any technical problems of obtaining those matrices from the environments of existing OODBMS.

3 Discovery of schema conflicts

As discussed above, the both relationships R and R1 are semantically comparable which enables us to use them as input for algorithms of automatic detection of schema conflicts and construction of a consistent object and class lattices.

General framework of our algorithms expects the existence of 2 matrices. The first matrix M1 is discovered from object base by constructing a binary relationship R on $O1 \times C1$, where $O1 = \{Oid_1,..., Oid_n\}$ and $C1 = \{C_1, ... , C_m\}$. Object identifiers are denoted by Oid-s and C-s are classes to which objects belong. Equal rows in matrix are glued together and corresponding rows represent a set of object's with the same values of "belong to" relationship. The second matrix M2 is discovered from class library by constructing a binary relationship R1 on $O2 \times C2$, where C2 is a set of class names, O2 is a set of abstract object identifiers of potential objects which may belong to a corresponding classes from C2.

We assume that elements of C1 and C2 are names of columns and elements of O1 and O2 are names of rows in the matrices M1 and M2 correspondingly.

It is easy to understand (from the previous discussion) that both matrices M1 and M2 represent a Galois lattice.

In order to discover schema conflicts we have developed algorithms for composition and comparison of the lattices represented in the form of matrices M1 and M2. We also created an algorithm for finding differences in these lattices. As a result, we have been able to propose an algorithm which makes it possible to automatically recover some conflicts found in lattices by correcting certain matrices and applying modifications made in matrices to objects from corresponding object base.

Complexity of proposed algorithms needs further investigations. In general, construction of a Galois lattice is a problem of exponential complexity. In practical applications, where the number of features per instance (number of classes for each object in our case) is usually bounded, the worst case complexity of the structure (lattice) is linearly bounded wrt to the number of instances [1].

References

1. R. Godin and H. Mili, Building and Maintaining Analysis-Level Class Hierarchies Using Galois Lattices, In: Proc. of OOPSLA'93, ACM Press,1993, pp 395-410
2. A. Guenoche, I. Van Mechelen, Galois Approach to the Induction of Concepts, In: Categories and Concepts. Theoretical Views and Inductive Data Analysis, Eds. I. Van Mechelen, J. Hampton, R.S. Michalski, P. Theuns, Academic Press, 1993, pp 287-307
3. Haav H-M, An Object Classifier Based on Galois Approach, In: H. Kangassalo, J. F. Nilsson, H. Jaakkola, S. Ohsuga, Information Modelling and Knowledge Bases VIII, IOS Press, 1997, pp 309-321
4. R. J. Peters, M. T. Özsu, An Axiomatic Model of Dynamic Schema Evolution in Objectbase Systems, ACM Transactions on Database Systems, Vol 22 No 1, 1997, pp 75-114

On the Ordering of Rewrite Rules
(Extended Abstract)

Joachim Kröger[1], Stefan Paul[2], and Andreas Heuer[1]

[1] University of Rostock, Computer Science Department, DB Research Group,
D–18051 Rostock, Germany
{jo, heuer}@informatik.uni-rostock.de
http://wwwdb.informatik.uni-rostock.de/Research/CROQUE.engl.html
[2] c/o SAG Systemhaus GmbH, Brandstücken 18, D–22549 Hamburg, Germany
stp@software-ag.de

Abstract. The conceptual development of the rule–based component of
the CROQUE query rewrite and optimization system led to the derivation of an ordering of the rules present in the rule base according to their
"optimization potential" in order to increase the efficiency of the logical term rewriting [5]. This heuristic may indeed be used for any other
rule–based optimizer, too.

The major contribution of our approach is a combination of three ideas:
(1) limit the search space of query optimization by grouping and ordering
rules (for rule–based optimizers), (2) use of "offline" pre–optimization
ordering instead of dynamic ordering during the optimization process,
(3) taking into consideration more than one ("n–best") alternatives for
further evaluation.

1   Motivation

The CROQUE project[1] [4, 2] is concerned with different aspects of optimization
and evaluation of object–oriented queries. Starting point of all our considerations
are queries in ODMG's OQL ([1], formalized in [6]), that are first represented
internally employing a hybrid approach of calculus and algebra [3] before being
transformed using a rule– and cost–based optimizer.

In general, equivalence rules may be applied in both directions. Since in
most cases a heuristically preferred direction of application can easily be distinguished, we only consider *directed* rules (transformation rules) in the framework
of the CROQUE project. Certain normalization steps are separately realized
first, splitting the rule set in smaller subsets. Thus, not all defined rules are part
of the rewriting according to the described concept.

An "exhaustive matching" of *all* rules against *every* operator node does not
make sense since most of the rules may not match successfully against most of

---

[1] CROQUE (*C*ost- and *R*ulebased *O*ptimization of object–oriented *QUE*ries) is a joint
research project of the universities of Rostock and Konstanz funded by the German
Research Association (DFG) under contracts He 1768/5–2 and Scho 554/1–2.

the considered nodes. Efficiency is increased by dividing the rule set up into rule classes using the root node of the left hand side of the rule for classification. In this way, the set of rules to be considered in a (sub–)query tree rewriting may be reduced to exactly one rule class by only one single function call. The overhead needed for pattern matching will hereby be cut down considerably.

2 Ordering Rewrite Rules

Realizing the real need of a heuristic search space pruning we developed a heuristic that is the present focus of our interest: per (sub–)query tree rewriting no more than the n *best* rules shall be applied. Therefore, we have to order the rules. Additionally, this strategy also succeeds in minimizing the number of pattern matcher calls. The ordering of rules is not a new idea but in other approaches the ordering has to be programmed in general or estimation of the rule ordering is done online. A somewhat more detailed discussion of other approaches comprising the systems COKO-KOLA, Volcano, EXODUS, Starburst, GOM, and Gral may be found in the full paper [5].

The realization of the rewriting in CROQUE is as follows. A given logical expression is rewritten by the rewrite engine according to a given strategy thus spanning a logical search space. Therefore, each call to the pattern matcher supplies a (sub–)query tree t and an ordered list r of rules. The elements of r are matched against t in order. User queries, successfully applied rules, and associated rewriting results (which altogether define the system's query load) are passed to the adaptation component which may then possibly influence the rule ordering.

In order to minimize the overhead we avoid an online ordering during the query evaluation, i.e. the rules are applied according to their order in the considered rule classes' list. An initial ordering of the rules is done only once in the beginning. Afterwards, the ordering is modified during distinguished adaptation phases. These steps may be done according to any policy, the only request we demand for is that the adaptation is done offline. By means of the adaptation, possible mistakes or inaccuracies of the initial ordering shall be remedied and additionally the ordering shall be adapted to cover the characteristics of the considered database, e.g. the used schema, present instances, and the observed query load.

2.1 Initial Rule Ordering

The initial ordering of the rules is realized according to a very simple method: two rules are comparable, i.e. may be ordered, if there exist a smallest common pattern that is contained in both rules. Applying both rules to this pattern will lead to two expressions that may easily be ranked "by a human query optimization expert" (e.g., the DBA). Moreover, the ordering is assumed to be transitive. Incomparable rules are ordered randomly in the initial ordering phase. The isolated rule orderings obtained in this way are integrated for every rule class by determining their topological order.

2.2 Rule Order Adaptation

The adaptation of the initial ordering is done by the help of selected statistics. Furthermore, a combination of benchmarks and specific user queries is utilized for an offline rule assessment. Statistics are mainly intended as a means to help ordering incomparable rules since a random ordering is not really satisfying. Rules that may be used very often with a noticeable success are ranked higher than rarely useable rules that only result in small cost reductions. So-called benchmarks are used to correct the ranking done by hand in the initial rule ordering phase.

3 Overall Optimization Process

Optimization in CROQUE is not restricted to algebraic rewriting. The rewriting of expressions is done in a hybrid approach consisting of a calculus and an algebra notation [3]. Rewriting calculus expressions is done in the same way as rewriting algebraic expressions by means of rules and pattern matching. Thus, the results are transferable. The use of heuristics therefore integrates well into the related work of the CROQUE project.

Evaluation of all our concepts will be done on the basis of our query optimizer prototype. Most parts of its implementation are already complete so that the optimizer is nearly fully operational. There will be further work in improving our heuristics. Above all, the (automatic) adaptation of the rule ordering will be a topic of our ongoing investigations as well as investigations about further opportunities for adaptation on other optimizer layers.

References

[1] R.G.G. Cattell, editor. *The Object Database Standard: ODMG-93, Release 1.2.* Morgan-Kaufmann, San Mateo, CA, 1996.

[2] D. Gluche, T. Grust, C. Mainberger, and M.H. Scholl. Incremental Updates for Materialized Views with User-Defined Functions. In *Proc. of the Fifth Int. Conference on Deductive and Object-Oriented Databases (DOOD'97), Montreux, Switzerland,* December 1997.

[3] T. Grust, J. Kröger, D. Gluche, A. Heuer, and M.H. Scholl. Query Evaluation in CROQUE — Calculus and Algebra Coincide. In *Proc. of the 15th British National Conference on Databases (BNCOD 15), London, UK, LNCS 1271, Springer,* pages 84–100, July 1997.

[4] A. Heuer and J. Kröger. Query Optimization in the CROQUE Project. In *Proc. of the 7th Int. Conference on Database and Expert Systems Applications (DEXA '96), Zurich, Switzerland, LNCS 1134, Springer,* pages 489–499, September 1996.

[5] J. Kröger, S. Paul, and A. Heuer. Query Optimization: On the Ordering of Rules. Preprint CS-09-98, CS Dept., University of Rostock, 1998.
Available at http://wwwdb.informatik.uni-rostock.de/~jo/CS-09-98.html

[6] H. Riedel and M.H. Scholl. A Formalization of ODMG Queries. In *Proc. of the 7th Int. Conference on Database Semantics (DS-7), Leysin, Switzerland,* October 1997.

Towards Data and Object Modelling
(Extended Abstract)

Jaroslav Pokorny

Charles University, Department of Software Engineering,
Malostranske nam. 25, 118 00 Praha 1, Czech Republic
pokorny@ksi.ms.mff.cuni.cz

Abstract. In the paper we survey research results of the Database Research Group at Charles University Prague during last 10 years. Its activities have been focused mainly on applying a functional approach to conceptual modelling and modelling of objects via relational databases. The former research direction influenced also an approach to a formalization of object-oriented models and, recently, OLAP and data warehouses modelling. The latter research concerned a persistence of objects and a study, how to implant high-level query capabilities in C++. In the context of the ADOORE project, a practical implementation – a general library (GENLIB) is now at disposal, where objects are stored in a relational database. To enhance queering objects, high-level query capabilities are possible.

1 Introduction

Data modelling at various level of abstraction is a common denominator of any data base technology. The research of the Database Research Group at Charles University Prague has been focused on developing a sound and rigorous approach to data modelling during last 10 years. As a formal construction a function has been chosen and a version of typed lambda calculus has provided a powerful manipulation tool. The new approach has led to several research directions, e.g. a development of new conceptual and data models, a proving formal properties of attributes, a comparing the expressive power of various conceptual models etc.

Some attempts towards an object-orientation have been also done in mid-1990's. Later, according to the trends in object-relational orientation, we have developed a general library (GEN-LIB) for ensuring persistence of C++ objects. Both research directions are discussed in more detail in Sections 2 and 3, respectively.

2   Functional approach to data modelling

The notion of attribute (see, e.g., [1,2]) has been introduced in 80ties as a universal construct for describing conceptual and databases models. This notion conceives the basic data structure as a very general function dependent on possible worlds and time moments. Consequently, unifying tools based on the typed lambda calculus gave possibilities to define appropriate notions for expressing queries, integrity constraints as well as mappings for proving an equivalency of schemes in different data models. The particular data models could be compared with respect to their expressiveness [4], [8], [11]. To measure „information content" of attributes, the notions such as information capability, distinguishing capability, and comparison based on cardinality are defined in this framework and some important theorems are proved [11].

This research contributed significantly to a development of a practical methodology of database design via attributes. As a result the data model HIT has been introduced and used in number large projects in Czech Republic.

A taxonomy of conceptual and database models based on these notions has been also proposed [10].

The functional approach has been shown as appropriate for integrating heterogeneous environment [3]. Practical consequences of the theory developed can help in constructing so called co-operative information systems as well as in transforming user requirements between two different kinds of information environment. How to add behaviour to objects is discussed in [5] and [9].

3   Objects via relations: The ADOORE approach

The GEN.LIB (General Library) system [12,13], being developed at Charles University in Prague, addresses many of features typical for object-relational databases. The main goal of the library is to make objects persistent via a relational database. The associated object model adopted is the one used in OMT methodology.

The library gives at least these possibilities: (1) handle persistent and transient objects via C++ programs, (2) conceive rows of relations as C++ objects, (3) use high-level query facilities in C++ programs, (4) use many of database-oriented features on the level of C++ programming.

The GEN.LIB is originally a part of the ADOORE project that was solved in Charles University during 1995-1997 [6, 7].

References

1. P. Materna, J. Pokorný. Applying simple theory of types to databases. *Information Systems*, Vol. 7, No. 4, Pergamon Press, pages 283-300, 1981.

2. J. Pokorný. A function: Unifying mechanism for entity-oriented database models. *Entity-Relationship Approach*, (Ed. C. Batini), Elsevier Science Publishers B.V. (North-Holland), pages 165-181, 1989.

3. J. Pokorný. Integration of functional, relational and logical databases. *In Proc. of Intern. Conf. on Engineering Information in Data Bases and Knowledge Based Systems (TECHNO-DATA '90), Berlin*, December 1990.

4. J. Pokorný. Semantic relativism in conceptual modeling. In *Proc. of 4th Int. Conf. Database and Expert Systems Applications (DEXA'93), Prague, CR, LCNS 720, Springer*, pages 48-55, September 1993.

5. J. Pokorný. On behaviour modeling using a functional approach. *In Proc. of Int. Conf. Information System Development (ISD '94), (Eds. J. Zupančič, S. Wrycza), Bled, Slovenia*, September 1994.

6. J. Pokorný, M. Prokeš. Object-Relational Databases. Res. Rep., ADOORE Consortium , NOT2-CU-POK51009, Praha, 1995.

7. Z. Farkas, Y. Hamon, J. Pokorný, J. Valenta. The ADOORE Software Engineering Framework. Res. Rep., ADOORE Consortium, RR01-OT-96.1581, Paris, 1996.

8. J. Pokorný. Conceptual Modeling of Statistical Data. In *Proc. of 7th Int. Conf. Database and Expert Systems Applications (DEXA'96), IEEE, Zurich, Switzerland,* September 1996.

9. J. Pokorný. A Functional Information Modeling in an Object-Oriented Environment. In *Proc. of Int. Conf. Information System Development (ISD'96), (Eds. S. Wrycza, J. Zupančič), Sopot, Poland*, September 1996.

10. J. Pokorný. Database semantics in heterogenous environment. In *Proc. of 23rd Seminar SOFSEM'96: Theory and Practice of Informatics, (Eds. K.G. Jeffery, J. Král, M. Bartošek.), LCNS 1175, Springer*, pages 125-142, November 1996.

11. M. Duží, J. Pokorný. Semantics of General Data Structures. In *Proc. of Seventh European-Japanese Seminar on Information Modelling and Knowledge Bases, Toulouse, France*, May 1997.

12. M. Kopecký, J. Pokorný. Objects Through Relations: the ADOORE Approach. In *Systems Development Methods for the Next Century (Eds. W.G.Wojtkowski, S. Wrycza, J. Zupančič), Proc. of Sixth Int. Conf. on Information Systems, Boise, Idaho, Plenum Press*, pages 1-14, August 1997.

13. M. Kopecký, J. Pokorný. Towards the Object Persistence via Relational Databases. In *Proc. of the First East-European Symposium in Advances in Databases and Information Systems (ADBIS'97), St. Petersburg, Russia*, September 1997.

14. J. Pokorný. Conceptual Modelling in OLAP. In *Proc. of 6th European Conference on Information Systems (ECIS '98), (Ed. W.R.J. Baets), Aix-en-Provence, France,* June 1998.

Propagation of Structural Modifications to an Integrated Schema *

Regina Motz

Instituto de Computación, Universidad de la República,
Montevideo, Uruguay
rmotz@fing.edu.uy

Abstract. This paper addresses the problem of propagating local structural schema changes to an already acquired integrated schema of a federation. Our approach is to regard this problem from a schema integration point of view. The main contribution is the development of a framework for performing evolution of an integrated schema without information loss and avoiding as much as possible re-integration steps.
Keywords: Federated Databases, Schema Evolution, Schema Integration.

1 Introduction

Considering the importance of schema integration methodologies as well as the growing use of cooperative engineering the relevance of evolution of an integrated schema in a federation becomes very important and necessary.

In the context of a 'tightly coupled' federated schema [4] one is interested in achieving schema evolution of the already integrated schema as a consequence of: (a) changes in the structure of the local schemas, or (b) changes in the semantics of correspondences between the local databases. The former case is referred to as *structural modifications* while the latter as *semantic modifications*. This paper addresses the study of schema evolution of an integrated schema due to structural modifications. (The treatment of semantic modifications can be found in [11].)

Recent work [1, 3, 2] addresses the automatic propagation of local schema changes to an integrated schema. They present schema integration methodologies that permit the propagation of structural and semantic changes, but only when these involve a single class. However, this turns out to be very restrictive, mainly if we take into account that local schemas may evolve in a complex way. One contribution of this paper is thus the proposal of a framework for efficient propagation of local schema evolution which adopts the complete schema level as the granularity of change, allowing changes to involve multiple classes or relationships in the local schemas.

Since modifications in corresponding subschemas may also involve a modification to the existing vertex/path correspondences, they cannot be directly

---

* This work was developed while at IPSI-GMD, Darmstadt University of Technology, Darmstadt, Germany.

propagated. Moreover, local schema evolutions may invalidate correspondences established in some previous integration step. The challenge is thus how to manage this fact without information loss and avoiding as much as possible re-integration steps.

The paper is organized as follows. Section 2 presents background material. We start briefly presenting a formal representation for ODMG schemas, called *schema graph*, our common data model for integration. Afterwards, we present the main features of the schema integration methodology SIM. In Section 3 we explain the procedure that permits the semi-automatic propagation of structural correspondences to an already integrated schema. Finally, some concluding remarks are given in Section 4.

2 Preliminaries

2.1 Schema Graph

One approach to integrating databases with heterogeneous data models is to apply syntactic transformations that map the local schemas to schemas in a uniform model. A relevant aspect of these transformations is that they also permit to map each local schema modification to schema modification operations in the common data model. For this reason it is sufficient to study schema evolution issues on the common data model.

In our case, we assume that the common data model is ODMG [9]. We use a formal representation for ODMG schemas, called schema graph, which provides a formal basis for the treatment of both schema integration and schema evolution. A *schema graph* $G = (V, E, S, K)$ is a directed graph that captures the inheritance hierarchies and relationships of a schema. The vertices of a schema graph are of two kinds, $V = C \cup T_I$, where C is a finite set of classes and T_I is a set of immutable types. $E = E_R \cup E_A$ is a set of labelled edges. E_R corresponds to a set of relationship edges between classes. We will denote relationship edges by $p \xleftrightarrow{a} q$, where $p, q \in C$ and $a \equiv (\alpha, \beta)$, for $\alpha, \beta \in L_E$ (a set of edge labels). $E_A \subseteq C \times L_E \times V$ is a set of attribute edges. $S \subseteq C \times C$ is a finite set of specialization edges, which will be denoted by $p \Longrightarrow q$, meaning that p is a specialization of q. We will write $p{=}q$ to denote an arbitrary edge. Finally, $K = K_R \cup K_A$ is a function which associates cardinality constraints to relationship and attributes edges.

Not every schema graph specifies a valid ODMG schema. A schema graph $G = (V, E, S, K)$ is said to be a *proper schema* when it satisfies the following restrictions:

1. **Uniqueness in the context of a class.** The occurrence of a relationship/attribute edge in the context of a class is unique.
2. **Acyclicity of subtyping.** Class specializations are acyclic.
3. **Monotonicity of Inheritance.** Specialization is preserved along equal attributes / relationships.

A detailed formalization of ODMG in terms of the concept of schema graph as well as a complete description of its features can be found in [10].

2.2   The Schema Integration Methodology. SIM

Our theoretical framework for propagating local semantic modifications is based on a declarative schema integration methodology called SIM [5, 6]. This methodology reduces schema integration to the resolution of a set of vertex/path correspondences between (arbitrary) subschemas of the local databases. ¿From such a set of correspondences, SIM semi-automatically derives schema transformations, called *schema augmentations*, from each local schema to the integrated one, in such a way that corresponding data among local databases is mapped to the same structure in the integrated database.

The generated schema augmentations enhance the schemas with classes and paths, such that the resulting integrated schema is a non-redundant proper schema graph. Formally, this means that it is the least upper bound $(G_1 \sqcup_A G_2)$ of the local schemas G_1 and G_2 under the augmentation ordering that we present next.

Definition 1. (Schema Augmentation and Augmentation Ordering)
Two proper schema graphs $G_1 = (V_1, E_1, S_1, K_1)$ and $G_2 = (V_2, E_2, S_2, K_2)$ are in an augmentation ordering, denoted by $G_1 \sqsubseteq_A G_2$, iff $V_1 \subset V_2$, $S_1 \subset S_2$ and there exists a mapping, denoted by $A : G_1 \to G_2$[1] and called an **augmentation**, *that maps each vertex/edge of G_1 to a proper subschema of G_2, satisfying the following conditions:*

(1) The mapping of the empty graph is the empty graph.
(2) Each class $p \in V_1$ is mapped to a (connected) subschema of G_2 which contains at least p.
(3) The augmentation of two distinct classes in G_1 do not contain a common class in G_2.
(4) Each specialization $p \Longrightarrow q$ in G_1 is mapped to a specialization path $p \overset{*}{\Longrightarrow} q$ in G_2.
(5) Each relationship $p \overset{a}{\longleftrightarrow} q$ in G_1 is mapped to a path in G_2 with begin and end given by p and q, respectively, and of this form: $p \Longrightarrow p' \overset{r_1}{\longleftrightarrow} A_1 \overset{r_2}{\longleftrightarrow}$ $... \overset{r_n}{\longleftrightarrow} A_n \overset{r_{n+1}}{\longleftrightarrow} q' \overset{*}{\Longleftarrow} q, n \geq 0$.
Additionally, if the relationship occurs in the path of G_2 as $p' \overset{a}{\longleftrightarrow} q'$, then $p \overset{*}{\Longrightarrow} p'$ and $q \overset{*}{\Longrightarrow} q'$, and $K_1(p \overset{a}{\longleftrightarrow} q) \leq K_2(p' \overset{a}{\longleftrightarrow} q')$.
(6) Each attribute edge $p \overset{a}{\to} q$ in G_1 is mapped to a path in G_2 of the form: $p \Longrightarrow p' \overset{r_1}{\longleftrightarrow} A_1 \overset{r_2}{\longleftrightarrow} ... \overset{r_n}{\longleftrightarrow} A_n \overset{a}{\to} q$, with $n \geq 0$, such that the path $p \overset{*}{\Longrightarrow} p' \overset{r_1}{\longleftrightarrow} A_1 \overset{r_2}{\longleftrightarrow} ... \overset{r_n}{\longleftrightarrow} A_n$ is included in the mapping of p.

Operationally, the methodology is able to recognize the existence of an inconsistent set of correspondences for which there is no augmentation possible, presenting this set to the user in order to discard one of the correspondences. On the other hand, in ambiguous cases the methodology guides the user in determining adequate augmentations, while for an unambiguous, consistent set of

---

[1] Actually, the proper type of A is $\mathcal{P}(G_1) \to \mathcal{P}(G_2)$, as it maps subschemas of G_1 to subschemas of G_2. Even so, we shall often write it as $G_1 \to G_2$ to remark which schemas are the source and target in the transformation.

correspondences, it generates appropriate augmentations fully automatically. An important aspect is that all path correspondences that overlap in some subpath are grouped as a pair of trees and resolved together recursively. The following diagram illustrates this fact graphically:

$$
\begin{array}{ccc}
& & C \quad T_{11} \\
& a_{21} \nearrow & \\
A \xrightarrow{\ a_1\ } B & \vdots & \\
& a_{2m} \searrow & \\
& & D \quad T_{1m}
\end{array}
\quad \sqcup_A \quad
\begin{array}{ccc}
& & X \quad T_{21} \\
& b_{11} \nearrow & \\
A & \vdots & \\
& b_{1n} \searrow & \\
& & Y \quad T_{2n}
\end{array}
$$

$$
= \left\{
\begin{array}{l}
\mathcal{A}_2(A) = A \xleftrightarrow{a_1} B \\[4pt]
\mathcal{A}_2(A \xleftrightarrow{b_{11}} X) = A \xleftrightarrow{a_1} B \xleftrightarrow{b'_{11}} X \\[4pt]
\vdots \\[4pt]
\mathcal{A}_2(A \xleftrightarrow{b_{1n}} Y) = A \xleftrightarrow{a_1} B \xleftrightarrow{b'_{1n}} Y
\end{array}
\right\} \ \cup
$$

$$
\begin{array}{ccc}
& & C \quad T_{11} \\
& a_{21} \nearrow & \\
B & \vdots & \\
& a_{2m} \searrow & \\
& & D \quad T_{1m}
\end{array}
\quad \sqcup_A \quad
\begin{array}{ccc}
& & X \quad T_{21} \\
& b''_{11} \nearrow & \\
A & \vdots & \\
& b''_{1n} \searrow & \\
& & Y \quad T_{2n}
\end{array}
$$

A complete description of SIM can be found in [6].

3 Propagation of Local Structural Modifications

We observe that, in general, the propagation of local structural modifications to the integrated schema can be accomplished by adopting one of the following alternatives:

1. Re-integrate from the beginning using the whole set of schema correspondences; or
2. Identify the augmentations affected by the evolution and deduce from them the involved corresponding subschemas. Then, re-integrate only on these subschemas; or
3. Identify the augmentations affected by the evolution and modify them directly without any new integration step.

Alternative (1) compounds to a brute force strategy, as it implies to redo the whole integration process each time a local schema change is produced. Alternative (2), on the other hand, reduces the number of correspondences used for re-integration, since only those correspondences deducible from the schema augmentations affected by the local evolution are considered. For instance, if a new class is added in the middle of an already existing path, then all path correspondences that contain this portion of the evolved path must be deduced, and the re-integration is performed on the local subschemas that these path correspondences determine. Finally, alternative (3) is clearly the most desirable solution, as it does no imply any extra integration step. However, it is applicable only in case of such modifications that do not generate inconsistent or ambiguous correspondences.

We adopt the combination of alternatives (2) and (3). The crucial point is then how to identify the augmentations that an evolution affects and from them deduce the affected overlapping subschemas (which are presented in the form of a set of path correspondences).

Since every structural modification essentially involves the addition/deletion of vertices or edges, the identification of the local subschemas that a modification affects can be factorized into the identification of those local subschemas that single vertices or edges affect.

3.1 Subschemas Affected by a Local Edge

Given an edge $x{=}y$ from a local schema, say G_0, the affected local subschemas are determined by those path correspondences containing that edge and those path correspondences that overlap with these ones.

By definition of edge augmentation [6], $x{=}y$ has one of the following types of augmentations:

(1) If the edge is in correspondence with an edge in the other local schema then $\mathcal{A}_0(x{=}y) = \mathcal{A}_1(x{=}y)$;

(2) If the edge is in correspondence with a vertex r in the other local schema then $\mathcal{A}_0(x{=}y) = x{=}r{=}y$ such that $r \notin \mathcal{A}_0(x)$, $r \notin \mathcal{A}_0(y)$;

(3) If the edge belongs to a path that is in correspondence with an edge in the other local schema then $\mathcal{A}_0(x{=}y) = \mathcal{A}_1(x{=}y)$ and there exists $u{=}v \in G_1$ such that $x{=}y \in \mathcal{A}_1(u{=}v)$;

(4) If the edge is in correspondence with a path in the other local schema then it is augmented by edge(s) from the other local schema, $\mathcal{A}_0(x{=}y) = x \overset{+}{=} s{=}t \overset{+}{=} y$, such that $x \overset{+}{=} s \in \mathcal{A}_0(x)$ and $t \overset{+}{=} y \in \mathcal{A}_0(y)$;

(5) If the edge does not belong to any subschema in correspondence then $\mathcal{A}_0(x{=}y) = x{=}y$ and there exists no $u{=}v \in G_1$ such that $x{=}y \in \mathcal{A}_1(u{=}v)$.

We write AS to denote the set of path correspondences that form (and we regard as representing) the corresponding affected subschemas of G_0 and G_1. The identification of the affected subschemas for the cases (1), (2) and (5) is straightforward:

Case (1): $AS = \{(x{=}_0y, x{=}_1y)\}$
Case (2): $AS = \{(x{=}_0y, x{=}r{=}_1y)\}$
Case (5): $AS = \{(x{=}_0y, \text{empty})\}$

Cases *(3)* and *(4)* require a more elaborated process, as their sets AS may be composed by several path correspondences and these need to be calculated. Moreover, in these cases the set of affected subschemas may contain path correspondences that do not contain the given edge. By augmentation construction, all those pairs of path correspondences that overlap in some subpath produce a tree in the integrated schema. Thus, correspondences belonging to such a tree affect the whole tree. The affected subschemas are then the source trees of G_0 and G_1 from which the augmentation tree was generated. These trees are computed as the union of the subschemas affected by the given edge. For each edge, the subschema that it affects is derived in two steps. First, we derive the set of path correspondences through the given edge. And secondly, we derive the whole tree to which these path correspondences belong, i.e. the affected subschemas.

Identifying path correspondences through a local edge Given an edge $x{=}y \in G_0$, the path correspondences in the affected subschemas are given by the *proper extension* of the edge, which is calculated as the componentwise concatenation of the paths pairs belonging to the right and left extension of the edge. By *right extension* of an edge $x{=}y$, we understand the set of path pairs (p_0, p_1), with $p_0 \in G_0$, $p_1 \in G_1$ and $p_0 = (x{=}y) \cdot p_0'$, which are derived by simultaneously traversing the graphs G_0 and G_1 following those paths indicated by the augmentations $\mathcal{A}_0$ and $\mathcal{A}_1$. The *left extension* of $x{=}y$ is defined analogously except that, instead of at the beginning, $x{=}y$ appears at the end in all paths derived from G_0 in the extension, i.e. for each path pair (p_0, p_1), $p_0 = p_0' \cdot (x{=}y)$.

The existence of such a proper extension of an edge is ensured by construction of augmentations. In fact, augmentations $\mathcal{A}_0$ and $\mathcal{A}_1$ are built from sets of path correspondences, where each set can be regarded as a pair of corresponding trees with roots in vertex correspondences (see diagram on Section 2.2). When building the extension of an edge $x{=}y$, we are essentially walking in parallel on such a pair of trees, determining those path pairs, connecting the root of the corresponding tree with a leaf, such that they contain the edge $x{=}y$.

The right and left extensions of an edge are calculated by the functions *RExtension* and *LExtension*, respectively (see algorithm *RExtension* of Figure 1, LExtension is performed in a similar way). We assume that $x{=}y \in G_0$.[2] In the description of the algorithm, we write $a \mapsto b$ to denote an *association pair*. A set $\{a \mapsto b\}$ denotes a singleton mapping, meaning that a maps to b. Sometimes we will construct finite mappings by set comprehension, $\{a \mapsto b \mid P(a,b)\}$, where P is a predicate. Note that, instead of union, we use overriding ($\oplus$) between augmentations mappings, e.g. $\mathcal{A} \oplus \mathcal{A}'$. This results in a mapping where the associations in $\mathcal{A}'$ have priority over those in $\mathcal{A}$. We write $A \otimes B$ to denote a form of cartesian product between sets of paths correspondences A and B. It is

---

[2] The case that $x{=}y \in G_1$ is completely symmetrical.

Function $REextension(x{=}y, e)$;
// **Input**: A searching edge $x{=}y$. A connection edge e.
// **Output**: Affected subschemas AS on the right of $x{=}y$. Affected augmentations $\widehat{\mathcal{A}}_0$ and $\widehat{\mathcal{A}}_1$.

Begin $AS := \emptyset$; $\widehat{\mathcal{A}}_0 := \emptyset$; $\widehat{\mathcal{A}}_1 := \emptyset$;
If $y \in VC$ **then** $AS := AS \cup \{(e, y)\}$
else $E := \{(u{=}v, y \overset{\bullet}{=} l, l{=}v) \mid \mathcal{A}_1(u{=}v) = u \overset{\bullet}{=} x{=}y \overset{\bullet}{=} l{=}v\}$;
$\quad\widehat{\mathcal{A}}_1 := \widehat{\mathcal{A}}_1 \oplus \{u{=}v \mapsto \mathcal{A}_1(u{=}v) \mid (u{=}v, c, d) \in E\}$;
$\quad$**For each** $(u{=}v, c_1, l{=}v) \in E$ **do**
$\qquad$**If** $v \in VC$ **then** $AS := AS \cup \{(e \cdot c_1 \cdot l{=}v, u{=}v)\}$
$\qquad$**else** $E' := \{(l{=}w, v \overset{\bullet}{=} t, t{=}w) \mid \mathcal{A}_0(l{=}w) = l{=}v \overset{\bullet}{=} t{=}w\}$;
$\qquad\quad\widehat{\mathcal{A}}_0 := \widehat{\mathcal{A}}_0 \cup \{l{=}w \mapsto \mathcal{A}_0(l{=}w) \mid (l{=}w, c, d) \in E'\}$;
$\qquad\quad$**For each** $(l{=}w, c_2, t{=}w) \in E'$ **do**
$\qquad\qquad AS := AS \cup \{(e.c_1.p_1, u{=}v \cdot c_2 \cdot p_2) \mid$
$\qquad\qquad\qquad (p_1, p_2) \in AS.REextension(t{=}w, l{=}w)\}$;
$\qquad\quad$**For** i = 0, 1 **do** $\widehat{\mathcal{A}}_i := \widehat{\mathcal{A}}_i \oplus \widehat{\mathcal{A}}_i.REextension(t{=}w, l{=}w)$;

// *Augmentations of affected vertices x and y*
If $(\mathcal{A}_0(x{=}y) \cap_{path} \mathcal{A}_0(x)) \neq \emptyset)$ **then** $\widehat{\mathcal{A}}_0 := \widehat{\mathcal{A}}_0 \oplus \{x \mapsto calA_0(x)\}$;
If $(\mathcal{A}_0(x{=}y) \cap_{path} \mathcal{A}_0(y)) \neq \emptyset)$ **then** $\widehat{\mathcal{A}}_0 := \widehat{\mathcal{A}}_0 \oplus \{y \mapsto calA_0(y)\}$;
// *Augmentations of internal affected vertices.*
For i = 0, 1 **do**
$\quad\widehat{\mathcal{A}}_i := \widehat{\mathcal{A}}_i \oplus \{z \mapsto \mathcal{A}_i(z) \mid z{=}w \in Dom(\widehat{\mathcal{A}}_i) \text{ and } \mathcal{A}_0(x{=}y) \cap_{path} \mathcal{A}_0(x)\}$;

Return $(AS, \widehat{\mathcal{A}}_1, \widehat{\mathcal{A}}_0)$;
End

Fig. 1. Derivation of the right extension of an edge.

defined by, $A \otimes B = \{(p_a \cdot p_b, p'_a \cdot p'_b) \mid (p_a, p'_a) \in A, (p_b, p'_b) \in B\}$ where $p \cdot p'$ to denote path concatenation, for paths p and p' with a common extreme. Note that, any edge may be regarded as a path of length one.

An outline of the algorithm for identifying the correspondences through a local edge and their augmentations is depicted in Figure 2.

Identifying Affected Subschemas So far, we have explained how to derive from augmentation tables the path correspondences that contain a given edge. By augmentation definition, an edge may belong to at most one tree.[3] In some cases, the subschemas affected by an edge are formed by more path correspondences

---

[3] This is not the case with a vertex in vertex correspondence, as it may belong to several trees.

Function *FindCorr*(x==y);
// **Input**: A searching edge x==y.
// **Output**: Set of path correspondences AS by x==y and their corresponding augmentations $\widehat{A}_0$ and $\widehat{A}_1$.

Begin
//*Initialize the augmentations*
$\widehat{A}_0 := \{x{=}{=}y \mapsto A_0(x{=}{=}y)\}$; $\widehat{A}_1 := \emptyset$;
//*The edge augments some edge(s) in the corresponding local schema.*
If $(A_0(x{=}{=}y) = x{=}{=}y$ and $\exists u{=}{=}v \in G_1 \mid x{=}{=}y \in A_1(u{=}{=}v))$
   then $AS_R := AS.RExtension(x{=}{=}y, x{=}{=}y)$;
        $AS_L := AS.LExtension(x{=}{=}y, x{=}{=}y)$;
        $AS := AS_R \otimes AS_L$;
        $\widehat{A}_0 := \widehat{A}_0 \oplus \widehat{A}_0.RExtension(x{=}{=}y, x{=}{=}y) \oplus \widehat{A}_0.LExtension(x{=}{=}y, x{=}{=}y)$;
        $\widehat{A}_1 := \widehat{A}_1.RExtension(x{=}{=}y, x{=}{=}y) \oplus \widehat{A}_1.LExtension(x{=}{=}y, x{=}{=}y)$;
        Return $(AS, \widehat{A}_1, \widehat{A}_0)$;

// *The edge is augmented by edge(s) from the corresponding local schema.*
If $(A_0(x{=}{=}y) = x{=}{=}l \overset{*}{=} l'{=}{=}y)$
   then let $x{=}{=}l \overset{*}{=} l'{=}{=}y = A_0(x{=}{=}y)$ **in**
        $AS_R := \{(p_1, l \overset{*}{=} l'.p_2) \mid (p_1, p_2) \in AS.RExtension(l'{=}{=}y, x{=}{=}y)\}$;
        $AS_L := \{(p_1, p_2) \mid (p_1, p_2) \in AS.LExtension(x{=}{=}l, x{=}{=}y)\}$;
        $AS := AS_R \otimes AS_L$;
        $\widehat{A}_0 := \widehat{A}_0 \oplus \widehat{A}_0.RExtension(l'{=}{=}y, x{=}{=}y) \oplus \widehat{A}_0.LExtension(x{=}{=}l, x{=}{=}y)$;
        $\widehat{A}_1 := \widehat{A}_1.RExtension(l'{=}{=}y, x{=}{=}y) \oplus \widehat{A}_1.LExtension(x{=}{=}l, x{=}{=}y)$;
        Return $(AS, \widehat{A}_1, \widehat{A}_0)$;

End

Fig. 2. Derivation of path correspondences through an edge.

than only those in the extension of the given edge. To derive the whole local trees, we need to determine which vertex is the root of the calculated extension of the given edge. After having the root, we can calculate the extension of the edge with extremity in the root, obtaining the whole local trees, since all paths correspondences from the root towards the leaves necessarily traverse this edge. The next example illustrates this case.

Example 1. Consider the following corresponding schemas:

Suppose that the initial path correspondences are (ABC, AC) and (ABD, AD).[4] Vertices with equal name are in vertex correspondence. The integrated schema is then given by G_0. Now, suppose that the edge AC of G_1 evolves to the path AMC. Suppose we consider that the subschema affected by AC is only formed by the extension of the edge, i.e. the path correspondence (ABC, AC). In that case, if we integrate only on the path correspondence (ABC, AMC), obtained from the evolution of the edge AC, an ambiguity arises because all these alternatives are equally valid: the augmentation of A from G_0 is AM, or the augmentation of A from G_1 is AB, or B and M are in vertex correspondence. On the contrary, if we consider that the subschemas affected are formed by the complete augmentation tree to which belongs the given edge AC, then no ambiguity arises and automatically it is deduced that the augmentation of A from G_1 is AB.

However, the criterion of maintaining the previous augmentation is not a good approach. Consider, for instance, when the evolution consists of the objectification of C and D of G_1. In this case we would like to have the possibility to choose again between all alternatives.

The problem then reduces to find the root. When the extension of the given edge is formed by several path correspondences, it reduces to find the overlapping parts of the paths in hand. On the other hand, when the extension is formed by a single path correspondence we need to test all four begin/end edges of the paths in the path correspondence in order to determine the desired root. The procedure for finding the complete trees is described in [10].

3.2 Subschemas Affected by a Local Vertex

Let v be a vertex of G_0 which belongs to a subschema that is in correspondence with G_1. By definition of schema augmentation, a vertex $v \in G_0$ is in an overlapping part with G_1 when it is in the augmentation of another vertex or it is in the augmentation of an edge. That v is already in an augmentation means that it belongs to an augmentation tree. Therefore, the affected subschemas are the source trees of G_0 and G_1 from which the augmentation tree was generated. These trees are computed as the union of the subschemas affected by the edges with extremity on v.

3.3 Kinds of Local Structural Modifications

The local structural modifications we handle are within the following categories:

1. *Modifications that extend an edge to a path*
   (a) Refinement of a specialization hierarchy An edge $x \Leftarrow y \in G_i$ evolves to a path : $x \Leftarrow z \Leftarrow y$.
   (b) Generalization of multiples classes Edges $x \Leftarrow y_n \in G_i$ evolve to paths : $x \Leftarrow z \Leftarrow y_n$.

---

[4] We have denoted edges by simple juxtaposition of vertices.

(c) **Objectification of attributes/relationships** An edge $x = y_n \in G_i$ evolves to a path: $x = z = y$.

(d) **Generalization of relationships** An edge $x \overset{r}{\leftrightarrow} y \in G_i$ evolves to a path: $x \overset{+}{\Rightarrow} x' \leftrightarrow y' \overset{+}{\Leftarrow} y$ such that $x', y' \notin VC$.

(e) **Specialization of relationships** An edge $x \overset{r}{\leftrightarrow} y \in G_i$ evolves to a path: $x \overset{+}{\Leftarrow} x' \overset{r}{\leftrightarrow} y' \overset{+}{\Rightarrow} y$ such that $x', y' \notin VC$.

2. *Addition of a new vertex or edge*
3. *Deletion of an existing vertex or edge*
4. *Modifications that compress a path to an edge*

   (a) **Flatting of a specialization hierarchy** A path $x \overset{+}{\Leftarrow} z \overset{+}{\Leftarrow} y \in G_i$ evolves to the edge $x \Leftarrow y$.

   (b) **Des-Objectification of attributes/relationships** A path $x \overset{+}{=\!=} z \overset{+}{=\!=} y \in G_i$ evolves to the edge $x = y$.

In the following we describe the procedure to the propagation of these kinds of local structural modifications. Due to space limitations we do not include the description of the corresponding algorithms, they can be found in [10].

Extension of an edge to a path. In case an edge $x = y \in G_0$ evolves to a path $x \overset{+}{=\!=} y \in G_0$ composed by already existing edges, the affected subschemas are calculated as the union of the subschemas that each of the edges in the path affect. Recall that affected subschemas are presented as sets of path correspondences holding before the evolution. The new path correspondences, i.e. those involving the edges in the path $x \overset{+}{=\!=} y$, are obtained by substituting everywhere in the previous path correspondences the edge $x = y$ by the path $x \overset{+}{=\!=} y$.

The affected subschemas are identified using the procedure given in the previous section. Then, affected subschemas are updated replacing the edge for its evolved path and SIM invoked to re-integrate on these evolved affected subschemas.

Addition of a class, attribute or relationship edge. The addition of a class, attribute or relationship edge to a local schema does not entail any risk of incompatibility with the existing integrated schema. The propagation of this modification is thus performed in the same way as it is traditionally done in the context of schema evolution.

Addition of a specialization edge. The addition of a specialization edge between two classes which are not in equivalence correspondence with classes of the other local schema does not entail any risk of incompatibility and therefore this modification can be automatically propagated to the integrated schema. On the contrary, when the classes are in equivalence correspondence with classes of the other local schema, the evolution cannot be automatically propagated. The propagation would produce an integrated schema which is no more a proper schema graph, since the two classes become related by a specialization while their corresponding classes in the other schema continue to be disjoint. The user must thus decide which of the class correspondences must be removed.

Deletion of a class. Removing a local vertex from a schema graph implies that previous existing correspondences involving that vertex do not longer hold. This leads to the necessity to identify the subschemas affected by those correspondences. When the set of affected correspondences is composed by a unique path correspondence, we can directly undo the augmentations of the components of this correspondence. On the contrary, when the set of path correspondences affected by a given edge has cardinality greater than one, then it represents a pair of trees in correspondence. In that case, we remove the affected augmentations and the correspondences that originates the set of correspondence and re-integrate on that set.

Deletion of a relationship or attribute edge. Similar to the deletion of a class, this local modification may impact an already integrated spanning tree. Therefore, we first identify the subschemas affected by the removed edge and then proceed in the same way as in the deletion of a vertex.

Deletion of a specialization edge. When the removed specialization edge is between two classes that are in vertex correspondence with classes of the other schema then, like in the addition of a specialization edge, the automatic propagation of this evolution would lead to an unproper integrated schema, since the two classes would become disjoint whereas their corresponding ones (in the other schema) would continue in a specialization relationship. Again, the user must decide which of the class correspondences to remove. On the other hand, when the removed edge is between classes which are not in vertex correspondence the propagation of this modification proceeds like in the deletion of a relationship edge.

Compression of a path to an edge. The propagation of this modification is performed in the same way as the deletion of an edge. The main difference is that now the affected subschemas and augmentations are derived from all those edges contained in the compressed path, but these edges are not deleted. Affected subschemas are updated replacing the path for its evolved edge and SIM invoked to re-integrate on these evolved affected subschemas.

4 Conclusions

In this paper we developed a mechanism for the dynamic maintenance of an integrated schema driven by local structural modifications (also applicable for propagation of local semantical modifications, see [10, 11]). The propagation of local schema changes that dismiss schema information is neglected by existing schema evolution methodologies (see e.g. [3, 2]). An essential aspect of our approach is that we can propagate *pure structural changes, capacity augmenting changes* as well as *capacity reducing changes* in a uniform way.

It is worth remarking that from this procedure we achieve *confluent* local schema evolution propagation. That is, the result obtained from performing schema integration after having applied a local schema evolution is the same as the result obtained from propagating the local evolution to the already integrated schema.

There already exist several implementations of SIM, the current one has been done in the context of the ESPRIT-III project IRO-DB [8, 7]. The extension we are proposing implies straightforward modifications to the current version. It only implies the implementation of the algorithms for finding the affected subschemas.

Many issues remain unexplored, and some important aspects of OODB such as methods or instances are not covered by our framework. Future work will concentrate on extending the propagation mechanism to instances and methods.

References

1. J. L. Ambite and C. A. Knoblock. Reconciling Distributed Information Sources. In *Working Notes of the AAAI Spring Symposium on Information Gathering in Distributed Heterogeneous Environments*, Palo Alto, CA, 1995.
2. Zohra Bellahsene. Extending a View Mechanism to Support Schema Evolution in Federated Database Systems. In A. Hameurlain and A. Min Tjoa, editors, *8th. Int. Conf. on Database and Expert Systems Applications (DEXA)*, Toulouse, France, September 1997. Springer Verlag, Lectures Notes in Computer Science Nro. 1308.
3. J. M. Blanco, A. Illarramendi, and A. Goñi. Building a federated relational database system: An approach using knowledge based system. *International Journal of Intelligent and Cooperative Information Systems*, 1(1), 1997.
4. U. Dayal and H. Hwang. View definition and Generalization for Database Integration in Multibase: a System for Heterogeneous Distributed Databases. *IEEE Transactions on Software Engineering*, 10(6), 1984.
5. P. Fankauser, R. Motz, and G. Huck. Schema Integration Methodology. Deliverable D4-4/1, IRO-DB(P8629), 1995. Accesible via the following URL address: http://www.darmstadt.gmd.de/oasys/projects/irodb/home.html .
6. Peter Fankauser. *Methodology for Knowledge-Based Schema Integration*. PhD thesis, University of Vienna, Austria, December 1997.
7. P. Fankhauser, G. Gardarin, M. Lopez, J. Munoz, and A. Tomasic. Federating Databases with Iro-DB . In *Proc. of the Int. Conf. on Very Large Databases(VLDB'98)(Industrial Programm)*, New York, August 1998.
8. G. Gardarin, S. Gannouni, P. Fankhauser, W. Klas, D. Pastre, and R. Legoff. *IRO-DB: A Distributed System Federating Object and Relational Databases*. Prentice Hall, 1995.
9. M. Loomis, T. Atwood, R. Catell, J. Duhl, G. Ferran, and D. Wade. The ODMG Object Model. *Journal of Object-Oriented Programming*, 10(6), June 1993.
10. Regina Motz. *Dynamic Maintenance of an Integrated Schema* . PhD thesis, Darmstadt University of Technology, Germany, 1998. Forthcoming.
11. Regina Motz. Propagation of Semantic Modifications to an Integrated Schema. In *Third IFCIS Int. Conf. on Cooperative Information Systems (CoopIS'98)*, New York, August 1998.

Integration of Schemas Containing
Data Versions and Time Components

Maciej Matysiak[1], Tadeusz Morzy[1], Bogdan Czejdo[2]

[1] Institute of Computing Science, Poznan University of Technology
ul. Piotrowo 3a, 60-965 Poznan, Poland
matys@cs.put.poznan.pl, morzy@put.poznan.pl
[2] Department of Mathematics and Computer Science, Loyola University
St. Charles Ave., New Orleans, LA 70118
czejdo@loyno.edu

Abstract. Data processing in modern information systems often require access to data stored in multiple heterogeneous databases. Schema integration is an important step for providing database integration and interoperability of distributed database systems. The process of schema integration requires knowledge of the semantics of component database schemas and must be supported by a database designer. The paper presents various models containing data versions and time components used in business systems and their possible semantic heterogeneity. Also, the techniques for integration of schemas containing version models are discussed and the methodology for creating an integrated schema with versions is proposed.

1   Introduction

Timely and accurate access to information resources of an organization has become a critical component of gaining competitive advantage in today's business. Effective decision making require comprehensive and reliable access to data stored in multiple databases utilized by the organization. Integration of pre-existing databases is compromised due to their heterogeneity and the increasing complexity of component database schemas. The databases are heterogeneous in a sense that they use different database management software, run on different operating systems and on different computer hardware, and also store different types of data and represent data differently.

There are several approaches to integration of heterogeneous databases. The examples are multidatabase systems, federated database systems, integration through database migration, and data warehousing. Methodologies that use either of these approaches require logical schema integration in order to provide database interoperability. Schema integration is the process of creating the integrated schema from multiple component schemas. The integrated schema is represented using a common data model and hides heterogeneities due to schematic differences in the underlying databases or differences in data models.

The term schema integration is also used to refer to view integration phase of conceptual schema design, which takes several user views representing the information requirements of different users and integrates them into a single conceptual schema. Thus view integration is typically used in the design of a new database schema in top-down database design process and user views do not reflect existing data in a database. Schema integration of heterogeneous databases on the other hand is bottom-up process and it integrates schemas of existing databases. The context of database integration and view integration is different but they can both be described as the activities of integrating the schemas of existing or proposed databases into a global, integrated schema.

Schema integration is a time consuming problem and requires interaction with database designers to understand the semantics of the databases and to ensure that the semantics of the integrated schema do not violate the semantics of the underlying databases.

One of more complex concepts being modeled in business systems is historical data. Business models implemented in component databases often contain a variety of data versions and time components. Modeling of data versions was discussed in the literature [4] [5]. In the paper we describe a systematic method for modeling of various version models, semantic conflicts among them, and methods for integrating such schemas.

The paper is organized as follows. In Section 2 we review the basic concepts of an extended ER model and describe in detail modeling of versions. In Section 3 we discuss examples of integration of various version models. In Section 4 we present brief classification of version models and application of integration techniques. The Section 5 contains the summary.

2   Modeling of data versions

An extended entity-relationship (EER) model similar to [4] is used for modeling of versions. EER model consists of three classes of objects: entities, relationships and attributes. Entities are the principal data objects about which the information is to be collected (e.g. person, thing, event, department, part, etc.). Properties of entities (name, color, age, address, etc.) are described by attributes.

Relationship types represent associations among one or more entity types. Relationship types are described in terms of degree, cardinality ratio and existence dependency. The degree of a relationship type is the number of entity types participating in the relationship type [4]. The generalization relationship type specifies that several types of entities (called entity subtypes) with some common attributes can be generalized into an entity type (called an entity supertype). The resulting hierarchy we will call generalization hierarchy. The entity subtypes in a generalization hierarchy can contain either disjoint or overlapping subsets.

Modeling can describe either timeless data i.e. cities, countries, positions, carmakers, etc., or most current data i.e. current salary, current sale price, current address. In static modeling there is no time component involved. However, in many practical situations we need to properly model the data that change in time and include an explicit time component.

Generally, the time can be involved in the data model explicitly or implicitly. The explicit time component is described by the physical clock and contains either the time value or the time interval (the beginning time and the ending time) identifying when the data is valid. The implicit time component is described by a logical clock such as semester, budget year, academic year, and payment period. The logical clock usually is described by several attributes. For example, payment period at the university can have a number, semester, and academic year.

Using either the physical clock or logical clock (or both) results in data versioning. Versioning can be applied to different data model components that can change in time such as an attribute, an entity, a relationship type or the whole sub-schemas. Below we will discuss versioning of all components.

2.1 Attribute versioning

Let us consider the EER model shown in Figure 1.a. This is a static model that might need to be expanded to capture the changing situations.

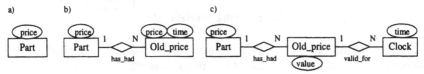

Fig. 1. Versioning of an attribute

Let us first consider the attribute versioning. Let us assume that a part used for producing a product has an attribute price and that for obvious reasons this value can be changed. First, we would like to include the information about when the new price was assigned. We can do this by simply adding time attribute to the original entity type. Next, we might want also to include in the model historical information about all previous prices and the time that they were actual. We can do this by applying the rules described below.

Here we have to deal with the physical clock component containing a time period. The modeling of such situation is done by creating a new entity type corresponding to the attribute being versioned. This new entity type has two types of attributes: the replication of the attribute being versioned, the time attributes describing the beginning and the end of the time period. This entity type is related to the original entity type containing attribute being versioned by a binary relationship type *has had*. Using this rule the EER model from Figure 1.a is transformed into EER model shown in Figure 1.b. Instead of using time attributes in entity type *Old Price* we can use a relationship type associated with logical clock, as shown in Figure 1.c.

2.2   Relationship set versioning

Now, let us consider the relationship type versioning. Let us assume that the departments can be managed by different employees in time. First, we would like to include the information indicating when the given department was assigned a new manager. We can do this by simply adding an attribute from to the original relationship type *managed by*.

Next, we might also want to include in the model historical information about all previous assignments of the departments to various employees. Let us assume that the physical clock component contains the description of a time period. The modeling of such situation is done by creating of a new relationship type corresponding to the original relationship type being versioned. This new relationship type has one or two time attributes describing the beginning and the end of the time period. Using the above described rule the EER model from Figure 2.a is transformed into EER model shown in Figure 2.b.

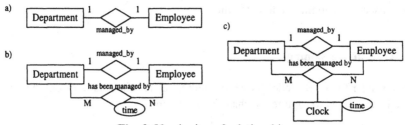

Fig. 2. Versioning of relationships

The similar transformation can be performed when versioning is applied to other relationship types such as parts produced by a department etc.

There are also some situations when we have to deal with the logical clock component when performing relationship type versioning. The modeling of such situation is done by creating a new entity type and a new relationship type. The new entity type describes the logical clock. The new relationship type is corresponding to the original relationship type being versioned. If the identical logical clock is used for versioning of many relationship types then the creation of the one logical clock entity type is sufficient.

2.3   Entity set versioning

So far we assumed that individual attribute values or relationship instances might change. There are situations when the versioning of a whole entity is needed. Let us consider the situation in a production department where parts used for producing goods are used only for some period of time and then new versions of parts may replace the old ones. So the entity representing a part is valid in a period of time. We also assume that a user wants to retrieve historical data about parts.

First, let us consider entity set versioning without relationship sets associated with it. Such versioning of static *Part* entity set from Figure 3.a with time attributes is shown in Figure 3.b. Figure 3.c shows part versioning with logical clock. Entity set *Part* in the hierarchy corresponds to the static entity set before versioning and it represents all current versions of parts. Entity set *Old Part* represents all old versions of parts. Super entity set *Super Part* is a generalization of current and old part versions. Relationship set *derived from* allows us explicitly associate new versions of parts with the old ones.

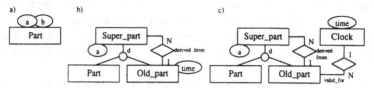

Fig. 3. Versioning of entities without N:1 relationship types

Each entity set has relationship sets associated with it, so while versioning entity sets we must also deal with relationship instances to old versions of entities. Let us assume that the entity set *Part* is related to the entity set *Product* with *consist of* relationship set as shown in Figure 4.a. Versioning of *Part* entity set together with associated relationship set *consists of* is shown in Figures 4.b and 4.c. The relationship set *consists of* in the new model represents all current instances of relationships between parts and products and the relationship set *consisted of* represents all historical relationship instances between products and parts.

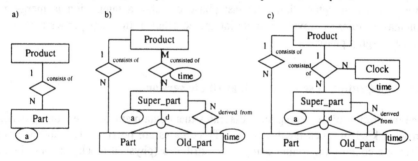

Fig. 4. Versioning of entities with N:1 relationship types attached

3 Integration of schemas with data versions

3.1 Schema integration process

The general objective of schema integration is to provide a single integrated database schema that will allow a user to view data distributed among component databases as if the data were stored in a single database. The issue of schema integration is difficult due to the semantic heterogeneity that appears in the form of schematic and data conflicts among component databases.

There are several classifications of schema conflicts proposed in the literature [6][8][2]. The examples of conflicts are as follows. Name conflicts occur when similar concepts have different names and different concepts have the same name. Data type conflicts occur when equivalent attributes have different types. Abstraction level conflicts occur when similar concepts are described at different level of abstraction. Missing data conflicts occur when a concept is described in two schemas by a different set of attributes. Integrity constraint conflicts occur when there are different constraints associated with the same concept. Scale and precision conflicts occur when similar attributes use different units of measure or different granularity. A schema integration process can be viewed as a set of steps to identify and resolve these conflicts.

Schema integration process in general consists of the following phases: 1) pre-integration, 2) comparison of schemas, 3) conformation of schemas, and 4) merging of schemas [1]. Pre-integration consists in analysis of component schemas, choosing the strategy of the integration and choosing the data model to describe the integrated schema. We use EER diagrams to construct the integrated schemas with hierarchies. Comparison of schemas consists in identifying schematic and data conflicts. Conformation of schemas consists in resolving existing conflicts by applying a set of primitive transformations to component schemas in order to make the schemas compatible and ready to merge. Transformations applied to a component schema may be viewed as actual modifications of the component schema in the case of view integration or as defining a virtual view over the underlying component schema in the case of database integration. The last phase of schema integration is merging of schemas in order to provide a single integrated schema. In this paper we concentrate on the merging phase.

3.2   Integration of schemas with attribute versions

The integration of two component diagrams that contain attribute versioning depends on what kind of clock has been used. Three cases are possible: 1. both component diagrams contain versioning using time attributes (physical clock), 2. one diagram uses time attributes and the other uses clock entity (logical clock), 3. both component diagrams contain versioning using logical clocks.

In the case that both component diagrams contain versioning using time attributes the integration consists in choosing one of the component diagrams as the integrated schema. The integrated schema represents the union of attribute versions from both component diagrams. As an example let us consider that we are given two separate versioning models of price of a part as shown in Figure 5.a and 5.b. The resulting diagram shown in Figure 5 contains the single entity type *Old Price* that represents a union of all entities from *Old Price(a)* and *Old Price(b)* entity type and the relationship *has had* represents a union of all instances of *has had(a)* and *has had(b)* relationship types.

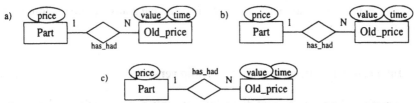

Fig. 5. Integration of two attribute versioning models that use time attributes

The integration of two component diagrams containing attribute versioning that use time attribute and logical clock consits in simple merging of the diagrams. The integrated schema contains both time attributes and clock entity type. The integrated entity type *Old Price* represents a union of all versions of prices from component databases. However, price versions taken from database *a* have time attributes and price versions taken from database *b* have instances of relationship type *valid at* instead. In a particular case, if we can find mapping between physical and logical clocks, all price versions may have both time attributes and relationships to clock entity type. Existance of such a mapping offers to a user more flexibility in querying the integrated database.

The integration of two component diagrams that contain attribute versioning using only logical clocks also consists in simple merging of the diagrams. Let us consider two component schemas shown in Figure 6.a and 6.b. In general, two logical clocks being integrated may not be compatibile. Thus we cannot make a union of instances of clock entity types and put a single entity type to the integrated schema. The integrated schema in this case contains both logical clocks from the component diagrams as shown in Figure 6.c. Neverthenless in a particular case when the logical clocks are compatible we can use only one logical clock on the integrated schema.

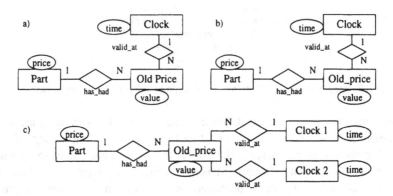

Fig. 6. Integration of two attribute versioning models that both use clock entity types.

Generally we have used two alternative techniques to integrate component schemas into one integrated schema: union – when component clocks are compatible and only union of instances is required, merge and union – when component clocks are incompatible and they both must be merged into the integrated schema before union of instances is performed

3.3 Integration of schemas with relationship versions

The integration of two component diagrams that contain relationship versioning also depends on compatibility of clocks used for versioning as presented in the previous section. There are also three possibilities of physical and logical clocks in the component diagrams: both use time attributes, one uses time attributes and the other uses logical clock, and both use logical clocks.

First, let us consider integration of schemas containing relationship versioning using time attributes. Let us assume that we have two component databases containing relationships between departments and employees as shown in Figure 7.a and 7.b and the historical instances of relationship type *managed by* are maintained using time attributes. Due to compatibility of the clocks we can use union without merging which produces the integrated diagram as shown in Figure 7.c. The relationship type *has been managed by* represents a union of all instances of relationships from *has been managed by(a)* and *has been managed by(b)* relationship types.

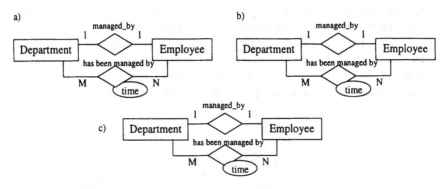

Fig. 7. Integration of two relationship versioning models that use time attributes

In the case that one component database contain relationship versioning using time attributes and the second one contain relationship versioning using the logical clock we must apply a different approach. In order to merge component diagrams we must transform the component relationship types M:N into entity types with relationship types N:1 according to rules described in the section *Primitive Integration Transformations*. Then we merge the diagrams and perform the union of entities from the newly created entity types. As an example let us consider two schemas shown in Figure 8.a and 8.b. The integrated schema after merging of transformed diagrams is shown in Figure 8.c.

Entity type *Old Dept* (czy nie lepiej to zmienic na OLD DEPT_EMP???) represents a union of all instances of *has been managed by(a)* and *has been managed by(b)* relationship types. Instances from *has been managed by(a)* relationship type use time attributes and instances *has been managed by(b)* relationship type use the logical clock. However, in the case that we can find a mapping between physical and logical clocks, all instances can use both methods for validating versions of relationships.

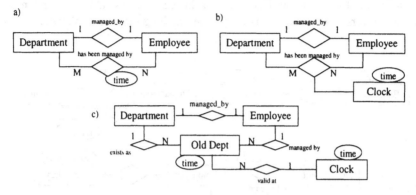

Fig. 8. Integration of the relationship versioning model that use time attributes with the relationship versioning model that use clock entity

In the case that both component schemas contain relationship versioning using logical clock we use the same approach as described above. First, we transform relationship types to entity types, then we merge diagrams and perform union operation over entities. Figures 9.a and 9.b show two example schemas that use logical entity types as logical clocks. The integrated diagram after transforming and merging of the component diagrams is shown in Figure 9.c.

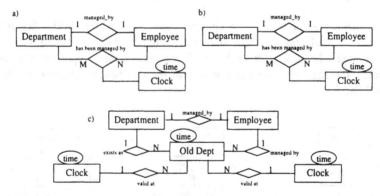

Fig. 9. Integration of two relationship versioning models that use logical clocks

3.4 Integration of schemas with attribute and relationship versions

Let us assume that we are given two database schemas, first containing attribute versioning and the second containing relationship versioning, both of them dealing with the same entity type. The examples of such component schemas are shown in Figures 10.a and 10.b. Versioning of the attribute is independent of versioning of the relationship, so the integration consists in simple merging of two component schemas. The union is not required and inadequate in this case because attribute versions and relationship versions are kept separately. The resulting diagram is shown in Figure 10.c.

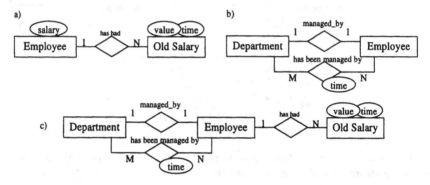

Fig. 10. Integration of the attribute versioning model and the relationship versioning model

This approach to integrating such schemas is independent of whether physical or logical clocks are used for versioning of relationships and versioning of attributes.

3.5 Integration of schemas with entity versions

Let us consider two databases containing versioning of whole entities that represent parts used for producing products, as shown in Figures 11.a and 11.b. In order to build the integrated schema we can apply simple merging of the component schemas. The integrated schema looks the same as one of the component schemas, as shown in Figure 11.c.

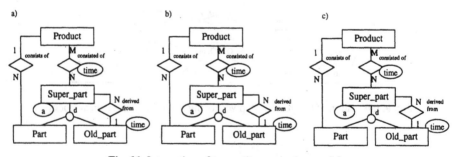

Fig. 11. Integration of two entity versioning models

Entity type *Old Part* on the integrated diagram represents a union of all versions of parts from *Old Part(a)* and *Old Part(b)* entity types. Relationship type *consisted of* on the integrated schema represents a union of all historical relationships from *consisted of(a)* and *consisted of(b)* relationship types.

3.6 Integration of schemas with attribute and entity versions

Let us assume that the first database being integrated is used in production department and contains versioning of entities that represent parts used for producing products, as shown in Figure 12.a. The second database, used in sales department, contains versioning of price of the same parts, as shown in Figure 12.b. Usually several versions of the attribute are created before creating a new version of the entity. The process of obtaining an integrated schema with entity and attribute versions of the same entity requires merging of component schemas. The example of integrated schema is shown in Figure 12.c.

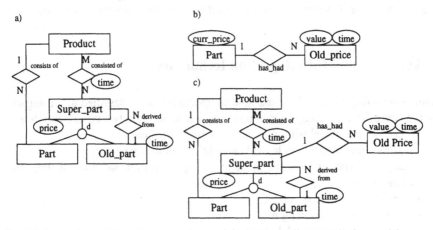

Fig. 12. Integration of the entity versioning model with the attribute versioning model

3.7 Integration of schemas with relationship and entity versions

Finally, let us assume that we are given two database schemas: the first one containing entity versioning and the second one containing relationship versioning, as shown in Figures 13.a and 13.b. Due to the fact that entity versioning includes versioning of connected relationships, as presented in section *Entity Versioning*, no merging is necessary in order to build an integrated schema. The example, integrated schema is shown in Figure 13.c and it is the same as the first component schema.

The relationship type *consisted of* represents a union of all historical relationships between parts and products as the result of whole entity versioning or only relationship versioning in component databases. The relationship *consists of* represents a union of all current relationships between parts and products in two component databases.

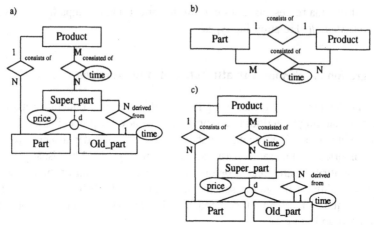

Fig. 13. Integration of the entity versioning model with the relationship versioning model

4 Application of the integration techniques

Schemas containing data versions and time components can be classified according to clock type used for versioning. Using this classification we have two types of models:
- versioning model with physical clock (time attributes)
- versioning model with logical clock (clock entity type).

According to type of schema element being versioned we can distinguish additional three types of models:
- attribute versioning model
- relationship versioning model
- entity versioning model

Building an integrated schema from component schemas requires resolving several conflicts, for example: name conflicts, data type conflicts, abstraction level conflicts missing data, integrity constraint conflicts, scale and precision conflicts, and others. Assuming that all basic conflicts among component schemas have been resolved, three additional techniques were used to construct an integrated schema with various version models: primitive integration transformations, simple merging of schemas, union of instances, as presented in sections 3.3 through 3.9.

Usage of these techniques depends on what types of component schemas are to be integrated. The application of the techniques according to types of component schemas is shown in the Figure 14.

types of component schemas	• Attribute versioning	• relationship versioning	• entity versioning
• attribute versioning	Union or Merge and Union		
• relationship versioning	Merge	Union or Transform, Merge, Union	
• entity versioning	Merge	Union	Union

Fig. 14. Integration techniques used while integrating various types of version schemas

5 Summary

Effective decision making require comprehensive and reliable access to data stored in multiple databases utilized by one or more organizations. In order to have such access well designed integration of pre-existing databases is critical. One of the most important components of database integration is logical schema integration. Schema integration is a time consuming problem and requires interaction with database designers to understand the semantics of the databases and to ensure that the semantics of the integrated schema do not violate the semantics of the underlying databases.

In the paper we discussed a systematic method of schema integration for a variety of attribute, relationship, and entity versioning models. For each type of versioning model we described an extended entity-relationship (EER) model to represent it as a component schema. Next we describe systematic methods for integrating component schemas also using EER model.

References

1. Batini C., Lenzerini M., Navathe S.B.: A comparative analysis of methodologies for database schema integration. ACM Computing Surveys, 18(4):323-364, 1986.
2. Coburn N., Larson P.A., Martin P., Slonim J.: Cords multidatabase project: Research and prototype overview. Proc. of CASCON'93, 767-778, Toronto, 1993
3. Czejdo B.D., Morzy T., Matysiak M. "Hierarchy and Version Modeling", Proc. Of Symposium on Expert Systems and AI, ESDA '96, Montpellier, France, 1996
4. Elmasri R., Navathe S.: Fundamentals of Database Systems, 2nd ed
5. Embley D.W., Kurtz B.D., Woodfield S.N.: Object-Oriented Systems Analysis: A Model-Driven approach. Yourdon Press, Englewood Cliffs, New Jersey, 1992.
6. Kim W., Seo J.: Classifying Schematic and Data Heterogeneity in Multidatabase Systems. IEEE Computer 24(12), 12-18 (Dec. 1991).
7. Matysiak M., Morzy T., Czejdo B.D.: Integrationg of Data Hierarchy Models. The Biennial World Conference on Integrated Desing & Process Technology, Berlin, Germany, July 1998
8. Missier P., Rusinkiewicz M.: Extending a Multiple Manipulation Language to Resolve Schema and Data Conflicts. Proc. of the Workshop on Interoperability of Database Systems and Database Applications, 19-37 (October 1993).
9. Navathe S., Elmasri R., Larson J.: Integrating User Views in Database Design. IEEE Computer 19,1, 1986, pp.50-62.
10. Teorey T. J.: Database Modeling and Design: The Fundamental Principles. 2nd ed., Morgan Kaufmann Pub. Inc., 1994.

Deriving Relationships between Integrity Constraints for Schema Comparison

Can Türker and Gunter Saake

Otto-von-Guericke-Universität Magdeburg
Institut für Technische und Betriebliche Informationssysteme
Postfach 4120, D–39016 Magdeburg, Germany
{tuerker|saake}@iti.cs.uni-magdeburg.de

Abstract. Schema comparison is essential for integrating different database schemata. Since the semantics of a schema is also represented by its integrity constraints, they must be considered by a correct schema comparison method. Especially the extensional relationships between classes are determined by the relationship between the corresponding integrity constraint sets. In this paper, we work out the relationships between different types of integrity constraints. As a result, we present rules for comparing integrity constraint sets. These rules can be used after a schema conforming step, where naming, type and structural conflicts are solved, to exactly fix the extensional relationship between object classes.

1 Introduction

Schema integration [1] is one of the central issues in logically integrating database systems [6]. Schema integration aims at deriving an integrated schema which is a virtual view on all database classes to be integrated. Traditionally, all existing schema integration methods, e.g. [4, 7, 3, 2, 5], assume that the database designer – as integrator – is an expert of the application domain who has complete knowledge about the semantics of the schemata to be integrated. Thus, the database designer should be able to exactly define the extensional relationship between two classes of different schemata in the schema comparison step. Obviously, this is a very hard task for the database designer.

A key point which is not regarded by the existing integration approaches is the correspondence between integrity constraints and extensional relationships. In case a schema captures all relevant integrity constraints occurring in the modeled real world, the extensional relationships between the classes are completely determined by the corresponding integrity constraints defined on these classes. Thus, our idea is to exploit the relationship between the integrity constraints of two classes to derive the correct extensional relationship between these classes.

In this paper, we work out the problem of relating different sets of integrity constraints. This issue is essential for comparing two classes of different schemata correctly. However, the comparison of arbitrary constraints is undecidable. Hence, we restrict ourselves to a certain set of constraint types. For these types we provide rules for computing the relationship between two integrity constraints. These rules can be used to extend existing schema comparison methods.

The paper is organized as follows: Section 2 investigates rules for comparing integrity constraint sets. The application of these rules is presented in Section 3. Finally, a short outlook on future work concludes the paper.

2 Relationships between Integrity Constraint Sets

Definition 1. A *set of object integrity constraints* $\mathcal{IC}$ restricts the set of possible objects, i.e. the database universe $\mathcal{U}$, to the semantically correct objects $\mathcal{U}^{\mathcal{IC}}$. In the sequel, we use the term *integrity constraint set* to refer to such a set. From a logical point of view, an integrity constraint set corresponds to a conjunction of integrity constraints. An integrity constraint itself is a formula. □

Objects with similar properties can be grouped into *classes*, i.e., classes are subsets of the database universe. The integrity constraint set of a class C, denoted as $\mathcal{IC}_C$, defines the semantically correct objects of that class. Additionally, we also consider uniqueness constraints which describes correct sets of database states.

Definition 2. Two constraints IC_1 and IC_2 defined on the same variables (attributes) are called *directly related* by one the following relationships:

$$IC_1 \oslash IC_2 :\Leftrightarrow \mathcal{U}^{IC_1} \cap \mathcal{U}^{IC_2} = \varnothing$$
$$IC_1 \equiv IC_2 :\Leftrightarrow \mathcal{U}^{IC_1} \equiv \mathcal{U}^{IC_2}$$
$$IC_1 \supset IC_2 :\Leftrightarrow \mathcal{U}^{IC_1} \subset \mathcal{U}^{IC_2}$$
$$IC_1 \,\mathbb{m}\, IC_2 :\Leftrightarrow \neg((IC_1 \oslash IC_2) \vee (IC_1 \equiv IC_2) \vee (IC_1 \subset IC_2) \vee (IC_1 \supset IC_2))$$

Two constraints defined on different variables can be *transitively* related if there is another constraint defined on both variables. Two constraints are called *unrelated* $(IC_1 \,\uplus\, IC_2)$ if they are neither directly nor transitively related. □

In order to relate integrity constraint sets to each other, *implicit constraints* must be considered. The following example illustrates the application of implicit constraints. Let there be two integrity constraint sets given as follows:

$$\mathcal{IC}_1 = \{(x < y), (y < z)\}$$
$$\mathcal{IC}_2 = \{(x < z)\}$$

Comparing each pair of constraints of the given sets, results that these sets must be unrelated. However, since the conjunction of $(x < y)$ and $(y < z)$ implies $(x < z)$, we can derive that $\mathcal{IC}_1 \supset \mathcal{IC}_2$ holds. For our following considerations we use the notion of *extended integrity constraint set* to denote an integrity constraint set capturing all its implicit constraints. Since the implication problem is not decidable for general constraints, we restrict our considerations to the following types of constraints[1]:

C1: $x_1 \,\theta\, c_1$

---

[1] We are aware of that there are other types of constraints which also decidable. However, this issue is not focused in this paper.

C2: $x_1 \theta x_2$

C3: $\mathbf{unique}(x_1, ..., x_n)$

C4: $C_i \Rightarrow C_j$, where C_i and C_j are constraints of type C1 or C2

The symbol $\theta \in \{<, \le, =, \ne, \ge, >\}$ stands for a comparison operator, $x_1, ..., x_n$ are variables (attributes), and c_1 is a constant.

Relationships between C1-Constraints. A C1-constraint restricts the possible values of exactly one attribute. Obviously, when we compare two C1-constraints, the resulting relationship between such two constraints depends on the respective comparison operators and constants:

$$\underbrace{(x_1 \, \theta_1 \, c_1)}_{IC_1} \wedge \underbrace{(x_2 \, \theta_2 \, c_2)}_{IC_2} \wedge (c_1 \theta_3 c_2) \Rightarrow (IC_1 \, \Theta_4 \, IC_2)$$

The comparison operators θ_1 and θ_2 are in $\{<, \le, =, \ne, \ge, >\}$, whereas the constant relationship operator θ_3 is in $\{<, =, >\}$. Thus, there are 108 ($6 \times 6 \times 3$) possible combinations (for the antecedent of the implication). Fig. 1 summarizes the rules for computing the relationship Θ_4 ($\in \{\varnothing, \supset, \equiv, \subset, \Cap\}$) between two given C1-constraints. The symbol ϑ stands for one of the comparison operators $\{<, \le, =, \ne, \ge, >\}$. The tenth row states that two C1-constraints are equivalent if and only if they have the same comparison operators and constants. In Fig. 1,

$(x_1 \, \theta_1 \, c_1) \wedge (x_2 \, \theta_2 \, c_2) \wedge (c_1 \, \theta_3 \, c_2) \Rightarrow (IC_1 \, \Theta_4 \, IC_2)$			
θ_1	θ_2	θ_3	Θ_4
$<, \le, =$	$=, \ge, >$	$<$	$\varnothing$
$<$	$=, \ge, >$	$=$	$\varnothing$
$\le$	$>$	$=$	$\varnothing$
$=$	$<, \ne, >$	$=$	$\varnothing$
$=$	$<, \le, =$	$>$	$\varnothing$
$<, \le, =$	$<, \le, \ne$	$<$	$\supset$
$<$	$\le, \ne$	$=$	$\supset$
$=$	$\le, \ge$	$=$	$\supset$
$=$	$\ne, \ge, >$	$>$	$\supset$
ϑ	ϑ	$=$	$\equiv$
$<, \le$	$<, \le, =$	$>$	$\subset$
$\le$	$<, =$	$=$	$\subset$
$<, \le$	$\ne, \ge, >$	$>$	$\Cap$
$\le$	$\ne, \ge$	$=$	$\Cap$

Fig. 1. Rules for Computing Relationships between C1-Constraints

we have only listed the rules for the combinations where at least one comparison operator is in $\{<, \le, =\}$. Based on these rules we can also derive relationships between constraints basing on the "complement" comparison operators $\{\ge, >, \ne\}$.

For that, we first have to build the complement constraints, i.e. change the comparison operators by their complements ($<$ for $\geq$, $\leq$ for $>$, and $=$ for $\neq$). Then, we compute the relationship for the complement constraints according to the rules depicted in Fig. 1. Finally, the result is "reversed" using the following complement rules for relationships: $(\varnothing \rightsquigarrow \text{ⓜ}), (\supset \rightsquigarrow \subset), (\equiv \rightsquigarrow \equiv)$.

Relationships between C2-Constraints. Similar to C1-constraints, rules can be derived for computing relationships between C2-constraints. Two C2-constraints are directly related if they are defined on the same variables. The relationship type is determined by the corresponding comparison operators, e.g. the constraint $(x > y)$ implies the constraint $(x \geq y)$:

$$\underbrace{(x\,\theta_1\,y)}_{IC_1} \wedge \underbrace{(x\,\theta_2\,y)}_{IC_2} \Rightarrow (IC_1\,\Theta_3\,IC_2)$$

The comparison operators θ_1 and θ_2 are in $\{<, \leq, =, \neq, \geq, >\}$. Fig. 2(a) summarizes the rules for computing Θ_3 ($\in \{\varnothing, \supset, \equiv, \subset, \text{ⓜ}\}$) between C2-constraints. The symbol ϑ stands for one of possible comparison operators. Analogously to Fig. 1, Fig. 2(a) contains only the rules for the operators $\{<, \leq, =\}$. Fig. 2(b) presents rules to derive an implicit C2-constraint from two C2-constraints:

$$(x\,\theta_1\,y) \wedge (y\,\theta_2\,z) \Rightarrow (x\,\theta_3\,z)$$

The comparison operators θ_1, θ_2, and θ_3 are in $\{<, \leq, =, \neq, \geq, >\}$, whereas x, y and z are variables (attributes). Please note that these rules also hold when z is a constant. In this case, we derive an implicit C1-constraint from a pair of (C2, C1)-constraints. Example 1 illustrates this fact.

$(x\,\theta_1\,y) \wedge (x\,\theta_2\,y) \Rightarrow (IC_1\,\Theta_3\,IC_2)$			$(x\,\theta_1\,y) \wedge (y\,\theta_2\,z) \Rightarrow (x\,\theta_3\,z)$		
θ_1	θ_2	Θ_3	θ_1	θ_2	θ_3
$<$	$=,\geq,>$	$\varnothing$	$<$	$<,\leq$	$<$
$\leq$	$>$	$\varnothing$	$<,\leq$	$<$	$<$
$=$	$<,\neq,>$	$\varnothing$	$\leq$	$\leq$	$\leq$
$<$	$\leq,\neq$	$\supset$	$=$	ϑ	ϑ
$=$	$\leq,\geq$	$\supset$	ϑ	$=$	ϑ
ϑ	ϑ	$\equiv$	$\geq$	$\geq$	$\geq$
$\leq$	$<,=$	$\subset$	$>$	$\geq,>$	$>$
$\leq$	$\neq,\geq$	ⓜ	$\geq,>$	$>$	$>$

Fig. 2. Rules for (a) C2-Constraints and (b) Implicit C2-Constraints

Example 1. Suppose that the following integrity constraint sets are given:

$$\mathcal{IC}_1 = \{(x \leq y)\}$$
$$\mathcal{IC}_2 = \{(x \geq y)\}$$

According to the last rule in Fig. 2, $\mathcal{IC}_1$ and $\mathcal{IC}_2$ are overlapping. □

Example 2. Assume that the following integrity constraint sets are given:

$$\mathcal{IC}_1 = \{(x > y), (y \geq 4)\}$$
$$\mathcal{IC}_2 = \{(x > 2)\}$$
$$\mathcal{IC}_3 = \{(x \geq y), (y \geq z)\}$$
$$\mathcal{IC}_4 = \{(x > z)\}$$

According to the last but one rule in Fig. 2(b), the constraints $(x > y)$ and $(y \geq 4)$ imply $(x > 4)$. Since $(x > 4)$ implies $(x > 2)$, we can state that $\mathcal{IC}_1 \supset \mathcal{IC}_2$ holds (cf. Fig. 1). Using rule six in Fig. 2(b) we can derive $(x \geq z)$ from the constraints $(x \geq y)$ and $(y \geq z)$. Since the constraint $(x > z)$ implies the constraint $(x \geq z)$, we may reason that $\mathcal{IC}_3 \between \mathcal{IC}_4$ holds (cf. Fig. 2(a)). □

Relationships between C3-*Constraints.* A uniqueness constraint (type C3) is defined on a set of attributes. The effect of a uniqueness constraint is that the values of the respective attribute combinations must be unique. The following theorem defines the relationships between two uniqueness constraints depending on the corresponding attribute sets.

Theorem 1 (Relationships between Uniqueness Constraints). Let x and y be two sets of attributes. Then the following rules hold:

$$(\textbf{unique}(x) \equiv \textbf{unique}(y)) \; \textit{iff} \; (x = y)$$
$$(\textbf{unique}(x) \supset \textbf{unique}(y)) \; \textit{iff} \; (x \subset y)$$

From (semantically) overlapping or disjoint attribute sets we can only reason that the respective uniqueness constraints overlap. □

Proof. A uniqueness constraint $\textbf{unique}(x_1, ..., x_n)$ can be expressed as follows:

$$(\forall o_1, o_2 \in U(o_1.x_1 = o_2.x_1 \wedge ... \wedge o_1.x_n = o_2.x_n \Rightarrow o_1 = o_2))$$

Such a formula is weakened by strengthen the antecedent of the implication. This can be done by considering further attributes, i.e., by adding further terms to the conjunction on the antecedent of the implication. In consequence, a uniqueness constraints is stronger than another uniqueness constraint if it is defined on a subset of the attributes of the other one. Considering this fact in both directions, we can derive that two uniqueness constraints are equivalent if and only if they are formulated over the same set of attributes.

In case the attribute sets are overlapping or disjoint, the antecedents of both implications contain attributes which occur only in one of the respective formulas. Thus, the antecedents are not comparable and we have to conclude that such kinds of uniqueness constraints are overlapping. □

Example 3. Let there be a class Employee with the attributes ssn, name, salary, and address. If a constraint **unique**(ssn) hold on class Employee, then the constraint **unique**(ssn, name, salary) must also hold on this class. In this case, the latter constraint is a specialization of the former one. On the other hand, the constraints **unique**(ssn) and **unique**(name, salary) overlap since the set of employee objects restricted by these constraints are overlapping. The same argument holds for the constraints **unique**(ssn, name) and **unique**(name, salary). □

Relationships between C4-Constraints. The relationship between C4-constraints is determined by the relationships between the antecedents and consequents of the implications. Let there be two C4-constraints IC_1 and IC_2 of the form $(X_1 \Rightarrow Y_1)$ and $(X_2 \Rightarrow Y_2)$, respectively, where X_1, X_2, Y_1, and Y_2 are constraints of type C1 or C2. Then, we can derive rules of the following form to compute the relationship between C4-constraints:

$$(X_1 \, \Theta_1 \, X_2) \wedge (Y_1 \, \Theta_2 \, Y_2) \Rightarrow (IC_1 \, \Theta_3 \, IC_2)$$

The most combinations of Θ_1 and Θ_2 result in an overlap relationship between IC_1 and IC_2. The table beside summarizes the combinations which lead to another relationship than overlap. We omit the proofs of these rules. Instead, we present an example to demonstrate some of these rules.

Θ_1	Θ_2	Θ_3
$\equiv$	$\equiv$	$\equiv$
$\equiv$	$\supset$	$\supset$
$\subset$	$\equiv, \supset$	$\supset$
$\supset$	$\equiv, \subset$	$\subset$
$\equiv$	$\subset$	$\subset$

Example 4. Let there be the following integrity constraints sets:

$$IC_1 = \{(\text{salary} > 10000) \Rightarrow (\text{age} > 35)\}$$
$$IC_2 = \{(\text{salary} < 5000) \Rightarrow (\text{age} < 25)\}$$
$$IC_3 = \{(\text{salary} < 2000) \Rightarrow (\text{age} < 40)\}$$

From the rules above follows that $IC_1 \, \text{ⓜ} \, IC_2$ hold (because the antecedents as well as the consequents of the implications are "disjoint"). For example, a forty year old employee with a salary of 2000 is conform to IC_1, but not to IC_2. On the other hand, a twenty year old employee with a salary of 30000 is conform to IC_2, but not to IC_1. However, there are employees which are conform to both integrity constraints, e.g. a fifty year old employee with a salary of 15000.

Comparing IC_2 with IC_3 lead to a superset relationship $IC_2 \supset IC_3$ (see the third rule in table above where the antecedents are in a subset relationship and the consequents are in a subset relationship). That is, the integrity constraint IC_2 is more restrictive than IC_3. For instance, IC_3 allows thirty year old employees with a salary of 4000, whereas IC_2 does not. □

Relationships between Different Types of Constraints. Up to now, we have discussed relationships between constraints of the same type. We worked out a set of rules for computing the corresponding relationships. Investigating relationships between constraints of different types, we come to the conclusion that, as a rule, the only possible relationship is overlap. We will not formally prove this fact. Instead, we present some examples for illustration.

Example 5. Suppose, there are the following integrity constraint sets given:

$$\mathcal{IC}_1 = \{(\text{salary} > 2000)\}$$
$$\mathcal{IC}_2 = \{(\text{salary} > \text{bonus})\}$$
$$\mathcal{IC}_3 = \{\textbf{unique}(\text{salary})\}$$
$$\mathcal{IC}_4 = \{(\text{salary} > 2000 \Rightarrow \text{bonus} < 1000)\}$$

Comparing the sets of possible objects restricted by the constraints $\mathcal{IC}_1$ and $\mathcal{IC}_2$, we see that $\mathcal{IC}_1$ allows employees to have an arbitrary value for the attribute bonus — since there is no restriction on this attribute. Thus, an employee may have a "fixed" salary higher than 2000 and bonus "salary" higher than 1000. Such a value combination is forbidden by the constraint $\mathcal{IC}_2$. However, this constraint allows employees to have a salary less than 2000. Since both constraints also allow same value combinations for salary and bonus, e.g. (salary=3000, bonus=500), we can state that these constraints are overlapping.

When we compare the constraints $\mathcal{IC}_1$ and $\mathcal{IC}_3$, we obtain the result that $\mathcal{IC}_1$ allows two employees with the same salary (which must be higher than 2000), whereas this is forbidden by $\mathcal{IC}_3$. On the other hand, $\mathcal{IC}_3$ allows employees to have a salary less than 2000. Since both constraints also allow same values for the attribute salary, we derive that these constraints are overlapping.

Finally, let us have a closer look at the relationship between the constraints $\mathcal{IC}_2$ and $\mathcal{IC}_4$. The constraint $\mathcal{IC}_2$ states that the "fixed" salary of an employee have to be higher than his bonus "salary". Hence, an employee may have a "fixed" salary higher than 2000 and bonus "salary" higher than 1000, e.g. (salary=5000, bonus=2500). Such an attribute value combination is forbidden by the integrity constraint $\mathcal{IC}_4$. However, the constraint $\mathcal{IC}_4$ allows employees to have a bonus "salary" which higher than their "fixed" salary, if the "fixed" salary is less than 2000, e.g. (salary=1000, bonus=2500). Since both constraints also allow same attribute value combinations for salary and bonus, e.g. (salary=3000, bonus=500), we can state that these constraints are overlapping. □

In contrast, when we consider integrity constraint sets containing at least two constraints, further relationships are possible. Sometimes, it is possible to derive an implicit constraint of type C2 from two constraints of type C1. In the following, we investigate the relation between a set of two constraints of type C1 and a constraint of type C2. We start with an illustrating example.

Example 6. Let there be the following integrity constraint sets:

$$\mathcal{IC}_1 = \{(\text{salary} > 2000), (\text{bonus} < 1000)\}$$
$$\mathcal{IC}_2 = \{(\text{salary} > \text{bonus})\}$$

The first integrity constraint set states that all employees must have a "fixed" salary higher than 2000 and a bonus "salary" which does not exceed 1000. The second integrity constraint set says that the "fixed" salary of each employee must be higher than his bonus "salary". Obviously, the latter constraint is also implicitly expressed by the conjunction of the two constraints of IC_1. Thus, we can state that IC_1 is stronger than IC_2, i.e. that $IC_1 \supset IC_2$ holds. □

Motivated by the example above, we have analyzed all combinations of comparison operators and constant relationships (of two C1-constraints). As a result, we found a set rules of the form

$$(x\,\theta_1\,c_1) \wedge (y\,\theta_2\,c_2) \wedge (c_1\,\theta_3\,c_2) \Rightarrow (x\,\theta_4\,y)$$

to derive an implicit C2-constraint from two C1-constraints. We have to point out that not all combinations of the comparison operators θ_1, θ_2, and θ_3 lead to an implicit C2-constraint. Fig. 3 depicts the combinations which lead to an implicit constraint. Furthermore, there are some cases where a relationship between an

$(x\,\theta_1\,c_1) \wedge (y\,\theta_2\,c_2) \wedge (c_1\,\theta_3\,c_2) \Rightarrow (x\,\theta_4\,y)$			
θ_1	θ_2	θ_3	θ_4
$<$	$=,\geq,>$	$<,=$	$<$
$\leq,=$	$=,\geq,>$	$<$	$<$
$\leq,=$	$>$	$=$	$<$
$\leq$	$=,\geq$	$=$	$\leq$
$=$	$\geq$	$=$	$\leq$
$=$	$=$	$=$	$=$
$=$	$\neq$	$=$	$\neq$
$=$	$\leq$	$=$	$\geq$
$=$	$<,\leq,=$	$>$	$>$
$=$	$<$	$=$	$>$

Fig. 3. Rules for Deriving Implicit C2-Constraints

integrity constraint set with (at least) two constraints of type C1 (or C2) and a C4-constraint exists. An C4-constraint $(x \Rightarrow y)$ can be expressed as $(\neg x \vee y)$. Since we know that generally

$$(IC_1 \wedge IC_2) \Rightarrow (IC_1 \vee IC_2)$$

holds, we can derive the following rules for computing relationships between an integrity constraint set IC_1 with two constraints x_1 and y_1 and an integrity constant set IC_2 with an C4-constraint of the form $(x_2 \Rightarrow y_2)$:

$$(IC_1 \supset IC_2) \Leftrightarrow (x_1\,\Theta_1\,x_2) \wedge (y_1\,\Theta_2\,y_2), \ \Theta_1, \Theta_2 \in \{\equiv, C\}$$

All other combinations of Θ_1 and Θ_2 lead to an overlap relationship between IC_1 and IC_2.

Example 7. Suppose the following two integrity constraint sets are given:

$$IC_1 = \{(\text{salary} > 2000), (\text{bonus} < 1000)\}$$
$$IC_2 = \{(\text{salary} \leq 2000) \Rightarrow (\text{bonus} < 1000)\}$$

Then, we can state that $IC_1 \supset IC_2$ holds, since IC_1 implies IC_2. □

Deriving Relationships between Integrity Constraint Sets. Up to now, our discussion was restricted to single integrity constraints or integrity constraint sets with specific constraint types. In the following, we extend our considerations to general integrity constraint sets which may contain constraints of different types. The following theorem provides the rules for computing the relationship between two general integrity constraint sets.

Theorem 2 (Relationship between Integrity Constraint Sets). For two extended integrity constraint sets $\mathcal{IC}_1$ and $\mathcal{IC}_2$ the following rules hold:

$$(\mathcal{IC}_1 \uplus \mathcal{IC}_2) :\Leftrightarrow (\forall IC_{1i} \in \mathcal{IC}_1(\nexists IC_{2j} \in \mathcal{IC}_2(IC_{1i} \; \vartheta \; IC_{2j}), \vartheta \in \{\varnothing, \equiv, \subset, \supset, \text{\textcircled{m}}\})$$

$$(\mathcal{IC}_1 \varnothing \mathcal{IC}_2) :\Leftrightarrow (\exists IC_{1i} \in \mathcal{IC}_1(\exists IC_{2j} \in \mathcal{IC}_2((IC_{1i} \varnothing IC_{2j}))))$$

$$(\mathcal{IC}_1 \equiv \mathcal{IC}_2) :\Leftrightarrow ((\forall IC_{1i} \in \mathcal{IC}_1(\exists IC_{2j} \in \mathcal{IC}_2((IC_{1i} \equiv IC_{2j}))) \wedge$$
$$(\forall IC_{2j} \in \mathcal{IC}_2(\exists IC_{1i} \in \mathcal{IC}_1((IC_{1i} \equiv IC_{2j})))))$$

$$(\mathcal{IC}_1 \supset \mathcal{IC}_2) :\Leftrightarrow (\forall IC_{2j} \in \mathcal{IC}_2(\exists IC_{1i} \in \mathcal{IC}_1((IC_{1i} \equiv IC_{2j}) \vee (IC_{1i} \supset IC_{2j}))) \wedge$$
$$(\exists IC_{2j} \in \mathcal{IC}_2(\exists IC_{1i} \in \mathcal{IC}_1((IC_{1i} \supset IC_{2j})))))$$

$$(\mathcal{IC}_1 \text{\textcircled{m}} \mathcal{IC}_2) :\Leftrightarrow \neg((\mathcal{IC}_1 \uplus \mathcal{IC}_2) \vee (\mathcal{IC}_1 \varnothing \mathcal{IC}_2) \vee (\mathcal{IC}_1 \equiv \mathcal{IC}_2) \vee (\mathcal{IC}_1 \subset \mathcal{IC}_2) \vee$$
$$(\mathcal{IC}_1 \supset \mathcal{IC}_2))$$

Please note that $IC \supset$ **true** always holds, if a corresponding related constraint does not exist in the other integrity constraint set. $\qquad \square$

Proof. In the following, we exemplary prove the "disjoint" rule. Since the proofs of the other rules can be shown analogously, we omit the proof of these rules in order to keep the paper concise.

The integrity constraint sets $\mathcal{IC}_1$ and $\mathcal{IC}_2$ can be represented as a conjunction of logical formulas where each term corresponds to an integrity constraint:

$$\mathcal{IC}_1 \rightarrow IC_{11} \wedge \dots \wedge IC_{1n}$$
$$\mathcal{IC}_2 \rightarrow IC_{21} \wedge \dots \wedge IC_{2m}$$

Since we assume that each integrity constraint set is consistent, the conjunction of the logical representation of the integrity constraint sets implies false if and only if there exists at least one pair of terms whose conjunction implies false:

$$((IC_{11} \wedge \dots \wedge IC_{1n}) \wedge (IC_{21} \wedge \dots \wedge IC_{2m}) \Rightarrow \textbf{false})$$
$$\Leftrightarrow (\exists IC_{1i}(\exists IC_{2j}(IC_{1i} \wedge IC_{2j} \Rightarrow \textbf{false})))$$
$$\leftrightarrow (\exists IC_{1i} \in \mathcal{IC}_1(\exists IC_{2j} \in \mathcal{IC}_2((IC_{1i} \varnothing IC_{2j}))))$$
$$\Leftrightarrow (\mathcal{IC}_1 \varnothing \mathcal{IC}_2)$$

Thus, we can conclude that the disjointness of two integrity constraints implies the disjointness of the corresponding integrity constraint sets. $\qquad \square$

Theorem 3. The relationship between integrity constraint sets containing constraints of type C1, C2, C3, and/or C4 is computable in polynomial time. $\qquad \square$

Proof. The rules can be realized by an algorithm consisting of two loops where each pair of constraints of the different sets are compared. Let the cardinality of the integrity constraints sets be n and m, respectively. Then, the cardinality of the extended integrity constraint sets is n^2 and m^2, respectively, in the worst case (for our constraint types). Hence, at most $n^2 \times m^2$ comparison operations are needed to determine the relationship between integrity constraint sets. □

3 Comparing Classes of Different Schemata

Suppose, the following three example schemata are given:

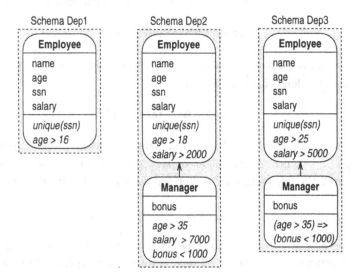

In the sequel, we relate the classes of these schemata using the rules previously introduced. First, we derive the integrity constraint sets of all classes existing in the three example schemata:

$$\mathcal{IC}_{\text{Dep1.Emp}} = \{\mathbf{unique}(\text{ssn}), (\text{age} > 16)\}$$

$$\mathcal{IC}_{\text{Dep2.Emp}} = \{\mathbf{unique}(\text{ssn}), (\text{age} > 18), (\text{salary} > 2000)\}$$

$$\mathcal{IC}_{\text{Dep2.Mng}} = \{\mathbf{unique}(\text{ssn}), (\text{age} > 35), (\text{salary} > 7000), (\text{bonus} < 1000)\}$$

$$\mathcal{IC}_{\text{Dep3.Emp}} = \{\mathbf{unique}(\text{ssn}), (\text{age} > 25), (\text{salary} > 5000)\}$$

$$\mathcal{IC}_{\text{Dep3.Mng}} = \{\mathbf{unique}(\text{ssn}), (\text{age} > 25), (\text{salary} > 5000),$$
$$(\text{age} > 35) \Rightarrow (\text{bonus} < 1000)\}$$

By definition of the class specialization concept the following relationships holds:

$$\mathcal{IC}_{\text{Dep2.Emp}} \subseteq \mathcal{IC}_{\text{Dep2.Mng}}$$
$$\mathcal{IC}_{\text{Dep3.Emp}} \subseteq \mathcal{IC}_{\text{Dep3.Mng}}$$

Comparing the integrity constraint sets of the employee classes leads to:

$$\mathcal{IC}_{\text{Dep1.Emp}} \subset \mathcal{IC}_{\text{Dep2.Emp}}$$
$$\mathcal{IC}_{\text{Dep1.Emp}} \subset \mathcal{IC}_{\text{Dep3.Emp}}$$
$$\mathcal{IC}_{\text{Dep2.Emp}} \subset \mathcal{IC}_{\text{Dep3.Emp}}$$

Below we exemplary sketch the derivation of the first relationship above:

1. Take the first integrity constraint in $\mathcal{IC}_{\text{Dep1.Emp}}$ and search for a related constraint in $\mathcal{IC}_{\text{Dep2.Emp}}$. Since the constraint **unique(ssn)** is in both integrity constraints sets, notice that there is an equivalent constraint:

$$\textbf{unique(ssn)} \equiv \textbf{unique(ssn)}$$

2. When we apply the same procedure on the second constraint of $\mathcal{IC}_{\text{Dep1.Emp}}$, we obtain the following relationship:

$$(\text{age} > 16) \subset (\text{age} > 18)$$

3. Since for all constraints in $\mathcal{IC}_{\text{Dep1.Emp}}$ there exists a related constraint in $\mathcal{IC}_{\text{Dep2.Emp}}$ which is equivalent or stronger, we can derive according to Theorem 2 the following relationship for the given integrity constraint sets:

$$\mathcal{IC}_{\text{Dep1.Emp}} \subset \mathcal{IC}_{\text{Dep2.Emp}}$$

In summary, we imply that class **Employee** of schema **Dep1** is a superclass of class **Employee** of schema **Dep2**. The class **Employee** of schema **Dep2**, on the other hand, is a superclass of class **Employee** of schema **Dep3**. Thus, class **Employee** of schema **Dep1** is transitively a superclass of class **Employee** of schema **Dep3**.

Comparing the integrity constraint sets of the manager classes, we obtain the relationship $\mathcal{IC}_{\text{Dep2.Mng}} \supset \mathcal{IC}_{\text{Dep3.Mng}}$:

$$\textbf{unique(ssn)} \equiv \textbf{unique(ssn)}$$
$$(\text{age} > 35) \supset (\text{age} > 25)$$
$$(\text{salary} > 7000) \supset (\text{salary} > 5000)$$
$$(\text{bonus} < 1000) \supset \textbf{true}$$
$$\{(\text{age} > 35), (\text{bonus} < 1000)\} \supset \{(\text{age} > 35) \Rightarrow (\text{bonus} < 1000)\}$$

For the first relationship see Theorem 1. The second and third relationships are derived using the negated result of rule 11 in Fig. 1. The fourth relationship is given by definition. The fifth relationship is computed by the rule given at Page 8 (see also Example 7). From the relationship $\mathcal{IC}_{\text{Dep2.Mng}} \supset \mathcal{IC}_{\text{Dep3.Mng}}$ immediately follows that the class **Manager** of schema **Dep2** is a subclass of the class **Manager** of schema **Dep3**. In consequence, the class **Manager** of schema

Dep2 is transitively a subclass of the other classes. In conclusion, the extensional relationships among the classes of the example schemata are as follows:

$$Dep1.Emp \supset Dep2.Emp \supset Dep3.Emp \supset Dep3.Mng \supset Dep2.Mng$$

These extensional relationships hold if all extensional restrictions are expressed by integrity constraints. Since extensional relationships are used as basic input information for a schema integration algorithm, we can state that the quality of the integrated schema (which should be conform to the modeled real world) also depends on the quality of the result of the schema comparison.

4 Conclusions

In this paper, we worked out the correspondence between integrity constraints as foundation for semantic schema comparison. We pointed out the relevance of a correct schema comparison as basis for a semantically correct schema integration. In particular, we have presented rules for computing the relationship between integrity constraint sets consisting certain types of constraints. These rules can be used to derive extensional relationships between classes of different schemata.

Currently, we are investigating how far rules for relating complex integrity constraints can be derived. There are also relationships between aggregation constraints and other types of integrity constraints. For instance, from the constraint (salary > 2000) we can derive the constraint (avg(salary) > 2000). In this case, the first constraint implies the second one.

Acknowledgments: We thank Kerstin Schwarz for useful hints. This work was partly supported by the German Federal State Sachsen-Anhalt under FKZ 1987/2527R.

References

1. C. Batini, M. Lenzerini, S. B. Navathe. A Comparative Analysis of Methodologies for Database Schema Integration. *ACM Computing Surveys*, 18(4):323–364, 1986.
2. Y. Dupont, S. Spaccapietra. Schema Integration Engineering in Cooperative Databases Systems. In [8], pp. 759–765.
3. M. Garcia-Solaco, M. Castellanos, F. Saltor. A Semantic-Discriminated Approach to Integration in Federated Databases. In S. Laufmann, S. Spaccapietra, T. Yokoi (eds.), *Proc. CoopIS'95*, pp. 19–31, 1995.
4. S. B. Navathe, R. Elmasri, J. A. Larson. Integrating User Views in Database Design. *IEEE Computer*, 19(1):50–62, 1986.
5. I. Schmitt, G. Saake. Schema Integration and View Generation by Resolving Intensional and Extensional Overlappings. In [8], pp. 751–758.
6. A. P. Sheth, J. A. Larson. Federated Database Systems for Managing Distributed, Heterogeneous, and Autonomous Databases. *ACM Computing Surveys*, 22(3):183–236, 1990.
7. S. Spaccapietra, C. Parent, Y. Dupont. Model Independent Assertions for Integration of Heterogeneous Schemas. *The VLDB Journal*, 1(1):81–126, 1992.
8. K. Yetongnon, S. Hariri (eds.). *Proc. 9th ISCA Int. Conf. on Parallel and Distributed Computing Systems, PDCS'96*, International Society for Computers and Their Application, Six Forks Road, Releigh, NC, 1996.

A Database Interface
Integrating a Query Language for Versions

Eric Andonoff[1], Gilles Hubert[1], Annig Le Parc[2]

[1] Laboratoire IRIT, 118 route de Narbonne, 31062 Toulouse cedex, France
{ando, hubert}@irit.fr
[2] Laboratoire TASC, Université de Pau, Avenue de l'Université, 64000 Pau, France
leparc@univ-pau.fr

Abstract. This paper describes an interface for querying databases integrating versions (DBiV). This interface gives a representation of the database schema as a graph of nodes and links and defines a graphic language for both querying versions and objects living together in the database. Expressing a query consists in selecting links and performing operations from nodes of the graph. The graphically performed operations are algebraic functions. This interface is intended for casual users.

1   Introduction

New database application fields such as computer aided design, software engineering or technical documentation emphasised the need of describing the evolution of real world entities over time. In this way, different states of an entity are kept in the database (not only the last one as in classical databases): these states correspond to the different versions of the considered entity.

Database systems which implement the version concept have proposed solutions for modelling versions. [8], OVM [12] and O2 [14] propose solutions to model instance versions. Orion [9,13], Encore [19] and Presage [16] also give solutions to model type versions in addition of instance versions. However, these database systems only propose partial solutions for querying versions. Indeed, some of them (Orion, O2) consider versions as simple objects while others [1] only give solutions for temporal querying of versions. But neither of them truly take into account the evolution these versions describe nor propose solutions for visual querying of versions.

Numerous works have been led about visual query languages in order to give access to databases to an increasing community of casual users. These languages, which may be tabular [17], graphic [2,3,4] or iconic [7], propose a more expressive representation of the semantics of the queried databases and offer an easier querying process than textual ones. They are more suitable for casual users [6]. But none of these visual query languages give solutions for versions querying.

This paper describes a database interface for querying DBiV. The interface lies upon a model which uses the type, class and link concepts to allow the description of both versions and objects living together in the database. The interface gives, through a graph of nodes and links, a graphic representation of the data described using the previous model. The interface also defines a graphic language, called VOHQL (Version and Object Hypertext Query Language), for querying the versions and objects stored in the database. Expressing a VOHQL query consists in selecting links and performing operations from nodes of the graph. The performed operations correspond to algebraic functions which define an algebra for DBiV. This algebra makes clear, in terms of algebraic functions, the graphical queries expressed by the users. Both the graphic language and the algebra give solutions that truly take into account the specificities of versions and notably the evolution they describe (exploiting the derivation links which exist between them).

This paper is organised as follows. Section 2 introduces the database model. Section 3 presents the algebra related to the model. It more particularly describes the main algebraic functions for querying versions and objects. Section 4 is dedicated to the graphic query language VOHQL. It notably illustrates, through examples, the solutions proposed by VOHQL to query versions and objects. It also gives the corresponding algebraic queries. Section 5 overviews related works while section 6 concludes the paper.

2 Modelling Databases Integrating Versions

2.1 Basic Model

A type gathers the attributes and functions (properties) available for its instances (objects). A class is defined for each user type: it describes the set of instances of a type. Types are organised into inheritance hierarchies. A sub-type inherits from properties of its super-type in addition to its own properties. The class of a sub-type is included into the one of the super-type. The model defines atomic types (Integer, String, Boolean...), a super-type (Object) and parameterised types such as the Set[T] and Tuple[(P1:T1),...,(Pn:Tn)][1] types to define new types. For example, the type of the class defined for each user type T is Set[T].

Links are explicitly modelled between (two) types. In order to specify a link, the concerned types and the corresponding cardinalities are given. A function, with the same name as the link, is automatically defined for each concerned type: it allows the instances linked by the link to an instance of a given type to be found. A class is also automatically defined for each link using the parameterised type Set. Its instances are couples specified using the parameterised type Tuple as Tuple[(L1:T1),(L2:T2)][2].

---

[1] P is a property (attribute or function) available for the parameterised type while T is the type on which the property P is defined.

[2] L1 and L2 are the names of the link while T1 and T2 are the names of the linked types.

2.2   Version Model

The version model resumes the main version models found in the literature [9,11,12,16, 19]. It allows the description of the evolution of entities through a set of versions. Each version corresponds to a significant state for the entity.

Versions are linked by derivation links and form a forest of versions (Fig 1). Derivation links between versions indicate that a version is derived from an existing one: a new state of an entity is created from an other state of the same entity (P.v1 is derived from P.v0). Versions derived from the same version are called alternatives (P.v1 and P.v4 are alternatives derived from P.v0).

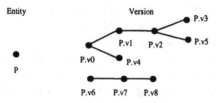

Fig. 1. Forest of Versions

Modelling the set of versions as a tree is inadequate because the result of a query may be a set of versions which are not linked by a derivation link (because of alternatives). That is the reason why our version model represents the set of versions of an entity as a forest (and not only as a tree like in some version models found in the literature).

2.3   Integrating the Version Model into the Database Model

This section illustrates how the basic model is extended in order to take into account the version model. Because of the word limit of the paper, we will only consider object versions (and not type versions).

Versions and Objects. Type instances are either objects or versions. If type instances are objects, only the last value of the modelled entities are kept. If type instances are versions, value evolutions for the modelled entities are kept: each version corresponds to a value of the modelled entities. The organisation of versions into forests is described through the class corresponding to the type using two new parameterised types: Forest[T] and Tree[T]. Forest[T] allows the description of forests of versions whose type is T while Tree[T] allows the description of trees belonging to forest of versions whose type is T. The type of the classes defined for each user type are either Set[T] if the instances of the considered type are objects or Set[Forest[T]] if the instances of the considered type are versions organised into forests of versions or Set[Tree[T]] if the instances of the considered type are versions organised into trees of versions. Each user type whose instances are versions inherit from a meta-type whose name is Versionable and which gathers the additional properties (such as date, successors, predecessors...) that each version has.

Historic Links. Taking into account versions requires the consideration of historic links. A link is historic when it is defined between types where one at least contains versions. In this way, the model distinguishes current links from past links. A current link is the last link defined between an instance (object or version) and a version, while a past link is a link defined before the current link. The following example illustrates these notions of past and current links.

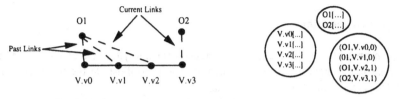

Fig 2. External and Internal Representation of Past and Current Links

The internal representation corresponds to the implementation of the external representation in the database. The parameterised type Tuple as Tuple[(L1:T1),(L2:T2),(PC:integer)] is used to implement historic links in their corresponding collection: the PC property indicates whether the considered link is past (0) or current (1). The function automatically defined in each type concerned by the link always returns a set of tuples. Therefore, for a link L defined between two types T1 and T2, the function L defined in the type T2 returns a set defined as follows: Set[Tuple[(L1:T1),(PC:integer)]].

3 Algebra

This algebra extends the algebra defined in [15] in order to take into account versions. [15] has been chosen as a basis of our work because it is a well-formalised and a closed algebra and it has a mathematically defined semantics [18].

3.1 Problematics of Querying Versions and Features of the Algebra

Query languages for versions must consider the evolution that the versions describe. This evolution is either expressed through the organisation of versions of entities or through the links existing between these versions of entities. Therefore, the algebra and VOHQL propose solutions to query versions independent of the others (without considering the derivation links which exist between them) or to query versions organised into forests or trees of versions (considering the derivation links which exist between them). Moreover, the algebra and VOHQL propose solutions to query past links, current links and both past and current links.

The algebra specifies a set of algebraic functions. An algebraic function is applied to a class and produces a class. The type of queried classes is Set[Forest[T]], Set[Tree[T]] or Set[T] that means that the instances of the type T are versions or objects. The type of the produced classes is also Set[Forest[T']], Set[Tree[T']] or Set[T'] according to the instances of T'. T' is either a new type defined using the parameterised type Tuple or an existing type of the database. The instances (versions or objects) belonging to the result are either new instances or existing instances of the database. The parameterised type Tuple is used to define the corresponding types of these instances and the create operation defined for this parameterised type is used to create the new instances.

3.2 Algebraic Functions

This section presents the main algebraic functions for querying versions and objects and pays particular attention to those which are useful to illustrate the translation of the VOHQL queries into algebraic functions.

The algebra distinguishes classical functions (such as select, project, join...) extended to take into account versions from specific functions specially defined for versions.

Specific Functions. Several specific algebraic functions are introduced in order to permit the expression of the previous type of queries. These functions are defined in the parameterised type Set. The forest, unforest, tree and untree functions permit the handling of forests and trees of versions while the past and current functions permit the handling of past and current links.

- unforest(Cs) -> Set[Tree[T]], where Cs is a class whose type is Set[Forest[T]],
- forest(Cs) -> Set[Forest[T]], where Cs is a class whose type is Set[Tree[T]],
- untree(Cs) -> Set[T], where Cs is a class whose type is Set[Tree[T]],
- tree(Cs) -> Set[Tree[T]], where Cs is a class whose type is Set[T],
- past(i.L) -> Set[Object], gives the set of past links from i following the link L,
- current(i.L) -> Object, gives the current link from i following the link L.

Classical Functions. These functions correspond to the classical querying functions found in many OODB algebra extended to take into account versions. Examples of queries illustrating these algebraic functions are given in section 4.

Select. This algebraic function implements the classical select operation. It creates a class of instances checking a predicate. This function is defined as follows:

Select (Cs, λi,p(i)) = {i / i$\in$Cs $\wedge$ p(i)}

where Cs is a class of objects or versions, i is an instance of the type corresponding to Cs and p(i) is a first-order predicate for the instance i. Select is applied to a class of a given type. If this type contains versions, the type of the corresponding class is Set[Forest[T]] or Set[Tree[T]]. If the type contains objects, the type of the corresponding class Set[T]. The result of the select function is a class whose type is Set[Forest[T]] or Set[Tree[T]] if T contains versions or Set[T] if T contains objects.

Others classical functions. The algebra also proposes the Project and Join functions which implement the classical project and join operations, the Union, Intersect and Difference functions which implement the classical set operations and the Flatten, Nest and Unnest functions to handle nested set and tuples. [5] gives a complete description of these functions.

4 The Graphic Language VOHQL

VOHQL gives a representation of the database as a graph of nodes and links. Expressing a query consists of selecting links and performing operations from nodes of the graph.

4.1 Database Representation

The graph which describes the database is composed of nodes corresponding to the classes associated to the user types, and of links corresponding to the links existing between the user types. Three kinds of links are described: inheritance, composition and relationship links. Bold lines represent inheritance links, plain lines relationship links and dotted lines composition links. The name of a link is indicated in an ellipse. A square indicates the composite class for a composition link. The link cardinalities are specified using usual notations (e.g. a servicing manual describes exactly one plane, and a plane is described by one or more servicing manuals).

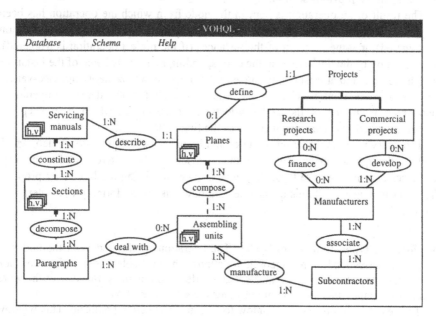

Fig 3. Database Representation

A button for a node indicates what kind of instances the corresponding type contains. If the type contains objects, there is no button while if the type contains versions, there is a button whom value is $h.v$ or v: $h.v$ indicates that the instances of the node are versions organised into forests of versions while v indicates that the instances of the node are versions organised independently ones from the others. Selecting the button produces the update of the versions organisation. Therefore, when the value of the button is $h.v$, the selection of the button implies that the value of the button becomes v and vice-versa. The selection of the button corresponds to a combination of algebraic functions. For the node Planes, the algebraic operations are untree(unforest(Planes)) to turn h.v into v and forest(tree(Planes)) to turn v into h.v.

4.2 Database Querying

VOHQL permits to query in the same way objects and versions living together in the database. It also takes into account the evolution the versions describe: historic links may be included into the scope of the query and versions may be considered either organised independently ones from the others or organised into forests of versions.

Querying Principle. VOHQL queries are expressed from the graph describing the database. Expressing a query consists in selecting links and performing operations from nodes of the graph. The operations which may be performed from the nodes permit a user to display the instances of the corresponding class and to query the instances that the corresponding class contains performing the algebraic functions presented in the previous section.

The result of an operation is kept in the node from which the operation has been triggered. Then, the node only contains the expected instances (if the select operation is triggered) or some property of the instances (if the project operation is triggered). The selection of the link allows in the corresponding nodes only some of the instances which are linked to at least one instance of the other node to be kept (and vice-versa). Moreover, when a link is selected, every new operation (notably the select operation) performed from one of the nodes affects the other nodes which only keep the instances linked to at least one instance of the first node.

The query result is a new set of nodes and links, visualised in reverse video, which replace the queried ones. The user may consult in the different nodes the kept instances and may browse through these instances following the links they propose. The user may also go on his query selecting new links or performing new operations from nodes.

Performing Operations from Nodes. The operations performed from the nodes of the graph correspond to the algebraic functions. The available algebraic functions are the select, project, join, union, intersect and difference functions. Because of the word limit of the paper, this section only presents the select operation.

The select operation uses a window to define the selection predicate. This window contains a predicate tree which describes the attributes (in rectangles), the system attributes (in italic rectangles), the functions (in rectangles) and the links (in grey rectangles) of the queried instances. The root of this tree gives the name of the queried instances and their organisation. The selection predicate is captured from this tree. A second window reminds the user of the selection predicate he is formulating.

The following of the section illustrates, through examples, the selection operation. For each example, the section gives the corresponding algebraic operation.

Querying Versions: "obtain the versions of the plane A320 whose manufacturing price is less than $200000" (Q1). This query concerns versions of planes. Therefore, the user first changes the organisation of the versions selecting the *h.v* button in the corresponding node Planes. Then the user performs the select operation and expresses a predicate composed of conditions. Defining each condition consists in selecting the name of the property or link, an operator (proposed by VOHQL according to the type of the property or the type of the link) and a comparison value. In the example, the predicate is composed of two conditions: the first concerns the attribute name while the second concerns the attribute manufacturing_price. Fig. 4. gives the graphical expression of the selection predicate. The corresponding algebraic operation is:

select(untree(unforest(Planes)), λp,p.manufacturing_price<200000)

The select function is applied to the class Planes whose type is Set[Forest[Plane]] since the type Plane contains versions organised into forests of versions. The untree and unforest functions are used to turn Set[Forest[Plane]] into Set[Plane] in order to consider versions of planes independent of others. Thus, p points out a version of a plane. The result is a class whose type is Set[Plane].

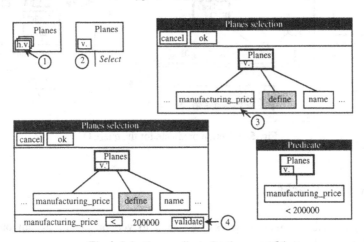

Fig.4. Selection predicate for the query Q1

Querying Forests of Versions: "obtain the planes which always have had a manufacturing price less than $200000" (Q2). This query concerns forests of versions of planes and keeps the forests of versions in which all the versions check the predicate manufacturing_price<200000. To express such a predicate, the user first has to select the attribute manufacturing_price to express the condition manufacturing_price <200000, and then has to indicate that this condition must be checked by all the versions of the considered forests. Fig. 5 gives the graphical expression of the selection predicate. The corresponding algebraic operation is:

Select(Planes, λt, forall[3](untree(t), λp, p.manufacturing_price<200000))

Querying Historic Links: "obtain the projects which have always end up to define planes whose manufacturing price is less than $200000" (Q3). This query concerns the node Projects and the link define which exist between the node Projects and the node Planes. More precisely, the query concerns the projects linked to the planes following past links. The condition manufacturing_price<200000 has to be checked by all the versions of planes linked to a project. To express such a predicate, the user first selects the link define from the node Projects and then the attribute manufacturing_price to express the condition manufacturing_price<200000. Then he indicates that this condition must be checked by all the versions of planes linked by a past link to a project. Fig. 6 gives the graphical expression of the selection predicate. The corresponding algebraic operation is:

Select(Projects, λpr, forall(past(pr.define), λp, p.manufacturing_price<200000))

The function past gives all the versions of planes (p) linked by the link define to a project pr. The function forall verifies that all the planes check the predicate p.manufacturing_price<200000. The result is a class whose type is Set[Project].

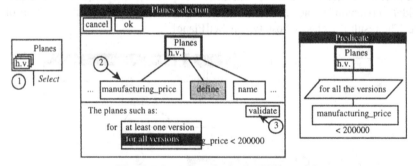

Fig. 5. Selection predicate for the query Q2

5   Related Works

Literature describes numerous works dedicated to version modelling but only few works dedicated to version querying.

With regards to version modelling works, two approaches exist: the entity version approach and the context version approach. In the entity version approach [9,11,12,16], entities evolution is described through a set of versions linked by derivation links. This approach considers entities independent of others. This

---

[3] The function forall(Cs,λi,P(i)) indicates if all the instances i in Cs check the predicate P(i).

approach was introduced to describe the evolution of objects notably during a computer aided design process. In the context version approach [8], entities evolution is described through the different contexts in which the versions of the considered entities belong to. This approach puts together versions of different entities (which are not considered independently one from the others). This approach was introduced in software engineering to both describe the global evolution of a system and to have multiple coherent representations of the same system.

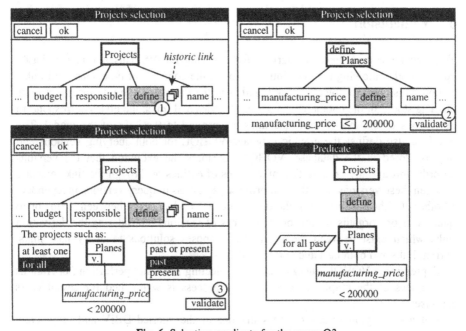

Fig. 6. Selection predicate for the query Q3

Our framework is the technical documentation in the aeronautic field. This framework leads us to define a model which permits us to handle, in a same context, several versions of an entity. Moreover the modelled entities are constantly evolving and the queries essentially concern the evolution of these entities. For these reasons, the model we define is relevant from the entity version approach (which responds to this kind of modelling).

With regards to version querying works, only partial solutions have been proposed in the literature. The systems implementing the entity version approach use the OQL-like query language they propose considering versions as simple objects (e.g. ORION[9]). The systems implementing the context version approach either use the OQL-like query language they propose to query versions in only one context (e.g. O2[14]) or define a new OQL-like query language to query versions in several contexts but only considering the temporal criteria when querying [1]. Moreover, these languages do not take into account the evolution that the versions describe.

The interest of visual query languages is not to be shown and the increasing number of casual users which consult databases leads researchers to work in this field. But, to the best of our knowledge, there does not exist any visual query language for versions. VOHQL satisfies this need. It permits the querying of both versions and objects living together in the database and takes into account the evolution which is inherent to versions. VOHQL defines also an algebra for object-oriented DBiV. This algebra formalises the VOHQL graphic queries because each VOHQL query corresponds to a set of algebraic functions.

6 Conclusion

This paper has presented an interface for querying DBiV[4]. This interface is based upon a model allowing the description, through the concepts of type, class and links, of both versions and objects living together in the database. The interface represents the data stored in the database as a graph of nodes and links: the nodes correspond to the classes of the model while the links correspond to the links of the model. The interface also defines the graphic language VOHQL for both querying versions and objects stored in the database. VOHQL considers the evolution that the versions describe through the organisation of versions of entities or through the links existing between these versions of entities. It proposes solutions to query versions independent of others (without considering the derivation links which exist between them) or to query versions organised into forests or trees of versions (considering the derivation links which exist between them). It also proposes solutions to query past links, current links and both past and current links.

Expressing a VOHQL query consists in selecting links and performing operations from nodes of the graph. Such a querying process is well-suited for casual users because:

- it gives a global view of the semantics of the queried DBiV and graphically indicates the consistent relationships which exists between the data contained in the database,
- it helps the user when querying the database proposing operations which are consistent with the kind of queried instances (versions or objects),
- it proposes a navigational and incremental querying process both for instances and classes (set of instances).

The graphically performed operations correspond to algebraic functions which formalise the semantics of the graphic queries. The set of algebraic functions defines an algebra for DBiV. This algebra is a well-formalised algebra, is closed since the algebraic functions are applied to classes and produce classes, and has a mathematically defined semantics [18].

VOHQL is implemented on the top of the object-oriented database systems O2. The interested reader will find in [10] further informations about the VOHQL architecture and about the principle used for translating algebraic queries into OQL queries. We now plan to adapt VOHQL in order to make it accessible to the web.

---

[4] VOHQL also proposes a language for defining and handling DBiV: the presentation of this language is out of the scope of this paper.

References

1. Abdessalem, T., Jomier, G.: VQL: un Langage de Requêtes pour Bases de Données Multiversions. 13th Nat. Conf. on Bases de Données Avancées, Grenoble, France, (1997)
2. Angellaccio, M., Catarci, T., Santucci, G.: Query By Diagram: a Fully Visual Query System. Visual Languages and Computing, 1(2), (1990)
3. Auddino, A;, Dennebouy, Y., Dupont, Y., Fontana, E., Spaccapietra, S., Tari, Z.: SUPER: Visual Interaction with an Object-Oriented Based Model. 11th Int. Conf. on the Entity-Relationship Approach, Kalrsuhe, Germany, (1991)
4. Andonoff, E, Morin, C., Mendiboure, C., Rougier, V., Zurfluh, G.: OHQL: An Hypertext Approach for Manipulating Object-Oriented Databases. Information Processing and Management, 28 (6), (1992)
5. Andonoff, E, Hubert, G., Le Parc, A., Zurfluh, G.: A Query Algebra for Object-Oriented Databases. 3rd Basque Int. Work. on Information Technology, Biarritz, France, (1997)
6. Batini, C., Catarci, T., Costabile, MF., Levialdi, S.: Visual Query Systems. Reserach Report, University of Roma, (1991)
7. Catarci, T., Massari, A., Santucci, G.: Iconic and Diagramatic interfaces: an Integrated Approach. Int. Work. on Visual Languages, Kobe, Japon, (1991)
8. Cellary, W., Jomier, G.: Consistency of Versions in Object-Oriented Databases. 16th Int. Conf. on Very Large DataBases, Brisbane, Australia, (1990)
9. Chou, HT., Kim, W.: Versions and Change Notification in an Object-Oriented database System. 25th Int. Conf. on Design Automation, Anaheim, USA, (1988)
10. Hubert, G.: Les Versions dans les Bases de Données Orientées Objet : Modélisation et Manipulation. PhD Dissertation, University of Toulouse, (1997)
11. Katz, R.: Toward a Unified Framework for Version Modeling in Engineering Databases. ACM Computing Surveys, 22(4), (1990)
12. Käfer, K., Schöning, H.: Mapping a Version Model to a Complex Object Data Model. 8th Int. Conf. on Data Engineering, Tempe, USA, (1992)
13. Chou, HT., Kim, W.: Versions of Schemas for Object-Oriented Databases. 14th Int. Conf. on Very Large DataBases, Los Angeles, USA, (1988)
14. O2Technology: The O2 User's Manual. Reference Manual, (1995)
15. Shaw, G., Zdonik, S.: A Query Algebra for Object-Oriented Databases. 6th Int. Conf. on Data Engineering, Los Angeles, USA, (1990)
16. Talens, G., Oussalah, C., Colinas, MF.: Versions of Simple and Composite Objects. 19th Int. Conf. on Very Large DataBases, Dublin, Ireland, (1993)
17. Vadaparty, K., Aslandogan, Y., Ozsoyoglu, G.: Towards a Unified Visual Database Access. Int. Conf. on the Management of Data, Washington, USA, (1993)
18. Yu, L., Osborn, S.: An Evaluation Framework for Algebraic Object-Oriented Query Models. 7th Int. Conf. on Data Engineering, Kobe, Japon, (1991)
19. Zdonik, S.: Version Management in Object-Oriented Databases. Int. Work. on Advanced Programming Environment, Trondheim, Norway, (1986)

nP-Tree: Region Partitioning and Indexing for Efficient Path Planning

Lusiana Nawawi, Janusz R. Getta, and Phillip J. McKerrow

School of Information Technology and Computer Science
University of Wollongong
Northfields Ave., Wollongong, NSW 2522
Australia
{102, jrg, phillip}@uow.edu.au

Abstract. This work describes a new method of two dimensional region partitioning and indexing. The method is based on recursive partitioning of a convex cell containing at most n polygonal obstacles into a number of smaller convex cells. Partitioning depends on the positions and shapes of the obstacles. The resulting cells are spatially indexed using a hierarchical data structure called nP-tree. Non-leaf nodes of an nP-tree represent convex cells that contain at most n obstacles and the leaf nodes represent empty cells. A new path planning algorithm in mobile robotics based on nP-tree representation of free cells is proposed.

1 Introduction

Path planning is one of the most important problems of mobile robotics and computer supported navigation. It involves construction of routes that a mobile object, e.g. mobile robot, can safely traverse to reach a given destination. The efficiency of a path planning algorithm strongly depends on the selection of the most appropriate spatial data structures [13] for modelling of free and occupied areas within two dimensional regions. A typical model of a huge environment is large enough to exceed the size of fast transient memory, therefore, either all or part of it must be stored in slower persistent memory. This is the main reason why persistent spatial data structures have a significant impact on efficiency of path planning methods.

A large number of spatial data structures has been proposed for representation of two dimensional regions. The "ad-hoc" approaches are based on linked lists of elementary paths, recorded motions, or landmark navigation points [10]. More complex techniques are based on partitioning free areas into polygonal cells. These are classified into two groups. The first one consists of all region partitioning methods which are independent of the position and shape of the obstacles [7]. This group includes the regular grid structures [6] and quadtree structures [8], [11], [15]. The second group consists of all methods where partitioning depends on the position and shape of obstacles. It includes R-trees and generalised cell trees [5], [4], [14], Voronoi diagrams [1], [3], overlapping generalised cones [2], [9], hypergraphs and road maps [12].

All these approaches to space modelling and indexing address one fundamental problem in path planning in mobile robotics. Given a description of a two dimensional region, start and destination points, and the spatial parameters of a mobile object, how can free areas of a region be partitioned and structured to:

(i) minimise the number of partitions a mobile object should go through from start to destination point,
(ii) keep information about adjacent free partitions, and
(iii) minimise the search and calculation time involved in path planning

A straightforward approach to the problem is to partition the free areas into a grid of small rectangular cells. The advantage of this method is that the computation of paths is relatively simple. This is due to the fact that physical space is directly mapped to the data structure. On the other hand, the large number of cells requires more storage, and computation upon large number of cells be time consuming. This is why grids are more suitable for local path planning in smaller regions. Quadtrees are designed to reduce the number of cells, with free areas represented by hierarchical structures of rectangular cells such that each cell is decomposed into four smaller rectangular cells until it reaches a reasonably accurate representation of the obstacles.

Another class includes irregular partitioning methods where partitioning is dependent on the positions and shapes of the obstacles. These methods require less storage but more time for numerical computations of the directions and distances. Thus, they are more suitable for modelling of large two dimensional outdoor regions where response time is not a critical factor.

The method of region partitioning and indexing proposed in this work (nP-Tree) integrates the properties of recursively defined region partitioning methods and irregular region partitioning methods with the properties of graph-based structures suitable for representation of adjacent free areas. Moreover, the method allows for adjustment of cell boundaries to the directions of the most frequently performed movements.

nP-Tree region partitioning and indexing method is based on the following principles:

(i) The obstacles are represented by polygons and free space is partitioned into convex polygons called *cells*.
(ii) A cell is decomposed into smaller free cells when it contains at most n obstacles, thus the notation n in nP-Tree.
(iii) A nested structure of cells is represented by a hierarchical data structure whose root node represents entire space and each of its child nodes represents a nested cell.
(iv) For any two points in the space, a path between them either does not exist or it is completely included within the smallest common cell both points are included in.

A structure of nested cells is represented by a hierarchical data structure called an *nP-tree* from *nPolygon-Tree*. The n denotes the maximum number of obstacles in one cell that will trigger the decomposition of that cell into smaller cells. A value of n of 1, i.e.1P-Tree, will be used for the examples in the rest of the paper.

A node of an nP-tree represents a convex cell and contains the description of the cell. Leaf nodes represent the cells that contain no obstacles i.e.*free cells*. Non-leaf nodes represent cells that contain at least one and not more than n obstacles and are called *occupied cells*. Occupied cells are decomposed into a number of smaller cells. The decomposition depends on the shape and position of all the obstacles included within that cell. Partitioning of a cell occupied by n obstacles is done using edges emanating from the convex corners of all obstacles to form smaller convex cells. The links between a non-leaf node of an nP-tree and its descendant nodes represent the nested structure of an occupied cell.

All nodes representing adjacent cells in an occupied cells are linked by *gateway links*. If all obstacles are convex polygons then for 1P-trees the gateway links form either a linked list or a linked ring. However, in the general case, i.e. for concave complex obstacles and for $n > 1$ the gateway links form a binary undirected graph. A sample partitioning of two dimensional space and its representation by a 1P-tree is given in Figure 1. The solid lines on tree structure on Figure 1(b) represent the nested structure of the 1P-tree while the dotted lines represent the gateway links between the nodes representing the cells on each level.

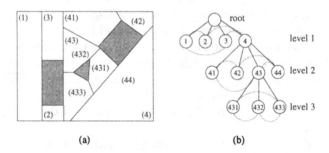

        (a)   (b)

Fig. 1. (a) A sample free space partitioning by 1P-tree and (b) The tree representation with gateway links shown as dotted lines

The nested structure of the nP-tree determines the choice of path planning algorithm. A path between two points in a two dimensional environment consists of a sequence of connected line segments across a number of nested cells. Therefore, the path may be planned at different levels of region granulation by the cells of an nP-tree. The path planning algorithm proposed in this work is based on a top-down decomposition, in much the same way as an nP-tree is constructed. The first approximation of a path is extracted from the topmost level of the nP-tree. Finer approximations are constructed by traversing down the tree. The process is repeated until the final path is obtained or it is proved that a path does not exist.

In the rest of the paper we present the nP-Tree method of free space partitioning and indexing and a path planning algorithm based on nP-trees. The next section describes the cell partitioning method. Section 3 discusses the construction and balancing of nP-trees. Section 4 presents a sample path planning algorithm using nP-trees. Finally, a brief evaluation of nP-trees and concluding remarks are sketched in Section 5.

2 Cell Decomposition

The nP-Tree partitioning method is based on recursive cell decomposition. To construct the partitioning, the descriptions of obstacles are read one by one. Every obstacle inserted may trigger the decomposition of one or more cells that it overlaps. Consider the following example of 1P-Tree where 1 obstacle triggers a cell decomposition (Figure 2(a)) We start with an empty space and insert the first object into it. The insertion decomposes the space into an obstacle region and a number of free cells. Then the second obstacle is read, triggering the decomposition of one or more free cells it overlaps. The process continues until all obstacles are inserted.

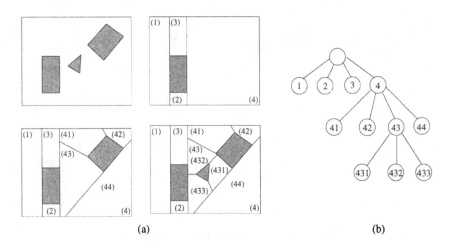

(a) (b)

Fig. 2. (a) Insertion of objects into space, and (b) The tree representation of the partition

When an obstacle overlaps more than one cell then the obstacle is decomposed into several smaller obstacles along the cells' edges with which it intersects. Each new obstacle triggers the decomposition of a cell it overlaps. Decomposition of a convex cell by an obstacle or part of an obstacle is performed by the straight lines called *dividing edges* emanating from the convex corners (smaller than π) of an obstacle. A new convex cell is formed from a combination of the adjacent dividing edges, the edges of a cell being partitioned and the edges of an obstacle, e.g. see Figure 3(a).

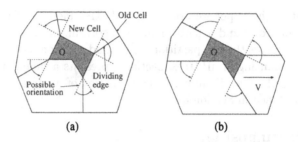

(a)   (b)

Fig. 3. (a) Decomposition of a cell triggered by obstacle O, resulting in 4 new cells, and (b) Cell decomposition with supplied preferred direction V

The direction of a dividing edge emanating from a convex corner should be included within a cone formed by expansion of the edges that create the corner. This constraint ensures that each new cell is a convex polygon. If the partitioning has to be consistent with an a priori given direction then the angle between each dividing edge and the given direction V should be minimal, see Figure 3(b).

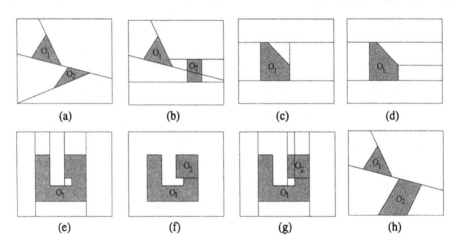

(a)   (b)   (c)   (d)

(e)   (f)   (g)   (h)

Fig. 4. Several cases for cell decomposition

A number of special cases must be considered when a cell is decomposed by an obstacle as illustrated in Figure 4. The sequence of object insertion in these examples is O_1, O_2, where applicable.

(i) If some of the obstacle's corners (vertices) are placed exactly on or very close to a border of a cell then, such corners have no dividing edges emanating from them, see Figure 4(a).

(ii) If an obstacle overlaps more than one cell then it is decomposed into the smaller obstacles, e.g. O_2 in Figure 4(b).

(iii) If two or more dividing edges intersect within a cell, as in Figure 4(c), then some of the resulting empty cells are adjacent to more than one other empty cell. In such a case, the gateway links do not form a list or a ring. To avoid this problem, the directions of dividing edges are changed so that they do not intersect within a common cell, as in Figure 4(d).

(iv) If an obstacle is concave then it is impossible to partition a cell so that the gateway links form either a list or a ring, see Figure 4(e). Then, an obstacle is decomposed into a number of smaller obstacles, see Figure 4(f) and Figure 4(g). However, it should be noted that decomposition of a convex obstacle is not beneficial because it increases the height of P-tree.

(v) An obstacle that partitions a cell into two or more disjoint cells, e.g. see Figure 4(h), violates the region partitioning assumption about the inclusion of a path between any two points inside the smallest common cell. Such a case requires reconstruction of the nP-tree described in the next section.

In the general form of an nP-Tree, i.e. when $n > 1$, the decomposition of an occupied cell is initiated when n obstacles are located within a cell. Having large n has the following advantages.

(i) It reduces a number of obstacles that have to be split because they overlap another dividing edge.

(ii) It allows for minimisation of a number of partitions when two convex corners of the opposite obstacles are joined with the same dividing edge.

(iii) It reduces the height of nP-tree and improves its balancing.

On the other hand, a larger value of n complicates the cell decomposition and the graph structure of the gateway links and increases path search time within the cells.

3   Construction of nP-trees

The nP-tree is constructed by means of sequential insertion of obstacles (recall Figure 2). At the beginning of the construction process, it is assumed that the entire environment is one empty convex cell. Such a cell is represented by an nP-tree containing a root node storing the coordinates of the vertices of the environment. In the next step, the descriptions of obstacles are read one by one and inserted into the root node. After the insertion of the n-th obstacle, the root cell is decomposed into a number of smaller cells. The description of each of these new cells is stored in the corresponding descendant node of the root node. Then, the descriptions of the next obstacles are read and inserted into one or more cells they overlap. Whenever a cell contains n obstacles, it is decomposed into a number of smaller cells. This process is repeated until the descriptions of all obstacles are read in. At the end, we may need to decomposed some cells that contain less than n obstacles.

This process of insertion is achieved with four algorithms: Build_Tree, Insert_Obstacle, Decompose and Overlap. Build_Tree starts from the root node, reads each obstacle's description and calls Insert_Obstacle to insert it. Insert_Obstacle recursively attempts to find the overlapping cell(s) and inserts the obstacle or parts of obstacle into the suitable cell(s). The algorithm uses Overlap to obtain a list of the region of obstacle and the cell it overlaps. The algorithm Decompose decomposes a cell into a number of smaller cells using the obstacles contained within that cell. In addition, Do_Insert registers the description of an obstacle into a cell, while No_Of_Obstacle returns the number of obstacles inside a cell.

```
Algorithm Build_Tree(Root_Node, Obstacle_List)
   for each Obstacle in Obstacle_List
      Insert_Obstacle(Root_Node, Obstacle)
   end


Algorithm Insert_Obstacle(Cell_Node, Obstacle)
   if Is_Leaf(Cell_Node) then
      Do_Insert(Cell_Node, Obstacle)
      if No_Of_Obstacle(Cell_Node) = N then
         Decompose(Cell_Node)
      end
   else
      Overlap_List = Overlap(Cell_Node, Obstacle)
      for each Cell, Obstacle_Part in Overlap_List
         Insert_Obstacle(Cell, Obstacle_Part)
      end
   end
```

Figure 2(a) shows the process of cell partitioning for the configuration of obstacles given in Figure 1. The final 1P-tree for this case is given in Figure 2(b).

The recursive nature of the partitioning process maps nicely to a hierarchical representation of the cells. The intermediate nodes of the tree represent the convex cells that contain one or more obstacles and are further decomposed. When a cell is decomposed, the resulting cells of that decomposition are represented as the descendant of that node. The leaf nodes of the tree represent the cells that do not contain any obstacle, i.e. the empty space in the environment.

Usually, the nodes at one level of a tree represent the free space polygons that surround an obstacle. Thus, there is either a direct connection between the cells (they are adjacent) or an indirect connection between the cells (via adjacent cells) represented by the nodes at that level. This is in fact an implication of the principle stating that whenever two points are included within the same cell, then a path between them either does not exist or it is completely included within that cell. This is desirable for some application purposes (see next section).

However, on insertion of an obstacle, it is possible that a large obstacle triggers a decomposition of a cell into two or more disjoint cells. Consider the Figure 5 where obstacle O_2 decomposes cell (3) into disjoint cells (31) and (32) that are are indirectly connected but not within the same level. To enforce the above principle we have to reorganise the tree representation as shown in Figure 5(b) to that shown in Figure 5(c), so that cells (31) and (32) are indirectly connected within a same level.

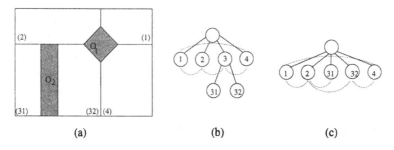

Fig. 5. Elimination of disjoint cells (31) and (32) caused by the insertion of O_2

In an nP-Tree construction, the order in which the obstacles are inserted plays an important role. Sometimes a random order is the reason why nP-tree is not well balanced. As an example, consider the partitioning and indexing of the environment in Figure 6. Insertion order of O_1, O_2 and O_3 in Figure 6(a) gives a less balanced tree than the insertion order of O_2, O_1, O_3 in Figure 6(b). Thus, sorting the obstacles according to certain criteria, e.g. their topology and size, is useful to achieve good partitioning.

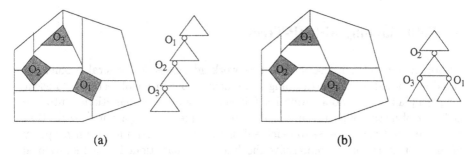

Fig. 6. Balancing of 1P-Tree by different insertion order of obstacles : (a) O_1, O_2, O_3, and (b) O_2, O_1, O_3

Deletion of an obstacle is a complex operation. Moreover, in the general case, the problem of moving an obstacle reduces to the problem of deletion and re-insertion of the obstacle. The deletion is considered a complex problem because it requires re-organisation of the subtree whose root is to be deleted. Consider the Figure 7(a) where obstacle O_1 is to be deleted. The subtrees with roots (1) and (4) have to be re-arranged. One way to perform this is by re-inserting the obstacles contained in the subtree, as shown in the example, where obstacles are re-inserted in the order of O_2, O_3 and O_4. However, this operation can be expensive, especially when the node containing the obstacle to be deleted has a deep subtree. Alternatively, a candidate obstacle from the subtree is selected to replace the deleted obstacle as the root of the subtree, and rearrrangement of the subtree can be performed relatively simpler.

220

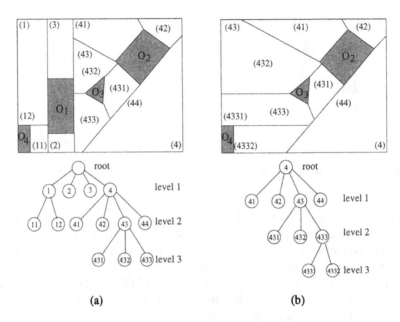

(a)   (b)

Fig. 7. Deletion of an obstacle in nP-Tree

4   Path Planning with nP-Trees

Although the method described in this work addresses the general problem of
two dimensional region partitioning and indexing, our prime objective is to use it
for path planning in mobile robotics. Given an environment partitioned into free
cells, the objective of path planning is to find a sequence of adjacent free cells that
a mobile robot can traverse to reach a destination point. An important property
of an nP-tree is that it represents the free space partitioned in a hierarchical
manner. This means that the higher levels of an nP-tree represent a rougher
approximation of free space than the lower levels. Therefore, the traversal of
an nP-tree in a top-down manner provides more precise information about the
positions of obstacles and free areas as we descend to the lower levels.

The path planning algorithm presented here is based on this feature of nP-
Trees. The first approximation of a path between two given points is a straight
line that links these points. In the next step, level 1 of nP-Tree is accessed to find
all cells that overlap the initial path. If the path is completely included within
one free cell then it is adopted it as the final solution. Otherwise, the gateway
links are traversed to obtain a sequence of adjacent cells that overlap the initial
path, i.e. a sequence of cells that connect the start and end points. According to
our space partitioning principle, a path between two points either does not exist
or it is included within the smallest common cell. If a sequence of cells between
the start and destination node does not exist then a path cannot be found.

Otherwise, we construct a polyline across all cells found. The polyline is
constructed in such a way that each line sections are completely included within

the cells and their connections are on the borders of adjacent cells. This polyline is adopted as the second approximation of the path. The next step considers each line segment of the polyline in turn. If a segment is contained within an empty cell, then it is adopted as a part of the final path. Otherwise, as before, we go down one level on the tree and traverse the gateway links on that level to find the sequence of connecting cells. The procedure is repeated for all segments of the path until free cells, i.e. leaf nodes of the tree, are reached.

The algorithm `Expand_Path` presented below starts with the root node on the tree. It checks if the node is a leaf node. If it is a leaf node, a line segment between the two points is returned. Otherwise, it calls `Find_Segment` to obtain the sequence of adjacent segments and their containing cells that connects the points. For each segment obtained, the procedure `Expand_Path` is then recursively called to obtain the final path.

```
Algorithm Expand_Path(Node, Start_Point, End_Point)
   if Is_Leaf_Node(Node) then
      Segment = Straight_Segment(Start_Point, End_Point)
      return segment
   else
      Segment_List = Find_Segment(Node, Start_Point, End_Point)
      for each Segment, C_node in segment_List
         Segment = Expand_Path(C_node, Segment.Start, Segment.End)
      end
   end
```

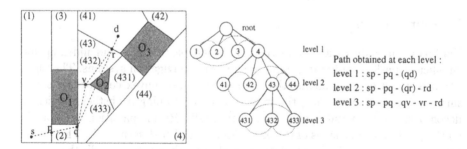

Fig. 8. Construction of a path

As an example, consider Figure 8, where we want to find a path from point s to point d. The procedure starts from the highest level of granulation of free areas, namely $level1$. Analysis of the gateway links between the nodes (1), (2), (3), (4) provides two possible paths of connected cells: $(1) - (2) - (4)$ and $(1) - (3) - (4)$. We consider the first one. At this $level1$, our path consists of line segments sp - pq -qd. The next analysis finds that the segment qd can still be further refined because it is included in the cell (4) which is not an empty cell. We traverse one level down from node (4), and use the sub-tree of cell (4) at *level2* to decompose the segment *qd* into segments *qr* and *rd*. The resulting path at this stage consists of segments *sp - pq - qr - rd*. The next analysis finds that cell (43) is not an empty cell, thus the segment it contains, namely segment *qr* can be further refined into segments *qv* and *vr*. Thus, we obtain the path that consists of segments *sp - pq - qv - vr - rd*. Each of these segments are now included in empty cells, therefore we have obtained the final path. The procedure described above finds a path, which is not necessarily the shortest path.

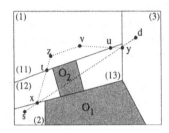

Fig. 9. Moving a path away from obstacle by inserting points *z* and *v*

For a mobile robot to execute the given path, some considerations have to be taken. Consider the example in Figure 9 . To avoid the problem of the mobile robot getting too close to an obstacle, the path of segments *sx - xt - tu - uy - yd* needs to be expanded to path *sx - xt - tz - zv- vu - uy - yd*. Moreover, path smoothing is required to deal with the crooked path.

5   Conclusion

This paper introduces a new method of region partitioning and indexing for an efficient path planning in computer supported navigation systems. The algorithm is based on partitioning the environment into convex cells of free space surrounding obstacles. Thus, the map is a cell containing n obstacles which is decomposed into a number of smaller convex cells. Region partitioning depends on the positions and shapes of the obstacles included within the cells. This adaptive partitioning algorithms results in a smaller number of empty cells than other space partitioning methods such as regular grid and quadtree structures. Partitioning is performed recursively over the original workspace and the resulting cells are spatially indexed by a hierarchical data structure.

Path planning is based on the partitioning method. A path is constructed in a similar way to the partitioning construction. Initially, the path is roughly approximated by a sequence of empty and non-empty cells. Each non-empty cell is then further expanded into a sequence of non-empty and empty cells. This process is performed recursively for every non-empty cell until every cell in the sequence is an empty cell. The final path is a sequence of line segments across empty cells that connect the start to the destination point.

Our region partitioning and indexing method has a number of positive impacts on efficiency of path planning. First, because it is an adaptive partitioning method, the number of partitions is minimised, hence the time required to analyse the workspace is less. Second, path construction is a simple recursive expansion of an initial rough approximation of the path. Because the cells are hierarchically indexed, every cell expansion requires only a substitution of an intermediate node on the tree by its children nodes.

References

1. Aurenhammer F., "Voronoi Diagrams - A Survey of Fundamental Geometric Data Structure", *ACM Computing Surveys*, vol. 23, no. 3, 1991, pp. 345-405
2. Brooks R.A., "Solving the Find Path Problem by Good Representation of Free Space", *IEEE Transactions on Syst. Man and Cybernetics*, SMC-13, no. 3, 1983, pp. 190-197
3. Choset H., Konukseven I., and Burdick J., "Mobile Robot Navigation: Issues in Implementing the Generalized Voronoi Graph in the Plane," *Proceedings of the 1996 IEEE/SICE/RSJ International Conference on Multisensor Fusion and Integration for Intelligent Systems*, 1996, pp.241-248
4. Gunther O., "The Design of the Cell Tree: An Object-Oriented Index Structure for Geometric Databases," *Proceedings of Fifth International Conference on Data Engineering*, 1989, pp.598-605
5. Guttman A., "R-trees: a dynamic index structure for spatial searching," *Proceedings of the SIGMOD Conference*, Boston, June 1984, pp. 47-57.
6. Jarvis R. and Byrne J.C., "Robot Navigation: Touching, Seeing and Knowing," *Proceedings of 1st Australian Conference on Artificial Intelligence*, 1986
7. Keil J.M., Sack J.R., "Minimum Decomposition of Polygonal Objects", in Computational Geometry, Elsevier Science Publishers, North Holland, 1974, pp. 197-216
8. Kambhapati S., Davis L.S., "Multiresolution Path Planning for Mobile Robots", *IEEE Journal of Robotics and Automation*, vol.RA-2, No.3, September 1986, pp.135-145.
9. Kuan D.T., Zamisha J.C., Brooks R. A., "Natural Decomposition for path Planning", *Proceedings of the IEEE Intl. Conference on Robotics and Automation*, New York, 1985, pp. 168-173
10. McKerrow P., *Introduction to Robotics*, Addison Wesley, Wollongong, 1991.
11. Noboria H., Naniwa T., Arimito S., "A Feasible Motion Planning Algorithm for a Mobile Robot on a Quadtree Representation", *Proceedings of IEEE Int. Conference on Robotics and Automation*, 1989, pp. 484-489
12. Rueb K.D., Wong A.K., "Structuring Free Space as a Hypergraph for Moving Robot Path Planning and Navigation", IEEE Transactions on Pattern Analysis and Machine Intelligence, PAMI-9, no. 2, 1987, pp. 263-273
13. Samet H., "The Design and Analysis of Spatial Data Structures", Addison Wesley, 1990
14. Sellis A., Roussopoulos N., and Faloutsos C., " The R^+-tree: A dynamic index for multi-dimensional objects," *Proceedings of the Thirteenth International Conference on Very Large Data Bases*, Brighton, 1987.
15. Zelinsky A., "Environment Exploration and Path Planning Algorithms for Mobile Robot Navigation using Sonar," PhD Thesis, Department of Computer Science, University of Wollongong, Australia, 1991.

Replication in Mirrored Disk Systems

Athena Vakali and Yannis Manolopoulos

Department of Informatics, Aristotle University
54006 Thessaloniki, Greece
{avakali,manolopo}@athena.auth.gr

Abstract. In this paper we study data replication in a mirrored disk system. Free disk space is exploited by keeping replicas of specific cylinders at appropriate disk locations. Assuming an organ-pipe arrangement we calculate the expected seek distance by varying the probability cylinder access under different distributions. Also, analytic formulae are derived for the expected seek distance under replication and comparison with the conventional (without replication) mirrored disk system is performed.

1 Introduction

The "access gap", i.e. the fact that processor and disk speeds differ by three orders of magnitude, has attracted attention towards minimizing this effect by developing efficient storage subsystems. Seeking is the most important factor in disk operations, therefore we focus on this issue in the sequel. A technique to minimize seeking is the *organ-pipe* arrangement, which places the most frequent data in the central cylinder, whereas the less frequent data are stored alternatively in decreasing order to the left and right of the latter cylinder. It has been proven that this scheme is optimal with respect to seeking [12].

Recently, there has been a considerable interest in shadowed/mirrored disks, where all disks are identical and store the same data. In such systems, enhanced fault tolerance and disk performance are achieved at the expense of storage space. In [3, 4, 8, 10] analytic models have been developed to study the performance of seeking. Also, in [6] the average seek time is estimated when multiple data access streams from different disks are merged into a target disk.

Disk rearrangement and adaptive block reorganization have been studied for single disks, in order to reduce seeking either by considering request probability distributions [5, 11] or by applying data replication in free disk space [1, 2]. The rearrangement techniques have been based on trace driven simulations and seek improvement has been reported for conventional disk configurations.

In this paper, a mirrored disk system (i.e. with two identical disks) is studied for specific replication schemes. We assume that single requests arrive under a distribution which supports the organ-pipe scheme. The structure of the remainder of the paper is as follows. In Section 2 the model and the system variables are described. In Section 3 we perform the analysis for three replication policies in a mirrored disk system, and derive estimates for the expected seek. In Section 4 we present the algorithm for the evaluation of the expected seek, we run several models for each of the replication strategies and compare the expected seek found with the corresponding expected seek distance derived for the non-replicated mirrored disk model. Comparisons between all the aforementioned disk configurations are discussed. Finally, future work areas are suggested in Section 5.

2   The Replicated Mirrored Disk Model

As mentioned in the previous, the organ-pipe arrangement is an efficient data placement technique. Figure 1 depicts the cylinder access probabilities of a disk with $N=100$ cylinders under the organ-pipe arrangement, where probabilities obey a normal distribution with variances $\sigma=15$ and $\sigma=40$. Such an arrangement is used in our replicated mirrored disk model.

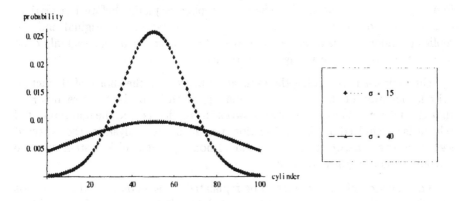

Fig. 1. Organ-pipe data placement scheme.

In a mirrored disk system identical data are stored in both disks. This way, an immediate backup service is supported, while data are accessible whenever at least one disk is available. The choice of the disk to satisfy a read request is made by applying the *nearer-server* rule, i.e. the disk on which the appropriate r/w head is closest to the required cylinder will perform the service.

Here, we propose a mirrored disk model supporting cylinder replication in each disk, in order to increase data availability. Our model is based on the following heuristics:

- the R most frequent cylinders are chosen for replication, R being a parameter in our model,
- a single replica is kept for each of the chosen cylinders, and
- the replica cylinder position has enough storage space in order to host the data of the original cylinder.

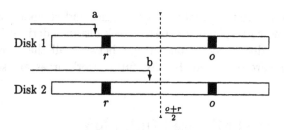

Fig. 2. Nearer-server rule for request servicing - Left Replication Technique.

Suppose that cylinder o is chosen for replication, and its replica is placed on cylinder r at both disks. Thus, if a request refers to the o-th cylinder, it can be satisfied by the r-th one as well. Since there are two disks, we have two heads (namely a and b) available for servicing. According to the nearer-server rule the head that is closer to the requested cylinder will perform the service. Figure 2 represents the model where the replica is placed before the original cylinder position o. The middle of the interval between the original and the replica cylinders $\frac{o+r}{2}$ is a crucial point regarding the choice of the original or the replica cylinder while servicing a read request.

The main issue regarding the replication process, is the choice of the actual cylinder location of the replica r. A first approach is to place the replica r so that the difference in expected seek between the replicated and the non-replicated scheme is maximized. In the next section, we deliver the analysis for the expected seek differences between the conventional non-replicated disk system and the introduced here replicated model.

The selection of the cylinder to be replicated is based on the cylinder access probabilities. Suppose that $p(x)$ is the probability that a request refers to a block of cylinder x. We introduce b_p to be a random variable (in a non-replicated mirrored disk system) for the seek distance traveled from the cylinder where the nearer head lies towards the current requested cylinder. Similarly, b_r is the corresponding random variable in a replicated mirrored disk system. Then, the difference between the non-replicated and the replicated disk system is $d_1 = b_p - b_r$. Similarly, we define n_p to be a random variable in a non-replicated mirrored disk system, referring to the distance traveled from the current cylinder towards the next requested cylinder. Again, n_r is the corresponding random variable in our replicated scheme. As before, the corresponding difference is: $d_2 = n_p - n_r$. Thus, the overall difference in expected seek is:

$$E[d] = E[d_1] + E[d_2] \tag{1}$$

The derivation of $E[d]$ depends on the various replication strategies and is presented in the following section.

3 Replication Strategies

Three replication strategies are presented in the next subsections. The first strategy called *Left Replication*, places the replica in a cylinder to the left of the original cylinder, the second strategy (called *Right Replication*) places the replica to the right of the original cylinder, whereas the third strategy applies either Left or Right Replication policy depending on the position of original cylinder compared to the central cylinder. The expected seek differences are evaluated for each of these strategies. In each case, we need to first evaluate both $E[d_1]$ and $E[d_2]$.

3.1 Left Replication Technique

Calculation of $E[d_1]$

The calculation of $E[d_1]$ is based on the cylinder positions of the replica r and the original copy o, as well as on the positions a and b where the r/w head lies at each disk. Suppose that an arriving request refers to data stored at cylinders o and r, whereas the previous request was for the block residing at a (since one head lies on top of the previous requested cylinder). The other head lies on top of b (by the service of another prior request).

The general formula for the calculation of $E[d_1]$ is:

$$E[d_1] = \sum_{a=a_l}^{a_u} \sum_{b=b_l}^{b_u} p(a)\, p(b)\, [d_p - d_r] \tag{2}$$

where, a_l, a_u represent the lower and the upper limit respectively of the range where a lies, and b_l, b_u represent the lower and the upper limit respectively of the range where b lies. Variables d_p and d_r are the distances traveled when there is no replication and with replication. In order to calculate $E[d_1]$ all the possible cases of a and b locations related to the locations of the replicas r and the originals o are considered. Obviously, we deal with all cases which contribute to the seek difference derived by the replica's use.

1. $a < b \leq r < o$. The introduction of the replica reduces seeking since the position r is closer to the heads location b. The difference is:

$$\sum_{a=1}^{r} \sum_{b=a+1}^{r} p(a)p(b)[(o-b)-(r-b)] = (o-r)\sum_{a=1}^{r} \sum_{b=a+1}^{r} p(a)p(b) \tag{3}$$

2. $a < r < b < \frac{r+o}{2} < o$. Contribution to the expected seek may result from either head a or b, depending on which results in the minimum distance to be traveled. Thus, if $x=\min(b{-}r, r{-}a)$ the difference is:

$$\sum_{a=1}^{r} \sum_{b=r}^{\lfloor \frac{r+o}{2} \rfloor} p(a)\, p(b)\, [(o-b) - x] \tag{4}$$

3. $a < r < \frac{r+o}{2} < b < o$. In this case, there is contribution from the replica only when $o\text{-}b > r\text{-}a$. Thus, the difference is:

$$\sum_{a=1}^{r} \sum_{b=\lceil\frac{r+o}{2}\rceil}^{o} p(a)\, p(b)\, [(o-b) - (r-a)] \qquad (5)$$

4. $a < r < o < b$. There is contribution from the replica only when $b\text{-}o > r\text{-}a$. In this case the difference is:

$$\sum_{a=1}^{r} \sum_{b=o}^{N} p(a)\, p(b)\, [(b-o) - (r-a)] \qquad (6)$$

5. $r < a < b < \frac{r+o}{2} < o$. The contribution to the expected difference is:

$$\sum_{a=r}^{\lfloor\frac{r+o}{2}\rfloor} \sum_{b=a+1}^{\lfloor\frac{r+o}{2}\rfloor} p(a)\, p(b)\, [(o-b) - (a-r)] \qquad (7)$$

6. $r < a < \frac{r+o}{2} < b < o$. There is contribution from the replica only when $o\text{-}b > a\text{-}r$. In this case the difference is:

$$\sum_{a=r}^{\lfloor\frac{r+o}{2}\rfloor} \sum_{b=\lceil\frac{r+o}{2}\rceil}^{o} p(a)\, p(b)\, [(o-b) - (a-r)] \qquad (8)$$

7. $r < a < \frac{r+o}{2} < o < b$. There is contribution from the replica only when $b\text{-}o > a\text{-}r$. In this case the difference is:

$$\sum_{a=r}^{\lfloor\frac{r+o}{2}\rfloor} \sum_{b=o}^{N} p(a)\, p(b)\, [(b-o) - (a-r)] \qquad (9)$$

If both a and b are on top of cylinders located after the cylinder $\frac{r+o}{2}$, the service will be done by the head (either a or b) which is nearer to the original cylinder location o. Thus, the service is performed by the original cylinder, and there is no difference between this case and a non-replicated system. We emphasize the fact that the above analysis holds when heads lie on top of two distinct cylinders a and b. Equation 2 if derived by adding the above Expressions 3-9.

Calculation of $E[d_2]$

The calculation of $E[d_2]$ depends on whether the original copy o or the replica r was used to service the previous request. Since there is no change in seeking if it was served by o, $E[d_2]$ will be measured by considering all possible cases of serving the request from the replica, i.e.:

$$E[d_2] = p(r \text{ is used})\, E[d_2/r \text{ is used}] \qquad (10)$$

where $p(r \text{ is used}) = \sum_{i=1}^{\lfloor\frac{r+o}{2}\rfloor} p(i)$. Suppose that n is the location of the block referenced after the service of the current request by the replica's position. Thus, one head is on top of the r-th cylinder, whereas the other head lies on top of the b-th cylinder. The positions of the heads compared to the requested location, specify the value of the $E[d_2 \, / \, r$ is used] which is given by the following general formula:

$$E[d_2/r \text{ is used}] = \sum_{n=n_l}^{n_u} \sum_{b=b_l}^{b_u} p(n) \, p(b) \, [d_p - d_r]$$

where n_l, n_u represent the lower and the upper limit of the n's range, b_l, b_u the lower and the upper limit of the b's range and d_p, d_r the previous and the new distance traveled in a non replicated disk system and in our replicated model, respectively. The following cases represent the combinations of positions resulting in new contribution to seeking and there is special reference to the negative contributions derived in some of the cases:

1. $b < n < r < o$. There is contribution from the replica when $n-b > r-n$. In the non-replicated scheme, the seek distance traveled is $d_n = \min(o-n, n-b)$ whereas in our replicated mirrored disk system the seek distance traveled is $d_r = \min(r-n, n-b)$. Thus, the expected seek difference is:

$$\sum_{b=1}^{r} \sum_{n=b}^{r} p(b) \, p(n) \, (d_n - d_r) \qquad (11)$$

2. $b < r < n < \frac{r+o}{2} < o$. There is contribution from the replica only when $o-n > n-r$. The difference in expected seek is:

$$\sum_{b=1}^{r} \sum_{n=r}^{\lfloor \frac{r+o}{2} \rfloor} p(b)p(n)[(o-n)-(n-r)] = (o-r) \sum_{b=1}^{r} \sum_{n=r}^{\lfloor \frac{r+o}{2} \rfloor} p(b)p(n) \qquad (12)$$

3. $b < r < o < n$. There is always negative contribution from the replica's use. This negative difference is given by:

$$\sum_{b=1}^{r} \sum_{n=o}^{N} p(b) \, p(n) \, [(n-o)-(n-r)] = (r-o) \sum_{b=1}^{r} \sum_{n=o}^{N} p(b) \, p(n) \qquad (13)$$

4. $b < r < \frac{r+o}{2} < n < o$. The difference in expected seek is:

$$\sum_{b=1}^{r} \sum_{\lceil \frac{r+o}{2} \rceil}^{n=o} p(b) \, p(n) \, [(o-n)-(n-r)] \qquad (14)$$

There is always negative contribution from this replica use since $o-n < n-r$.
5. $n < r < b < o$.

$$\sum_{b=r}^{o} \sum_{n=1}^{r} p(b) \, p(n) \, [(b-n)-(r-n)] = \sum_{b=r}^{o} \sum_{n=1}^{r} p(b) \, p(n) \, (b-r) \qquad (15)$$

6. $n < r < o < b.$

$$\sum_{b=o}^{N} \sum_{n=1}^{r} p(b)\, p(n)\, [(o-n) - (r-n)] = (o-r) \sum_{b=o}^{N} \sum_{n=1}^{r} p(b)\, p(n) \quad (16)$$

7. $r < n < b < o.$

$$\sum_{b=r}^{o} \sum_{n=r}^{b} p(b)\, p(n)\, [(b-n) - (n-r)] = \sum_{b=r}^{o} \sum_{n=r}^{b} p(b)\, p(n)\, (b+r) \quad (17)$$

8. $r < n < o < b.$

$$\sum_{b=o}^{N} \sum_{n=r}^{o} p(b)\, p(n)\, [(o-n) - (n-r)] = (o+r) \sum_{b=o}^{N} \sum_{n=r}^{o} p(b)\, p(n) \quad (18)$$

9. $r < b < o < n.$

$$\sum_{b=r}^{o} \sum_{n=o}^{N} p(b)\, p(n)\, [(n-o) - (n-b)] = (b-o) \sum_{b=r}^{o} \sum_{n=o}^{N} p(b)\, p(n) \quad (19)$$

10. $r < o < n < b.$ The seek distance for the non-replicated scheme is: $d_n = \min(n-o, b-n)$. Thus, there is negative contribution from the replica's use when $n-o > n-r$. The difference is:

$$\sum_{b=o}^{N} \sum_{n=o}^{b} p(b)\, p(n)\, [d_n - (n-r)] \quad (20)$$

Equation 10 if derived by adding the Expressions 11-20.

3.2   Right Replication Technique

The Right Replication technique places the replica to the right of the original cylinder, i.e. from cylinder locations $o+1$ to N. As before, the appropriate replica location is found by the value maximizing the expected seek expressed by Formula 1.

Calculation of $E[d_1]$

$E[d_1]$ is expressed by Equation 2, by summing the corresponding quantities. Similarly to the previous subsection, we end up with the expression:

$$E[d_1] = (r-o) \sum_{a=r}^{N} \sum_{b=a+1}^{N} p(a)\, p(b) + \sum_{a=\lceil \frac{r+o}{2} \rceil}^{r} \sum_{b=r}^{N} p(a)\, p(b)\, [(a-o) - x]$$

$$+ \sum_{a=o}^{\lfloor \frac{r+o}{2} \rfloor} \sum_{b=r}^{N} p(a)\, p(b)\, [(a-o) - (b-r)]$$

$$+ \sum_{a=1}^{o} \sum_{b=r}^{N} p(a)\, p(b)\, [\min(b-o, o-a) - (b-r)]$$

$$+ \sum_{a=\lceil \frac{r+o}{2} \rceil}^{r} \sum_{b=a+1}^{r} p(a)\, p(b)\, [(a-o) - (r-b)]$$

$$+ \sum_{a=o}^{\lfloor \frac{r+o}{2} \rfloor} \sum_{b=\lceil \frac{r+o}{2} \rceil}^{r} p(a)\, p(b)\, [(a-o) - (r-b)]$$

$$+ \sum_{a=1}^{o} \sum_{b=o}^{r} p(a)\, p(b)\, [\min(b-o, o-a) - (r-b)].$$

Calculation of E[d_2]

Similarly, E[d_2] is expressed by Equation 10 by adding the following summations:

$$E[d_2] = \sum_{b=1}^{o} \sum_{n=b+1}^{o} p(b)\, p(n)\, [\min(o-n, n-b) - \min(r-n, n-b)]$$

$$+ \sum_{b=o}^{r} \sum_{n=b}^{r} p(b)\, p(n)\, [(n-b) - \min(r-n, n-b)]$$

$$+ \sum_{b=1}^{o} \sum_{n=r}^{N} p(b)\, p(n)\, (r-o) \; + \; \sum_{b=1}^{o} \sum_{n=o}^{r} p(b)\, p(n)\, [(n-o) - (r-n)]$$

$$+ \sum_{b=o}^{r} \sum_{n=1}^{o} p(b)\, p(n)\, (o-b) \; + \; \sum_{b=r}^{N} \sum_{n=1}^{o} p(b)\, p(n)\, (o-r)$$

$$+ \sum_{b=n}^{r} \sum_{n=o}^{r} p(b)\, p(n)\, [\min(b-n, n-o) - (b-n)]$$

$$+ \sum_{b=r}^{N} \sum_{n=o}^{r} p(b)\, p(n)\, [\min(b-n, n-o) - (r-n)]$$

$$+ \sum_{b=n}^{N} \sum_{n=r}^{N} p(b)\, p(n)\, [\min(b-n, n-o) - \min(n-r, b-n)].$$

Again, the total seek E[d] equals the sum of quantities E[d_1] and E[d_2].

3.3 Symmetric Replication Technique

This technique applies either Left or Right Replication technique depending on the original cylinder location compared to the middle of the disk. Thus, Symmetric Replication is governed by the following rule:

if original $\leq \frac{N}{2}$ then use Right Replication

if original $> \frac{N}{2}$ then use Left Replication

Evaluation of the expected seek is based on the adopted policy, i.e. in case of Left Replication we use the formulae derived in Subsection 3.1, whereas in case of Right Replication we use the formulae derived in Subsection 3.2.

4 Expected Seek Distance

The algorithm used for the evaluation of the expected seek for each of the replication schemes, in our replicated mirrored disk model, follows:

1. Use normal distribution for the data placement
2. Choose the R most frequent requested cylinders
3. For each of the R chosen evaluate their $E[d]$ and find the cylinder r which maximizes $E[d]$
4. Re-estimate the probabilities for cylinders o and r
5. Evaluate expected seek distance

After replication the probabilities of the original cylinder (o) and the replica cylinder (r) are updated since the distribution is affected by the introduction of the replica. The probability of the replica position is increased by an amount pr, whereas the probability of the original cylinder position is decreased by the same amount (pr). We have run the above algorithm for a model consisting of $N=100$ cylinders. The cylinder access probability obeys the normal distribution, whereas the organ-pipe placement scheme has been adopted. Two variations of the normal distribution are applied ($\sigma=15$ and $\sigma=40$). The expected seek is evaluated for each of these placement schemes by the algorithm described above. Figures 3 and

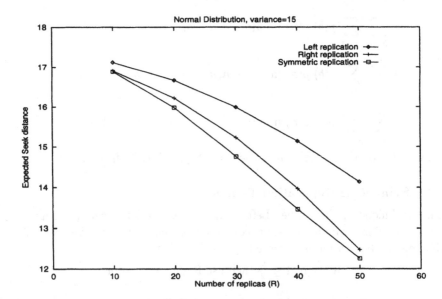

Fig. 3. Expected seek distance as a function of the number of replicas (for $\sigma=15$).

4 represent the expected seek distance metric for Organ-pipe arrangement which is expressed by Normal Distribution with variance $\sigma=15$ and $\sigma=40$ respectively. These results are compared with the corresponding expected seek derived for the non-replicated mirrored disk model. In [4] the expected seek was found to be $\frac{N}{5}$ for a mirrored disk system with no replication. For our deterministic model of $N=100$ cylinders the non-replicated model will result in an expected seek of 20 cylinders. This seek distance is used for comparisons with our results.

Left Replication

Here, the amount to be added/subtracted to the original probabilities is estimated by the probability of using the replica i.e.

$$pr = p(r) \sum_{i=1}^{\lceil \frac{r+o}{2}-1 \rceil} p(i)$$

Compared to the mirrored disk models with no replication, our model shows significant seek improvement. When using normal distribution with variance $\sigma=40$, we have a range of expected seeks from 18.5 cylinders for $R=10$ replicas to 16.8 cylinders for $R=50$. Thus, there is an improvement rate from 8% to 16% approximately. When using normal distribution with variance $\sigma=15$, we have a range of expected seeks from 17.1 cylinders for $R=10$ to 14.1 cylinders for $R=50$. Thus, there is an improvement rate from 14% to 30% approximately.

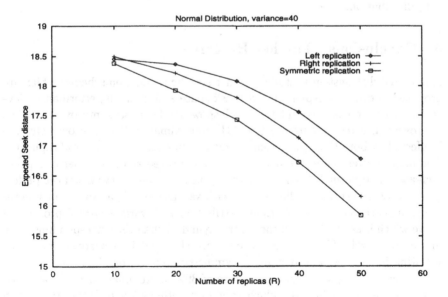

Fig. 4. Expected seek distance as a function of the number of replicas (for $\sigma=40$).

Right Replication

Here, the amount to be added/subtracted to the original probabilities is:

$$pr = p(r)\,(1 - \sum_{i=1}^{\lfloor \frac{r+o}{2} \rfloor} p(i))$$

When using normal distribution with variance $\sigma=40$, we have a range of expected seeks from 18.5 cylinders for $R=10$ to 16.2 cylinders for $R=50$. Thus there is an improvement rate from 8% to 19% approximately. When using normal distribution with variance $\sigma=15$, we have a range of expected seeks from 16.9 cylinders for $R=10$ to 12.5 cylinders for $R=50$. In this case, the improvement rate ranges from 15% to 38% approximately.

Symmetric Replication

In this case, when using normal distribution with variance $\sigma=40$, we have a range of expected seeks from 18.4 cylinders for $R=10$ to 15.8 cylinders for $R=50$. Thus, there is an improvement rate from 8% to 21% approximately compared to the non-replicated mirrored disk system. When using normal distribution with variance $\sigma=15$, we have a range of expected seeks from 16.9 cylinders for $R=10$ to 12.3 cylinders for $R=50$. Thus, there is an improvement rate from 16% to 39% approximately. Thus, the Symmetric Replication scheme shows a better behavior since it takes advantage of both techniques and exploits better the data distribution.

5   Conclusions - Further Research

A mirrored disk system is studied, under specific replication schemes which are proposed in order to exploit the free disk space and improve performance. Several analytic models are evaluated which show significant seek improvement. The improvement rates vary from 8% to 39% approximately. The improvement rate is affected by both the data placement distribution and the number of replicated cylinders. In every case, the performance is improved as the number of replicas increases. The normal distribution with variance $\sigma=40$ shows a weaker performance than the corresponding model with variance $\sigma=15$, as shown in Figures 3-4. This is the case, since Normal distribution with variance $\sigma=15$ produces a curve which is skewer(around the central cylinder) than the corresponding curve of variance $\sigma=40$. So, when $\sigma=15$ data are clustered in a narrower disk area resulting in reduced seek distances. Symmetric Replication shows the best behavior by reaching an improvement rate of 39% approximately. It is concluded that Symmetric Replication which combines both Left and Right Replication reduces seeking significantly.

Further research should extend the replication schemes presented here, by introducing adaptive block replication in mirrored disks. The analysis could be supported by simulation experiments. Also, issues like the number of replicas, as well as "high" priority positions to place replicas could extend the presented models. The organ-pipe placement could be replaced by other data placement policies in order to compare different methods and possibly come up with a more efficient scheme. The replication idea could be adapted to modern optimal data placement strategies applied to technologically advanced large-scale storage media such as Tertiary Storage Libraries discussed in [7]. Also, the camel-arrangement [9] is a data placement scheme which can be applied to the models studied in the present work since there are two mirrored disks suitable for the two peaks of the camel-arrangement scheme.

References

1. S. Akyurek and K. Salem: Adaptive Block Rearrangement, *ACM Transactions on Computer Systems*, Vol.13, No.2, pp.89-121, 1995.
2. S. Akyurek and K. Salem: Adaptive Block Rearrangement Under UNIX, *Software - Practice and Experience*, Vol.27, No.1, pp.1-23, 1997.
3. D. Bitton: Arm Scheduling in Shadowed Disks, *Proceedings IEEE COMPCON 89 Conference*, pp.132-136, 1989.
4. D. Bitton and J. Gray: Disk Shadowing, *Proceedings 14th VLDB Conference*, pp.331-338, 1988.
5. S. Carson and P. Reynolds: Adaptive Disk Reorganization, Technical Report UMI-ACS TR-89-4, University of Maryland at College Park, MD, 1989.
6. C. Chien and N. Bourbakis: Approximation of Seek Time for Merged Disks, *Transactions of the Society for Computer Simulation* Vol.12, No.3, pp.245-260, 1995.
7. S. Christodoulakis, P. Triantafillou and F. Zioga: Principles of Optimally Placing Data in Tertiary Storage Libraries, *Proceedings 23rd VLDB Conference*, pp.236-245, 1997.
8. R.W. Lo and N.S. Matloff: Probabilistic Limit on the Virtual Size of Replicated Disc Systems, *IEEE Transactions on Knowledge and Data Engineering*, Vol.4, No.1, pp.99-102, 1992.
9. Y. Manolopoulos and J.G. Kollias: Optimal Data Placement in Two-headed Disk Systems, *BIT*, Vol.30, pp.216-219, 1990.
10. A. Vakali and Y. Manolopoulos: An Exact Analysis on Expected Seeks in Shadowed Disks, *Information Processing Letters*, Vol.61, pp.323-329, 1997.
11. P. Vongsathorn and S. Carson: A System for Adaptive Disk Rearrangement, *Software - Practice and Experience*, Vol.20, No.3, pp.225-242, 1989.
12. C. Wong: *Algorithmic Studies in Mass Storage Systems*, Computer Science Press, 1983.

Clustering Techniques for Minimizing Object Access Time

Vlad S. I. Wietrzyk, Mehmet A. Orgun

Department of Computing, Macquarie University ~ Sydney
Sydney, NSW 2109, Australia
vlad@mpce.mq.edu.au

Abstract. We propose three designs for clustering objects: a new graph partitioning algorithm, Boruvka's algorithm, and a randomized algorithm for object graph clustering. Several points are innovative in our approach to clustering: (1) the randomized algorithm represents a new approach to the problem of clustering and is based on probabilistic combinatorics. (2) All of our algorithms can be used to cluster objects with multiple connectivity. (3) Currently applied partition-based clustering algorithms are based on Kruskal's algorithm which always runs significantly slower than Prim's and also uses considerably more storage. However in our implementation of clustering algorithms we achieved additional reduction in processing time of object graphs.
Keywords. *Object Database System, Performance, Clustering, and Buffering.*

1 Introduction

Clustering can have substantial impact on ODBMS performance; [1] finds that a factor of three improvement can be achieved by proper ODBMS object clustering for CAD applications. In [2] it is shown that optimal clustering is an NP complete problem. Clustering improves reference locality, it however, totally depends on clients' access patterns. Naturally, we cannot foresee all the clients in advance, and access patterns of clients may impose conflicting demands on clustering. Results of our experiments show that building the object list from MST (Minimum Spanning Tree) instead of the original object graph does not change the result of clustering. However it results in increased performance.

Suppose that a storage manager is capable of accepting commands, which enable the user to issue low-level hints on an object-by-object basis. However, this result in total user's responsibility for controlling the clustering structure, which directly violates the data-independence property for any DBMS especially because users should be unaware of the data's physical representation. Thus, a system should posses a clustering scheme that accepts higher level hints which can be based on configuration relationship of objects in the object net.

We propose three designs for clustering objects:

- *A New graph partitioning algorithm.*
- *Boruvka's algorithm..*
- *A Randomized algorithm.*

Our third algorithm represents a new approach to the problem of clustering and is based on probabilistic combinatorics.

Our main conclusion is that randomized algorithms can be successfully applied to the problem of clustering objects in ODBMS. To the best of our knowledge this novel approach hasn't been used as a clustering mechanism in persistent object systems.

2 Benefits of Clustering Objects

This section summarizes the main benefits of clustering objects in persistent systems, which have been discussed and quantified by many studies [3], [4], [5], [6].

The choice of placing objects to pages affects the performance of the ODBMS in terms of server load, server overhead, concurrency control, and recovery. Clustering significantly effects memory utilization and system load. Object placement affects the number of pages a transaction will need during its lifetime.

Data clustering is also an important means of increasing the performance of queries. A great deal of effort has been put into the research of optimal clustering methods for hierarchical objects [7], [8], [9], [10]. However, even the dynamic clustering method [34], while increasing performance of common queries, may result in a dramatic performance decrease of less common but still frequently used queries.

It is far more expensive to gather dynamic information on the access behavior of applications since this requires monitoring the applications. Also, dynamic monitoring of the system has some disadvantages that were pointed out by [11], [12] and hence they have suggested static dataflow analysis techniques as a way of deriving the access patterns of objects. We assume the weights of the edges of the object graph to be given - using one of the many techniques proposed in the literature [13], [14], [15], [6], [11], [12].

We use the VERSANT database management system developed at Versant Object Technology Corporation, California as the database in our experiments [16]. VERSANT is a fourth-generation DBMS combining the direct modeling of complex graph-structured data with the power of today's leading object programming languages. VERSANT has a few unique features which are relevant to our experiments, but our results should apply to more conventional databases as well [17].

An alternative to the VERSANT approach is the page server architecture, however study [3] showed that page caching can lead to inefficient use of client buffers in the page server architecture if clustering is poor.

In order to address those issues related to clustering we designed and implemented new clustering algorithms.

3 Clustering Algorithms Designs for Minimizing Object Access Time

In this section we describe three new clustering algorithms for persistent object systems, and discuss the complexity of these algorithms and the implication of each design on the ODBMS performance.

3.1 The New Greedy Graph Partitioning Heuristics

Now, we will present our first design of the clustering algorithm as follows: a clustering algorithm takes as input a random sequence of nodes of a configuration Directed Acyclic Graph (DAG), and generates a clustering sequence of nodes. Our approach is to generate and cluster a minimum spanning tree of the nodes of a given configuration DAG.

Our strategy for clustering objects is mainly based on the estimated inter-object communication volume represented by the weight between pairs of objects. In order to keep all clusters within a reasonable size, we impose a limit on cluster size: P_{max}, which is a page size. When the total size of objects of P_x and P_y is less than P_{max}; $P_x + P_y \leq P_{max}$, they can be clustered together by moving objects from P_y to P_x. The result of this clustering process is a set of pages P_1, P_2, ... , each of which is a set of o_i objects, $1 \leq o_i \leq N$, and the size of each page, P_i, satisfies the condition $1 \leq P_i \leq P_{max}$. Let N be the number of objects in the object net of application software system; w_{v_1,v_2} is the weight representing totality of references between objects v_1 and v_2.

In order to minimize intercluster connectivity and maximize concurrency, the objective function can be expressed as follows:

$$IR = \min \left[\sum_{i}^{N-1} \sum_{j}^{N} \sum_{k}^{P} w_{v_1,v_2} \, \lambda_{ik} (1 - \lambda_{jk}) \right]$$

where:

$\lambda_{ik} = 1$ *(if object is clustered on page k)*, 0 *(if not)*;

$1 \leq i \leq N$ and $1 \leq k \leq P$.

In the description of the first algorithm the following notations are used, see also [18], [19]. The edges of G are stored in the list E, i.e., E(i) is the pair of the end vertices of the i-th edge. The list W contains the edge weights: W(i) is the weight of the i-th edge. ET is the set of edges of the current forest T, p is the number of its components, E_1 is the set of minimum-weight edges for the current forest T. In order to improve the performance of the construction of the minimum-weight edge sets, the following scratchpad, auxiliary work lists are used: COMP(j) is the index of the component of the current forest which contains the vertex j; MWE(i) is the index of the minimum-weight edge for the i-th component of the growing forest; MW(i) is the weight of the edge MWE(i).

Algorithm Cluster Object Net
Input: Weighted, undirected graph G
    with n vertices and E edges
Output: Clustering Mapping
/* Compute MST (Minimum Weight Spanning Tree */
{

 1. Initialization step: Set ET ← ∅,
  COMP(i) ← i, MW(i) ← ∞ for i = 1,
  2, ..., n. p ← n.

    //Operations 2-8 gradually build-
    //up the set E_1 of minimum-
    //weight edges for the forest T.

 2. k ← 1.

 3. Let E(k) = uv; i ← COMP(u), j ← COMP(v) .

 4. If i ≠ j then go to step 5, otherwise go to step 7.

 5. If w(uv) = W(k) < MW(j) then MW(j) ← w(uv), MWE(j) = k.

 6. If w(uv) = W(k) < MW(i) then MW(i) ← w(uv), MWE(i) = k.

 7. If k = |EG| then go to step 8
   otherwise k ← k + 1 and go to step 3.

    //Immediately before the
    // execution of step 8, the first p
    //entries of MWE contain the
    //indices of edges from the
    //minimum-weight set for T

 8. Examine the first p elements of MWE
   and create the set E_1 of the minimum-
   weight edges for the forest T.

 9. ET ← ET ∪ E_1.

    //This is the edge set
    //for the "new" forest T'

 10. Using the depth-first search, extract
   the connected components of the
   "new" forest T' = T' + E_1.

    //The list COMP and the value
    //of p are updated

11. IF p = 1 then terminate
   //ET is the edge set of the
   //minimum spanning tree

   Otherwise go to step 2.

   RETURN M_{ST}
}

12. Using the output of MST algorithm generate
   list of tuples of the form $(v_1, v_2, w_{v1, v2})$
   where v_1, v_2 are pair of objects delimiting the
   edge taken from the edge list
   $w_{v1, v2}$ is the weight representing totality of
   references between objects v_1 and v_2
      // As a result of traversing MST objects in
      // the list will be in ascending order of
      // their weight */

13. Copy every object from MST to a new page

14. Assign those pages to blocks

15. while (there are unclustered objects)
      {
      // traverse the list of tuples in reverse
      // order */
      Cluster pair of object from the current
      tuple onto one page
      // Let Px, P_y be the pages containing
      // objects v_x, v_y
      If (Px <> P_y and the total size of objects
      of Px and P_y is less then P_{max}
      Move current object from P_y to Px
      If no object left in Py delete Py from the
      block;
      // end the while loop
                                    }

16. Compact the pages

17. Assign blocks to the disk
   // End of the *Algorithm Cluster Object Net*

The algorithm at the first iteration handles the spanning forest of a graph G consisting of n = |G| single-vertex components. The way our algorithm assigns objects to pages is like the algorithm presented in [20], however our algorithm doesn't require edges to be sorted.

   The complexity of the greedy graph partitioning algorithm is $O(|EG|log_2|G|)$ [18], [19].

3.2 Boruvka's Algorithm

Our second algorithm represents a partition-based approach to the clustering problem.

Later we show that using randomization in conjunction with this algorithm leads to a linear-time algorithm. The basic idea in Boruvka's algorithm is to contract simultaneously the minimum weight edges incident on each of the vertices in G. This process of contracting the minimum-weight incident edge for each vertex in the graph is called a *Boruvka phase* or *Boruvka step* [21], [22].

Boruvka's algorithm thus reduces the MST problem in an $|G|$-vertex graph with $|EG|$ edges to the MST problem in an $(|G/2|)$-vertex graph with at most $|EG|$ edges. The time required for the reduction is only $O(|EG| + |G|)$. It follows [23], that the worst-case running time of this algorithm is $O(|EG| \log |G|)$.

3.3 A Randomized Algorithm for the Object Graph Clustering

Our third design uses randomization in conjunction with Boruvka's algorithm which leads to a linear-time algorithm. The analysis of randomized algorithms should be distinguished from the *probabilistic* or *average-case* analysis of an algorithm, in which it is assumed that the *input* is chosen from a probability distribution. In case of a probabilistic algorithm, the analysis would typically imply only that the algorithm is good for *most* inputs but not for all [24]. The algorithm will recourse on subgraphs that are not necessarily connected. When the input graph G is not connected, a spanning tree does not exist and we generalize the notion of a minimum spanning tree to that of a minimum spanning forest (MSF) [23]. The only use of randomization in the MST algorithm is in the use of random sampling to identify and eliminate edges that are guaranteed not to belong to the MST. The random-sampling result is the key to the $O(|EG|)$ bound. For detailed, tightened high-probability complexity analysis of randomized algorithms see [23].

Algorithm Randomized Clustering
Input: Weighted, undirected graph G with n vertices and E edges
Output: Clustering Mapping
/* Compute Randomized MST (Minimum Weight Spanning Tree) */
{
1. Using four applications of Boruvka steps
    interleaved with simplification of the
    contracted graphs, compute a graph G_1 with at
    most G/16 vertices and let EG_c be the set of
    edges contracted during the four steps.

2. In the contracted graph G_1, choose a
    subgraph G_s by selecting each edge
    independently with probability ½.

3. Compute the minimum spanning tree T_M of
    the graph G_2 by recursively applying
    Randomized MST algorithm.

4. Identify the edges in G_1 which doesn't belong
   to the MST and delete them to obtain a graph G_3.

5. Compute the minimum spanning tree T_{MS} for
   the graph G_3 by recursively applying
   Randomized MST algorithm.

6. Return edges contracted in step (1); EG_c
   together with the edges of T_{MS}.
   }

7. Apply steps 12 - 17 from *Algorithm Cluster Object Net* in paragraph 4.1
/* End of the *Algorithm Randomized Clustering* */

In step 4 of our algorithm to identify the edges which doesn't belong to the MST we applied the verification algorithm based on [25].

The expected running time of *Algorithm Randomized Clustering* is $O(|G| + |EG|)$ [23]. However, the *Algorithm Randomized Clustering* runs in $O(|EG|)$ time with probability $1 - \exp(- \Omega (|EG|))$. For a detailed, tightened high-probability complexity analysis of this algorithm based on a Chernoff bound see: [24], [26], this probability is $\exp(- \Omega(|EG|))$ since $|EG| \geq |G/2|$.

4 Experimental Study Evaluation

In order to test our clustering approach, we conducted a series of object clustering experiments.

4.1 Clustering Methodology

Our first two clustering algorithms, like that of Lin-Kernighan [27], are trying to build an optimization algorithm on its *greediness*: building up the solution by making the best choice locally. But in most optimization problems, greed does not pay off; the greedy solution is not optimal in general. We may still use a greedy algorithm as a heuristic, to obtain a "reasonable" solution (and in practice it is very often used indeed).

Our approach grew out of a methodology for proving the existence of combinatorial configurations having certain desired properties based on the works of Erdos and Renyi, which is treated in [28]. Randomization is often used in conjunction with deterministic methods, and it is an important tool in avoiding "traps" (degenerates), in reaching tricky "corners" of the domain, and in many other situations.

4.2 Quantitative Clustering Analysis

Our experimental machine was based on the 82440FX Intel Premiere motherboard, with a 200-MHz Intel Pentium Pro processor.

We have adapted hypermodel benchmark [29] to test our clustering algorithms.

The results are displayed in Figures 1 through 6 in detail. In conclusion, the size of workstation buffer pool has no effect on the performance of the sequential scan query and the results are not included.

In our first set of experiments we measured the running-time of our algorithms as a function of the database size. The results are shown (in Fig. 1). The characteristic result of that experiment is that the performance in running-times of the tested algorithms are significantly different. We can conclude that *Algorithm Randomized* is competitive and is acceptable for large databases.

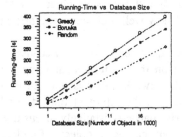 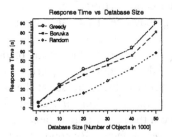

Fig. 1. Running-Time for Algorithms.   **Fig. 2.** Response Time v/s Database Size.

In this series of experiments, we varied the database initial size - [prime size before new instances were generated]. Mean response time to random read query for all algorithms is shown (in Fig. 2). Concerning the global database size, the algorithm random outperforms the other algorithm.

This probably is due to the fact that a random distribution of data over pages is the best way to guarantee balanced index trees and to avoid almost empty pages. Therefore, in a probabilistic number of cases the strategy random needs the smallest number of page transfers and its performance results for creating the initial database and for following randomly chosen paths through the database along mn-relationships are better than those for the other algorithm. We should also note that the performance of the clustering algorithm strongly depends on the internal fragmentation, which can be defined as the proportion of the space not used in a page to the page size.

This analysis is also supported by looking at the mean number of I/Os transactions, (see Fig. 3), function of the database initial size.

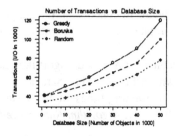

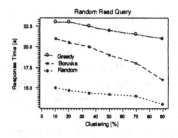

Fig. 3. Transactions v/s Database Size.   **Fig. 4.** Response Time vs Clustering Factor.

We can deduce (from Fig. 3) that the random algorithm clusters objects better than the greedy one. This also gives us an idea of how well a clustering algorithm places the objects on disk.

In (Fig. 4) we plotted the results of random read query experiments. Because of the VERSANT architecture, queries are executed on the platform containing the data and because locks are set at the object level, network traffic is reduced to a short query message from the client to the server and the return of only desired objects from the server to the client. Hence, its performance is relatively insensitive to the clustering factor. By contrast, a file/server query causes all objects of a class to be locked and passed over a network even if only one object is desired. These results are consistent with those reported in [3].

Fig. 5 displays the random update results of our tests. All objects selected for reading during the traversal are also at the same time updated. As expected, because of the VERSANT architecture, the test results confirm that object-server design is relatively insensitive to clustering factor. This can be explained by the fact that at the client level only those objects that are actually touched by the application are fetched and only the objects actually modified are written back.

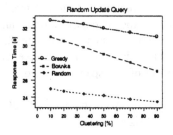

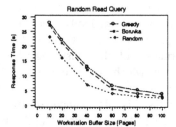

Fig. 5. Random Update Query.   **Fig. 6.** Random Read Query.

In our next set of experiments, we varied the size of the buffer pool on the workstation from 10 to 100 pages. The results are displayed (in Fig. 6).

While the performance of the greedy and random algorithms improve as the size of the buffer pool increases, the performance of the greedy algorithms levels off once the buffer pool has been increased to 60 pages. The only explanation we can offer is that at this point the cache size is no longer the limiting factor; the data referenced by the query will all fit in the buffer pool. This reduces the performance gains by the random algorithm since the effect of internal fragmentation on the disk is practically eliminated. The behavior of the greedy algorithm is conditioned by its construction heuristics - building up the solution by making the best choice locally. Therefore, because of the way in which the page size constraint is handled in those algorithms, the high gain moves may not be performed and thus the greedy algorithm may get stuck in a local minimum.

This also indicates that relatively large buffer sizes can to a certain degree compensate for the lack of effective clustering.

5 Related Work

Section 2 summarized the many benefits of using clustering to increased performance of persistent storage systems. In this section, we describe prior studies that have suggested methods for applying effective clustering.

The study most closely related to this paper was done by Bing, Cheng and Hurson [30] in the context of the Pennsylvania State University project. Tsangaris and Naughton [4] have presented a model for multi-client environments where clustering and caching is used.

It is very characteristic to note a lack of efficient control and tuning tools supporting clustering, although recent work by G. Moerkotte [31] takes significant steps in the right direction.

In research conducted by [11], [12] they proposed to exploit the knowledge about the objects' behavior for clustering decisions. The EXODUS system [32] supports clustering by means of file objects. A clustering strategy in the O_2 ODBMS built on top of WiSS [33] is a set of placement trees, which allows the Data Base Administrator to specify how the object of the class may be placed in physical storage.

This paper extends the previous work in the following ways:

- Our *clustering randomized algorithm* represents a new approach to the problem of clustering and is based on probabilistic combinatorics.
- All of our algorithms can be used to cluster objects with multiple connectivity. In applications with multiple level of connectivity among objects, this approach has improved the average access time for tightly connected objects.
- Currently applied partition-based clustering algorithms are based on Kruskal's algorithm which always runs significantly more slowly than Prim's.

However in our implementation of clustering algorithms we did achieve significant reduction in processing time of object graph.

In summary: we designed and applied a new generation of object graph partitioning algorithms whose the expected and worst-case running times are low while still yielding quality results in clustering.

6 Conclusion

Time-demanding and sophisticated clustering algorithms which depend on very specific assumption about application access patterns are able to compete with more heuristically working clustering strategies, but they will not scale their performance in the case of rapidly changing databases with dynamic applications. Extensive tests show that our algorithms are competitive and provide efficiency of access and resource utilization.

References

1. E. E. Chang, R. H. Katz, "Exploiting Inheritance and Structure Semantics for Effective Clustering and Buffering in an Object-oriented database system", in *Proceedings of the ACM SIGMOD Conference*, 1989.
2. Manolis M. Tsangaris and Jeffrey F. Naughton. Amnesia: a stochastic access model for object stores. *Unpublished Manuscript*, University of Wisconsin-Madison, August 1990.
3. D. DeWitt, S. Ghandeharizadeh, S. Schneider, D. Bricker, H. Hsiao, H. Rasmussen, "The Gamma Database Machine Project", *IEEE Transactions on Knowledge and Data Engineering, 2(1)*, March, 1990.
4. M. M. Tsangaris, J. F. Naughton, "A Stochastic Approach for Clustering in Object Bases", *ACM SIGMOD Conference, Denver, Colorado*, 1991, pp. 12-21.
5. J. R. Cheng, A. R. Hurson, "Effective Clustering of Complex Objects in Object-Oriented Databases", *ACM SIGMOD Conference, Denver, Colorado*, 1991, pp. 22-31.
6. V. Benzaken, "An Evaluation Model for Clustering Strategies in the O_2 Object-Oriented Database System", *Int. Conf. on Database Theory (ICDT)*, pp. 126-140. Springer-Verlag, 1990.
7. J. Banerjee, W. Kim, and J. F. Garza, "Clustering a DAG for CAD Databases", *IEEE Transactions on Software Engineering* 14(11) p. 1684, November 1988.
8. V. Benzaken, C. Delobel, "Dynamic Clustering Strategies in the O_2 Object-Oriented Database System", *Technical Report 34-89*, Altair, 1989.
9. E. E. Chang, R. H. Katz, "Exploiting Inheritance and Structure Semantics for Effective Clustering and Buffering in an Object-oriented database system", in *Proceedings of the ACM SIGMOD Conference*, 1989.
10. P. Drew, R. King, S. Hudson, "The Performance and Utility of the Cactis Implementation Algorithms", *Sixteenth VLDB Conference*, 1990.
11. K. Kemper, C. Gerlhof, "Clustering in Object Bases", *University of Karlsruhe, Technical Report 6/92*, June, 1992.
12. G. Moerkotte, C. Kilger, "Clustering in Object Bases", *University of Karlsruhe, Technical Report*, June, 1992.
13. J. Stamos, "Static Grouping of Small Objects to Enhance Performance of a Paged Virtual Memory", *ACM Trans. Comp. Syst.*, 2(2): 155-180, May 1984.
14. M. Carey, D. DeWitt, J. Richardson, and E. Shekita, "Object and File Management in the EXODUS Extensible Database System", *Conf. on VLDB, p. 91-100, Japan*, Aug 86.
15. Hudson, R. King, "Cactis: A self-adaptive, concurrent implementation of an Object-Oriented Database Management System", *ACM Trans. On Database Systema, 14(3)*: 291-321, Sep 1989.
16. VERSANT *System Manual, VERSANT Release 5.0*, February 1997

17. Wietrzyk, M. A. Orgun, "VERSANT Architecture: Supporting High-Performance Object Databases", *International Database Engineering & Applications Symposium,* IDEAS98, Cardiff, U.K., July 1998, (accepted to appear).

18. Melnikow, R. Tyshkevich, V. Yemelichev, V. Sarvanov, "*Lectures on Graph Theory*", *Moscow,* "Science", 1990.

19. Tyshkevich, N. Korneenko and V. Zemljachenko, "Graph Isomorphism Problems", *J. of Math, Moscow, "Science"*, 1990.

20. Kemper, G. Moerkotte, "*Physical Object Management*" in *Modern Database Systems, ACM Press,* New York, 1995, Won Kim, Editor.

21. R. Karger, "Approximating, verifying, and constructing minimum spanning forests", *Manuscript,* 1992.

22. R. Karger, "Random sampling in matroids, with applications to graph connectivityand minimum spanning trees", In Proceedings of *the 34th Annual IEEE Symposium on Foundations of Computer Science. IEEE* Computer Society Press, Los Alamitos, Calif., p. 84-93, 1993.

23. N. Klein, R. E. Tarjan, "A randomized linear-time algorithm for finding minimum spanning trees", In Proceedings of *the 26th Annual ACM Symposium on Theory of Computing. (Montreal,* Que., Canada, May 23-25). ACM, New York, p. 9-15, 1994.

24. N.Alon, J. Spencer, "*The Probabilistic Method*", Wiley, New York, 1992.

25. Komlos, "Linear verification for spanning trees", *Combinatorica 5 p.57-65,* 1985.

26. Chernoff, "A measure of the asymptotic efficiency for tests of a hypothesis based on the sum of observations", *Ann. Math. Stat. 23, p. 493-509,* 1952.

27. W. Kernighan, S. Lin, "An efficient Heuristic Procedure for Partitioning Graphs", *Bell System Technical Journal, 49(2),* pages 291-307, February 1970.

28. Erdos and A. Renyi, "*On the Evolution of Random Graphs*", Magyar Tud. Akad. Mat. Kut. Int. Kozl 5, 1960.

29. L. Anderson, A.J. Berre, M. Mallison et al, "The Hypermodel Benchmark" in Bancilhon, Thanos, Tsichritzis (Eds.): *Advances in Database Technology - EDBT'90,* LNCS 416, 1990.

30. Bing, R. Cheng, A. R. Hurson, "Effective Clustering of Complex Objects in OO Databases", in Proc. *ACM SIGMOD Conf., Denver,* CO. May 1991.

31. Moerkotte, C. Gerlhof, A. Kemper "On the Cost of Monitoring and Reorganization of Object Bases for Clustering", *SIGMOD Record, September* 1996.

32. M. Carey, D. DeWitt, "Storage Management for Objects in EXODUS", in W. Kim and F. H. Lochovsky, eds., *Object-Oriented Concepts, Databases and Applications, Addison-Wesley,* 1989.

33. T. Chou, D. Dewitt, R. Katz, A. Klug, "Design and Implementation of the Wisconsin Storage System", in *Software-Practice and Experience,* October 1985.

34. T. Keller, G. Graefe, D. Maier, "Efficient Assembly of Complex Objects", *ACM SIGMOD Conference, Denver, Colorado,* 1991.

Designing Persistence for Real-Time Distributed Object Systems*

Igor Nekrestyanov, Boris Novikov, and Ekaterina Pavlova

University of St.-Petersburg, Russia
igor@meta.math.spbu.ru, borisnov@acm.org, katya@meta.math.spbu.ru

Abstract. An implementation of persistent object store for real-time systems with strict processing time constraints is a challenging task, because many traditional database techniques, e.g. transaction management schemes, are not applicable for such systems.

This paper examines technical and business requirements for one particular class of such systems and describes an architecture based on distributed shared virtual memory. The major contributions are: use of distributed dynamic hashing to achieve load balancing and tight coupling of transaction and virtual memory management, which allows local scheduling of read-only transactions.

1 Introduction and Motivation

During past two decades the object orientation evolved from a useful programming paradigm to a widespread technology which now addresses virtually all layers of software (from operating systems to application programs), all application domains, and all phases of the system life cycle.

In particular, the requirements of non-traditional database applications (such as CAD) stimulated rapid development of object-oriented databases and appropriate models.

The need to reduce software development costs together with rapid growth of global networks brought up the ideas of interoperability and software reuse as one of the major directions of research and development. Both software interoperability and reuse involve several issues related to different layers from formal compatibility of data formats (e.g. low-level network protocols), and interfaces (e.g. OMG IDL) to very deep problems of semantic interoperability.

One of very popular approaches to facilitate interoperability is creation of open systems that can communicate with other systems over network. The majority of modern systems (e.g. operating systems and DBMSs) are designed as *open* in the above sense. However, to enable efficient software reuse it is necessary, in addition, to open some of system internal functionality.

One of widely accepted ways to interoperability is through OMG CORBA architecture [10]. In this architecture, the system functionality, available via

---

* This work was partially supported by Russian Foundation for Basic Research under grant 98-01-00436, and UrbanSoft Ltd. under contract 35/98.

Object Request Broker (ORB), is split into several object services and common facilities, so that application may use these components as needed.

Ideally, the services should be mutually orthogonal. However, the notion of orthogonality is not precisely defined and therefore may be viewed only as a desirable but not reachable in practice. Some services, even specified as completely independent, inevitably have strong implementation dependencies. In particular, several services related to different aspects of persistence are closely related. Further, different implementations are required for various applications so that domain-specific requirements can be satisfied.

In this paper we describe an approach to implementation of the persistence and related services which can be combined into a consistent OMA-compliant architecture, providing efficient support for heterogeneous persistent real-time object environments.

Each of the desired properties is addressed by existing approaches and even commercial systems, but neither of these currently addresses the whole set of requirements:

- Distributed object environments provide for scalable, reliable, and cost-efficient computations, but, in general, do not address neither persistence nor real-time.
- Open architectures such as OMG OMA/CORBA provide basic interoperability in heterogeneous systems, but the problems of persistence and real-time become much harder than for homogeneous distributed systems.
- Persistent object environments do not address real-time constraints.
- Object-oriented DBMSs cannot efficiently support heterogeneous environments with mixed applications (e.g. transactional and non-transactional).
- Research on real-time database systems is restricted to transaction management in the presence of deadlines and do not address complex objects and queries, which may cause unpredictable response times.
- Virtual main memory databases are useful for implementation of persistence for real-time distributed object environments, but many of traditional databases techniques should be revised for this kind of database systems.

The requirements of real-time, especially performance requirements, are extremely hard to meet. We are interested in application domains were critical parts of distributed system should exhibit very high performance: most of transactions should be completed in tens of milliseconds after arrival of a transaction.

This level of performance cannot be achieved within current OMG CORBA architecture, because the best ORB implementations implementations consume at least few milliseconds per request. The standard OMG services require several requests to be issued when transaction starts or commits, locks are acquired or released, and even persistent data are accessed.

To bypass these problems, a hybrid architecture should be used, with special (streamlined) processing of requests which can be performed entirely in the time-critical part of the system.

Fortunately, due to special features of the application domain, it is possible to rely on assumptions which make the solution feasible. The most important assumption is that all time-critical transactions in the system are read-only, and a special kind of transaction scheduling can be used to meet performance requirements.

Although this assumption looks overrestrictive, it holds for applications related to embedded real-time systems with soft deadlines, e.g. telephone switches.

The paper is organized as follows.

Next section lists the requirements for the system, then the basic architecture of the proposed implementation is described and motivated. Further, use of shared virtual memory in the system, concurrency control, and the prototype implementation are described. A brief review of related work is followed by conclusions.

2 Requirements and System Architecture

2.1 Requirements and Assumptions

In this section we identify the special requirements of real-time applications to persistence and issues to be resolved.

Typical real-time requirements include:

- extremely high reliability
- transactions have firm deadlines with tight time limits
- the system is essentially distributed, and each transaction may involve more than one site.

However, applications we have in mind have special features which allows to reduce drammatically the number of remote object requests, streamlining the implementation of persistence-related services.

In this paper it is assumed that the following properties of the target application domain are valid:

- most of transactions are very short
- most of transactions are read-only, end almost all time-critical transactions are read-only ones
- the database may reside entirely in the main memory
- significant portion of data is write-protected for almost all transactions
- the size of individual data objects is relatively small
- the memory is partitioned into pages, so that objects cannot cross page boundaries.

Actually, the target system should process two different types of requests.

The major part of requests (regular service requests), should be processed with very tight time constraints. Typically, these requests should be processed in less than 100 milliseconds. Usually requests of this type come from hardware (a kind of interruptions), and almost all of them require only read access to persistently stored data (however, they need to see consistent state, so transactions are still necessary).

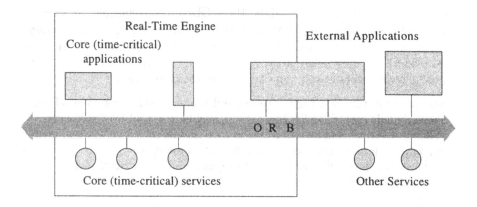

Fig. 1. The Basic Architecture

External requests without too strict time constraints. The of requests of this type normally come "from the network", that is, are issued from heterogeneous environment including different hardware architectures, operating systems, and language environments.

2.2 The Environment

Basically, the system consists of a *core engine* which processes all kinds of requests, and a set of *applications* which generate these requests (see Figure 1).

The external requests (including maintenance, statistics, analysis and other applications without strict real-time requirements) are issued from distributed heterogeneous environment via CORBA interfaces (this is a business requirement, rather than a designers' choice).

All time-critical requests come from hardware tightly connected with core engine, which is itself distributed (for scalability and reliability reasons).

The core stores significant amount of data permanently and thus may be considered as a database with usual requirements, such as consistency, data independence, etc.

In other words, the core engine may be considered as a real-time object-oriented DBMS with CORBA-compliant interfaces. It also contains significant amount of the application code for time-critical applications which also access data via CORBA type of interfaces.

However, as explained above, it is not possible to meet performance requirements within current CORBA implementations.

2.3 Performance Shortcuts

The architecture of the core engine follows the structure defined in CORBA, but the implementation relies on several *shortcuts* which provide fast inter-service interactions.

In order to tight time constraints, the OODB is implemented as a main memory database. The core engine is distributed, therefore, our main memory is actually a distributed shared virtual memory. Each process, however, runs in separate address space (which virtually includes the shared memory).

The following types of shortcuts are used in the core engine:

- Services may run as a single process and therefore share common address space. In this case, CORBA invocations may be replaced by direct calls.
- When both client and service reside in core engine, the shared virtual memory may be used to pass bulk amounts of data directly.
- Services may internally benefit from presence of shared virtual memory.

2.4 Objects

While the complete engine includes (relatively) high-level features and supports strongly-typed objects, only low-level storage aspects of the engine are considered in this study.

All objects in the core engine may keep (some portion of) their state in persistent memory area. In this project, we do not rely on a popular concept of *transparency of persistence* because it implies certain performance penalties, and actually significant percentage of all objects do not need it.

Instead, the (part of the) state of object which should persist is explicitly mapped to persistent memory area (implemented as shared virtual memory).

When an object needs to access it's persistent state, the appropriate portion of shared virtual memory is mapped to *the same address of* the process address space, so no pointer translation is needed. Thus the mapping of object state to persistent store does not imply performance penalties. However, this mapping is very important conceptually because it is a *forget* operator—it maps typed data objects representing persistent state to untyped *generic data objects*. The type information is stored as an attribute of generic object.

This dynamically typed (or untyped) objects layer was identified previously in other persistent object systems, e.g. Tycoon Storage Protocol [7] operates with a data structure very similar to generic data objects used here. The objects considered in [1] also possess dynamic type information and can be therefore viewed as untyped.

From this perspective, the CORBA persistence service may be described as a composition of mappings:

1. The application persistent object's (PO) transient state is mapped to a persistent state referred to by PID and represented with Data Objects.
2. Data Objects are mapped to untyped Generic Data Objects which may be handled directly in datastore.
3. The (transient) references to generic data objects are mapped to (persistent) locations in datastore.

Last mapping (usually called swizzling) was extensively studied in the literature and several options were evaluated and compared. We are considering this issue later in connection with the datastore structure 3.2.

3 Shared Virtual Memories

Significant performance gains (with respect to general purpose persistence as specified by OMG) can be obtained if the application persistent object is running on the site that can access the datastore memory. In this case the datastore memory may be shared between several clients.

Once the datastore memory is made accessible to client address space, the data can be accessed locally, either directly or via an advanced object request broker which can utilize this potential benefit.

The pre-requisite for this type of interaction is that datastore should run at the same site as application persistent object (PO). We cannot control the selection of the site for PO, hence it is necessary to relocate persistent store to gain from the potential benefits of co-location.

The straightforward solution, suggested in [1], is based on a concept of distributed shared virtual memory (DSVM). Although this solution is applicable only for homogeneous environments, which is not limiting restriction for time-critical applications.

The basic idea of the DSVM is to utilize huge virtual address space (64-bit addressable) and map it to address spaces of all sites that share this virtual memory. Some portion of the address space, should be, of course, reserved for private use of each particular site, but the size of address space provides a possibility to make this private part negligible.

With this type of environment, we may replicate data (on the virtual memory page level), so that each client can access it's persistent state locally, with additional advantages:

- The memory mapping is fixed, consequently addresses may be used as pointers, no swizzling is necessary.
- The conversions made by Type layer may be significantly simplified.

However, an attempt to implement this structure directly would face certain problems.

The first problem to mention is related to placement of persistent data in the virtual memory. If the object identifiers (represented as virtual addresses) are selected randomly, the address space will be extremely sparse, which cannot be efficient for any implementation of virtual memory. Other strategies may cause problems with load balancing. Under any allocation policy it is difficult to preserve load balancing.

Another problem is related to updates. If stored objects are claimed to be immutable (as in [1]), an additional directory is unavoidable on top of the described one (to manage references to objects representing the latest state of mutable objects), which results in extra indirection and hence performance penalties. Alternatively, if objects are relocatable, some expensive mechanizms (such as garbage collection) are un-avoidable.

Both problems mentioned above are the problems of location and identity. Next section explains how these problems can be addressed.

3.1 Object Identity and Location

The root cause of the problems listed above is that the functions of identity (provided by object identifier) and locality are often mutually exclusive. The identity should be immutable, while any dynamic environment will degrade if objects cannot be relocated for some reason.

The problem can be completely solved by additional indirection (with well-known disadvantages). To avoid extra indirection, this project relies on dynamic hashing. We are concerned with persistent object states, so the identifier in this section refers to identifier of a persistent object state in a datastore (to avoid mismatch with CORBA object reference).

The proposed structure is actually a combination of distributed shared virtual memory [1] and distributed dynamic hashing proposed in [6].

3.2 Distributed Hashing for DSVM

The shared virtual memory is segmented into pages of reasonable size. Actual locations are calculated from the values of identity using perfect hash function which yields the address of distributed shared virtual memory page where the corresponding persistent state is currently located. A small table in the header of each page is used to finally resolve the reference.

Modern hash schemes can avoid collisions, so there is no need in any overflow chains. Moreover, most of hashing schemes are dynamic, so the data will not be scattered over the whole address space. Instead, it will occupy reasonable amount of memory pages with controlled density.

An additional advantage is that the Identity space is not limited with address space size of the computer. The only requirement is that existing data should fit into available virtual memory address space.

The speed of modern connections is significantly greater than mechanical speed of disk storage. Therefore, it is reasonable to use main memory instead of disks to hold the pages. The amount of main memory in a distributed system should anyway sufficient to keep all data in the main memory.

So, instead of disk address, the hash function is used to calculate the address of a site which holds a primary copy of this page [6].

When the page is cached, the calculated pointer values may be re-used if refer to a page cached into the same address space, providing extremely fast access to persistent data.

In terms of address space, we assume that the virtually addressable space is huge, and distinguish the following ranges:

- private space of a process
- a range for cached pages of shared memory
- a space for pages hosted in this site.

Thus, the range to which a particular address belongs allows always easily decide if this address requires recalculation.

For the reasons of reliability, each page should be kept at more than one site. The modification of the hashing algorithm is also proposed in [6].

3.3 Concurrency Control for Shared Memories

The objective of any system that depends on persistent data is to preserve data consistency while providing best performance (e.g. maximal throughput or minimal response rime). The common way to improve performance, especially in distributed systems, is to increase degree of parallelism. This increase, however, is limited with requirement to preserve consistency, and concurrency control limits degree of parallelism in order to preserve consistency.

For this reason, we consider consistency as a primary objective, and the concurrency control as a tool which may be used to achieve it.

The Protocol. The concurrency control is a hard problem due to unacceptable processing overheads (e.g. locking of a single data element may require several remote procedure calls, each of which may consume few milliseconds.

On the other hand, the probability of conflicts is extremely low. For this reason, a concurrency control algorithm with low overhead is needed. Optimistic concurrency control protocol which can meet these requirements is briefly described here. More detailed discussion is available at [9].

The main idea of our protocol is to use virtual memory management to trace access to persistent data and to detect the inter-transaction conflicts.

To keep overhead minimal, we choose page-level granularity of access control. The objects are expected to be very small, hence object-level control would result in increased amount of processing necessary to keep track of accesses. This decision might lead to decrease of concurrency, but this is not for read-only transactions, which are our major concern.

The Model. In addition to system features that were outlined above we need few additional assumptions.

We assume that each transaction runs within a process and each process has it's own virtual 64-bit address space. Each address space have own page table and there is a common global page table.

The transaction manager can influence the page replacement policy of virtual memory manager through call-back functions. Finally, hardware can trap both read and write (to protected) page faults.

Data Structures. We assume that the transaction manager has access to page tables of all address spaces that are in use on the same processor. The transaction manager may either use separate process or may be invoked from regular application process (e.g. via exception handler), and in any case it can also access global page table.

The transaction manager maintains a transaction counter, which should be globally unique. This counter may be also used to define serialization order.

In this protocol, we use multiple versions of pages and allow read-only transactions to access previous states of updated pages.

To implement this feature the transaction manager should maintain additional data structures to keep track of existing versions for each (recently) updated page, and this data should be consistent for all transaction managers.

Each version of a page has associated version number, which is equal to global part of the transaction identifier (which is increased when writing transaction appears).

During the initialization of a transaction an interval of admissible version numbers for this transaction is calculated.

Transaction Identifiers. When the transaction manager registers new transaction, a globally unique transaction identifier is created.

Each transaction manager maintains local transaction counter, and the global counter is used only for writing transactions.

The transaction identifier should contain the value of global counter (advanced when a writing transaction commits), transaction manager identifier, and local sequential number (relative to the global number).

The advantage of this implementation is that the identifiers for most frequent read-only transactions can be assigned locally on each processor without any synchronization with other transaction managers.

Operations. To present the protocol, we further describe actions performed by transaction manager on certain events.

Read Operation: When a transaction attempts to read data from a page of shared persistent memory, the transaction manager looks for the page address in the global page table. If the page is found there, this page has only one version, which is made accessible to the requester.

Otherwise the transaction manager looks for appropriate version of a page in the list of versioned pages and selects a version which is suitable for the requesting transaction (the selection is based on the transaction identifier and the version number associated with each version of a page).

Write Operation: When a transaction attempts to update the data in shared persistent memory, an exception occurs, because initially each page is available in (at most) read-only mode.

If transaction attempts to write to the latest (or the only) version of a page then exception handler then creates a private copy of the page to be accessed and appropriately updates the local page table. This copy may or may not be allocated on the persistent memory. Otherwise the transaction is aborted.

In addition, the transaction is registered as writing transaction and the manager makes housekeeping records to be able to handle the private (shadow) copy properly when the transaction terminates.

Abort: In case of abort of the read-only transaction the information about this transaction is discarded. When writing transaction aborts all updated pages (that is, private copies) are simply discarded.

Commit: The read-only transaction can commit regardless of any other circumstances, because proper versions of each page it accessed were provided at the first access.

The validation of the writing transaction includes check of all updated pages. If for some pages which were updated by the transaction in question more recent versions exist the transaction should be aborted, otherwise it commits.

Rollback: In case of abort of the read-only transaction the information about this transaction is discarded. When writing transaction aborts (e.g. for it's internal reasons), all updated pages (that is, private copies) are simply discarded and all information about this transaction may be erased.

Correctness. The correctness of this protocol is obvious because every committed read-only transaction work with same state of database which was at the time of its start.

3.4 The Performance Model

Proposed concurrency control algorithm has little overhead, but may potentially result in high rate of transaction aborts (typical for all optimistic algorithms). To estimate the probabilities of successful transaction commits, a simple model was used.

For the case of read-only transaction the estimation is trivial, because they always commit, and $P_{read-only} = 1$. For updating transactions the model depends on the following parameters:

N — total number of data elements,

n — average number of data elements used by single update transaction,

l — average length of transaction,

k — average number of transactions per second.

Then the probability of successful commit is estimated as

$$P_{update} = \frac{1}{1 + (k * l - 1) * P}$$

where $P = \min(k * l * (1 - \frac{((N-n)!)^2}{(N-2n)! * N!}), 1)$.

Estimations obtained from this model show that the abort rate is very small, which is not surprising under our assumptions.

4 Implementation Environment and Prototype

The prototype was developed on a network consisting of SunSPARC 5 workstation and two Intel CPU-based computers running under Solaris 2.5, Windows NT 4.0 and Windows 95, respectively.

The development of a prototype was based on ILU - the Xerox Research implementation of [10], which implements (a subset of) CORBA 2.0.

To estimate potential performance gains, sometimes direct interaction of the objects that share common address space is used in the prototype, instead of regular ORB requests, when the placement of the objects in the same address space is reasonable.

The complete implementation of the datastore structure requires significant support from the operating system. The prototype only models some of the critical features. The implementation is based on Unix concept of mapped memory (mmap system call). This function effectively provides for persistence of main memory segments.

The limitation is that the addresses cannot be preserved in this approach, so this part of the engine is not modelled in the prototype.

The prototype includes persistence and transaction services, a virtual memory datastore implementation on UNIX system, and example clients.

The prototype exhibits expected performance and demonstrates feasibility of the reliable and efficient datastore implementation based on the concept of distributed shared virtual memory.

5 Related Work

Distributed object systems over virtual memory are described and implemented in several papers and projects, e.g. [4, 11, 12, 2]. however, neither load balancing nor object (de)clustering is considered in these projects.

Distributed persistent object directory based on shared virtual memory is described in [5, 8, 1], but the architecture proposed there does not take into account performance issues.

Distributed dynamic hashing schemes were described in series of papers, e.g. [6]. The structures described there are designed for performance and reliability, but applications to object systems are out of the scope of these papers.

Typeless representations for persistent objects in distributed heterogeneous systems are defined in [7]. This work does not consider neither real-time requirements nor performance issues.

Concurrency control protocols for real-time databases were studied in [3, 13, 14]. However, this work is mostly related to protocol enhancements that make response time predictable, and does not consider actual implementation.

6 Conclusions

The paper describes potential implementation of persistent object store for real-time systems with very tight time constraints. The implementation is based on distributed shared virtual memory combined with distributed dynamic hashing.

The major contributions of the approach are:

- The coupling of concurrency control with virtual memory management provides very efficient processing of time-critical transactions. Read-only transactions may be scheduled locally (without any remote calls).

- Use of dynamic hashing for object placement results in increased flexibility and load balancing.

The feasibility of this design was demonstrated on a prototype, but actual performance characteristics still need further investigation.

References

1. K. Barker, R. Peters, and P. Graham. Distributed Shared Memory for Interoperability of Heterogeneous Information Systems—*Position Statement*. In *OOPSLA Workshop on Interoperable Objects—Experiences and Issues*, Oct. 1995.
2. D. Hulse and A. Dearle. A Log Structured Persistent Store. In *Proceedings of the 19th Australasian Computer Science Conference*, pages 563–572, Jan. 1996.
3. L. Juhnyoung and H. S. Sang. *Performance of Concurrency Control Mechanisms in Centralized Database Systems*. Prentice-Hall, 1996.
4. E. Koldinger, J. Chase, and S. Eggers. Architectural Support for Single Address Space Operating Systems. In *Proceedings of the 5th International Conference on Architectural Support for Programming Languages and Operating Systems - ASPLOS*, Oct. 1992.
5. A. Lindstrom, A. Dearle, R. di Bona, A. Norris, J. Rosenberg, and F. Vaughan. Persistence in the grasshopper kernel. In *Proceedings of the 18th Australasian Computer Science Conference*, pages 329–338, Feb. 1995.
6. W. Litwin, M.-A. Neimat, and D. Schneider. RP*: A Family of Order Preserving Scalable Distributed Data Structures. In *Proceedings of the Twentieth International Conference on Very Large Databases*, pages 342–353, Santiago, Chile, 1994.
7. F. Matthes, R. Mueller, and J. W. Schmidt. Towards a unified model of untyped object stores: Experience with the tycoon store protocol. In *Proc. of the Third Intnl. Workshop on Advances in Databases and Information Systems - ADBIS'96*, pages 1–9, Moscow, Sept. 10–13 1996. MEPhI.
8. H. Moons and P. Verbaeten. Persistence in Open Distributed Systems: The COMET Approach. In *Proceedings of the Euromicro Workshop on Parallel and Distributed Processing*, pages 342–349, Jan. 1994.
9. I. Nekrestyanov, B. Novikov, E. Pavlova, and S. Pikalev. Concurrency Control Protocols for Persistent Shared Virtual Memory Systems. In *Proc. of the Workshop on Advances in Databases and Information Systems - ADBIS'97*, pages 035–039, St.-Petersburg, September 2–5 1997. Nevsky Dialect.
10. Object Management Group and X/Open. *The Common Object Request Broker: Architecture and Specification, Revision 1.1, OMG Document Number 91.12.1*. OMG, 1992.
11. R. Schmidt, J. Chase, and H. Levy. Using Shared Memory for Read-Mostly RPC Services. In *Proceedings of the 29th Hawaii International Conference on System Sciences*, Jan. 1996.
12. M. Shapiro and P. Ferreira. Larchant-RDOSS: a Distributed Shared Persistent Memory and its Garbage Collector. In *Proceedings of the 9th International Workshop on Distributed Algorithms*, Sept. 1995.
13. O. Ulusoy. Analysis of concurrency control protocols for real-time database systems. Technical Report BU-CEIS-9514, Bilkent University, 1995.
14. O. Ulusoy and G. Belford. A performance evaluation model for distributed real-time database systems. *International Journal of Modeling and Simulation*, 15(2), 1995.

Partial Replication of Object-Oriented Databases

Michael Dobrovnik and Johann Eder

Institut für Informatik-Systeme, Universität Klagenfurt
Universitätsstr. 65, A-9020 Klagenfurt, Austria
{michi,eder}@ifi.uni-klu.ac.at

Abstract. Partial replication is a well established technique for relational databases. The creation of partial replica of object-oriented databases is more complex due to the richer type schema and object references. We present a procedure for deriving schemas for partial replica of object-oriented databases which are minimal and self-contained and discuss the isomorphic mapping of objects from the original database to the replicated database.

1 Introduction

Partial replication of databases is a well known technique for relational databases [9]. Replication means to copy parts of a schema of a datadase and parts of the database instances to build a second database. Major application areas of replication are distributed databases and on-line analytical processing [8]. In distributed databases replication can significantly lower network traffic and increase availability of databases. In data warehouse and OLAP applications the database for analytical queries is separated from the database for on-line transaction processes. This allows the tuning of the two databases for the different transaction loads, reduces interferences between short update transactions and long read transactions, and enables load partitioning [12].

While replication is quite well understood for relational databases and research activities are mainly concerned with replica maintenance, building replica of object oriented databases is much more complex. This is due to two facts: First the type system of object-oriented databases is much richer than that of relational databases. In particular, type inheritance, methods, and late binding make the creation of correct partial schemas a complex task. Second, while instances of relational databases consist merely of values (of base types), instances of object-oriented databases also consist of references to other instances which are stored in form of object identifiers. Object identifiers are system controlled keys whose properties are strictly local, i.e. the properties hold only within the database. For replication not only the values have to be transfered but also an isomorphic mapping between the objects of the database and those of the replica has to be established.

In this paper we concentrate on the creation of a correct schema for the replicated database. The process starts from a view definition where the designer of the replica states all types and their components (attributes and methods) which should be included in the schema of the replica. We then compute a minimal schema which is self contained, i.e. which does not refer to types which are not included in the schema. It is our goal to provide a minimal schema in the sense that only types and components are included which are necessary.

The paper ist structured as follows. In the next section we discuss our data model and the specification of the replica in terms of types and instances. Then the meta schema used to hold the schema information needed to perform the generation of the replica schema is presented. In section 4, the mechanism for instance export and import is sketched. Section 5 discusses the five steps of the generation of the replica schema from the initial specification. Finally, we draw some conclusions and outline areas for further research.

2 Data Model and View Specification

In this section we will first present a sketch of our data model which can essentially be regarded as a subset of the ODMG proposal [2]. For a more detailed discussion we refer to [3–6]. Then the constructs for the view specification mechanism are discussed.

2.1 Basic Data Model

We distinguish between extensional and intensional concepts, so a schema in our data model consists of a set of types and a set of containers. The types describe the structural and behavioral aspects of the objects and values.

Some atomic value types (like boolean integer, string) are provided together with an atomic root object type. The type constructors *set* and *tuple* can be orthogonally applied to types to build set valued and tuple valued structured value types. For reasons of brevity and clarity, we will not elaborate on tuple types in the sequel.

Object types (also commonly referred to as classes) can be declared through the use of the object type constructor *object*. They are positioned in an inheritance lattice which supports conventional structural top down multiple inheritance semantics. By demanding an unambiguous origin of object type attributes and methods we circumvent conflicts from the multiple inheritance.

The definition of a subtype can make use of covariant redefinition of attributes and method signatures. The subtype relation also defines type substitutability and assignment compatibility, namely wherever an instance of a type can be used, it is also allowed to use an instance of one of its subtypes.

At the extensional level, we provide containers, which can be described as typed object sets. An instance of an object type can be added to any type compatible container and can also be removed from it. The containers are user defined object sets which also provide persistence. An object persists the current session when it is in at least one object container or when it is referenced by another persistent object (*persistence by reachability*). Currently, there is no hierarchy defined between the containers. The object types are the factories and the containers are the warehouses of the object instances.

We assume the existence of a Turing complete procedural language for the implementation of the methods and also of a declarative query language. All object types have to be *well formed*, a property which restricts overriding to the covariant case and forbids conflicts by multiple inheritance.

If all object type definitions in a schema are well formed, then the schema obeys the covariant subtyping principle. As usual, the object generating method new is treated differently, since it can already be bound at compile time.

2.2 Initial Replica Specification

A partial replica is specified on the basis of a well formed schema of the source database. We have to specify the types and containers the replica will consist of.
*Type Specification:*For each type of the source schema, at most one corresponding type in the replica can be specified and we can also include entirely new types in the replica. Types of the source schema can be incorporated in the replica in a completely unmodified manner, or we can make combined use use of type extension and type projection to restructure the type in the replica.

Type *extension* allows us to use a type of the source schema and to define new methods and attributes for the type in the replica. The newly defined type components must not interfere with the rest of the source schema. In particular, conflicts between additional attributes and methods and attributes and methods of subtypes in the source schema must be avoided. The new methods are included in the replica and must be compilable and executable just in this context and not in the source schema.

Attributes added through type extension may get a default value. This value is computed by means of a query expression. The query is formulated in terms of the source schema since it will be executed there. This mechanism particularly facilitates aggregation operations and the caching of complex navigation paths or method results in the replica.

Type *projection* is expressed by selecting a subset of the attributes and methods of an object type. By specifying a projection, we do not exclude the other elements of the object type but specify which of the attributes and methods are to be included in the replica, whether they are used or not by other schema elements. The projections are just an initial subset of the type structure which may be expanded later on by a schema completion phase.
Containers and Object Sets: In our data model, the containers are the entry points for queries and provide persistence like relations do in a relational DBMS. In the original database (source), each object is (directly or indirectly) reachable from a container, and a query can be used to retrieve it. We also use the notion of containers in the replica to provide for persistence and to serve as initial variables for queries. Containers in the source database are specified by their instance type and by a unique name. The set of instances is neither implicitly specified nor automatically maintained by the system. The set of objects of a

container must be build by the application by explicitly adding and removing the desired instances.

In the replica, containers can have attached an additional *initial query expression*. This query is used during the replica generation to construct the instance set of the corresponding container in the replica. The query is somewhat special, since it is used to fill a container in the replica, but it is specified within the scope and in the terms (types, containers) of the source schema. The initial query specifications are neither part of the source schema nor of the replica schema, they are somewhere in the middle of the two worlds. They are executed exactly once, namely at the point when a replica is generated; a user of the replica has no means to start those queries, she is not even aware of their existence.

During the replica generation process, which is described in greater detail in section 4, all initial query expressions are executed (one after the other) against the source database. The query results are then subject to the object export and import mechanism described in the next section. The results of this process are replica objects which are also added to the instance set of the container of the replica corresponding to the initial query expression. Thereby they gain persistence, become part of the replica and can be returned by appropriate queries against the replica container.

3 Meta Schema

The information needed for schema completion is stored and maintained in a database. The schema of this database (the meta-schema of the source database) is depicted in OMT notation in figure 1. For reasons of brevity we omit some minor details and concentrate on the central aspects. To facilitate navigation in the schema we make extensive use of qualifiers [10].

A schema is characterized through a name. As a shortcut, all methods and all attributes of object types in the schema can be accessed by means of the methods Attribs and Methods. The usages of attributes and methods can be computed by methods AUsages and MUsages in a similar manner. All types in the schema can be reached via the path schema.Types. Each type has an attribute in_view which is used to mark it if the type is included in the replica.

Types can be predefined types, set types or object types. Predecessors and successors of an object type along the inheritance hierarchy can be computed through the methods super* and sub*. Components of object types are represented by the classes Attribute and Method. In the following we will first focus on the representation of attributes. Each attribute has a name and a domain characterized by its Type. The relationship between attributes and object types is represented by a special class AUsage. An object of this class connects one attribute to an object type where it is defined. If an attribute is inherited from a supertype (and not redefined), then the attribute is used in both the supertype and the subtype. We do not just include the information about the attributes which are directly defined in an object type but also include all inherited components as well. The type of the direct definition of the attribute is denoted by

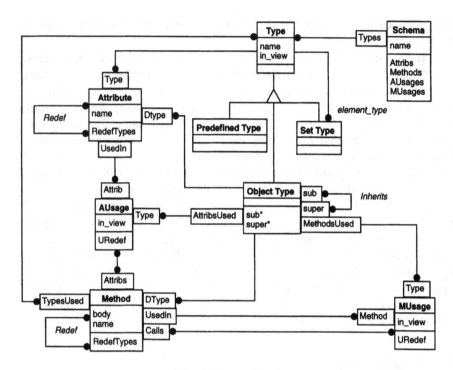

Fig. 1. Meta schema

Dtype. This specific representation is advantageous for the schema completion process as we will see later on. The field in_view of **AUsage** is again used to indicate if the attribute is used for this type in the replica. The relationship **Redef** connects attributes with their redefinitions. The Method **RedefTypes** returns all subtypes where the attribute is redefined and is just a convenient shorthand for a corresponding query. Another shorthand is method **URedef** in **AUsage**. It returns all attribute usages below the object type of the current usage where the used attribute is redefined.

The representation of methods for object types has a name and a method body. The types which are directly used in the method body or signature are reachable via **TypesUsed**. Method redefinitions and usage of redefined methods manifest themselves like it was the case for attributes. Attribute **Dtype** connects the method to the type where it is directly defined.

The usage of schema elements by methods has three aspects, namely types needed, method called and attributes used. Types used in a method body are connected to the method via **TypesUsed**. Those types can occur in the signature of the method or can be used for the definition of local variables. Methods used (called) by a method are reachable via **Calls**. The usage of a method does not only take into account the method name but also the most specific type of the object the method is applied to. Usage of attributes of other objects via navigation are expressed by the relation between **Method** and **AUsage** via **Attribs**. Usages of the special types **self** and **super** must be treated specially. The generic references are resolved during schema completion and are substituted by the appropriate object type. For a concise presentation we will not discuss this issue further.

We assume that this information is readily available through syntactic analysis of the structure of the source schema and the method bodies. Navigation paths are splited into atomic navigations (attribute selection, method call) and considered step for step. The specific information in the meta-schema allows us to determine the minimal subset of attributes of an object type that is needed by the methods in the schema. With this information we can then construct the appropriate projection of the source type for the replica type.

4 Extensional Aspects of Replica Generation

In the previous sections we were mainly concerned about the intensional aspects of the replica, namely the structure of the schema. In this section we will deal with the generation of the objects in the replica in a way which is consistent with the original database.

Queries in OODBs are commonly classified into object preserving queries, object generating queries and value returning queries. As the replica and the source database operate independently and have no common object space, all initial query expressions return new replica objects or values. Strictly speaking, the initial queries are object generating.

But we cannot simply generate a new replica object every time a object of the source database is to be referenced and included in the replica database. Since an object can be referred to many times by other objects and also included in many different containers, a significant increase in database size could occur by such a strategy. But whereas this reason is relevant, it is a rather subordinate problem to the issue of *identity preservation*. It must be possible to export identical objects from the source database and to import them as as identical objects to the replica. More exactly, references to identical objects in the source database must also result in references to identical objects in the replica.

While there are no object preserving queries, identity preserving object generating queries are needed. There must be a mapping from the objects in the source database to objects in the replica and vice versa. In the case of a replica which is never updated against the source database this mapping is only needed during the export/import phase itself. For the operation, the mapping is no longer relevant. While we do not consider object aggregations and replica updates for the time being, an identity preserving object export/import mechanism which provides a persistent mapping between source objects and replicated ones may be quite beneficial for those problems.

The replication mechanism has to deal with three object spaces. There are the object space of the source database and the object space of the target replica. The third object space is valid only in the replication generation subsystem. This system consists of an exporter and an importer. The exporter gets an object from the source database. The state of the object is extracted and (re)constructed in terms of the type system of the new database. The identity of the object is mapped into an replication alias. This alias should have all the properties of an object identifier, since it serves as an identification for the replicated object during the replica generation process. The exporter maintains a mapping between the source object identities and the replication aliases.

The importer gets the state of the object to be constructed, along with the appropriate type information and the objects replication alias. It constructs a replica based on this data and maintains a mapping between the replication alias and the identity of the replica object.

Whenever a source object being exported refers to another source object via its attributes (object aggregation), and the attribute should also be exported to the replica, the identity of the referenced object must also be preserved across the system boundaries. This object may already have been transferred to the replica or it may be the first time that a reference to this particular object is encountered in the replication process. If it has already been transferred to the replica database, both the exporter and the importer have the appropriate mapping information between source object identity, replication alias and replica identity. In this case, the exporter just sends the replication alias as the state for the referenced object to the importer, which transforms it into a reference to the replica object already generated. If the reference to the (sub)object was the first one within the replication process, the exporter generates a new replication alias for the object and sends this information along to the importer. The importer recognizes that the alias is a new one and constructs a preliminary replication object. This object has the appropriate type and a unique replication identity, but its state is uninitialized. Further references to the object originating in the source database will result in references to this preliminary replication object.

The exporter maintains a set of references to such objects which have been given a replication alias but have not been transferred to the importer. All those objects will be subject to transfer later on. This continues until there are no unresolved references left in the replica. When the importer receives the state for a preliminary replication object, it updates the state of this preliminary object with the received state. Thereby the preliminary replication objects becomes a fully functional replication object.

As already said the mappings between the identity spaces are primarily needed for replica generation and therefore can be of transient nature. But if the longer term operation of the replica is considered, updates will come into play. This requires that the mapping from a previous generation or update operation is still available later on. Persistence of the mapping can be achieved by storing the mapping between source object identities and replication aliases in the source database and preserving the mapping between replication aliases and replication identities in the replica database. Together with some meta data (source and target of replication, replication timestamp, ...) this mappings provide all necessary information to trace a replication object back to its origin and vice versa. Object deletion in the source database requires special treatment.

5 Replica Schema Generation

The starting point for the generation of the replica schema is a meta-schema as discussed in section 3. This schema has been filled with the appropriate information according to the schema structure of the source database. Then the designer of the replica defined the intended view on the source schema as an initial replica schema by means of type projection and extension (cf. section 2.2).

The schema generation takes 5 phases. In the first step, the schema is completed in the sense that necessary schema elements that where not explicitly included in the replica specification are included in the schema. Then, the schema is compressed by removing redundant indications of method and attribute usage. The third step generates the new inheritance relationships for the replica schema, while the fourth step is concerned with conflict resolution for multiple inheritance and the last step generates the replica schema and also specific information needed by the export import subsystem.

5.1 Schema Completion

The replica will operate fully autonomous from the source database. It cannot refer back to the source database and use schema elements or instances during its operation. Therefore, we strive for a closed replica schema in which all needed elements from the orginal schema are incorporated.

Approaches to schema completion in the context of object oriented views can be found in [3, 7, 11, 13]. All those proposals have a different goal than we have here. While they are also concerned with the definition of an external schema (view, subschema) of the source database, all of them assume that the source database and the external view do not operate autonomous from each other. Some propose even an integrated schema for the source database and the view schema. The approach in [1] can be used to determine the applicability of methods under type projection. It could be also used to some extend in the context of replicas as a support mechanism for the replica designer, who could see the consequences of a projection operation. The basis for this step in the schema generation process is a meta schema in which the replica designer selected the schema elements that are to be included in the replica. This is simply done my marking the types as well as the usage of attributes and methods through setting the in_view attribute of the corresponding object in the meta schema. The algorithm sketched in figure 2 does the schema completion. It computes new needed schema elements on the basis of the schema elements needed so far by means of a delta iteration.

The starting point are the set of types T_n, the set of attribute usages A_n, and the set of method usages M_n that were marked to be included in the replica schema. It is important to note that we do not deal with attributes and methods themselves, but with their *usages*. The sets T, A and M are used to store the schema elements already processed.

The main while-loop of the algorithm terminates when there were no more new elements computed in the last iteration.

```
method complete() in schema;
var T, Tₙ : set(Type);
var A, Aₙ : set(AUsage);
var M, Mₙ : set(MUsage);
begin
    T := {};  A := {};  M := {};
    Tₙ := {t ∈ self.Types | t.in_view = true};
    Aₙ := {a ∈ self.AUsages | a.in_view = true};
    Mₙ := {m ∈ self.MUsages | m.in_view = true};
    while Tₙ ≠ {} ∨ Aₙ ≠ {} ∨ Mₙ ≠ {} do
        T := T ∪ Tₙ;  A := A ∪ Aₙ;  M := M ∪ Mₙ;
        Tₙ := {a.Attrib.Type | a ∈ Aₙ} ∪ₘ∈ₘₙ m.Method.TypesUsed
            ∪ₐ∈ₐₙ a.Attrib.RedefTypes ∩ a.Type.sub*
            ∪ₘ∈ₘₙ m.Method.RedefTypes ∩ m.Type.sub* \ T;
        foreach t ∈ Tₙ do t.in_view := true; end
        Aₙ := ∪ₘ∈ₘₙ {m.Method.Attribs} ∪ₐ∈ₐₙ a.URedef \ A;
        foreach a ∈ Aₙ do a.in_view := true;  end
        Mₙ := ∪ₘ∈ₘₙ {m.Method.Calls} ∪ₘ∈ₘₙ m.URedef \ M;
        foreach m ∈ Mₙ do m.in_view := true;  end
    end
end
```

Fig. 2. Schema Completion Algorithm

The types to be included by the current iteration consist of the types of the new attributes of the last iteration, of the types used in the new methods of the last iteration and of all types where redefined attributes or redefined methods are used minus the types in T which were already processed. The inclusion of the redefinition points in the types guarantees that the most specific attributes and methods for each type are included in the replica. All the new types are marked as required elements of the replica schema.

Then the attribute usages and method usages through the methods in M_n are computed and marked. Here we also have to take into account the usages of redefined attributes and methods by marking them. When the algorithm terminates, all usages of types attributes and methods by the elements of the initial schema are marked to be in the view. The schema is closed, since it terminates if no new usages of schema elements are found.

5.2 Schema Compression

The schema compression phase removes unnecessary markings for usages of attributes and methods. A usage marking is not needed if the used schema element is already marked for usage in a supertype. In figure 3 an algorithm that removes those usage markings is depicted. We start with a list of object types topologically ordered by the inheritance hierarchy with the object root type first. For each of the object types and each of the marked usages for attributes (methods),

```
method compress() in schema;
var T : list(Type);
begin
  T :=/ * List of object types in schema topologically ordered
        by inheritance hierarchy relationship (root first) * /
  foreach t ∈ T do
    foreach a ∈ {t.AttribsUsed | a.in_view = true} do
      foreach t_s ∈ t.sub* do
        foreach a_s ∈ {t_s.AttribsUsed | a_s.Attrib = a.Attrib} do
          a_s.in_view := false;
        end
      end
    end
    foreach m ∈ {t.MethodsUsed | m.in_view = true} do
      foreach t_s ∈ t.sub* do
        foreach m_s ∈ {t_s.MethodsUsed | m_s.Method = a.Method} do
          m_s.in_view := false;
        end
      end
    end
  end
end
```

Fig. 3. Schema Compression Algorithm

we check all subtypes for usages of the same attribute (methods) and remove their markings. Redefined attributes (methods) are considered to be different. The removal of markings takes place only in part of the type lattice just between the topmost usage and all types where the attribute (method) is redefined.

The result of this step of the schema generation is a meta-schema where just the topmost usages of attributes and methods in the type hierarchy are marked.

5.3 Inheritance Relationship Generation

The step of inheritance generation is mainly concerned with the removal of unnecessary types from the inheritance hierarchy and with the construction of a type hierarchy for the replica schema. So the set of types and the set of inheritance links are minimized. We do not need to include a type T in the replica schema if it is not marked (T.in_view = false). We use the algorithm presented in figure 4 for this task. Basically, it traverses the type hierarchy from the types at the leaves and constructs the new hierarchy by storing the supertypes for the replica schema in the attribute new_inherits_from.

5.4 Conflict Resolution

During the construction of the new inheritance hierarchy, we removed unmarked types. The removal of such types can introduce conflicts via multiple inheritance.

```
method inheritgen() in schema;
var T, T_p, T_L, T'_L : set(Type);
begin
    T := {t ∈ self.Types | t.in_view = true};
    T_p := {};
    T_L := {t ∈ T | t.sub* ∩ T = {}};
    while T_L ≠ {} do
        T'_L := {};
        foreach t_l ∈ T_L do
            T_p := T_p ∪ {t_l};
            pred := torder(t_l.super*);  / * list of predecessors of t_l topologically sorted * /
            while pred ≠ {} do
                p := pred.first;  pred := pred.rest;
                if p ∈ T
                t_l.new_inherits_from := t_l.new_inherits_from ∪ {p};
                T'_L := T'_L ∪ {p};
                pred := pred.remove(p.super*);
            end
        end
    end
    T_L := T'_L \ T_p;
    end
end
```

Fig. 4. Inheritance Hierarchy Generation

Our data model avoids multiple inheritance conflicts by demanding a unique origin for attributes and methods of object types. If we remove a type T which has more than one subtype which have a common subtype S, and a component of T is used in two or more unrelated subtypes of T above S, then the origin of the component from the point of view of S is ambiguous. We propose a simple solution, which is to attach the problematic component at type S with the identical definition as in T. This is always possible since in the source schema S inherited the definition from T. Since there is no other possible way to introduce additional conflicts, we can simply check all the object types for such a conflicting component and then define an additional component according to its definition in one of its origins.

5.5 Final Schema Generation

In this final phase, the marked object types are traversed from the root downwards in topological order according to the new inheritance hierarchy constructed in the previous step. For each marked usage of attributes and methods we have to include the used components in the resulting type definition.

But not only the resulting replica schema should be generated here, we also construct appropriate mapping schemes to support the export/import process.

This information mainly consists of the query expressions used to derive the replica instances and to determine the values for the new attributes in the replica.

6 Conclusions

The main contribution of this paper is a procedure for deriving a minimal self-contained schema for a replica of an object-oriented database starting from a view definition. Furthermore, we sketched how instances of an object-oriented database can be transfered to the replica. We view this results as a starting point to provide replication for object-oriented databases. There are still many issues to be approached. Extension of the replicated database in particular with the results of aggregation queries, and most important the maintenance of the instances in the replica - the propagation of updates on the original database to the replicated database.

References

1. R. Agrawal and L.G. DeMichiel. Type derivation using the projection operation. In M. Jarke, J. Bubenko, and K. Jeffery, editors, *Advances in Database Technology - EDBT'94*, pages 7–14, Cambridge, UK, March 1994. Springer.
2. R. Catell and D. Barry, editors. *The Object Database Standard: ODMG 2.0*. Morgan-Kaufmann, 1997.
3. M. Dobrovnik. *Externe Schemata in objektorientierten Datenbankmanagementsystemen; Logische Datenunabhängigkeit durch Änderungen über Sichten*. PhD thesis, Institut für Informatik, Universität Klagenfurt, August 1995.
4. M. Dobrovnik. *Externe Schemata in objektorientierten Datenbankmanagementsystemen; Logische Datenunabhängigkeit durch Änderungen über Sichten*, volume 25 of *DISDBIS*. Infix, February 1997.
5. M. Dobrovnik and J. Eder. Adding view support to odmg-93. In I. A. Mizin, L. A. Kalinichenko, and Y. I. Zhuralev, editors, *Proc. Intl. Workshop on Advances in Databases and Information Systems*, pages 74–81, Moscow, Russia, May 1994. Moscow ACM SIGMOD Chapter.
6. M. Dobrovnik and J. Eder. Logical data independence and modularity through views in oodbms. In A. Dogac, H. Toroslu, S. Tosunoglu, S. Kalaycioglo, and L. Seneviratne, editors, *Proc. Engineering Systems Design and Analysis Conference*, volume 2, pages 13–20, 1996.
7. S. Heiler and S. Zdonik. Object views: Extending the vision. In *Proc. 6th Intl. Conf. on Data Engineering*, pages 86–93, 1990.
8. W. H. Inmon. *Building the Data Warehouse*. John Wiley, 2nd edition, 1996.
9. R. Ramakrishnan. *Database Management Systems*. McGraw-Hill, 1997.
10. J. Rumbaugh, M. Blaha, W. Permerlani, F. Eddy, and W. Lorensen. *Object-oriented Modelling and Design*. Prentice-Hall, 1991.
11. E. Rundensteiner. Multiview: A methodology for supporting multiple views in object-oriented databases. In *Proc. 18th VLDB Conference*, pages 187–198, Vancouver, Canada, August 1992.
12. D. Sasha. *Database Tuning: A principled Approach*. Prentice-Hall, 1992.
13. B. Schiefer. *Eine Umgebung zur Unterstützung von Schemaänderungen und Sichten in objektorientierten Datenbanksystemen*. PhD thesis, Universität Karlsruhe, December 1993.

Optimizing Knowledge Discovery over the WWW

Matthew Montebello

Computer Science Department, Cardiff University, Wales.
m.montebello@cs.cf.ac.uk
http://www.cs.cf.ac.uk/User/M.Montebello

Abstract. The rapid growth in data volume, user base, and data diversity render Internet-accessible information increasingly difficult to be used effectively. In this paper we discuss the issues involved with knowledge discovery in knowledge bases, in particular the WWW, by presenting a general architecture and describing how it has been instantiated in a functional system we developed. The system attempts to concurrently maximize and optimize the resource/knowledge discovery, and custimize the information to individual users. A number of machine learning techniques have been employed in the development of the system for comparative reasons - results are presented and discussed.

1 Introduction

The World-Wide Web's (WWW) [1] exponential growth is resulting in a dramatic rapid increase in the volume of data on the Internet, requiring techniques and tools that reduce users' information overload and improve the effectiveness of online information access. As more users come on the net, they provide their own information which in turn encourages even more people to join in. With this massive increase of the Internet usage, a vast array of networks services is growing up around the Internet and huge amounts of information is added everyday. Users can now access enormous amounts of information in various forms, thereby creating an equally massive problem. This rapid growth in data volume, user base, and data diversity render Internet-accessible information increasingly difficult to be used effectively, thereby rendering the task of resource and knowledge discovery highly critical. This triggered off the development of techniques for building indexes such as Altavista [2] and Excite [3], to help users during their search. These massive search engines seem to solve the problem but have a number of limitations [4], which pushes the problem back to the users [5].

The rest of the paper is organized as follows. In Section 2 we analyse in some detail major knowledge discovery systems over the web, particularly we attempt to contrast data mining and machine learning techniques. We argue that data mining is the least suitable for the discovery of knowledge over the WWW and justify our reasons for employing machine learning techniques. Use of machine learning techniques has been widely used with heterogeneous document databases to learn user interests [6, 7], and data mining to extract knowledge from databases and/or knowledge bases [8, 9]. In Section 3 we argue that machine learning is an important factor towards a solution to drastically improve knowledge discovery over the WWW. Different techniques are underlined and discussed to set the stage for the current implementation of our system. We present a general architecture in Section 4 and describe how we attempt to concurrently maximize and optimize the resource/knowledge discovery, and custimize the information we present to individual users by applying machine learning techniques. Finally, Section 5 presents our conclusions.

2 Data Mining versus Machine Learning

It is a well known fact that in this decade there has been an explosion of information available on the Internet, and a corresponding increase in usage. This is particularly true of the WWW and its associated browsers which allow easier access to the information available, and thus make it accessible to a wider audience. The WWW is the major knowledge dissemination system that makes the world's staggering wealth of knowledge and experience, stored on server machines scattered across the internet, accessible to the on-line world. The effective organization, discovery and use of the rich resources in the global information network poses great challenges to the database and information system researchers. Current resource discovery techniques rely on the user knowing the location of information, or the location of a meta-information system that will return locations holding information of interest. The user than has to access the information site and retrieve the information. Knowledge discovery using this methodology is not practical especially with the ever increasing volume of data. This brings into context the need of search engines, as outlined in the introduction. Their far from satisfactory services triggered further research to develop more sophisticated search engines and agent-like systems that made use of user profiles to personalize the service they provide. The artificial intelligence research community had been working in this area long before the exponential explosion of the WWW, and the systems developed and techniques implemented have evolved over time [10].

Data mining is the search for relationships and global patterns that exist in large knowledge bases, but are hidden amongst the vast amounts of data. These relationships represent valuable knowledge about the objects in the knowledge base and of the world registered by the knowledge base. On the other hand machine learning inductively learns and constructs models by observing the environment and recognizing similarities among objects and events within this environment. A machine learning system does not interact directly with its environment but makes use of coded observations. Although data mining and machine learning in general may seem very similar, there are important distinctions. Knowledge bases are often designed for purposes different from data mining. That is, the representation of the objects in the knowledge base have been chosen to meet the needs of applications rather than the needs of data mining, and hence, the properties or attributes that would simplify the learning task are not necessarily present giving a net advantage to machine learning. Another important difference is that knowledge bases are invariably contaminated by errors, resulting in noisy and contradictory data with values for attributes often missing. Moreover, the data represents only a small set of all possible behaviour, and a data mining system cannot manipulate its environment to generate interesting examples as in machine learning. Hence, it is harder to discover relationships and patterns than in the ideal conditions found in machine learning[11].

3 Optimizing Knowledge Discovery

The use of AI and the application of machine learning techniques to optimize services provided by existing internet search technologies is one way to control and manage the immense and ever-increasing volume of data published on the WWW. Users demand effective and efficient on-line information access to reduce information overload via efficient and effective knowledge discovery methodologies.

We employ *Machine Learning* [12] techniques to automatically generate a user profile by extracting information from documents which the user gives feedback on. This achieves a satisfactory level of personalisation because it adapts over time as new information is processed by the system. The user profile is continually being refined and augmented, thereby improving the targeted end-user requirements. In our present implementation we make use of four machine learning techniques in order to be able to compare their performance and also their effectiveness when applied to knowledge discovery over the WWW. The four different measures of term significance which have been applied so far are Term Frequency, Boolean , Term Frequency Inverse Document Frequency, and Term Frequency Discrimination Value.

The following notations are used in the rest of the paper:

W_i is weight of the term i	F_i is number of occurrences of term i
N_w is total number of words	D_T is total number of documents
D_i is number of documents containing term i	DV_i is difference between the space densities before and after term i is added

The term frequency (TF) measure (1) assumes that the importance of a term is directly proportional to the frequency with which it appears within a document.

$$W_i = \frac{F_i}{N_w} \tag{1}$$

The second technique applied is based on the simple boolean retrieval model (binary) where the occurence or absence of the term within the document determines the weight of the term. 1 if the term is present, 0 otherwise.

The term frequency inverse document frequency (TFIDF) measure (2) assigns a greater significance to terms that are good discriminators between documents in a collection. It compares how frequently a term appears in a document against the number of other documents which contain that term.

$$W_i = F_i * ln\frac{D_T}{D_i} \qquad (2)$$

Finally, the term frequency discrimination value (TFDV) measure (3) is based on the hypothesis that a good term is one which on removal from the collection of documents leads to an decrease in the average dissimilarity (adding it would hence lead to an increase), whereas a bad term is one which leads on removal to an increase.

$$W_i = F_i * DV_i \qquad (3)$$

The machine learning techniques employed were compared to evaluate and assess the overall performance of our approach. A set of data tests on a number of different topics were performed, once on documents returned from a single search engine[1] and consecutively on our system. The results (Figure 1) indicate that the machine learning techniques performed well and a significant improvement on the single search engine data set is visibly noticable. This cannot be said for the boolean model which is too elementary for our purposes. Clearly, as the number of documents selected by the user increased (from 10 to 100 in steps of 30) the better the results that were obtained due to the greater size of the training data set which progressively improves the predictions.

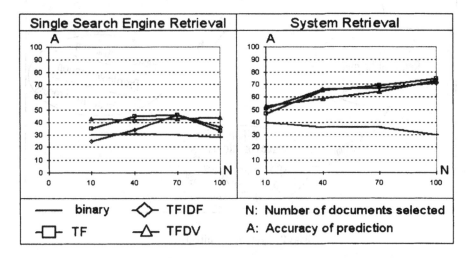

Fig. 1. Comparison of Machine Learning Techniques

---

[1] AltaVista was selected during the tests because it averaged most frequently in the top three search engines ranking list (source: http://searchenginewatch.internet.com)

4 Implementation

In order to optimize knowledge discovery over the WWW we make use of major knowledge bases on the WWW and apply machine learning techniques to achieve the required objectives. Important to note that the system performs knowledge discovery on specific items of interest individual users show interest in, rather than the whole knowledge base of the entire WWW.

To maximize the management and exploit the potential of the WWW's vast knowledge-base we require to efficiently and effectively search and retrieve specific information for specific users. By making use of what other systems generate, we ensure that we get all the information that all of them would retrieve at the same time. To add value to the retrieved results we generate user profiles to be able to predict and suggest the most suitable information to specific users. Through various interactions the system will be able to optimize the targeting and predicting of what users are interested in.

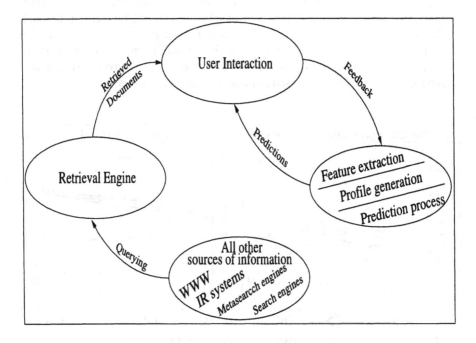

Fig. 2. System Architecture

The basic outline of our architecture, in Figure 2, depicts the major four components that perform the tasks our approach requires in order to achieve the objectives set. Resource and knowledge discovery is performed on the knowledge bases that the major information systems on the Internet meticulously accumulate. All relevant resources and knowledge discovered is retrieved, aggregated and collated appropriately. When a user accesses this information, there is no need to go through all information, but the feedback given will be utilised to extract features, generate a profile and predict further sources that fit this profile from the pool of information generated by the retrieval engine. In the eventuality that the user accepts the suggestion, this will help in the further refinement of the profile and eventually in the precise prediction of additional information.

5 Conclusion

In this paper we have tackled the optimization of knowledge discovery over the WWW. We argued that machine learning has distinct advantages over traditional data mining when applied to a knowledge base like the WWW. A system that we developed to implement our novel approach was presented - it parasites major knowledge bases and applies machine learning techniques to achieve the required objectives, rendering the process of resource and knowledge discovery using the Internet even more efficient and effective. In the future we will be investigating ways to improve the accuracy of information presented. This will be achieved by analysing feedback given from a group of users who are presently making use of the system, determining the relevancy of the information presented and helping in the evaluation of the system.

References

1. T Berners-Lee, R Caillian, A Luotonen, H F Nielsen, and A Secret. The World-Wide Web. *Communications of the ACM*, 37(8):76–82, 1994.
2. Digital Equipment Corp. *AltaVista*. http://altavista.digital.com/.
3. Excite Inc. *Excite*. http://www.excite.com/.
4. H Berghel. Cyberspace 2000: Dealing with information overload. *Communications of the ACM*, 40(2):19–25, 1997.
5. H Chen, C Schuffels, and R Orwig. Internet categorization and search: A self-organizing approach. *Journal of Visual Communication and Image Representation*, 7(1):88–102, 1996.
6. C Knoblock and Levy (eds). Agent-based knowledge discovery. *AAAI Spring Symposium on Information Gathering*, 1995.
7. B Krulwich. Learning user interests across heterogeneous document databases. *AAAI Spring Symposium on Information Gathering*, 1995.
8. W H E Davies and P Edwards. Distributed learning: An agent-based approach to data-mining. In *ML95 - workshop on agents that learn from other agents*, 1995.
9. G Piatetsky-Shapiro and W J Frawley. *Knowledge Discovery in Databases*. MIT press, 1991.
10. D Bayer. A learning agent for resource discovery on the world wide web. Master's thesis, University of Aberdeen, 1995.
11. C L Green and P Edwards. Using Machine Learning to enhance software tools for internet information management. In A Franz and H Kitamo, editors, *AAAI-96, Workshop on Internet-Based Information Systems*, pages 48–55. AAAI Press, 1996.
12. G Salton and M J McGill. *Introduction to Modern Information Retrieval*. McGraw-Hill, 1983.

Data Mining Query Language
for Object-Oriented Database

Vladimir Novacek*

Department of Computer Science, TU Brno
Bozetechova 2, 612 66 Brno
Czech Republic
novacekv@dcse.fee.vutbr.cz

Abstract. Knowledge discovery in databases (KDD) and data mining represent very important tools for processing and analysing data in large databases. The combination of powerful KDD and data mining techniques and sophisticated resources of object-oriented database systems brings even more considerable results. These emerging tools and techniques require a powerful data mining query language serving as an interface between applications and data mining tools. This motivates us to design an object-oriented data mining query language for mining different kinds of knowledge from object-oriented databases. We introduce an overview of this language, its syntax and semantics in this paper and some examples of practical use will be shown too.

1 Introduction

Knowledge Discovery in Databases (KDD) is general process of useful knowledge discovery from data. This process involves data pre-processing, data mining itself and then interpretation of mined patterns. Data Mining is only one part of KDD process. It analyses pre-processed data and produces information patterns which are then interpreted and convenient ones are considered as knowledge.

Development of modern database systems, e.g. object-oriented databases (OODB), has advanced considerably. It is naturally then to investigate knowledge discovery in OODB ([1]) offering richer structure and semantics which can be employed in the KDD process.

In the present time there is a lot of practical applications employing or based on the KDD technology. These applications require introducing certain standard which could be called Data Mining Query Language (DMQL). DMQL language would offer standard interface between application and the KDD system. Design of such language for data mining in relational databases is described in [2].

---

* Supported by grant of the Czech Grant Agency Object-oriented Database Model No. 102/96/0986 and grant of the Advancement fund of MSMT Data Mining in Object-Oriented Database No. 243.

Join of modern object-oriented database technology and data mining with conjunction of the request of creating query language for data mining leads us to development of object-oriented query language (OOQL) for data mining. Such language for OODB hasn't been designed yet namely. This language would enable an application to get knowledge from OODB in certain standard simple way similar to getting stored data from OODB using OOQL. A language ODAMIL (Object-oriented DAta MIning query Language) is the result of research in this area and is described in this paper.

The second chapter deals data mining input, i.e. OODB being used. In the third chapter there is described the data mining output, i.e. particular types of mined rules. The language ODAMIL itself is described in the fourth chapter.

2 Database Description

Object-oriented database ([3]) is to be input for data mining process. OODB is described in the VDL language ([4, 5]). There are no additional adaptations of database required for data mining purposes, no completion or adding of attributes, methods or objects. There are no required changes of already existing data or metadata.

Data mining program takes the OODB as is. It doesn't worry about a database structure, type or origin of stored data, etc. It retrieves data from OODB using OOQL in the same way as any other application. So from the data mining point of view no other changes of the OODB are required.

It is necessary to give the data mining program access to metadata. Data mining program needs to get description of analysed data, i.e. description and structure of classes analysed objects belong to. It needs to know information about object attributes and their types, about methods and their parameters. This information is important for proper choice of data mining techniques and algorithms, for proper treating analysed data.

Knowing analysed objects metadata data mining program can choose optimal data mining strategy and mine interesting knowledge effectively.

3 Knowledge Representation

Data mining output is represented by newly obtained knowledge in the form of mined rules. Formally, the rule is expression E in language L describing facts in certain subset of data from database ([6]). For example, the expression "If a customer buys bread he will buy also milk with probability of p percent" can be rule for appropriate choice of threshold p.

Rules are characterised by two parameters, namely support and confidence ([6]). The *rule support* expresses generally the rule strength. Thus the higher the rule support is the lower the probability of accidental rule deducing only from a few of transactions is. The *rule confidence* expresses generally the measure of correlation in the database among items of the left and right side of the rule. Higher confidence means again higher rule quality.

There are various rule types ([6]) focusing on particular aspects of relations among data, data structure and content. It is not necessary to involve all these rule types into the ODAMIL language. In the case of ODAMIL language mining only limited number of rule types is supposed. Association, sequential and classification rules are to be mined.

Concept of knowledge and rule specified in this formal way must be expressed and defined by means of OODB now, i.e. described in the VDL language. In the case of OOQL the output is a collection of objects of some already defined class. In the case of data mining the output is a set or collection of rules. These rules we must first describe in the VDL language and their definitions, in other words rule metadata, add to the OODB. Mined rules are formally treated as objects returned as a query result. That's why it is necessary to know rule metadata in advance.

3.1 Association Rules

Mining of association rules is motivated by often case of market basket analysis. A retailer needs to identify sets of items that are purchased together (during one customer's visit in a shop) and needs to know how purchase of one item influences purchase of another one.

The association rule ([6]) has then a form of LHS $\Rightarrow$ RHS where both LHS and RHS are itemsets. The item is meant here as for example particular commodity purchased by a customer. Meaning of the rule is that if a customer buys items stated on the left side of the rule then it is likely he will buy also items stated on the right side of the rule in the same shop visit.

3.2 Sequential Rules

So called sequential rules are next often rule type, i.e. rules describing some phenomenon process in the time, e.g. items purchased by customers during their particular visits in a shop. This enables us to identify often purchases patterns or purchases stereotypes over time, e.g. changes of market basket during a week, etc.

Sequential rule ([6]) we can describe as a sequence of itemsets. The rule $\{s_1, s_2, ..., s_n\}$ says that if a customer purchases items from itemset s_1 then he'll purchase items form the set s_2 in the following shopping, then items from the set s_3, etc.

3.3 Classification Rules

Classification rules ([6]) are used for records or objects classification into beforehand given categories. The classification rule has form $(l_1 \leq X_1 \leq h_1)$ AND ... AND $(l_n \leq X_n \leq h_n) \Rightarrow Y = c$. Attributes X_1 to X_n are used for prediction or classification of attribute Y value. Both sides of rule can be understood as conditions put on attributes of given class(es).

The left side of the rule expresses the rule assumption that given attributes values are constrained in a reputed way. The right side of the rule expresses conclusion that determined attribute has value c. This fact can also be understood that determined attribute or object belongs to the category determined by attribute c.

For example following rule ClassificationRule(Set[...], Customer, 'Good credit') means that having fulfilled the conditions on the left side of the rule the customer belongs to the category of good customers and a bank can give him a loan.

4 The Data Mining Language

The ODAMIL language is proposed as an extension of object-oriented query language Object Comprehensions ([7]). The ODAMIL language enables mining of association, classification and sequential rules. It is also possible to specify necessary auxiliary components of data mining algorithms, such as various thresholds.

The standard mathematical notation was inspiration for the Object Comprehensions language. We introduce here one example of query written in this language : Set [s ← Student, s.address.city = "Prague" | s]. This query returns a collection of all students from the class Student living in Prague as its result.

The Object Comprehensions language contains also other constructs for entering various query types. It enables to use user defined functions with parameters in queries. These functions work with objects in the OODB and return collections of objects as their results. They behave as subqueries then.

Just this feature of Object Comprehensions language is employed in the ODAMIL language design. The ODAMIL language newly defines function MineRules which represents a command for data mining. Mined rule types, target data set and other information is entered through parameters of this function.

```
MineRules (RuleType: TRuleType;
           TargSet: Set Of Object;
           Thresholds: Tthresholds;
           RelatedAttr: Set Of String) : Set Of Rule;
```

The function MineRules has four parameters with following description :

- Parameter RuleType defined as enumerated determines type of mined rules. Particular values determine type of mined rules according to its name.
- Parameter TargSet defines target data set. It is a query in the Object Comprehensions language which is evaluated and resulting collection of objects represents target data set. The target data set contains data which are interesting for data mining at the moment and from which rules are mined.
- Parameter Thresholds can contain particular thresholds definitions. If this parameter is empty implicit thresholds are used. Otherwise it contains set of records each of which setting one threshold.

There are two threshold types, namely minimal support (determined by keyword minsupp) and minimal confidence (determined by keyword minconf). It means there will be put as knowledge into an output of result of MineRules function only those rules with support and confidence greater than given minimal thresholds. Threshold's value itself entered in percents but written as a number within 0 to 1 interval.

- Parameter RelatedAttr contains a list of attributes according to which classification of a target data set will be done. It is meaningful only for classification rules mining. In this case target data set is processed by classification algorithm ([8, 9]) at first which classifies it, i.e. divides it, into categories according to entered attributes. After this suitable data mining algorithm is executed which will mine classification rules for each data category.

In the OODB being used there is not possible for a function to have various number of parameters. That's why function MineRules has parameters necessary for mining all rule types even if some of them are redundant during some rule types mining. Instead of proposing one function for each mined rule type we decided to propose only one common function for all rule types mining because of similarity of that functions and design simplicity.

4.1 Examples of Mined Rules

The function MineRules is used in queries in a normal way as other query functions. Usage of the ODAMIL language will be demonstrated on following examples of queries written in the Object Comprehension language.

```
Set [ r ← MineRules(association, Set [ p ← Purchases,
    p.total ≤ 100 | p ], Set [], Set []| r ]
```
This query returns as its result collection of association rules r mined from data about potty purchases. The target data set will be collection of transactions p, i.e. particular customer purchases, which total doesn't exceed $100. Implicit thresholds will be used during data mining.

```
Set [ r ← MineRules(sequential, Set [ p ← Purchases,
    p.date ≥ 1.1.1997, p.date ≤ 31.12.1997 | p ],
    Set [Thr(minsupp, 0.75), Thr(minconf, 0.8)], Set []) |
    r ]
```
This query will mine sequential rules from data about transactions performed in 1997. Thresholds will be set so that minimal support of mined rules will be 75% and minimal confidence will be 80%.

```
Set [ r ← MineRules(classification, Set [ p ← Purchases,
    c ← Customers, p.date ≥ 1.1.1997, p.date ≤ 31.12.1997
    | p ], Set [], Set ['Customer.Spending']) | r ]
```
This query will mine classification rules from data about transactions performed in 1997 using implicit thresholds. The target data set will be divided according to customer's spending and then classification rules for each category will be mined, e.g. what goods buy rich and poor customers which could be useful for marketing, etc.

Conclusions

Data mining and KDD represent very important area for further research, especially in the environment of new progressive database systems such as OODB. These database systems are capable to hold large amounts of data but also involve their structure and mutual relationships. Just these features can be successfully employed in data mining.

In the time of rapid development in this area there is increasing need for data mining query language which would enable simple and uniform entering of various data mining tasks and which would represent standard interface between application and data mining system.

Future research will continue probably towards development of new effective algorithms for data mining in the OODB and towards employing of the deductive object-oriented databases as progressive tools for handling data and knowledge.

References

1. Han, J., Nishio, S., Kawano, H.: *Knowledge Discovery in Object-Oriented and Active Databases*. In Knowledge Building and Knowledge Sharing, ed. F. Fuchi and T. Yokoi, 221-230. Ohmsha, Ltd. and IOS Press 1994.
2. Han, J., Fu, Y., Wang, W., Koperski, K., Zaiane, O.: *DMQL: A Data Mining Query Language for Relational Databases*.
   Available at ftp://ftp.fas.sfu.ca/pub/cs/han/kdd/dmql96.ps
3. Beneš, M., Hruška, T.: *Objektově orientovaná databáze*. In: Sborník celostátní konference EurOpen.CZ '97, Borová Lada na Šumavě 22.-25.6.1997, Česká společnost uživatelů otevřených systémů 1997, pp. 5-18
4. Beneš, M.: *Jazyk pro popis údajů objektově orientovaného databázového modelu*. In: Sborník konference Některé nové přístupy při tvorbě informačních systémů, ÚIVT FEI VUT Brno 1995, pp. 28-32
5. Beneš, M.: *Object-Oriented Model of a Programming Language*. In: Proceedings of MOSIS 96 Conference, Krnov 1996 MARQ Ostrava and Department of Computer Science Technical University Ostrava 1996, pp. 33-38
6. Fayyad, U. M., Piatetsky-Shapiro, G., Smyth, P., Uthurusamy, R.: *Advances in Knowledge Discovery and Data Mining*. Menlo Park, Calif.: AAAI / MIT Press 1996.
7. Chan, D. K. C., Trinder, P. W.: *Object Comprehensions: A Query Notation for Object-Oriented Databases*. In Directions in Databases, LNCS 826, Springer-Verlag, 1994
8. Mehta, M., Agrawal, R., Rissanen, J.: *SLIQ: A fast scallable classifier for data mining*. In Proc. International Conference on Extending Database Technology (EDBTí96), Avignon, France, March 1996
9. Winstone, L., Wang, W., Han, J.: *Multiple-level data classification in large databases*. In submitted for publication, March 1996

Itemset Materializing for Fast Mining
of Association Rules

Marek Wojciechowski, Maciej Zakrzewicz

Institute of Computing Science
Poznan University of Technology
ul. Piotrowo 3a, 60-965 Poznan, Poland
{marek, mzakrz}@cs.put.poznan.pl

Abstract. Mining association rules is an important data mining problem. Association rules are usually mined repeatedly in different parts of a database. Current algorithms for mining association rules work in two steps. First, the most frequently occurring sets of items are discovered, then the sets are used to generate the association rules. The first step usually requires repeated passes over the analyzed database and determines the overall performance. In this paper, we present a new method that addresses the issue of discovering the most frequently occurring sets of items. Our method consists in materializing precomputed sets of items discovered in logical database partitions. We show that the materialized sets can be repeatedly used to efficiently generate the most frequently occurring sets of items. Using this approach, required association rules can be mined with only one scan of the database. Our experiments show that the proposed method significantly outperforms the well-known algorithms.

1 Introduction

Data mining, also referred to as database mining or knowledge discovery in databases (KDD), is a new research area that aims at discovery of useful information from large datasets. Data mining uses statistical analysis and inference to extract interesting trends and events, create useful reports, support decision making etc. It exploits the massive amounts of data to achieve business, operational or scientific goals. An important goal of current research is to provide methods for on-line analytical mining (OLAM) [6]. On-line analytical mining implies that data mining is performed in a way similar to on-line analytical processing (OLAP), i.e. mining can be performed interactively, for different portions of a database and at different conceptual levels. On-line analytical mining requires a high-performance and rapid-response environment that assists users in data selection, rule generation and rule filtering [5], [8], [11].

One of the most significant data mining problems is mining association rules. Association rules are interesting class of database regularities, introduced by Agrawal,

Imielinski, and Swami in [1]. Association rules approaches address a class of problems typified by a market basket analysis. Classic market basket analysis treats the purchase of a number of items (the contents of a shopping basket) as a single transaction. Basket data usually consists of products bought by a customer along with the date of transaction, quantity, price, etc. Such data may be collected, for example, at supermarket checkout counters. The goal is to find trends across large number of purchase transactions that can be used to understand and exploit natural buying patterns, and represent the trends in the form of association rules. Each association rule identifies the set of items that is most often purchased together with another set of items. For example, an association rule may state that "80% of customers who bought items A, B and C also bought D and E". This information may be used for promotional displays design, optimal use of shelf and floor space, effective sales strategies, target marketing, catalogue design etc.

1.1 Association Rules

Let $L=\{l_1, l_2, ..., l_m\}$ be a set of literals, called items. Let a non-empty set of items T be called an *itemset*. Let D be a set of variable length itemsets, where each itemset $T \subseteq L$. We say that an itemset T *supports* an item $x \in L$ if x is in T. We say that an itemset T *supports* an itemset $X \subseteq L$ if T supports every item in the set X.

An *association rule* is an implication of the form $X \rightarrow Y$, where $X \subset L$, $Y \subset L$, $X \cap Y = \emptyset$. Each rule has associated measures of its statistical significance and strength, called *support* and *confidence*. The support of the rule $X \rightarrow Y$ in the set D is:

$$support(X \rightarrow Y, D) = \frac{\left|\{T \in D \mid T \text{ supports } X \cup Y\}\right|}{|D|}. \tag{1}$$

In other words, the rule $X \rightarrow Y$ holds in the set D with support s if $s\%$ of itemsets in D support $X \cup Y$. The confidence of the rule $X \rightarrow Y$ in the set D is:

$$confidence(X \rightarrow Y, D) = \frac{\left|\{T \in D \mid T \text{ supports } X \cup Y\}\right|}{\left|\{T \in D \mid T \text{ supports } X\}\right|}. \tag{2}$$

In other words, the rule $X \rightarrow Y$ has confidence c if $c\%$ of itemsets in D that support X also support Y.

1.2 Previous Work on Association Rules

The problem of generating association rules was first introduced in [1] and an algorithm called *AIS* was proposed. In [13], an algorithm *SETM* was proposed for mining association rules using relational operators. In [3], Agrawal and Srikant presented two new algorithms, called *Apriori* and *AprioriTid*, that are fundamentally different from the previous ones. The algorithms achieved significant improvements over *SETM* and *AIS* and became the core of many new algorithms for mining association rules

In the existing approaches [3], [6], [7], [9], [12], [14], [15] the problem of mining association rules is decomposed into the following two steps:

1. Discover the large itemsets, i.e. the sets of itemsets that have support above a predetermined minimum support σ.
2. Use the large itemsets to generate the association rules for the database.

It is noted that the overall performance of mining association rules is determined by the first step. After the large itemsets are identified, the corresponding association rules can be derived in a straightforward manner.

Much research has focused on deriving efficient algorithms for discovering large itemsets. Generally, to show that an itemset is large we can count its occurrences in the database D. If the count is greater than σ $|D|$, then the itemset is large. The problem is that the number of all possible itemsets is huge and it is infeasible to count them all (e.g. for 1000 different items there are: c.a. 500 000 of possible 2-itemsets, c.a. 160 000 000 of possible 3-itemsets, etc.). If we knew, say, a few thousands of itemsets which are *potentially* large we could count them in only one scan of the database. All well-known algorithms rely on the property that an itemset can only be large if all of its subsets are large. It leads to a level-wise procedure. First, all possible 1-itemsets (itemsets containing 1 item) are counted in the database to determine *large 1-itemsets*. Then, large 1-itemsets are combined to form potentially large 2-itemsets, called *candidate 2-itemsets*. Candidate 2-itemsets are counted in the database to determine *large 2-itemsets*. The procedure is continued by combining the large 2-itemsets to form *candidate 3-itemsets* and so forth. A disadvantage of the algorithm is that it requires K or $K+1$ passes over the database to discover all large itemsets, where K is the size of the greatest large itemset found.

Since it is costly to discover association rules in large databases, there is often a need for techniques that incrementally update the discovered association rules every time the database changes. In general, database updates may not only invalidate some existing strong association rules but also turn some weak rules into strong ones. Thus it is nontrivial to maintain such discovered association rules in large databases. In [4], Cheung, Han, Ng and Wong presented an algorithm called *FUP* (Fast Update Algorithm) for computing the large itemsets in the expanded database from the old large itemsets. The major idea of *FUP* algorithm is to reuse the information of the old large itemsets and to integrate the support information of the new large itemsets in order to reduce the pool of candidate itemsets to be re-examined. Unfortunately, the method cannot be used to mine association rules in a part of a database because the large itemsets that hold in the entire database may not hold in a part of it.

Another way of reducing the number of database passes was proposed by Savasere, Omiecinski and Navathe in the algorithm called *Partition* [14]. *Partition* algorithm reads the database in portions into main memory and discovers large itemsets inside each portion. Then, by scanning the whole database, the actual support values for these itemsets are computed.

1.3 Problem Description

Given a database of sets of items, the problem of mining association rules is to discover all rules that have support and confidence above the user-defined minimum values. In practice, association rules can be mined repeatedly in different parts of the database. A straightforward, though ineffective way to solve this problem is to run (each time) a well-known algorithm for mining association rules on the part of the database. Note that if the large itemsets could be precomputed and stored in a database, the algorithm for mining association rules would be simpler and more efficient. This is known as the *itemset materializing*.

In this paper, we propose a new method that addresses the issue of discovering the most frequently occurring sets of items. Our method consists in materializing precomputed sets of items discovered in logical partitions of a large database. We show that the materialized sets of items can be repeatedly used to efficiently generate the sets of items that most frequently occur in the whole database or only in a part of it. Using this approach, the required association rules can be interactively mined with only one scan of the database.

1.4 Outline

The structure of the paper is the following. In Section 2, the method of itemset materializing is described and the algorithm for mining association rules is given. In Section 3 we give our experimental results showing the performance of the new method. Section 4 contains final conclusions.

2 Itemset Materializing Method

The key idea behind itemset materializing is the following. Recall that the reason that limits the well-known algorithms is that if itemset counting should be done in a single scan of a database, the number of itemsets to count would be exponentially large. However, if we could easily select a small set of *potentially* large itemsets, say a few thousand itemsets, then they could be counted in only one scan of a database. We present the method that uses materialized itemsets to select potentially large itemsets that can be verified in a single database scan.

Itemset materializing method divides the database into user-defined, non-overlapping partitions and discovers all large itemsets inside each partition. The positive borders of the large itemsets are computed and stored along with the partitions in the database. We use the positive borders as a condensed representation of the itemsets. Later on, when association rules are to be discovered in a set of database partitions, the positive borders for those partitions are merged to generate the *global positive border*. Then all the itemsets described by the global positive border (potentially large itemsets) are counted in the database partitions to find their supports. Thus, the itemsets materialized only once can be used repeatedly to efficiently select potentially large itemsets.

2.1 Basic Definitions

Positive border
The concept of the positive border was introduced by Manilla and Toivonen in [10]. Given a set S of itemsets, the *positive border $BD^+(S)$* consists of those itemsets from S which are not contained by any other itemsets from S:

$$Bd^+(S) = \{ X \in S \mid for\ all\ Y \in S,\ we\ have\ X \not\subset Y \} . \tag{3}$$

The positive border can play a role of the condensed representation of the itemsets.

Combination of positive borders
Combination $\theta (S_1, S_2)$ of the two positive borders S_1 and S_2 is the positive border of $S_1 \cup S_2$:

$$\theta (S_1, S_2) = Bd^+(S_1 \cup S_2) . \tag{4}$$

We will use the combination of the positive borders to generate the global positive border for the partitions.

2.2 Generation of Materialized Positive Borders

Given is a database D and a minimum support value σ. The minimum support value σ should be less or equal to a predicted minimum value that users can set on support of their mined association rules.

We divide the database D into a set of non-overlapping partitions: $d_1, d_2, ..., d_n$. The database can be divided according to e.g. dates, locations, customer types. For each partition d_i all large itemsets $L_1^i, L_2^i, ..., L_k^i$ are discovered be means of a well-known algorithm (L_1^i refers to large 1-itemsets in the partition d_i, L_2^i refers to large 2-itemsets in the partition d_i, etc.). Then, for each partition d_i a positive border Bd^+_i of $L_1^i \cup L_2^i \cup ... \cup L_k^i$ is computed and stored in the database together with the partition. The algorithm is shown in Figure 1.

for each partition d_i of D **do**

> **begin**
>
> > discover all itemsets whose support > σ
> >
> > compute the positive border $Bd^+{}_i$ for the discovered itemsets
> >
> > store $Bd^+{}_i$ together with d_i
>
> **end**

Fig. 1. Generation of materialized positive borders

Example 1

To illustrate the generation of materialized positive borders, consider the database D in Figure 2. Assume that σ is 0.2. Let us first divide the database D into three partitions: d_1, d_2, d_3. For each partition all itemsets with support ≥ 0.2 are discovered (not depicted here). Then the positive borders of the itemsets are computed. For the partition d_1 we have the positive border $Bd^+{}_1 = \{\{4,5,6\}, \{1,3,5,7\}, \{2,3,4,7\}\}$, for the partition d_2 we have $Bd^+{}_2 = \{\{1,3,7\}, \{2,3,5\}, \{1,2,5,7\}\}$ and for the partition d_3 we have $Bd^+{}_3 = \{\{1,4,6\}, \{3,5,7\}, \{2,4,6,7\}\}$. Then, the positive borders are stored together with the partitions in the database.

D

TID	Item
100	1 3 5 7
101	2 3 4 7
102	4 5 6
103	1 2 5 7
104	2 3 5
105	1 3 7
106	3 5 7
107	1 4 6
108	2 4 6 7

d₁

TID	Item
100	1 3 5 7
101	2 3 4 7
102	4 5 6

d₂

TID	Item
103	1 2 5 7
104	2 3 5
105	1 3 7

d₃

TID	Item
106	3 5 7
107	1 4 6
108	2 4 6 7

Fig. 2. Example database and its partitions

2.3 Generation of Large Itemsets from Materialized Itemsets

Given is the database D, divided into the set of n partitions d_1, d_2, .., d_n, and the positive borders for the partitions $Bd^+{}_1$, $Bd^+{}_2$, ..., $Bd^+{}_n$, derived for the minimum support value σ. Let $I = \{i_1, i_2, ..., i_l\}$ denote a set of partition identifiers. Below we present the algorithm that discovers all large itemsets that hold in $d_{i1} \cup d_{i2} \cup ... \cup d_{il}$ with support above σ', $\sigma' \geq \sigma$. Once the large itemsets and their supports are determined, the rules can be discovered in a straightforward manner [1].

First, the positive borders of all the partitions described in I are *combined* to form the *global positive border* S. Then, for each itemset in S all unique subsets are generated to form the set of *potentially large itemsets* C. In the next step the partitions $d_{i1}, d_{i2}, ..., d_{il}$ are scanned to count the occurrences of all the itemsets in C. The result of the algorithm consists of the itemsets in C with support greater or equal to σ', i.e. large itemsets. The algorithm is shown in Figure 3.

> $S = \varnothing$
> **for each** partition identifier i_k in I **do**
> $\quad S = \theta\,(S,\ Bd^+_{ik})$
> C = all unique subsets of the itemsets in S
> **for each** transaction $t \in d_{i1} \cup d_{i2} \cup ... \cup d_{il}$ **do**
> $\quad$ increment the count of all itemsets in C that are contained in t
> Answer = all itemsets in C with support $\geq \sigma'$

Fig. 3. Mining association rules

Example 2

To illustrate the large itemset generation algorithm, consider the database partitions and the positive borders from Example 1. We are looking for all association rules that hold in the database partitions d_1 and d_3 with support ≥ 0.4. First, the positive borders $Bd^+_1 = \{\{4,5,6\},\ \{1,3,5,7\},\ \{2,3,4,7\}\}$ and $Bd^+_3 = \{\{1,4,6\},\ \{3,5,7\},\ \{2,4,6,7\}\}$ are combined to form the global positive border $S = \{\{1,4,6\},\ \{4,5,6\},\ \{1,3,5,7\},\ \{2,3,4,7\},\ \{2,4,6,7\}\}$. Then, for each itemset in S all unique subsets are generated to form the set of potentially large itemsets C. Thus we get $C = \{\{1\},\ \{2\},\ \{3\},\ \{4\},\ \{5\},\ \{6\},\ \{7\}, \{1,3\},\ \{1,4\},\ \{1,5\},\ \{1,6\},\ \{1,7\},\ \{2,3\},\ \{2,4\},\ \{2,7\},\ \{2,6\},\ \{3,4\},\ \{3,5\},\ \{3,7\},\ \{4,5\}, \{4,6\},\ \{4,7\},\ \{5,6\},\ \{5,7\},\ \{6,7\},\ \{4,5,6\},\ \{1,4,6\},\ \{1,3,5\},\ \{1,3,7\},\ \{1,5,7\},\ \{3,5,7\}, \{2,3,4\},\ \{2,3,7\},\ \{2,4,7\},\ \{3,4,7\},\ \{2,4,6\},\ \{2,6,7\},\ \{4,6,7\},\ \{2,3,4,7\},\ \{2,4,6,7\}\}$. Now, the partitions d_1 and d_3 are scanned and all the itemsets in C are counted. The itemsets in C with support greater or equal to 0.4 are returned as the result. In this example the resulting large itemsets are: $\{3\}$, $\{4\}$, $\{5\}$, $\{6\}$, $\{7\}$, $\{3,7\}$, $\{4,6\}$. The association rules that can be derived from those large itemsets are the following:

$3 \rightarrow 7$, support = 0.50, confidence = 1.00
$7 \rightarrow 3$, support = 0.50, confidence = 0.75
$4 \rightarrow 6$, support = 0.50, confidence = 0.75
$6 \rightarrow 4$, support = 0.50, confidence = 1.00

Note that the database has been scanned only once to get this result.

Correctness

Our algorithm relies on the property that an itemset can only be large if it is large in at least one partition. To prove this property formally, we show that if an itemset is not large in any of the partitions, then it is not large in the whole database.

Let s_i denote the count of the itemset in the partition d_i. If the itemset is not large in any of the database partitions, then:

$$s_1/|d_1| < \sigma \wedge s_2/|d_2| < \sigma \wedge ... \wedge s_n/|d_n| < \sigma,\qquad(5)$$

therefore:

$$s_1 < \sigma |d_1| \wedge s_2 < \sigma |d_2| \wedge ... \wedge s_n < \sigma |d_n|.\qquad(6)$$

When we add those inequalities together we get the following:

$$s_1 + s_2 + ... + s_n < \sigma |d_1| + \sigma |d_2| + ... + \sigma |d_n|,\qquad(7)$$

therefore:

$$(s_1 + s_2 + ... + s_n)/(|d_1| + |d_2| + ... + |d_n|) < \sigma.\qquad(8)$$

The last inequality says that the itemset is not large. Thus, we have shown that an itemset that is not large in any of the partitions can not be large in the whole database.

2.4 Database Partitioning

Let us now consider how the database can be divided into partitions to efficiently use the presented method. The limitation of the method is that association rules can be mined in union of selected database partitions only, not in whichever part of the database. However, it is obvious that in real systems users usually mine association rules in semantic ranges of a database - i.e. in data from selected weeks, months, supermarkets. Then, each partition can refer to a week or to a supermarket and flexible queries over the partitions can be formulated. The similar problem is often discussed in OLAP communities.

Flexibility of the presented method is greater when the number of the database partitions is large. On the other hand, large number of partitions results in storage overhead. Thus, users can evaluate the number and size of the partitions individually, depending on the storage cost and flexibility requirements. We evaluated that a real-life number of database partitions in which users mine association rules is 20-50.

Another important feature of the itemset materializing method is that it is easy to maintain the materialized positive borders for the database partitions. When a database or data warehouse is *updated*, the materialized positive borders for the updated database partitions should be updated too. When new partitions are *appended* to a database or data warehouse, then the positive borders for the new partitions must be computed, however, none of the previously materialized positive borders need to be updated. Besides, computing the positive borders for a partition can be done fast, because the whole partition is likely to fit in main memory.

3   Experimental Results

To assess the performance of the proposed method, we conducted several experiments on large itemset discovering by using a 2-processor Sun SPARCserver 630MP with 128 MB of main memory. The database was implemented in Oracle 7.3.1 DBMS. Experimental data sets were generated by the synthetic data generator *GEN* from Quest project [2]. *GEN* generates textual data files that contain sets of numerical items. Several parameters affect the distribution of the synthetic data. These parameters are shown in Table 1. To load the contents of the data files into the database, *Oracle SQL*Loader* program was used.

Table 1. Synthetic data parameters

parameter	value	parameter	value
n_{trans}	number of item sets, 1,000 and 10,000	n_{pats}	number of patterns, 50 and 500
n_{items}	number of different items, 100	patlen	average length of maximal pattern, 6
t_{len}	average items per set, 10 and 15	corr	correlation between patterns, 0.25

Figures 4 and 5 show the execution time of discovering the large itemsets in the synthetic database for different minimum support values. The positive borders were materialized before the experiment with the traditional *Apriori* algorithm. We have compared the performance of our method (for different numbers of partitions) with the performance of the algorithm *Apriori*. Our method, for 5-20 partitions and minimum support > 0.05, beat out *Apriori*, running 2-3 times faster. As we expected, its performance decreases for decreasing the minimum support value and for increasing the number of partitions. This behavior can be explained by larger number of itemsets that are described by the global positive border.

Figure 6 shows the storage overhead for the materialized positive borders for different numbers of partitions. The space needed to store the positive borders is linearly proportional to the number of partitions. In our experiments, the storage overhead for 30 partitions and minimum support = 0.1 was c.a. 50% of the size of the database. This is the cost of faster mining association rules.

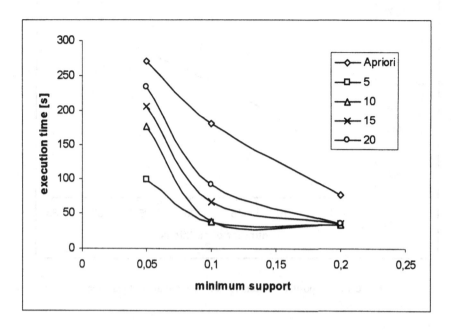

Fig. 4. Execution time for different minimum support values

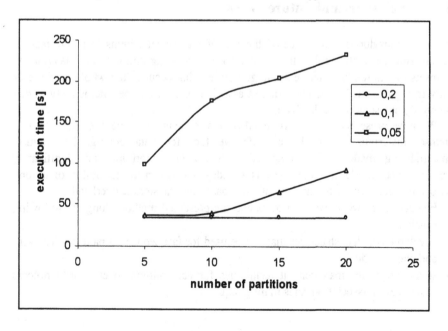

Fig. 5. Execution time for different numbers of partitions and different minimum supports

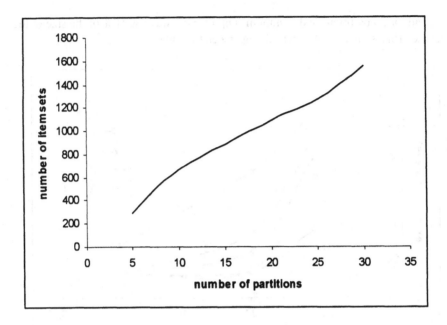

Fig. 6. Size of positive borders for different numbers of partition

4   Conclusions and Future Work

We have introduced and discussed the use of materialized itemsets in the task of discovering association rules in large databases. Our algorithm uses the materialized itemsets to efficiently generate the large itemsets that occur in the whole database or only in a part of it. Thus, the required association rules can be interactively mined with only one scan of the database.

We have presented our experimental results for synthetic databases to show that itemset materializing can be an effective tool for data mining. The itemset materializing method was compared with *Apriori* algorithm and significantly outperformed it. We note that there is a trade-off between the flexibility of mining association rules (in different parts of a database) and the storage overhead.

For the future work, we plan to extend the presented method along the following dimensions:

- develop other data structures that can be used for fast sequential patterns discovery and classification,
- study the buffer management techniques for data mining to efficiently process sequences of association rules mining requests.

References

1. Agrawal R., Imielinski T., Swami A., "Mining Association Rules Between Sets of Items in Large Databases", Proc. ACM SIGMOD, pp. 207-216, Washington DC, USA, May 1993
2. Agrawal R., Mehta M., Shafer J., Srikant R., Arning A., Bollinger T., "The Quest Data Mining System", Proc. of the 2nd Int'l Conference on Knowledge Discovery in Databases and Data Mining, Portland, Oregon, August 1996
3. Agrawal R., Srikant R., "Fast Algorithms for Mining Association Rules", Proc. 20th Int'l Conf. Very Large Data Bases, pp. 478-499, Santiago, Chile, 1994
4. Cheung D.W., Han J., Ng V., Wong C.Y., "Maintenance of Discovered Association Rules in Large Databases: An Incremental Updating Technique", Proc. Int'l Conf. Dana Eng., New Orleans, USA, February 1996
5. Fayyad U., Piatetsky-Shapiro G., Smyth P., "The KDD Process for Extracting Useful Knowledge from Volumes of Data", Communications of the ACM, Vol. 39, No. 11, Nov. 1996
6. Han J., "Towards On-Line Analytical Mining in Large Databases, SIGMOD Record", Vol. 27, No. 1, March 1998
7. Houtsma M., Swami A., "Set-Oriented Mining of Association Rules", Research Report RJ 9567, IBM Almaden Research Center, San Jose, California, USA, October 1993
8. Imielinski T., Manilla H., "A Database Perspective on Knowledge Discovery", Communications of the ACM, Vol. 39, No. 11, Nov. 1996
9. Manilla H., Toivonen H., Inkeri Verkamo A., "Efficient Algorithms for Discovering Association Rules", Proc. AAAI Workshop Knowledge Discovery in Databases, pp. 181-192, July 1994
10. Manilla H., Toivonnen H., "Levelwise Search and Borders of Theories in Knowledge Discovery", Report C-1997-8, University of Helsinki, Finland
11. Morzy T., Zakrzewicz M., " SQL-Like Language For Database Mining", ADBIS'97 Symposium, St. Petersburg, September 1997
12. Park J.S., Chen M.-S., Yu P. S., "An Effective Hash-Based Algorithm for Mining Association Rules", SIGMOD'95, San Jose, CA, USA, 1995
13. Piatetsky-Shapiro G., Frawley W.J., editors, Knowledge Discovery in Databases, MIT Press, 1991
14. Savasere, E. Omiecinski, S. Navathe, "An Efficient Algorithm for Mining Association Rules in Large Databases", Proc. 21th Int'l Conf. Very Large Data Bases, pp. 432-444, Zurich, Switzerland, September 1995
15. Toivonen H., "Sampling Large Databases for Association Rules", Proc. 22nd Int'l Conf. Very Large Data Bases, Bombay, India, 1996

Schema Derivation for WWW Information Sources and Their Integration with Databases in Bioinformatics[*]

Michael Höding, Ralf Hofestädt, Gunter Saake and Uwe Scholz

Otto-von-Guericke-Universität Magdeburg
Institut für Technische und Betriebliche Informationssysteme
Postfach 4120, D–39016 Magdeburg, Germany
{hoeding|hofestae|saake|uscholz}@iti.cs.uni-magdeburg.de

Abstract. In this paper we discuss first experiences and results of current work on the Bio_{Bench}, an integrated information system for Bioinformatics. Since the major part of Bioinformatic data is distributed in many heterogeneous systems all over the world one has to deal with problems of integration of heterogeneous systems. Especially semi-structured data, presented via WWW-interfaces has to be integrated. Therefore, we focus on the aspects of acquisition, integration and management of the data for the Bio_{Bench}. First we give a short motivation of the project and an overview of the system. In the main follows a discussion of schema derivation for the WWW-interfaces. Thereby, we discuss the application of domain knowledge and automatic grammar generation. Finally we briefly describe an automatic wrapper generation approach, supporting high quality wrappers as well as wrapper modification according to local schema or format evolutions.

1 Introduction

Nowadays biotechnology is becoming a key technology for the future. The research covers topics from advanced agriculture to medicine. Many researchers all over the world are collecting information about genes, metabolic pathways, diseases, etc. Commonly each task or application scenario owns a dedicated software system. These systems have to manage huge data collections. However, many systems are focused on a specific application of data only. Often, the vital data is stored in flat files, using an own file format. Fewer systems are based on database management systems. We have to point out, that many researchers have a specific application scenario and their own systems are quite suitable to solve the essential research problems.

Nevertheless an integration of data from different systems containing information from the same or from related domains is a quite promising task

---

[*] This research was partially supported by the German State Sachsen-Anhalt under FKZ: 1987A/0025 and 1987/2527B and the Kurt-Eberhard-Bode-Foundation under FKZ: T 122/4

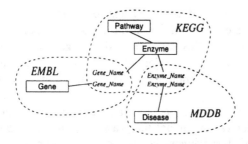

Fig. 1. Overlapping databases from different application domains

for biotechnology research. To illustrate this fact in figure 1 we sketched the overlapping domains referring to the main entities which are contained in the KEGG-System (enzymes and metabolic pathways) [14, 9], our MDDB-System (metabolic diseases), and the EMBL-Database (genes) [20]. (The figure simplifies the situation because commonly we neither have database-like access to the data nor equivalent attributes available.) Obviously, an integrated view can support new approaches for biotechnology. For instance, the integrating of the mentioned systems enables complex queries concerning diseases and genes. On the other hand, the integration of different systems containing data of the same domain could be provide more complete databases. Moreover, the detection of existing redundancies offers opportunities for error detection. Based on an integrated database new kinds of applications can be developed.

2   The Bio$_{Bench}$ Project

The current work of our research group is focused on the application area as well as on the database integration field. The applications can be classified into

- applications for intuitive and high level data presentation, e.g. presentation of pathways with annotations and links to data from distributed and heterogeneous data sources, and
- applications for data processing, e.g. analysis or simulation tools processing related data (cf. [12]).

Beside this, we maintain an own database containing information about metabolic diseases, the MDDB database. However, for advanced applications, e.g. data-mining techniques for knowledge acquisition, a well structured database with as many as possible data is necessary. To support such a database we started the Bio$_{Bench}$ project [13]. The current system architecture (cf. figure 2) is based on the ideas of federated database systems (FDBS) [19] and mediator systems [22, 5, 10]. The local systems are covered by a virtual interface supporting homogeneous access to the heterogeneous and distributed data. Since we are using JAVA as the implementation language we choose an appropriate object-oriented data model as the data model of the virtual integrated interface. For each system that should be integrated, a specific adapter or mediator [22] presenting the data with the common data-model has to be designed. The integration of existing database systems with different data models was discussed in numerous publications concerning FDBS [19, 15, 6]. Adapter generation and access to files and semi-structured data were subject of [1, 11, 21, 4]. Based on the interface of the adapters an integration component merges and unifies the data of different systems.

Due to the fact that the important databases in Bioinformatics are permanently growing a logical or virtual integration approach seems to be suitable. However, in case of slow network connections caching or data import can improve the performance of the system, perhaps with a reduction of information quality. We have to mention, that in contrast to traditional FDBS scenarios no writing access to the distributed systems has to be supported. Therefore the virtual integrated interface is a simple subset of a federating database management system.

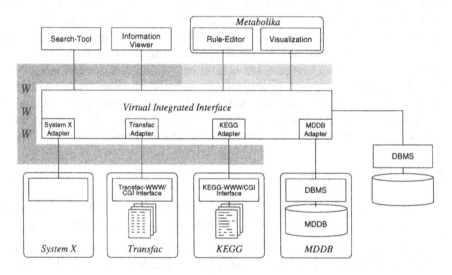

Fig. 2. The current architecture of the Bio$_{Bench}$

Current activities focus on the development of system specific adapters (cf. section 4), translating data from the heterogeneous systems into a common representation, and on the design of an integrated schema. For the design of the integrated schema, methods and tools of FDBS design are used [17, 6].

3 Heterogeneous Data Sources in Bioinformatics

As mentioned before, the information sources in Bioinformatics are distributed and heterogeneous. In this section we discuss classes of information systems we have found. Our classification is based on the experiences and results from pre-studies in the Bio$_{Bench}$ project. For each class we briefly discuss the aspects *kind of access interface* and *availability of schema information.* The kind of the access interface (this can be an application programmers interface as well as a user interface) is essential for the implementation of adapters and their performance. The availability of schema information[1] determines the cost of adapter generation.

- *Class A: Database systems offering common access to their data*

  If the owner of an information system based on a real database management system offers such an interface a comfortable access to the data is possible. Complex queries are optimized by the database system. This could provide high performance - also in distributed systems using wide area networks, e.g. the Internet. This is a precondition for efficient data processing for new approaches or algorithms in Bioinformatics.

  The schema-information, essential for the necessary integration, can be taken from the schema catalogue which is commonly supported by database management systems.

- *Class B: Information systems offering own interfaces for specific queries and navigating access*

  Nowadays, many groups offer WWW interfaces to their databases. Commonly these interfaces allow specific queries for a dedicated application scenario, mostly with navigating access. The interfaces are designed for human interaction and data-presentation. Therefore, they are less suitable for the automated access and effective processing of data. Such an interface has to be wrapped by a system specific adapter module.

  For the implementation of adapters we need schema information describing the structure of the WWW pages. Commonly this information is not available. However, the presentation information can help to derive schema information automatically. We will discuss this question in more detail in the following sections.

- *Class C: Systems without an interface offering flat files*

  Traditionally information systems developed for specific research applications are based on own file formats. Flat files can also be a database dump in a specific export file format. As argued before, the stored information might also be relevant for other application fields. Therefore, adapters, wrapping the file cluster are necessary for a database-like access. The derivation of schema information and the design of adapters is commonly more complex than in the former case, because the files are not associated with the presentation format HTML. However, local copies of dedicated files allow better performance for data processing.

Our view to existing systems that should be integrated in the Bio$_{Bench}$ shows that the majority of the systems belongs to class B (KEGG, Transfac) and class C (Transfac, EMBL). Class A contains our local database system as part of the MDDB-System.

---

[1] information about the syntax and semantics of the information delivered by a data sources

Another aspect is the data change frequency. Commonly we can distinguish systems changing data very frequently (many times in every hour), often (daily), rare (monthly) or never. Databases in Bioinformatics belong commonly to the last two or three groups. Moreover, mainly the set of stored information is growing and not changing. This situation offers possibilities for caching or import-architectures without major loss of data quality.

4 Schema Derivation for Semi Structured Data

In this section we discuss our approach for the design of adapters to the semistructured data-sources of class B and class C according to the classification presented in the previous section. The the design of adapters is a quite expensive task. Therefore a systematical approach is necessary [2].

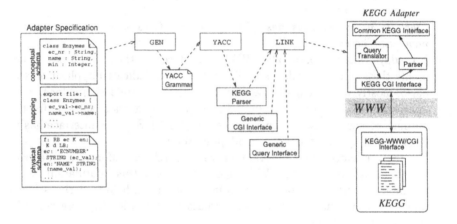

Fig. 3. Automatic generation of an adapter

For the conceptual design of adapters we propose the use of two schema levels and a mapping between the schemata of these levels. The first level describes the physical structure or the syntax of the file-cluster. Mapping this schema to the schema of the second level, which specifies semantics in a common data model, allows the automatic generation of adapters (cf. figure 3). We can refer to these schemata as physical schema and conceptual schema similar to the 3-level-architecture of ANSI-SPARC [7]. As mentioned before, an object-oriented data model is used as the common data model. The choose of a data model for the physical schema level is more sophisticated. It strongly depends on the concepts which are used by the local file formats. To illustrate possible problems we briefly list concepts that can be combined and used to express semantics in files:

- query names: e.g. path names for files or HTTP addresses for WWW pages can contain attribute values (especially keys)

- positions: absolute or relative position determines the meaning of data
- order: similar to 'position' the order can be used to express semantics
- data: tokens, e.g. attribute names, determine the meaning of the following data

In many cases a grammar is suitable for the physical schema. This could be a grammar as necessary for the parser generator YACC [1] or a SGML document type definition [3, 11]. The former one allows an easy implementation with tools like YACC whereas the latter one offers more intuitive grammars with a smaller set of rules. A compromise solution was proposed in [8] combining YACC grammars with set operators known from SGML.

The resulting question is: How can we derive the schemata for both levels? Due to the fact, that we have very large databases (in our case numerous or large files) this step has to be supported by tools. This could reduce the necessary efforts and improve the quality of the derived schemata. There are two thinkable approaches (cf. figure 4):

- *Description, mapping and evaluation [8]*
  For this approach the designer specifies the conceptual schema first. The quality of the result strongly depends on the knowledge about the information system and the domain knowledge. Then she or he specifies the mapping from the classes of the designed schema to elements in example files. This leads to grammar fragments which have to be completed. The next step is the evaluation of the grammar and the conceptual schema.
- *Analysis, grammar generation and annotation [18]*
  This approach is based on the formal methods of pattern recognition and grammatical inference. Starting with results of a syntactical analysis which determines specific symbols, e.g. delimiters or brackets, a tool generates a grammar according to given example files. The grammar has to be annotated by the designer with mappings to a conceptual schema.

Commonly the approaches should be combined.

For both methods the designer needs good domain knowledge. On one hand, she or he should know the essential entities and their attributes to find their names (or synonyms of them) as tokens in files or WWW pages. On the other hand, knowledge of typical data is also quite useful, especially if the data source format does not include tokens. For that case the integration scenario can support the designer with data or meta data. For instance, if a local database exists (in our case the MDDB system), a tool can search the WWW pages for attribute names given by the schema of the available database. In that way it is possible to find the (relative) position of the attributes.

Another possibility is the use of data contained in the available database, e.g. if the database contains a class `Diseases` with the attribute **name** and the values 'gout', 'albinism', or 'diabetis mellitus' and the tool recognized the relative or absolute position of these strings in given WWW pages it implies grammatical rules and mappings to the conceptual schema.

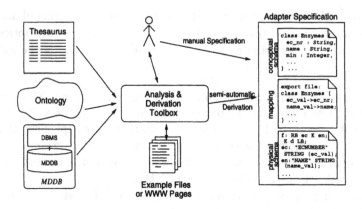

Fig. 4. Manual specification and semi-automatic derivation of schemata

In a similar manner a knowledge base, e.g. an ontology or a thesaurus, describing the the most important entities of the application scenario can support semi-automatic grammar and schema derivation.

Another potential source for the derivation of schema information are constructs for data presentation. Good examples can be found in the HTML-Format. E.g. a list construct for the presentation of WWW pages commonly contains elements which can be represented as objects of the same class. Another example is the use of tables. A table in a WWW page can be transformed into an extension of a class. Every column number determines the attribute name and a row refers to an object. However, it could also be vice versa. Moreover, the first row can contain possible attribute names. Obviously such presentation oriented formats commonly support only hints which have to be evaluated.

Besides, it is necessary to point out some restrictions of the approach. It is not guaranteed that the given example files or WWW pages of the explored information systems represent all possible data or meta data. It is only a current database state! Usually, grammar generation and schema derivation still needs a lot of user interaction. For that a suitable and intuitive presentation of data and meta data is necessary. Solutions and tools supporting automatic and interactive steps are part of the currently developed FDBS design framework Sigma$_{Bench}$ [16]. Applying existing tools in adapter design for the Bio$_{Bench}$ shows the possible benefits of the approach.

5 Conclusion and Outlook

In this work we introduced demands and solutions for an integrating information system in Bioinformatics. We emphasized the problems of the virtual integration of distributed and heterogeneous data sources, especially of semi-structured data, accessible via WWW interfaces. We briefly presented the goals and the architecture of the Bio$_{Bench}$ project. Then we discussed an approach to a semi-automatic derivation of schema information for adapter design. Adapters can be generated automatically according to a given specification describing syntax and semantics of local data sources. The derivation of schema information which is necessary for the adapters should be supported by tools, but can not be completely automated. For the semi-automatic derivation or specification of the schema information we briefly discussed two ways, using formal methods as well as domain knowledge or information from other related databases.

The current implementation of the Bio$_{Bench}$ allows specific queries to the virtual interface, e.g. to metabolic pathway data. This integrated data can be viewed using an WWW based graphical user interface. Moreover, the simulation tool for metabolic pathways Metabolika now has a transparent access to distributed data. However, the current solution needs a lot of maintenance. The implemented adapter strongly depends on the formats of WWW pages or files generated by the integrated systems. Every change of this formats causes a re-design and a re-implementation of the adapter. Moreover, the current solution supports only a restricted view to the distributed data which is designed for our applications.

Future work will tackle this problems and improve the methods for semi-automatic schema derivation and adapter generation.

References

1. S. Abiteboul, S. Cluet, and T. Milo. Querying and Updating the File. In *Proc. of the 19th VLDB Conference*, pages 73–84, Dublin, Ireland, August 1993.
2. S. Abiteboul, D. Quass, J. McHugh, J. Widom, and J.L. Wiener. The Lorel query language for semistructured data. *Int. Journal on Digital Libraries*, 1(1):68–88, 1997.
3. H. Ahonen, H. Mannila, and N. Nikunen. Generating Grammars for SGML Tagged Texts Lacking DTD. In *Proc. of PODP'94 – Workshop on Principles of Document Processing*, 1994.
4. N. Ashish and C. Knoblock. Wrapper Generation for Semi-structured Internet Sources. *ACM SIGMOD Record*, 26(4):8–15, December 1997.
5. S. S. Chawathe, H. Garcia-Molina, J. Hammer, K. Ireland, Y. Papakonstantinou, J. D. Ullman, and J. Widom. The TSIMMIS Project: Integration of Heteregenous Information Sources. In *Proc. of IPSI Conf.*, 1994.
6. S. Conrad, M. Höding, G. Saake, I. Schmitt, and C. Türker. Schema Integration with Integrity Constraints. In C. Small, P. Douglas, R. Johnson, P. King, and N. Martin, editors, *Advances in Databases, 15th British National Conf. on Databases, BNCOD 15, London, UK, July 1997*, volume 1271 of *Lecture Notes in Computer Science*, pages 200–214, Berlin, 1997. Springer-Verlag.
7. Database Architecture Framework Task Group (DAFTG) of the ANSI/X3/SPARC Database System Study Group. Reference Model for DBMS Standardization. *ACM SIGMOD Record*, 15(1):19–58, March 1986.
8. A. Ebert. Enhancement of the ODMG Data Definition Language for the Integration of Files into Database Federations (In German). Master's thesis, University of Magdeburg, Faculty of Computer Sciences, September 1997.
9. S. Goto, H. Bono, H. Ogata, T. Fujibuchi, T. Nishioka, K. Sato, and M. Kanehisa. Organizing and Computing Metabolic Pathway Data in Terms of Binary Relations.

In R. B. Altman, A. K. Dunker, L. Hunter, and T. E. Klein, editors, *Pacific Symposium on Biocomputing '97*, pages 175–186. Singapore et al: World Scientific, 1997.

10. Hammer, J. and Garcia-Molina, H. and Nestorov, S. and Yerneni, R. and Breunig, M. and Vassalos, V. Template-Based Wrappers in the TSIMMIS System. In J. M. Peckman, editor, *Proc. of the 1997 ACM SIGMOD Int. Conf. on Management of Data, Tucson, Arizona, USA*, volume 26 of *ACM SIGMOD Record*, pages 532–535. ACM Press, June 1997.

11. M. Höding. An Approach to Integration of File Based Systems into Database Federations. In *Heterogeneous Information Management, Prague, Czech Republic, 4–5 November 1996, Proc. of the 10th ERCIM Database Research Group Workshop*, pages 61–71. ERCIM-96-W003, European Research Consortium for Informatics and Mathematics, 1996.

12. R. Hofestädt and F. Meinecke. Interactive Modelling and Simulation of Biochemical Networks. *Computers in Biology and Medicine*, 25(3):321–334, 1995.

13. R. Hofestädt and U. Scholz. Information Processing for the Analysis of Metabolic Pathways and Inborn Errors. In *Biosystems*, 1998. *im Druck*.

14. M. Kanehisa. Toward pathway engineering: a new database of genetic and molecular pathways. *Science & Technology Japan*, 59:34–38, 1996.

15. B. Rieche and K. R. Dittrich. A Federated DBMS-Based Integrated Environment for Molecular Biology. In J. C. French and H. Hinterberger, editors, *Proc. of Seventh International Working Conference on Scientific and Statistical Database Management*, pages 118–127, Charlottesville, USA, September 1994. IEEE Computer Society Press.

16. I. Schmitt, A. Ebert, M. Höding, and C. Türker. SIGMA$_{Bench}$ – A Tool-Kit for the Design of Federated Database System (In German). In W. Hasselbring, editor, *Kurzfassungen zum 2. Workshops "Föderierte Datenbanken", Dortmund, 12.-13. Dezember 1996*, number 90, pages 19–26. Fachbereich Informatik, Universität Dortmund, 1996.

17. I. Schmitt and G. Saake. Integration of Inheritance Trees as Part of View Generation for Database Federations. In B. Thalheim, editor, *Conceptual Modelling — ER'96, Proc. of the 15th Int. Conf., Cottbus, Germany, October 1996*, volume 1157 of *Lecture Notes in Computer Science*, pages 195–210, Berlin, 1996. Springer-Verlag.

18. B. Schroeder. Concepts for Schema Extraction from File for the Integration in Database Federations (In German). Master's thesis, University of Magdeburg, Faculty of Computer Sciences, September 1997.

19. A. P. Sheth and J. A. Larson. Federated Database Systems for Managing Distributed, Heterogeneous, and Autonomous Databases. *ACM Computing Surveys*, 22(3):183–236, September 1990.

20. P. J. Stoehr and G. N. Cameron. The embl data library. *Nucleic Acids Research*, 19, 1991.

21. Suciu, D. Management of Semistructured Data. *ACM SIGMOD Record*, 26(4):4–7, December 1997.

22. G. Wiederhold. Mediators in the Architecture of Future Information Systems. *IEEE Computer*, 25(3):38–49, March 1992.

Component-Based Information Systems Development Tool Supporting the SYNTHESIS Design Method

Dmitry Briukhov and Leonid Kalinichenko

Institute for Problems of Informatics
Russian Academy of Sciences
Vavilova 30/6, Moscow, V-334, 117900
{brd,leonidk}@synth.ipi.ac.ru

Abstract. An approach intended to fill in the gap between the existing Object Analysis and Design (OAD) methods applying mostly top-down technique and the demand of the middleware architectures (OMG CORBA) for the information system development based on composition of pre-existing interoperating components is discussed. An overview of the SYNTHESIS method for component-based interoperable information systems design is presented. The heuristic procedure for the most common reduct construction for a pair of ontologically relevant type specifications is outlined. The refinement property of the common reduct leads to a justifiable identification of reusable component fragments. The process of design is based on such identification driven by ontologically relevant pairs of types. The common reducts discovered are composed further to construct specifications serving as concretizations of the required types. The structure and functions of the design tool supporting the SYNTHESIS method and a process of design under the tool are considered.
vspace0.1 in
Keywords: component-based information system development, interoperable systems.

1 Introduction

Main objective of the component-based information systems development consists in deviating of production of handcrafted lines of code to system construction based on object-oriented components and automated processes. DCOM ActiveX and SunSoft JavaBeans solutions show a practical way for component-based software development. Enterprise JavaBeans bring interoperable server components into consideration. Object Analysis and Design Methods are consolidating around UML diagrammatic representation with the serious moves to component-based software reuse solutions [9].

The industrial trends in component-based development are characterized by low level specifications (actually, conventional programming techniques) hidden by the visualization tools. These approaches are good to support local libraries assuming good knowledge of their components by programmers, programming with reuse becomes unsafe [10] due to low level of specifications and unability to justify the adequacy of components to specification of requirements.

In this paper we present structure, interfaces and functionality of the prototype supporting component-based information development in frame of the SYNTHESIS method [1] [11, 3, 12].

The SYNTHESIS method brings more semantics into the component-based design to fill in the gaps mentioned and to make process of reusable component identification and composition more automated, controllable and justifiable. Interoperability (as in the architectures like the OMG CORBA) is considered in the project as a universal paradigm for compositional information systems development (technically interoperability implies composition of behaviours) in the range of systems scaling from non-distributed object-oriented systems to large systems composed of heterogeneous, distributed software components. Correct compositions of information systems components should be semantically interoperable in contexts of specific applications.

The overall goal of the SYNTHESIS project is to provide a uniform collection of modeling facilities suitable for different phases of the forward engineering activities (that lead to construction of new information systems on the basis of pre-existing reusable components) as well as for the reverse engineering phases (that deal with the extraction of components from existing software or legacy system descriptions with the provision for these parts of homogeneous and equivalent specifications for further reuse). The SYNTHESIS method emphasizes the semantic interoperation reasoning (SIR) process [3] that should lead to the concretization of specification of requirements by compositions created over the pre-existing information resources. We intend to build information systems from existing components primarily by assembling, replacing, wrapping and adapting the interoperable parts. Components in their turn may have similar structure.

SYNTHESIS method belongs to *formal and knowledge-based techniques* that are focused on component composition process by means of combination of formal and semi-formal methods. The formal approach relies on independently developed components (pre-existing resources that may also result from a re-engineering of legacy systems) by negotiating their interoperability on the basis of domain knowledge and component semantics.

The problem of components is that they do not have sufficiently clean semantic specifications to rely on for their reuse. We distinguish between application semantics and object model semantics. The latter we represent in frame of a "canonical" semi-formal object model used for uniform representations of various object and data model specifications in one paradigm. To give the canonical model exact meaning, we construct a mapping of this object model into the formal one (we choose for that Abstract Machine Notation (AMN) of the B-Technology [1, 2]).

---

[1] The SYNTHESIS project developed at the Institute for Problems of Informatics of the Russian Academy of Sciences (IPI RAS) is partially supported by the INTAS grant 94-1817 and the Russian Foundation for Basic Research grant 97-07-90369

Such canonical model provides capabilities of consistency check of specifications and supports concept of *refinement* of requirements by pre-existing components [3] that is crucial for component-based development. Specifying components developed in different object models, we should preserve information and operations of their types while mapping them into the canonical types. The required state-based and behavioural properties of the mappings lead to a proof that a source type model is a refinement of its mapping into the canonical type model [14]. Related researches [18, 21] are applied to storing and retrieving software components based on formal specifications of components and on the refinement ordering between specifications.

Application semantics of specifications we consider separately in frame of the ontological approach. The ontological model introduced is based on the canonical object model. For each of the component specification suspected to be relevant to the application the reconciliation of its ontological context with the application domain ontological context should be made.

According to SYNTHESIS, a process of the component-based information system development arranged around the middleware concept is considered as a CASE-like activity. The requirement planning and analysis phases of the conventional system development process are augmented with ontological specifications and complete specifications of type invariants and operations defined in the canonical model. The design phase is completely reconsidered: this is the design with reuse of the pre-existing components homogeneously specified in the canonical model.

The steps of the design process include integration of application domain and of information resource ontological contexts establishing the ontological relevance of constituents of requirements and components specifications, identification of component types (classes) and their fragments suitable for the concretization of an analysis model type (class) capturing its structural, extensional and behavioural properties, composition of such fragments into specifications concretizing the requirements, justification of a property of concretization of requirements by such compositions.

Type specifications and their reducts are chosen as the basic units of specification manipulation. Taking common type reduct for a pair of ontologically relevant types is a basic operation of manipulation and transformation of type specifications. Reducts of the component type specifications can be used as minimal fragments potentially reusable for the respective reducts of the analysis model types. The identification of the fact of type reducts reusability is the main concern of the design. Operations of type algebra are used to produce specifications of respective compositions of their operands. Correctness of the results of design can be verified using formal facilities of the canonical level.

Different aspects of the SYNTHESIS approach were considered in [12, 3–5, 14, 15]. This paper concentrates mostly on the facilities of the prototype supporting component-based design according to SYNTHESIS and is structured as follows. The first part of the paper presents a brief overview of the SYNTHESIS methodology. The SYNTHESIS modeling framework based on well-defined canonical model is introduced. Basic constituents of the SYNTHESIS methods are presented: an approach providing for ontological integration of different application domains contexts, the concepts of the most common reducts for the abstract data types, the method for common reducts identification, the method for reusable fragments composition into a specification refining the requirements. The second part of the paper shows how the SYNTHESIS method is supported by the SYNTHESIS design tool. The processes of ontological integration, common reduct identification, conformant type structure paths detection, concretizing type composition construction are considered.

2 SYNTHESIS Methodology

2.1 SYNTHESIS Modeling Framework

The following specification models and respective macro layers are constituents of the SYNTHESIS modeling framework:

1. *Ontological model.* The model is used for definition of application contexts of problem domains providing for their terminological and conceptual specifications. The modeling facilities for ontological definitions include a combination of natural language verbal specification facilities and canonical object model facilities used for the concept definitions.

2. *Requirement planning / Analysis models.* Requirement planning is aimed at thorough description of the problem domain and detailed specification of the information system requirements. Analysis modeling leads to the development of specification of the system in accordance with the requirements. We assume that the modeling facilities for both models are based on the canonical object model and its mapping into the formal notation.

3. *Design model.* Design modeling is oriented on a component-based design in the heterogeneous interoperable information resource environment (HIRE) according to the analysis model specifications. For the design the canonical modeling facilities are extended with specific features for specification of component type compositions to serve as a refinement of the analysis model types and for verification of such refinements. Specific features are provided also for the ontological specifications reconciliation.

4. *Implementation model.* An implementation model describes how the logical design of the system is mapped onto physical realization. Basic notions of the implementation model are servers, adapter types, implementation types. The model supplies information about distribution of implementations over the set of servers of HIRE which make up the system. In particular, we should decide which design type should be supported by which component adapters, how implementation types should be arranged into groups implementing a single design type, how implementations are hosted by different machines. The required adapters and the respective interface specifications supporting core interoperation level should be implemented.

5. *Information resource specification model.* The model provides for complete specification of pre-existing components. The facilities are a combination of ontological, design and implementation modeling.

The semantics behind any of these models is provided by one and the same descriptive canonical object model treated in a semi-formal style and having a formal interpretation. Canonical model should provide for the integrated support of various functions, including (i) semi-formal representation of the specification of requirements and analysis models of information systems; (ii) description of ontological contexts of application domains and justification of their coherence; (iii) uniform (canonical) representation of specifications of heterogeneous components; (iv) support of semantic reconciliation and adaptation of components to form their reducts and compositions serving as concretizations of analysis models of information systems.

The semi-formal canonical model should have a formal model-theoretic interpretation. Mapping of semi-formal specification into a formal one allows to develop a formal model of an application domain and of components reflecting their static and dynamic properties. Formal specifications and respective tools create a basis for provable reasoning on the specification consistency and provable concretization of specification of requirements by pre-existing components compositions.

A general picture showing logical functioning of the SYNTHESIS framework is presented on Fig. 1. Here we emphasize that for the forward development phase (the flow at the left side of the picture) as well as for the backward development phase (the flow at the right side of the picture) we should have in mind an application domain that subsumes application semantics for specification of requirements or for specification of a pre-existing component (an information resource). We can meaningfully interprete pre-existing components in context of some application. Therefore, we should establish a coherence of the respective application contexts. Ontological specifications for both phases should be introduced for that.

The picture does not show explicitly steps of requirement planning, system analysis and reverse engineering. A possibility of relying on various existing object analysis and design or reverse engineering methods for these purposes is emphasized. We assume that these methods can be properly adjusted to reflect complete specifications required for SYNTHESIS. Results of the Forward and Backward processes serve as an input to the design with reuse that is the the key phase to reach component reuse and semantic interoperability.

For our approach it is of crucial importance that whatever notations could be used by the methods on the layers listed, we supply this notation with a clean object semantics given by the underlying object model – one and the same for different specification layers and models. This model is the canonical semi-formal object model [12] and its mapping into a formal notation - Abstract Machine Notation of the B Method [1]. Metaobject repository serves as an input for the process of the formal specification generation.

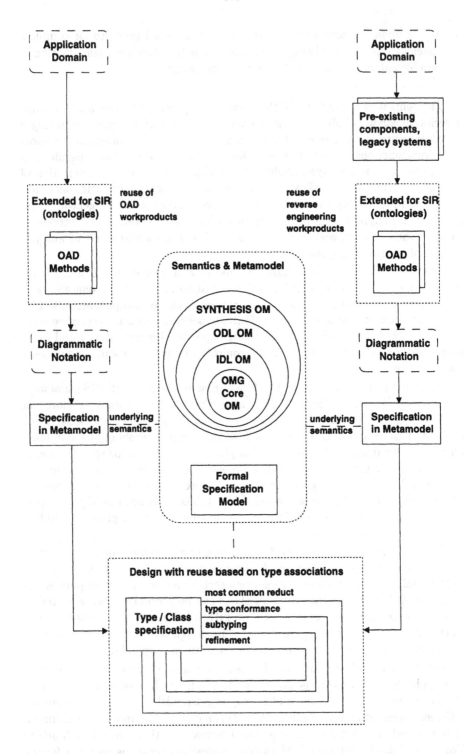

Fig. 1. SIR Framework

The following principles for the model definition on various layers are exploited:

1. provision of possibly various suitable notations for different layers of the development process;
2. separation of notations, the descriptive model used and the process of development;
3. structuring of the design procedure as an autonomous phase independent of other development phases providing for its embedding into various object analysis and design tools;
4. focusing implementation phase on the core (technical) interoperation environment (such as CORBA) to provide for the structuring of implementation in clients and servers so that one specification type can span borders of several servers or a server can include implementations of several types.

Formal specifications are intended to be used:

1. at the analysis phase to check consistency of type specifications obtained (a type specification should have a model and operations of the specifications should not violate invariants);
2. at the design phase to check a refinement relationship of constructions obtained for different design purposes (such as, e.g., producing of common reducts, their compositions or concretization views construction);
3. at the backward phase to justify that original component specifications refine their mapping into the canonical model.

An introduction into basic constituents of the SYNTHESIS method is given in this section. Examples illustrating the approach can be found in the next section presenting the SYNTHESIS design tool.

2.2 Interconcept Correlation Based on Their Verbal Descriptions

We assume that ontological definitions are provided for specification of requirements (collected in Application Ontology Modules – AOM), for specification of information resources (collected in Resource Ontology Modules – ROM) and for common domain-specific ontology (collected in Common Ontology Modules – COM). Each ontology module consists of the respective concept specifications. Each concept specification consists of the verbal description of the concept and positive and superconcept/subconcept association with other concepts.

We also introduce the *similarity functions* to establish positive associations between application and resource concepts. A constituent I_r of a resource specification is *loosely* ontologically relevant to a constituent I_s of a specification of requirements of the same kind (type, class, function, attribute, etc.) if I_r name has a positive association to I_s name or if I_r name is a hyponym of I_s name.

Similarity functions are introduced as follows. Let C be a n-component vector, where n is the number of linguistic terms characterizing terms in the system, and C_i, $1 \le i \le n$, denote its i-th component, namely the i- th term. The association of a set of terms with a term X can be represented by an n-component vector Cx, where $Cx_i = 0$ if term C_i is not associated with X, otherwise $Cx_i = 1$. Given two vectors Cx and Cy of two terms X and Y, a similarity function can be defined as follows:

$$sim(Cx, Cy) = \frac{(Cx*Cy)}{\sqrt{(|Cx|*|Cy|)}}$$

where $*$ is the vector product and $|Z|$ is the number of components in the vector Z. This correlation function calculates cosinus of the angle between vectors Cx and Cy. For two identical vectors the angle is equal to 0; for two vectors having no common terms cosinus of the angle is equal to 0. More details on that can be found in [4].

Based on the verbal concept definitions, a *loose* interconcept correlation is established. *Tight* correlation is formed specifying concepts as interrelated types in the canonical model. Tight correlation will not be considered here.

2.3 Type Specification Reuse and Compositions

Most Common Reduct Information system development is a process of construction and refinement of type specifications. Considering development with reuse, we need operations on type specifications leading to transformation of their specifications - decomposition and composition.

We remind here basic definitions of reusable fragments for a type as they were given in [13]. A *type reduct* R_T can be considered a *subspecification* of a specification of a type T. The specification of R_T should be formed so that R_T becomes a supertype of T. Decomposing a type specification, we can get its different reducts on the basis of various type specification subsignatures. Reducts create a basis for their further compositions.

A **common reduct** for types T_1, T_2 is such reduct R_{T_1} of T_1 that there exists a reduct R_{T_2} of T_2 such that R_{T_2} is a refinement of R_{T_1}. Further we refer to R_{T_2} as to a *conjugate* of the common reduct.

Operations of the type T_1 are suspected to belong to its common reduct with T_2 if operations with similar signatures can be found in T_2 up to the parameter type relationship (contravariant for the argument types and covariant for the result types).

A specification of an operation of T_1 to be included into the resulting reduct is chosen among such pre-selected pairs of operations of operand types if the operations in a pair are in a refinement order (for the common reduct (resulting supertype) more abstract operation should be chosen). If the pre-selected operations in the pair are not in a proper refinement order then they are considered to be different operations and will not be included into the common reduct.

A **most common reduct** $R_{MC}(T_1, T_2)$ for types T_1, T_2 is a reduct R_{T_1} of T_1 such that there exists a reduct R_{T_2} of T_2 that refines R_{T_1} and there can be no other reduct $R_{T_1}^i$ such that $R_{MC}(T_1, T_2)$ is a reduct of $R_{T_1}^i$, $R_{T_1}^i$ is not equal to $R_{MC}(T_1, T_2)$ and there exists a reduct $R_{T_2}^i$ of T_2 that refines $R_{T_1}^i$.

The notion of a common type reduct is fundamental for the component-based design: it constitutes a basis for determining reusable fragments. An approach for searching for such fragments and most common reduct formation will be shortly considered further.

Other operations providing for creation of composition of reusable specification fragments are join, meet and product applied to complete type specifications as their arguments. The operations are based on a concept of a common type reduct and a refinement condition. More details on these operations can be found in [16].

Common Reduct Identification For each pair of type specifications Ts and Tr (each Tr should be ontologically relevant to Ts) we try to construct their common reduct. We start with identification of their *common signature reduct*. This procedure takes into account only signatures of types ignoring their complete specifications. After that most common reducts are constructed. This makes possible to identify the common reduct for Ts, Tr and the respective *concretizing* reduct of Tr that can be imagined as a conjugate of a common reduct that incorporates also necessary conflict reconciliation with Ts specifications. Finally, if required, we can justify the concretizations constructed so far by formal proofs.

Here and further the notion of *concretizing* specification (of reduct, type, class) means that the refining specification includes required mediating functions resolving value, structural or behavioural conflicts with the respective specification of the analysis level.

To identify common signature reducts, we should find for each pair of ontologically relevant types Ts, Tr a maximal collection A of pairs of attributes (a^i_{Ts}, a^j_{Tr}) that are also ontologically relevant and satisfy the type constraints so that a^j_{Tr} could be reused as a^i_{Ts}. General approach to form A for the pair of ontologically relevant types Ts and Tr is the following:

1. All ontologically relevant pairs of immediate state attributes (a^i_{Ts}, a^j_{Tr}) of the types belong to A if type of a^j_{Tr} is a subtype of type of a^i_{Ts}. This requirement can be completely checked for built-in attribute types. For the user defined types a pair of ontologically relevant attributes is conditionally included into A: final check is postponed until user defined attribute types relationship will be clarified.

2. All ontologically relevant pairs of immediate functional attributes (a^i_{Ts}, a^j_{Tr}) of the types belong to A if signatures of functions a^i_{Ts} and a^j_{Tr} satisfy the following requirements:

   (a) they have equal numbers of input parameters and of output parameters pairwise ontologically relevant;

   (b) for each ontologically relevant pair of input parameters their types should be in a contravariance relationship;

   (c) for each ontologically relevant pair of output parameters their types should be in a covariance relationship.

3. A pair of immediate attribute a^i_{Ts} of type Ts and of immediate attribute $a^j_{Tr'}$ of a component type Tr belongs to A if they do not satisfy conditions 1) or 2) above but $Ts, Tr, a^i_{Ts}, a^j_{Tr'}$ are included into reusable structures (paths) suggested by the reusable path detecting rules.

Structural conflicts deserve specific attention: they are resolved in a process of reusable path detecting process (3.1). This process resembles the processes developed for the database schema integration approaches [17].

On analysis of attribute pairs we recognize and resolve the various conflicts between the application and component type specifications. This resolution is reflected in specification of a concretizing reduct (3.1) that is a common reduct mediated to the specification of requirements level.

For common reducts the refinement condition is established using mapping of participating types and their reducts into AMN, specifying and proving the respective refinement machines. The mapping and proving procedure used for that were illustrated in [3].

Construction of Concretizing Types and Views Main task of the design with reuse phase is to specify views and concretizing types refining each application class and type specification. Up to now we have seen how reusable fragments for original types can be identified and specified. Using reusable fragments of the lowest level (common reducts specified just above the pre-existing components (information resources)), we try to apply operations of type algebra and their compositions to form intermediate and final type specifications refining the required types. Further coercions and mediation may be required in this process leading to creation of concretizing type specifications over compositions of specifications of the lower level. The hierachy of specifications formed in this process is shown on Fig. 2. Only one level of type compositions is shown here. Obviously, several levels are possible leading to further compositions of concretizing types (reducts).

The process of specification compositions according to such hierarchy is being developed along the following scheme. We consider a type t_s together with a collection of component types t_r related to t_s through most common reducts. We call this collection the *most common conformance* of $t_s - MCC(t_s)$.

Constructing further our type compositions we would like to cover t_s with minimal number of concretizing reducts. For participation in a composition, we select from $MCC(t_s)$ the reducts by the following procedure:

1. choose in $MCC(t_s)$ a concretizing reduct having maximal common reduct (covering maximal number of t_s attributes) with t_s, exclude it from $MCC(t_s)$ for participation in a composition;
2. find a residue of the t_s interface; exit if residue is empty; go to 1.

If after the procedure the residue of the t_s interface is not empty then we treat a reduct corresponding to this residue as a specification of the new component to be developed. To construct compositions of selected specifications refining t_s we

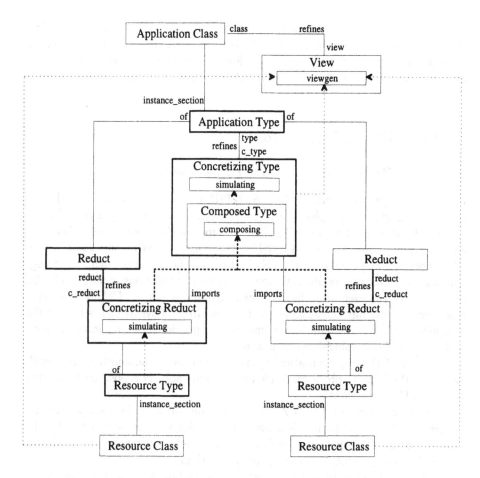

Fig. 2. Type (class) refining hierarchy formed during the design phase

apply type algebra operations (meet, join, product) [16] to concretizing reducts (types) to form types that are closer to the required type.

After that we construct a concretization type specification over the composition obtained before:

1. Construct an abstraction function mapping the state attributes of the composition type into the state attributes of the required type.
2. Construct wrapping operations based on the operations of participating types (if required).
3. Justify the refinement condition.

If our objective is to construct concretizations of required classes (views) then the criteria for choice of fragments included into type compositions supporting instance type t_s of the required class c_s is different. For each $t_r \in MCC(t_s)$ that can be selected as a candidate for further analysis, a class c_r that can make the most significant data contribution to c_s among other classes should correspond.

Now, the most common reduct of t_s and such t_r should contain collections of state attributes that may form class instance keys (several keys may be identified). Thus we make fragments of t_r instances joinable into instances of t_s. After that we use formulae of the canonic model object calculus to specify the required view.

3 SYNTHESIS Design Tool

3.1 SYNTHESIS Method Prototype Architecture

Fig.3 shows a general structure of the SYNTHESIS prototype supporting the design and implementation phases of the component-based development in HIRE.

We choosed the ParadigmPlus [20] to support the Requirement Planning and Analysis phases (the SYNTHESIS tool is independent on this choice). The UML notation augmented with SYNTHESIS specific features, such as ontological specifications and predicative specifications of operations is used. Actually any standard representation facilities can be suitable (as the UML subset with some extensions) but the approach is different from conventional one, it is the canonical model that has primary importance providing proper interpretation and meaning for graphical representation.

Using the CDIF representation [6] taken out of the ParadigmPlus, the specifications of the analysis phase are loaded into the metaobject repository supported by the PSE ObjectStore.

For formal modeling the B Abstract Machine Notation is used [1] that together with B-Toolkit [2] provides for type specification consistency check, adequacy of component specifications [14], establishment of a refinement condition, generating and proving respective proof obligations.

SYNTHESIS prototype is implemented using Java 1.1 under Windows NT 4.0. The tool is oriented on work in a CORBA-like interoperable environment: the tool generates an IDL specifications and CORBA-based adapters code.

During the rest of the paper we demonstrate our approach on an example (Fig. 4) showing parts of two schemas: schema of the specification of requirements and schema of the pre-existing component.

Ontological Integration Step The first step of the design phase consists in construction of vectors of terms for each verbally defined constituent of schema in AOM, ROM. An example of verbal concept definitions in AOM, ROM, COM follows.

Example of the ontological definitions represented in a SYNTHESIS language:

```
AOM:
{Organization;
 def: {group of people working cooperatively with a special purpose}
 }
```

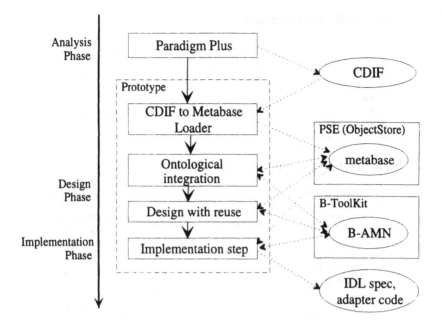

Fig. 3. SYNTHESIS Prototype Structure

```
ROM:
{Company;
 def: {group of employees joint for special business}
}

COM:
{Organization;
 def: {group of people joint to work together}
}
```

For each name definition a vector of terms included into the respective verbal specification is extracted. Then each vector is mapped to co-names in COM to get the map-to-concept vector. In this process a stop-word dictionary is used (SWD). If it appears that the word from a verbal definition is not in a set of the COM co-names, then we should check whether this word is included into SWD. If the word is not there, then it is appended to the logOfTerms file. This file is used afterwards by the experts maintaining COM to decide whether COM should be extended with a new co-name.

Example of component vectors for application type Organization and resource type Company. These vectors are presented in a map_to_concept slot.

```
{Organization;
 def: {group of people working cooperatively with a special purpose}
 map_to_concept: {council, staff, professor, organization, proposal}
```

Schema of requirements:

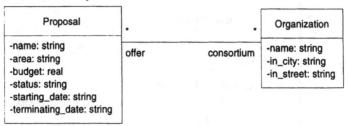

Schema of pre-existing component:

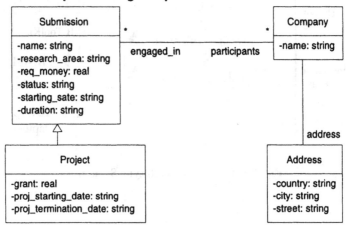

Fig. 4. Example

```
}

{Company;
 def: {group of people joint to work together}
 map_to_concept: {council, staff, professor, human, organization,
         specialist, proposal}
}
```

The second step consists in evaluation of correlations of AOM/ROM names using the term correlation function explained above (2.2). For each AOM name (for each schema constituent) we get a list of relevant ROM names sorted by the correlation factor.

After that the ROM names denoting another kinds of elements of the ROM schema will be filtered out from each list. The third step consists in manual work (Fig. 5): an expert can browse relevant AOM/ROM name pairs and eliminate the pairs that are not relevant.

Common Reducts Specifications Identification of candidates for most common signature reducts for pairs of ontologically relevant types Ts, Tr is provided

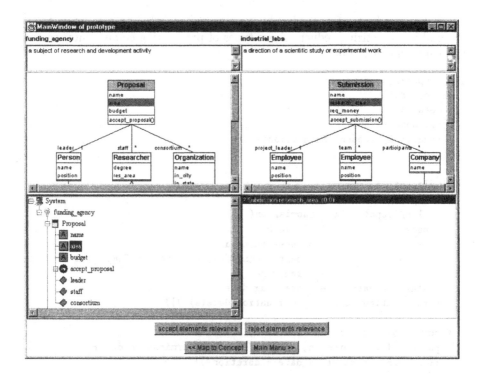

Fig. 5. GUI for confirmation of relevance of application and resource elements

by the tool automatically. Further work of a developer is required to produce more detailed specifications of the most common reducts to justify the required conditions.

The most common reducts and their concretizing reducts are specified as SYNTHESIS types. The specific metaslots and attributes are used to represent the specific semantics. The following example shows definition of the Proposal reduct intended as a common Proposal - Submission reduct.

```
{R_Proposal_Submission;
    in: reduct;
      metaslot
        of: Proposal;
        taking: {name, area, consortium, budget};
        c_reduct: CR_Proposal_Submission;
      end
}
```

A list of attributes of the reduced type in the slot taking contains names of its attributes that are to be included into the reduct. A starting list of attributes is taken from the common signature reduct obtained previously. Further the list can be properly adjusted.

A slot c_reduct refers to the concretizing reduct based on a resource type. We add a concretizing reduct (above types of pre-existing components) as the following type definition:

```
{CR_Proposal_Submission;
  in: c_reduct;
    metaslot
    of: submission;
    reduct: R_Proposal_Submission;
    end;

  simulating: {
    in: predicate;
    {all p/Proposal ex s/Submission(
    p.name              = s.name &
    p.area              = s.research_area &
    p.consortium        = s.participants/CR_Organization_Company &
    p.budget            = s.req_money &
    p.starting_date     = s.starting_date &
    p.termination_date = f_termination_date(s) )}};

  f_termination_date: {in: function;
    params: {+s/Submission, -return/Proposal.termination_date}
    {{ return = s.starting_date+s.duration }}}
}
```

In this case a slot reduct refers to the reduct based on an analysis model type. The predicate simulating provides an abstraction function showing how the concretizing state is mapped to the reduct state.

p.area = s.research_area defines that values of attribute area of reduct R_Proposal_Submission are taken from values of attribute research_area of resource type Submission. f_termination_date presents the mediating function resolving the conflict.

s.participants/CR_Organization_Company defines s.participants as a variable typed by the common reduct for types Organization and Company.

Common Reduct Construction Step Constructing common reducts we start with a procedure detecting conformant paths in the compositional structures of relevant application and component types. The algorithm for this procedure will be considered in the next section. After that the tool constructs signature reducts for all relevant pairs of the application and resource types.

For each pair of the relevant application type Ts and resource type Tr a developer should refine the common reduct and its concretizing reduct definitions. The developer may edit these specifications using the GUI shown in Fig. 6.

The tool generates the initial filling of this form. Tool detects the conflicts and constructs the corresponding mapping functions. For structural conflicts the specifications of mapping functions are generated. For other conflicts tool fill the mapping function specification with helping information.

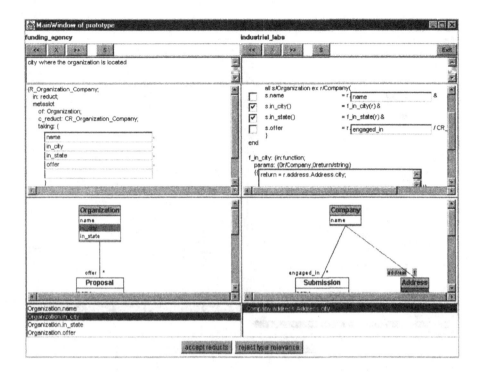

Fig. 6. GUI for reducts construction

Conformant Paths Detection Algorithm The main goal of the algorithm is to find the conformant paths in application and resource type composition schemas. The conformant paths are used to resolve the structural conflicts in application and resource schemas. The search is based on the list of relevant elements obtained after the ontology integration step. The process also allows to find additional relevant elements missed in the ontology integration step.

Briefly, the algorithm of finding the conformant paths is the following.

1. Take an arbitrary pair - application type Ts_0 and resource type Tr_0 from the list of ontologically relevant types.
2. Try to find application type Ts_1 and resource type Tr_1 such that the paths $Ts_0..Ts_1$ and $Tr_0..Tr_1$ meet one of the rules of paths conformance (see example for one such rule below). If a rule has been detected then the tool requests a developer (item 3) otherwise the tool goes to the first item.
3. If types Tx_1 and Ts_1 or Ty_1 and Tr_1 are not the same, a developer is requested if these types are relevant or not. If the developer accepts the relevance of types Tx_1 and Ts_1, and of types Ty_1 and Tr_1, these pairs are added to the list of ontologically relevant types.
4. If types Tx_1 and Ts_1, Ty_1 and Tr_1 are relevant or the same, the developer is requested if the paths $Ts_0..Tx_1$ and $Tr_0..Ty_1$ are conformant or not. If the

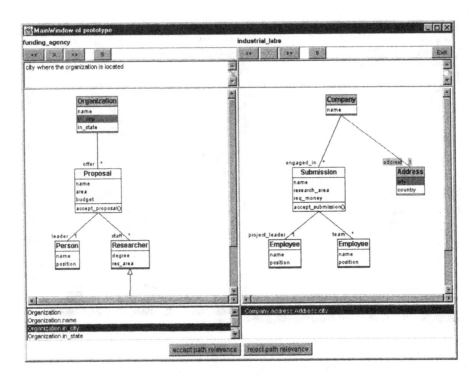

Fig. 7. GUI for confirmation of paths conformance

developer accepts the conformance of paths $Ts_0..Tx_1$ and $Tr_0..Ty_1$ (Fig. 7), these pairs are added to the list of conformant paths.

As an example we give one of the rules of path conformance. Other rules are similar to those considered in researches on database schemas integration [17]. **Rule of path conformance: Structural abstraction.**

The application path $Ts_0..Ts_1$ is conformant to resource path $Tr_0..Tr_1$, if

a) application path has the form: $Ts_0 - a1- > Tx_1..Ts_1$
b) resource path has the form: $Tr_0 - b0- > Tr_3 - b1- > Ty_1..Tr_1$
c) application type Tx_1 is relevant to resource type Ty_1
d) application path $Tx_1..Ts_1$ is conformant to resource path $Ty_1..Tr_1$

where

$Ts_0 - a1- > Tx_1$ – single-valued attribute having a user-defined type (Ts_0 has an attribute $a1$ of type Tx_1)

$Tx_1..Ts_1$ – any path (may be with zero length)
Example of conformant paths:

```
Organization -> in_city == Company -address-> Address -> city
```

The tool automatically generates a list of conformant paths which the developer should accept or reject using the GUI shown in Fig. 7.

Concretizing Type Specification A concretizing type plays for the analysis model type the same role as a concretizing reduct plays for its abstraction reduct counterpart. A concretizing type may be defined as follows:

```
{CT_Proposal;
  in: c_type
    metaslot
    type: Proposal;
    imports: {CR_Proposal_Submission, CR_Proposal_Project};
    composing: {{COMP_Proposal = CR_Proposal_Submission [name,
      area, s_budget/budget, s_starting_date/starting_date,
      s_termination_date/termination_date, accept_proposal] |
      CR_Proposal_Project[name, area, p_budget/budget,
      p_starting_date/starting_date,
      p_termination_date/termination_date]}}
    end;
  simulating: {
    in: predicate;
    {all  p/Proposal ex  c/COMP_Proposal(
    p.name                = c.name &
    p.area                = c.area &
    p.budget              = f_budget(c) &
    p.starting_date       = f_starting_date(c) &
    p.termination_date    = f_termination_date(c)}};

  f_budget: {in: function;
    params: {+c/COMP_Proposal, -return/Proposal.budget};
    {{return = (c.p_status = null & budget' = c.s_budget) |
      (c.p_status <> null & budget' = c.p_budget)}}
  f_starting_date: {in: function;
    params: {+c/COMP_Proposal, -return/Proposal.starting_date};
    {{return = (c.p_status = null &
      starting_date' = c.s_starting_date) |
      (c.p_status <> null & starting_date' = c.p_starting_date)}}
  f_termination_date: {in: function;
    params: {+c/COMP_Proposal, -return/Proposal.termination_date};
    {{return = (c.p_status = null &
      termination_date' = c.s_termination_date) |
      (c.p_status <> null &
      termination_date' = c.p_termination_date)}}
}
```

We assume that the import list can show what operations are to be promoted to the c_type from each imported c_reduct or c_type. Such operations can be used to specify operations of the defined type.

composing is a slot showing how the importing reduct types are arranged with type algebra expression into an intermediate composed type. In this example COMP_Proposal is defined as the join [16] of two concretizing reducts specifications.

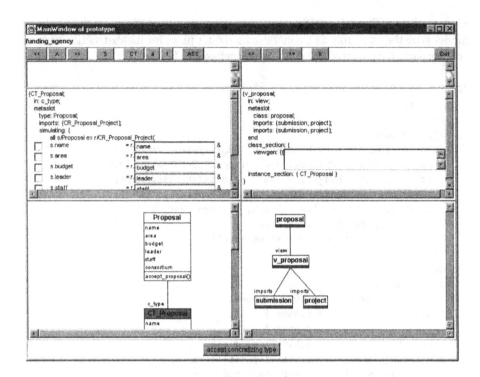

Fig. 8. GUI for concretizing types construction

To create proper analysis type instances we should define a `simulating` predicate to indicate how states of the composed type are mapped into the states of the more abstract type. `f_budget`, `f_starting_date`, `f_termination_date` present the mediating functions resolving conflicts.

In function definitions input (output) parameters are denoted with + (-) characters respectively. In predicative specifications apostroph denotes state of the variables after function computation.

Concretizing Type Construction Step Briefly, the process of creating the concretizing type (Fig. 2) for an arbitrary application type is the following.

We start with constructing of a composed types over all or several concretizing reducts. Then we can construct the concretizing types (Fig. 8) over the concretizing types we have obtained and other concretizing reducts. And so on, while we construct the concretizing types refining analysis model types.

The process of creating the view for arbitrary application class is the following. For types of instances of the application class and relevant component classes, we construct reducts, concretizing reducts and concretizing types as said above (2.3). Then we can construct views over the component classes with type instances corresponding to the concretizing reducts and/or concretizing types for the target class instance type. We also can construct views over the views we get while we construct view for the considered application class over all relevant component classes.

The result of the design phase is a collection of specified reducts, concretizing reducts, concretizing types and views which will be used further during the implementation phase. Mapping of type specifications into AMN and using B-Toolkit can be done during different steps of design when a developer needs formal justification of consistency and refinement properties of results.

4 Conclusion

Broad industrial scale of the interoperation technologies creates a strong demand for component-based information systems development based on the provided middleware. New information systems development methods are required to take advantage of the new capabilities. Current industrial trends in component-based development (e.g., DCOM ActiveX and SunSoft JavaBeans solutions) can be characterized as overemphasizing low level specifications (actually, conventional programming techniques) hidden by visualization tools.

Standardization consortiums (like OMG) continue unscaleable and unsafe trends in componentware [7, 19] applying ad hoc solutions. UML is just one example of such recent solutions by OMG [8]. Due to that the gap between the existing Object Analysis and Design (OAD) methods applying mostly top-down technique and the demand of the middleware architectures and methodologies for the development based on a composition of interoperating components remains to be large.

Developing well grounded strategy for the componentware infrastructure for survival in more durable perspective is required. Sound understanding of the essence of component-based development and reusability problem leading to proper component modeling, compositions and design in HIRE is required. The paper presents the decisions of the SYNTHESIS project that is focused on such strategy at the Russian Academy of Sciences.

SYNTHESIS addresses the design with reuse phase in a process of the interoperable information system development organized around the middleware concept. We base the development process on conventional object analysis and development methods. The requirement planning and analysis phases of the conventional process are augmented with ontological specifications and complete specifications of type constraints and operations in the canonical model. The conventional design phase is completely reconsidered: in SYNTHESIS this is the design with reuse of pre-existing components homogeneously and completely specified in the canonical model.

The SYNTHESIS canonical model is a semi-formal object-oriented model with a provision of type specifications mappings into formal notation (currently AMN of J.-R.Abrial B Method). Such canonical model provides capabilities of consistency check of specifications on different phases of the information system development. But what is more important is that the concept of refinement of the specifications relying on the pre-existing components becomes inherent for the model.

In SYNTHESIS information system development is considered as a process of systematic transformation of specifications. SYNTHESIS focuses on the component-based development as a transformation from the analysis model to the design model constructing compositions of relevant fragments of pre-existing components specifications that should finally serve as concretizations of requirements.

Type specifications and their reducts are chosen as the basic units of specification manipulation. For their manipulation, the algebra of type specifications is introduced. The algebra includes operations of *reduct, meet, join* and *product* of type specifications [16]. These operations are used to produce specifications of the respective compositions of their operands.

The paper presents functionality and process of the SYNTHESIS design tool supporting suitable notation and making specification transformation manageable and justifiable. The tool is implemented independently of existing OAD tools to complement them. An augmented subset of UML notation sufficient for representing the SYNTHESIS model is used for conventional specification of requirements and analysis phases. B-Toolkit supporting B technology is used as a part of the prototyping architecture.

Basic steps and functionalities of the process supported by the SYNTHESIS design tool are considered: an approach for application contexts reconciliation and integration, a procedure for common reducts identification and construction, aspects of structural conflict reconciliation used for this procedure, assistance for construction of specification compositions concretizing specifications of requirements.

Further plans in SYNTHESIS include more tight integration of formal facilities into the tool and investigation of scaleability of the approach to the broad component providers market.

References

1. Abrial J.-R. *The B Book: assigning programs to meaning*, Cambridge University Press, 1996
2. Abrial J.-R. B-Technology. Technical overview. BP International Ltd., 1992
3. Berg K. and Kalinichenko L.A. Modeling facilities for the component-based software development method. In *Proceedings of the Third International Workshop ADBIS'96*, Moscow, September 1996
4. Briukhov D.O., Shumilov S.S. Ontology Specification and Integration Facilities in a Semantic Interoperation Framework, In *Proc. of the International Workshop ADBIS'95*, Springer, 1995
5. Briukhov D.O. Interfacing of Object Analysis and Design Methods with the Method for Interoperable Information Systems Design, In *Proceedings of the Third International Workshop ADBIS'96*, Moscow, September 1996
6. EIA Interim Standard: CDIF-Framework for Modeling and Extensibility. EIA, 1991
7. CORBA Component Imperatives. ORBOS/97-05-25. IBM Corporation, Netscape Communications Corporation, Oracle Corporation, Sunsoft, Inc.

8. M.Fowler *UML Distilled*, Addison-Wesley, 1997
9. Jacobson I., Griss M., Jonsson P., *Software Reuse*, ACM Press, 1997
10. Jezequel J.-M., Meyer B. Design by Contract: The Lessons of Ariane, http://www.tools.com/doc/manuals/technology/contract/ariane/index.html
11. Kalinichenko L.A. Emerging semantic-based interoperable information system technology. In *Proceedings of the International Conference Computers as our better partners*, Tokyo, March 1994, World Scientific
12. Kalinichenko L.A. SYNTHESIS: the language for desription, design and programming of the heterogeneous interoperable information resource environment. Institute for Problems of Informatics, Russian Academy of Sciences, Moscow, 1995
13. Kalinichenko L.A. Workflow Reuse and Semantic Interoperation Issues. In *Advances in workflow management systems and interoperability*. A.Dogac, L.Kalinichenko, M.T. Ozsu, A.Sheth (Eds.). NATO Advanced Study Institute, Istanbul, August 1997
14. Kalinichenko L.A. Method for data models integration in the common paradigm. In *Proceedings of the First East European Workshop 'Advances in Databases and Information Systems'*, St. Petersburg, September 1997
15. Kalinichenko L.A. Component-based Development Infrastructure: A Systematic Approach *OMG-DARPA-MCC Workshop on "Compositional Software Architecture"*, Monterey CA, January 6 - 8, 1998
16. Kalinichenko L.A. Composition of type specifications exhibiting the interactive behaviour. In *Proceedings of EDBT'98 Workshop on Workflow Management Systems*, March 1998, Valencia
17. Wolfgang Klas, Peter Fankhauser, Peter Muth, Thomas Rakow, Erich J. Neuhold. Database Integration using the Open Object-Oriented Database System VODAK Omran Bukhres, Ahmed K. Elmagarmid (Eds.): Object Oriented Multidatabase Systems: A Solution for Advanced Applications. Chapter 14. Prentice Hall, Englewood Cliffs, N.J., 1996
18. Mili R., Mili A., Mittermeir R. Storing and retrieving software components: a refinement based systems. IEEE Transactions on Software Engineering, v. 23, N 7, July 1997
19. *ODP Trading Function - Part 1: Specification*, ISO/IEC IS 13235-1, ITU/T Draft Rec X950 - 1, 1997
20. Paradigm Plus Reference Manual. Protosoft, 1997
21. Zaremski A.M., Wing J.M. Specification matching of software components. ACM Transactions on Software Engineering and Methodology, v. 6, N 4, October 1997

Translating Relational Queries to Object-Oriented Queries According to ODMG-93

Ahmed Mostefaoui[1] and Jacques Kouloumdjian[2]

[1] Laboratoire de l'Informatique du Parallélisme (L.I.P)
Ecole Normale Supérieure de Lyon
46 Allée d'Italie 69364 Cedex 07, France
Ahmed.Mostefaoui@ens-lyon.fr
[2] LISI- Laboratory for Information Systems Engineering
Dpt of informatics, INSA
20 AV. A.Einstein, FR-69621 Villeurbanne CEDEX France
koulou@lisisunk1.insa-lyon.fr

Abstract. With the advent of object-oriented database systems there is a need to migrate/integrate old systems, mainly relational ones, to/into object-oriented systems. In this paper we propose a method to automatically translate SQL queries to OQL ones. The method is based on a graph representation of SQL queries. This graph is enriched and transformed in a series of stages which take into account the caracterics of the object schema with respect to the relational one (new entity type, ISA relationship, class hierarchy, etc.). This semantic enrichment allows an optimized translation of the SQL queries compared with a purely syntaxic translation.

1 Introduction

During the last two decades, many database management systems (DBMS) based on different data models have been built. Todays, in a large organization different types of DBMSs often coexist and such coexistence presents problems for users to access data from different systems with ease. Schema transformers [1–3] and query translators [4,5] are then critical components of heterogeneous database systems. In addition, the process of reverse engineering of the old systems requires also such components [6]. Using objet-oriented systems as the front-end systems has been widely approved. Unfortunately, there was no common data model for those object-oriented systems, consequently translations were specifically tailored towards the target systems. The ODMG proposals [7] provide now a standard for a uniform schema and query translation. So it is possible to do schema conversion and query translation in a system independent way! with the ODMG as a target. The problem of schema translation from relational to object data model has been addressed in a number of works [1,3,8]. It has been shown that exploiting equijoins in SQL queries together with data examination allow the discovery of the semantics of data and the building of an object conceptual schema which correctly reflects this semantics (with new entity type and ISA relationships)[9, 10]. In this paper we address the issue of SQL query translation. As examplified in section 1.1 a purely syntaxic translation, even if it is correct, is not always satisfactory since it does not take into account the whole semantics of the object schema (for example classes which are image of no relation). Our approach consists in building a graph representing the SQL query and to gradually enrich this graph to include elements specific to the object schema. This enrichment is based on the use of predicates expressing correspondences between items of the relational and object schemata. This approach leads to a more meaningful translation of SQL queries.

1.1 Motivation

Many relational systems are confronted to the problem of integration/migration into/to Object-Oriented systems. As the object models are semantically richer than relational one, this integration/migration is not straightforward. This issue has been widely studied in the literature through schema transformation [11]. However, to the best of our knowledge, few researches have focussed on the query translation [4, 5]. In this paper, we propose a new approach that addresses this issue. Note that the translation from relational query to object query according ODMG-93 can be done in a *ad hoc* manner without exploiting any of the additional semantics captured by the object schema. However, because of the semantic expressiveness of the object schema, query translation can be more *"meaningful"* as illustrated in the following example :

Example 1. We consider the relational schema of the figure 1 on which is defined the query of the figure 2. The semantics of such query is to *"list the names of all teachers who are department managers, have salary less than 15000 FF and do not work on project which budgets exceed 200000 FF"*. Note that the entity *department-manager* which is implicit in the relational schema was expressed by the sub-query **EXISTS**. Such an entity is explicit in the object schema of the figure 5. Two translations of the query are presented in the figures 3 and 4. The first one is a systematic translation, whereas the second one takes profit of the semantic expressiveness of the object schema ,i.e, the entity *department-manager* is explicit.

Our aim is to propose a query translator which is capable of detecting such entities and optimize the translated query.

The rest of the paper is organized like follows. Section 2 discusses schema transformation and requirements needed by the query translator. In section 3 we present the proposed approach illustrated by an example. Section 4 concludes this paper.

TEACHER(<u>ssn</u>, name, address, sal, dno)
DEPARTMENT(**<u>Dnumber</u>**, dname, dlocation, <u>dheadssn</u>, headstdate)
PROJECT(**<u>Pnumber</u>**, pname, pbudget, pstdate)
WORKS-ON(**<u>tssn, pno</u>**)

Teacher.dno $\subseteq$ Department.Dnumber
Department.dheadssn $\subseteq$ Teacher.ssn
Works-On.tssn $\subseteq$ Teacher.ssn
Works-On.pno $\subseteq$ Project.Pnumber

Fig. 1. Example relational schema with inclusion dependencies

```
SELECT  name
FROM  Teacher
WHERE sal<15000 AND
        EXISTS (
                SELECT  *
                FROM  Department
                WHERE  dheadssn=ssn )
        AND
        ssn NOT IN  (
                    SELECT  tssn
                    FROM  Works-On, Project
                    WHERE  pno=Pnumber AND budget > 200000)
```

Fig. 2. Example query

```
SELECT  name
FROM  x in Teacher
WHERE  x.sal<15000 AND
        EXISTS (y in department : y.head.ssn=x.ssn )
        AND
        NOT EXISTS  (p in x.projects : p.budget<200000)
```

Fig. 3. systematic translation of the studied query.

```
SELECT  name
FROM  x in Dept-Manager
WHERE  x.sal<15000 AND
        NOT EXISTS  (p in x.projects : p.budget>200000)
```

Fig. 4. *"Intelligent"* translation of the studied query.

2 Schema transformation

Schema transformations between different models (from conceptual models to logical models or vice versa) were well studied in literature [1, 8, 12]. In a design process, a conceptual schemata (E-R schema for instance) is transformed to a logical schema (relational schema for example) in a straightforward manner. This is due to the fact that conceptual models are semantically richer than logical models. However, when doing schema transformation from logical models to semantically richer models, as it is the case in the reverse engineering process, some problems arise. Indeed, several conceptual schemata can be derived from one logical schema [2], and the difficulty consists in choosing the *"meaningful"* conceptual schema. In the context of this paper, we deal with transformation from relational schema into object schema. Several methods for (semi)-automatic transformation of a relational schema to an Object-Oriented schema have been proposed ! itefahrner2,caste,petit2. Such methods try to exploit the modelling power of the semantic model used to obtain a more meaningful schema. We assume that the relational schema on which the input query is defined has been transformed into an ODMG-93 object schema by using one of those methods. We also assume that they are able of detecting so-called *missing entities*, which are implicit in the relational schema, and infer a *class hierarchy*. Generally, the input for a schema transformation method consists of relations, informations on keys, and inclusion dependencies between different attributes. Figure 1 shows an example input to a schema transformation method. The corresponding object schema expressed in ODMG-93 is shown in the figure 5. The example shows the non-trivial mapping from relations to classes. Whereas **Teacher** is mapped to a single class, **Works-On** has been transformed to the set-valued object references *! Teacher.projects* and *Project.Teachers*. Also, the relation **Department** yielded two classes *Department* and *Dept-Manager*, the latter being a *missing entity*, detected due to the extraneous secondary key *dheadssn*. Furthermore, based on the inclusion dependency defined between their key attributes, an **isa**-relationship between *Dept-Manager* and *Teacher* has been inferred.

2.1 Schema annotation

Although we make abstraction on the schema transformation method used, we define an annotation on the resulting object schema to be able to perform the query translation. Such an annotation allows to take profit of the semantic expressiveness of the object model, especially the detected missing entities and isa-relationships. Thus, we define two predicates, similar to those defined in [4], as follows :

Definition 1 : (predicate Image)
The predicate IMAGE is defined by the triplet (C,R,T) where :
C is a class of the object schema,
$R = \{R_1,...,R_n\}$ is a subset, not empty, of relations of the relational schema,

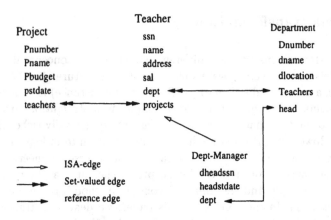

Fig. 5. The ODMG-93 object schema of the studied example

$T = \{Att_1,...,Att_n\}$ is a set, possibly empty, of attributes of R relations.

This predicate defines for each class of the object schema the set of relations and attributes invoked in its detection. It allows the query translation process to take into account missing entities and isa-relationships. Figure 6 shows the annotation related to the studied example.

Definition 2 : (predicate Reference)
The predicate *"reference"* is defined by the triplet (C_1, C_2, T) where :
C_1 and C_2 are two classes of the object schema,
$T = \{Att_1,...,Att_n\}$ is a non-empty set of attributes of the relational schema.

This predicate defines for every reference between two classes C_1 and C_2 the set of attributes invoked in its detection. In the relational context, such references are materialized by joins between attributes in queries. On the contrary, they are explicit in the object schema (reference attributes for example *Teacher.projects*). By defining this predicate, the query translator can make difference between explicit joins and those materializing references between classes in the relational query. The figure 6 shows the annotation related to the studied example.

IMAGE (Teacher,{Teacher}, {})
IMAGE (Department,{Department}, {})
IMAGE (Project,{Project}, {})
IMAGE (Dept-Manager,{Teacher,Department}, {ssn,dheadssn})

REFERENCE (Teacher,Department,{dno,Dnumber})
REFERENCE (Teacher,Project,{ssn,tssn,pno,Pnumber})

Fig. 6. Annotation defined on the example relational schema

3 Query translation

As shown in the example above, the translation of relational query to object query can exploit the additional semantics captured by the object schema especially the class hierarchy to optimize parts of the relational query. Indeed, in a relational query, there are parts which materialize implicit structures. However, those structures are explicit in the object schema and therefore there is no need to translate them. The proposed query translator takes into account this fact and optimizes the resulted object query.

In the following, we discuss the translation of relational queries, expressed in SQL, submitted against the transformed relational schema to OQL (Object Query Language) against the underlying object schema expressed in the standard ODMG-93. We focus on the translation of **Select-From-Where** statements and also the clauses **In, Exists, Not In** and **Not Exists**. The translation consists in four steps. In the first step, a relational query graph (RQG) of the given query is constructed. In the second step, the RQG is transformed to an Object Graph (OG) which is considered as a intermediate graph representation. In the third step, the OG is translated to an Object Query Graph (OQG). Finally, the Select-From-Where clause of the object query, expressed in the standard OQL, is constructed. The above four steps are discussed in the following four subsections.

3.1 Constructing a RQG

We use a representation formalism for SQL-queries comparable to the one used in [13, 4]. As shown in [13], the conditions **In** and **Exists** can be represented by semijoins whereas **Not In** and **Not Exists** conditions correspond to a special kind of antijoins[1].

Definition 3 : for a given relational query Q, we define its RQG as an annotated graph : RQG(Q)=RQG(RV,RE1,RE2), where RV is a set of vertices, $RE1$ is a set of undirected edges and $RE2$ is a set of directed edges. Each vertex v in V corresponds to a Relational Tuple Variable (RTV) annotated with the set of selection on this RTV. A undirected edge e between vertex v_1 and vertex v_2 with label $<a\ op\ b>$ where a and b correspond to attributes and op to an operator ('=','>', etc.) represents a regular join. A directed edge e from vertex v_1 to vertex v_2 represents semijoin or the special kind of antijoins. Figure 7 shows the RQG associated with the example query of figure 2.

3.2 Translating an RQG to an OG

The Object Graph (OG) is an intermediate graph between the RQG and the OQG. It allows the representation of the isa-relationships and the missing entities. Thus it will be possible to optimize the query translation latter.

---

[1] Such antijoins should always be computed after the computation of the regular joins.

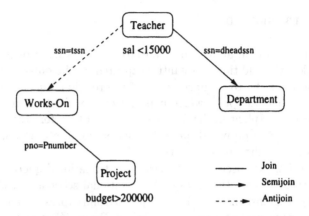

Fig. 7. The Relational Query Graph of the studied example

Definition 4 : given a RQG(RV,RE1,RE2), we define by construction the OG (OV,OE1,OE2) like fellows :

- *OV* is a set of vertices. Each vertex v represents a Class Instance Variable (CIV). Each CIV correspond to a RTV in the RQG. The annotations defined on the RTV are reported on the corresponding CIV. The RTVs representing relations transformed, during the process of schema transformation, to set-valued references are ignored. In our example the RTV corresponding to the relation **Works-On** is ignored.
- *OE1* is a set of undirected edges. An edge e that does not correspond to a reference in the object schema is preserved with its annotation in the OG. Such edges represents explicit joins.
- *OE2* is a set of directed edges constructed as follows :
  - the edges to/from RTV in the RQG whose corresponding relations were transformed to set-valued references between classes are replaced in the OG by edges between the corresponding CIV. Edges representing antijoins have priority on edges representing semijoins. The latters have priority on edges representing joins. In the example the antijoin between *Teacher* and *Project* is kept.
  - the edges in the RQG which materialize references between classes are replaced by edges having same direction in the object schema.
  - the edges representing antijoins in the RQG are preserved in the OG.
  - the edges representing semijoins in the RQG are preserved in the OG.
  - ISA-edges : the annotation defined on the edges of the RQG and the one defined above on the object graph allow to detect ISA edges by analizing the attributes (key, candidate key, etc.). In the example, the semijoin edge between Teacher and *Department* is annotated by the two attributes *ssn* and *dheadssn*. In addition, those two attributes are invoked in the predicate
    IMAGE (Dept-Manager,{Teacher,Department}, {ssn,dheadssn}).
    So, this edge is transformed into a ISA-edge.

Figure 8 shows the OG constructed from RQG of the figure 7.

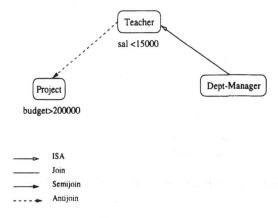

Fig. 8. The Object Graph of the studied example

3.3 Translating an OG to an Object Query Graph

Until now, the OG can not be mapped to an object query because of the presence of ISA-edges which are explicit in the object schema. Therefore the translation of the OG to an OQG is done by eliminating such ISA-edges.

Definition 5 : given a OG (OV,OE1,OE2), the OQG (OV,OE1,OE2) is constructed by the following algorithm :

Algorithm
Input : OG
Output : OQG

Foreach ISA-edge e from subclass C_1 to superclass C_2
        remove the edge e from the graph and consult the edge in the RQG which
        was invoked in its creation
        If it was a semijoin edge **then**
            All selection predicates defined on the superclass C_2 are reported on
            the subclass C_1
            All edges to/from C_2 are directed to C_1.
            If there are other ISA-edges from C_i, ..., C_j to the superclass C_2 **then**
                Make explicit joins between C_i,...,C_j and C_1.
        If it was a antijoin edge **then**
            Remove the vertex corresponding to the superclass C_2
End For
Remove all unconnected vertices.

Figure 9 shows the resulted OQG after transformation of the OG of the figure 8.

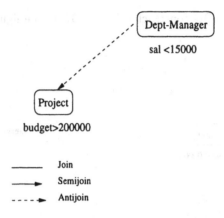

Fig. 9. The Object Query Graph of the studied example

3.4 Constructing the query expression from the OQG

At this stage, an OQL expression of the Select-From-Where form can be derived from the OQG. This is done by travelling the OQG graph. Below, we present the different steps of construction. The expression is constructed gradually while travelling the OQG in a depth-first manner, starting at the top of the graph.

Obtaining the clause Select The clause **Select** selects the attribute(s) that will be returned by the query. Its semantic is the same in both the relational query and the object query. Therefore, its translation is straightforward.

Obtaining the clauses From-Where The clause From contains the different path-expression [5] of the OQG. Those path-expressions are explicited by using nammed variables which represent the reference attributes. By travelling the OQG, only the semijoin and antijoin edges are considered because they materialize references between classes. Below we consider those two kinds of edges

- **Travelling an antijoin edge :** here the direction of the materialization in the object schema does play a role. Assume an antijoin edge e from CIV C_1 to C_2 and a reference r between the two classes [2] C_1 and C_2. Below, we discuss the two cases :
  - The edge e and the reference r are in the same direction : the semantics of this query construct is such that every object of C_1 not referencing an object of C_2, after application of the selection predicates on the latter, satisfies the specification of the query. So, it is translated to **Not Exists** clause in the where clause in the following manner :
  Not Exists var *in* $C_1.r$: < *list_of_conditions* >
  Where *var* is a C_2 variable and < *list_of_conditions* > is the conjonction of selection predicates applied to the variable *var*

---

[2] To simplify notation we assume that a CIV and class are interchangeable.

- The edge e is the opposite direction of the reference r : the semantics of this query construct is such that every object of C_1 not referenced by a object of C_2, after application of the selection predicates on the latter, satisfies the specification of the query. So, it is translated to **Not Exists** clause in the where clause, as in the precedent case, but by including a additional variable that *"nominates"* the class C_1.
  Not Exists *var in C_2: var.r=x and <list_of_conditions>*
  x corresponds to the additional variable related to the class C_1
- **Travelling a semijoin edge** : here the direction of the materialisation in the object schema does not play a role[3]. Assume an semijoin edge e from CIV C_1 to C_2 and a reference r between the two classes C_1 and C_2. Travelling an edge e is translated as follow :
  - if the reference r is from C_1 to C_2 then the translation is of the form :
    From *var1 in C_1, var2 in var1.r*
  - if the reference r is from C_2 to C_2 then the translation is of the form :
    From *var1 in C_2, var2 in var1.r*

Finally, all selection predicates corresponding to vertices in the OQG not present in the blocs **Not Exists** are added in the clause **Where**. The example 4 shows the query expression derived from the OQG of figure 9.

4 Conclusion

Translating queries from SQL to OQL in an automatic and satisfactory way requires to take into account all the semantic aspects of the object schema derived from the relational one. Several points make this task difficult. Indeed, paths are expressed explicitly in the object model while by means of joins in queries in the relational one, relationships are expressed in different manner in each model, ISA relationships have no counterpart in the relational model. Moreover, new *missing* entities (not explicited in the relational schema) can be added to the object schema. Our method for translating SQL queries is based on graph representations of queries. These representations are progressively transformed to include semantic aspects of the correspondence between the two schemata. Although we have not considered here all the possible forms of SQL queries, we believe that our method is general enough to be extended to other clauses.

References

1. C. Batini S. Ceri and S.B Navathe. *Conceptual DatabaseDesign- An Entity-Relationship Approach*. Benjamin/Cumming Redwood city, 1992.
2. C. Fahrner and G. Vossen. A survey of database design transformation based on the entity-relationship model. *Data and Knowledge Engineering*, 15:213–250, 1995.
3. R. Elmasri and S. B. Navathe. *Fundamentals of database systems*. Benjamin/Cummings redwood city, 1994.

---

[3] Semantically speaking.

4. M. Vermeer and P. Apers. Objet-oriented views of relational databases incorporating behaviour. In *the fourth International Conference on Database Systems for Advanced Applications (DASFAA'95)*, 1995.

5. W. Meng C. Yu W. Kim G. Wang T. Pham and S. Dao. Construction of a relational front-end for object oriented database systems. In *The 9th International Conference on Data Engineering*, pages 476–483, vienna 1993.

6. J-L Hainault. Database reverse engineering : models technics and strategies. In *The 10th International Conference on Entity-Relationship Approach*, pages 729–741, 1991.

7. R.G.G Cattell. *ODMG-93 : Le standard des bases de donnes objets*. Thomson Publishing, 1995.

8. C. Fahrner and G. Vossen. Transformation of relational schemas into object-oriented schemas according to odmg-93. In *fourth International Conference on Deductive and Object-Oriented Database DOOD'95*, pages 429–446, 1995.

9. J-M Petit F. Toumani J-F Boulicaut and J. Kouloumdjian. Towards the reverse engineering of denormalized relational databases. In *the 12th International Conference on Data Engineering ICDE'96*, 1996.

10. J.M. Petit, F. Toumani, and J. Kouloumdjian. Relational database reverse engineering : a method based on query analysis. *International Journal of Cooperative Information Systems*, 4(2, 3):287–316, 1995.

11. M. Castellanos F. Saltor and M. Garcia-Salaco. Semantically enrichment of relational databases into an object-oriented semantic model. In *The 5th International conference on Database Applications DEXA'94*, 1994.

12. W. Kim. On optimizing an sql-like nested query. *ACM TODS*, pages 443–469, 1982.

13. U. Dayal. Of nests and trees : A unified approach to processing queries that contain nested subqueries, aggregates and quantifiers. In *13th Very Large DataBases (VLDB) Conference*, pages 197–208, 1987.

A Flexible Framework
for a Correct Database Design

Donatella Castelli, Serena Pisani

Istituto di Elaborazione dell'Informazione
Consiglio Nazionale delle Ricerche
Via S. Maria, 46 Pisa, Italy
e-mail: {castelli,serena}@iei.pi.cnr.it

Abstract. This paper presents a flexible database schema transformational framework. Flexibility is achieved by adopting a generic model for describing database schemas and a transformational language able to represent all the correctness preserving schema transformations. This framework, originally defined for schema design, is also applicable for supporting other activities related to the database life-cycle. As an illustrative example, this paper shows how it can be used to support a database reverse engineering process.

1 Introduction

The correctness of a database design is often obtained by fixing the set of schema transformational operators that can be used for carrying out the design and by associating a set of applicability conditions to each of these operators. These conditions must be checked when the operators are applied. If they are satisfied, then the design step is guaranteed to be correct. A drawback of this solution is that the set of schema transformational operators is often too rigid: the operators work for particular models and they can only execute particular refinement steps.

This paper proposes a correctness preserving schema transformational framework that, unlike to the previous proposals [2–5, 12], is also adaptable to different situations. This framework relies on a database schema model, called *Database Schema* (DBS) [6] and a design language, called *Schema Refinement Language* (SRL). SRL consists of a set of primitives (with associated the set of their applicability conditions) for transforming DBS schemas and a composition operator. A rule is given for deriving the applicability conditions of any transformations from the applicability conditions of its component transformations. The composition operator renders the language complete, i.e., able to express all the schema transformations.

The genericity of the model employed and the completeness of the transformational language render the framework suitable for different kinds of database applications. This paper shows how the SRL framework can be exploited to point out incorrect database reverse engineering processes.

The next three sections of this paper introduce the design framework. In particular, Section 2 presents DBS and the primitive operators of SRL. Section

3 introduces the composition operator. Section 4 introduces the rule for deriving the applicability conditions of a composed schema transformation. This rule is given in detail in the Appendix. Section 5 shows how the framework introduced can be exploited in a database reverse engineering process. Finally, Section 6 contains concluding remarks.

2 Schema Refinement Language

The Schema Refinement Language (SRL) assumes that the whole design relies on a single notation which is sufficiently general to represent semantic and object models. This notation, illustrated briefly through the example in Figure 1[1], allows to model the database structure and behavior into a single module, called *Database Schema* (DBS). This module encloses classes, attributes, is-a relations, integrity constraints and operations specifications. A graphical representation of the schema *StoneDB* is given in Figure 4(a).

---

database schema *StoneDB*
class *exterior* of *MARBLE* **with** (*e_name:NAME; e_tech_char:TECH_CHAR*)
class *interior* of *MARBLE* **with** (*i_name:NAME; i_tech_char: TECH_CHAR*)
constraints
    $\forall\ m \cdot m{\in}(interior{\cup}exterior) \Rightarrow \exists\ n \cdot n{=}(e\_name{\cup}i\_name)(m)$
initialisation
    exterior, interior, e_tech_char, i_tech_char, e_name, i_name := **empty**
operations
    assign_tech_char(n,t) = **pre** $n{\in}ran(e\_name{\cup}i\_name) \wedge t{\in}TECH\_CHAR$
    then *i_tech_char* := *i_tech_char* ⩤ $\{(x,t)\ |\ i\_name(x){=}n\}$ ∥
        e_tech_char := *e_tech_char* ⩤ $\{(x,t)\ |\ e\_name(x){=}n\}$

Fig. 1. A Database Schema

The notation of Database Schema is formalised in terms of a formal model introduced within the B-Method [1]. This formalisation allows to exploit the B theory and tools for proving expected properties of the DBS schemas.

The SRL primitive operators that transforms DBS schemas are given in Table 1. The equality conditions that appear as a parameter in the add/rem transformations specify how the new/removed element can be derived from the already existing/remaining ones. These conditions are required since only redundant components can be added and removed in a refinement step. The language does not permit to add or remove schema operations. It only permits to change the way in which an operation is defined. Note that the operation definitions are also automatically modified as a side effect of the transformations that add and remove schema components. In particular, these automatic modifications add appropriate updates for each of the new schema components, cancel the occurrences of the removed components and apply the proper variable substitutions.

---

[1] ⩤ stands for the overriding between relations; ∥ represents the parallel assignment.

Table 1. SRL language

add.class (*class.name, class.name =expr*)
rem.class (*class.name, class.name =expr*)
add.attr(*attr.name, class.name, attr.name =expr*)
rem.attr (*attr.name, class.name, attr.name =expr*)
add.isa(*class.name1, class.name2*)
rem.isa (*class.name1, class.name2*)
mod.op (*op.name, body*)

A transformation can be applied when its *applicability conditions* are verified. These are sufficient conditions, to be verified before the execution of the transformation, that prevent from applying meaningless and correctness breaking schema design. The criterion for the correctness of schema design is based on the following definition (for a formal definition see [7]):

Definition (DBS schema refinement relation) A DBS schema S_1 refines a DBS schema S_2 if:

(a) S_1 and S_2 have the same signature;

(b) there exists a 1:1 correspondence between the states modelled by S_1 and S_2;

(c) the database B_1 and B_2, modelled by S_1 and S_2, when initialised and submitted to the same sequence of updates, are such that each possible query on B_1 returns one of the results expected by evaluating the same query on B_2. $\square$

The applicability conditions consist of the conjunction of simple conditions. In that follows, these conditions will be called *applicability predicates*.

Let us outline that the main objective in defining this framework has been the flexibility. In order to fulfill this objective the model and the schema refinement language have been provided with very primitive mechanisms.

SRL, as presented above, is not still suitable enough to be used in the real applications. Indeed, the applied schema transformations are usually more complex of those listed above. In order to overcome this limitation, a composition operator for SRL is introduced in the next section.

3 Composition Operator

The composition operator permits to define complex transformations from simpler one. The following preliminary definition is needed before introducing the composition operator (the corresponding formal definition is given in [7]).

Definition (Consistent operation modification) A set of SRL schema transformations specifies *consistent operation modifications* if, for each operation that is modified by more than one transformation, the replacing bodies can be totally ordered with respect to the refinement relation. $\square$

Intuitively, this definition means that all the bodies that are specified for the same operations by different transformations must describe the same general behaviour. They can only differ for being more or less refined.

The SRL composition operator can be now defined as follows. **Definition (Composition operator "o")** Let t_1, t_2, ..., t_n be a set of SRL schema transformations that specify consistent operation modifications. Let $<Cl,Attr,IsA,Constr,Op>$ be a DBS schema where: Cl, $Attr$, IsA, $Constr$ and Op are, respectively, the set of classes, attributes, is-a relationships, integrity constraints and schema operations. Op always contains an operation $Init$ that specifies the schema initialisation. The SRL schema transformation composition operator is defined as follows:

$$t_1 \circ t_2 \circ \ldots \circ t_n \ (<Cl,Attr,IsA,Constr,Op>)=$$
$$<Cl \cup ACl\text{-}RCl, Attr \cup AAttr\text{-}RAttr, IsA \cup AIsA\text{-}RIsA,$$
$$[\text{RemSubst}^*](Constr \wedge AConstr), [\text{RemSubst}^*]Op'>$$

where ACl/RCl, $AAttr/RAttr$ and $AIsA/RIsA$ are sets formed, respectively, by the set of classes, attributes and is-a relationships that are added/removed by t_1, t_2, ..., t_n. $RemSubst^*$ is the transitive closure of the variable substitutions $x:=E$ dictated by the conditions that are specified when an element is removed. If we have, for example, $rem.class(c, c=E) \circ rem.class(d, d=f(c)) \circ rem.class(e, e=F)$ then $RemSubst^*$ is the parallel composition of the substitutions $c:=E$, $d:=f(E)$ and $e:=F$. $[RemSubst^*]X$ is the expression that is obtained by applying the substitution $RemSubst^*$ to X. For example, $[x:=E]R(x)$ is $R(E)$. This substitution permits to rephrase integrity constraints and operation definitions by removing the cancelled schema components. $AConstr$ are the conjunction of the inherent constraints associated with the new schema components and the conditions that specify how an added element relates to the remaining ones. Finally, Op' is the new set of operation definitions. These result from the modifications that are required explicitly and from the automatic adjustments caused by the addition and removal of schema components. When more than one of the component transformations modifies an operation, the more specialised behavior is selected.□

SRL is a complete DBS schema refinement language. This property ensures that SRL is powerful enough to express every DBS schema transformation. The following example illustrates how new transformations can be build.

Example. Let us define the transformation illustrated graphically in Figure 2. This transformation adds a new class, C, as superclass of n already existing classes, C_1, $\cdots$, C_n, and moves a set of attributes shared with the subclasses to the new class. The designer can built this transformation as composition of simple SRL transformations[2]:

$$add.superclass(C, (C_1, \cdots, C_n), \{((a_1, \cdots, a_n), a), \cdots, ((b_1, \cdots, b_n), b)\}) =$$
$$add.class(C, C=C_1 \cup \cdots \cup C_n) \circ add.isa(C_1, C) \circ \cdots \circ add.isa(C_n, C) \circ$$
$$add.attr(a, C, a=a_1 \cup \cdots \cup a_n) \circ$$
$$rem.attr(a_1, C_1, a_1=C_1 \lhd a) \circ \cdots \circ rem.attr(a_n, C_n, a_n=C_n \lhd a)) \circ \cdots \circ$$
$$add.attr(b, C, b=b_1 \cup \cdots \cup b_n) \circ$$

---

[2] $\lhd$ indicates the domain restriction.

Fig. 2. add_superclass

$$rem.attr(b_1, \ C_1, \ b_1 = C_1 \lhd b) \ \circ \cdots \circ \ rem.attr(b_n, \ C_n, \ b_n = C_n \lhd b))$$

The transformation *add.superclass* can be used as any other SRL transformation. For example, it can be applied to the database schema *StoneDB* of Figure 1, generating the DBS schema of Figure 3, as follows:

$$add.superclass(marble,(exterior,interior),\{((e\_name,i\_name),name)\})(StoneDB)$$

The change brought to the static part of the schema are shown in Figure 4.

---

database schema *StoneDB_1*
class *marble* **of** *MARBLE* **with** (*name:NAME*)
class *exterior* **is-a** *marble* **with**(*e_tech_char:TECH_CHAR*)
class *interior* **is-a** *marble* **with**(*i_tech_char:TECH_CHAR*)
constraints
    $\forall \ m \cdot m \in (interior \cup exterior) \Rightarrow \exists \ n \cdot n = name(m)$
initialisation
    marble, name, exterior, interior, e_tech_char, i_tech_char := **empty**
operations
    assign_tech_char(n,t) = **pre** $n \in ran(\ name) \wedge t \in TECH\_CHAR$
    then *i_tech_char* := *i_tech_char* $\Lleftarrow \{(x,t) \mid (name \lhd interior)(x) = n\}$ ||
        e_tech_char := *e_tech_char* $\Lleftarrow \{(x,t) \mid (name \lhd exterior)(x) = n\}$

Fig. 3. StoneDB_1

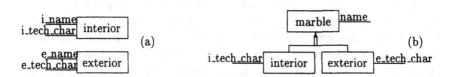

(a)   (b)

Fig. 4. *StoneDB* schema

The next section presents the mechanisms that allow to dynamically associate, to each of the new defined transformations, its applicability conditions.

4 Applicability Conditions

The applicability conditions of a composed transformation are sufficient conditions for ensuring that the application of the transformation to a schema results in a correct design. These conditions are generated constructively by an algorithm, called *Applicability Condition Generating Algorithm* (ACGA), given in Appendix. ACGA generates the applicability conditions by considering the schema structure and the changes brought by the component transformations.

As far as the applicability conditions of composed transformations, the following property holds [7]:

Property (SRL is a refinement language) Let t_1, t_2, ..., t_n be SRL schema transformations and S be a DBS schema. The application of the transformation $t_1 \circ t_2 \circ \ldots \circ t_n(S)$, when its applicability conditions are verified, produces a refinement of S.□

This property ensures the correctness of any database SRL design.

By reasoning on the applicability conditions generated by the ACGA algorithm, it turns out that some of them can be solved without instantiating the parameters; others can be discharged by simply comparing the values of the parameters. This suggest us to automatically prune these predicates and associate to the instance of a transformation only the simplified set of applicability predicates. The pruning is done at different stages. When the transformation is defined, with parameters $p_1, \ldots, p_n$, the set of applicability predicates is scanned and, for each predicate P_{ij} of the set, the proof of $\forall p_1, \ldots, p_n, S \cdot P_{ij}$ is attempted, where S is a DBS schema. If the proof is successful, P_{ij} is inserted in the set of the applicability predicates that have not to be proved anymore. The second kind of pruning, is executed when the transformation is instantiated. By reasoning on the structure of any transformations and the values of the parameters, several applicability predicates are discharged. The ACGA algorithm, reported in the Appendix, actually implements a mix between the generation of the applicability conditions and the second pruning. The result of the second pruning is the set of applicability predicates that the designer has to prove for a particular application of the transformation. Notice that no much effort is usually required for this proof. This is because the set of applicability predicates returned by the ACGA algorithm is often very small. Moreover, since the SRL framework and its application conditions are formalised, an automatic, or at least guided, discharge of the applicability conditions that are generated is possible.

Let us see an example of dynamic generation of the applicability conditions of a composed transformation. Table 2 lists the applicability conditions of the transformation *add.superclass*, as invoked in the example of Section 3[3].

Those above are the only applicability conditions that are returned to the designer. The others are checked and discharged automatically either when the *add.superclass* is defined or when the transformation is applied.

---

[3] *NewConstr* stands for the constraints generated by the ACGA algorithm for each condition to be proved; C_2 is-a-reach C_1 is a predicate that indicates, if verified, the existence of an is-a path between C_1 and C_2.

Table 2. Applicability conditions of the add.superclass

$NewConstr \Rightarrow \neg(\text{marble is-a-reach exterior})$
$NewConstr \Rightarrow \neg(\text{marble is-a-reach interior})$
$NewConstr \Rightarrow \text{dom}(e\_name \cup i\_name) \subseteq \text{marble}$
$NewConstr \Rightarrow e\_name = (\text{exterior} \triangleleft name)$
$NewConstr \Rightarrow i\_name = (\text{interior} \triangleleft name)$

5 Exploiting SRL in a Reverse Engineering Process

The genericity of the employed model, the completeness of the SRL language and the definition of the ACGA algorithm render the transformational framework a general instrument for supporting a correct database design. The designer can thus build a personalised set of transformations and use them as primitive operators. This can be done without giving up the support for correctness.

The above three characteristics provides also the ground for a wider use of the framework. As an example of possible use, below it is illustrated how the presented framework can be profitably employed for supporting a reverse engineering process.

Several approaches, either systematic or informal, are available for carrying out database reverse engineering processes [10, 14]. They permit to produce a plausible high level model of an existing logical schema by employing different heuristics and rules. These approaches exhibit different levels of automatic treatments. Generally, the more automatic they are, the more limitations they impose on the original form of the logical schema. Actually, most authors consider impracticable a rigid compiling approach. They recommend, instead, informal approaches driven by frequent interactions with the designer that is responsible of taking semantic decisions. These informal approaches, if more applicable in practice, are, however, unable of ensuring that the semantic interpretation embedded in the reverse engineering process is correct. This limitation regards both the static part of the schema, and, more remarkably, the behavioural part.

In what follow we illustrate, by an example, how the schema transformational framework, that has been presented in the previous sections, can be used to overcome the above limitation.

Consider the schema depicted in Figure 5(a). Imagine that this is the logical schema of a particular database and that the following operation is associated to this schema.

$assign_tech_char(n,t) = $ **if** $n \in ran(e\_name)$
$\qquad\qquad$ **then** $e\_tech\_char := e\_tech\_char \triangleleft \{(x,t)|\ e\_name(x) = n\}$

Imagine, now, that a reverse engineering approach is applied to this schema and that the conceptual schema returned after this application is that given in Figure 5(b).

Fig. 5. Reverse engineering

By observing both the data and the operations during the reverse engineering process the existence of a superclass of *exterior* and *interior* has been extrapolated. The attributes of these two classes have been moved to the superclass[4].

We now employ the SRL transformational framework to verify the correctness of the reverse engineering process. To do this, we move forward from the reverse process, i.e., we derive from the two schemas a transformation that, when applied to the schema in Figure 5(b), produces the logical schema and the operation defined on it. If such transformation can be safely applied, then we can conclude that the logical schema is a correct implementation of the conceptual schema, and, vice versa, that the chosen conceptual schema is a correct specification of the logical schema. This transformation can be easily defined by considering the difference between the set of components in the two schemas and the assumptions on the semantics of the logical schema that have driven the reverse engineering process:

$$
\begin{aligned}
&\text{add.attr}(i\_name, interior, i\_name=name \triangleleft interior) \circ \\
&\text{add.attr}(e\_name, exterior, e\_name=name \triangleleft exterior) \circ \\
&\text{rem.attr}(name, marble, name=(e\_name \cup i\_name)) \circ \\
&\text{add.attr}(e\_tech\_char, exterior, e\_tech\_char=tech\_char) \circ \\
&\text{rem.attr}(tech\_char, marble, tech\_char=e\_tech\_char) \circ \\
&\text{rem.isa}(interior, marble) \circ \text{rem.isa}(exterior, marble) \circ \\
&\text{rem.class}(marble, marble=(interior \cup exterior)) \circ \\
&\text{mod.op } (assign\_tech\_char, \textbf{if } n \in \text{rane\_}(name) \textbf{ then} \\
&\qquad tech\_char := tech\_char \triangleleft\!\!\!+ \{ (x,t) | \; e\_name(x)=n \})
\end{aligned}
$$

Notice that assumptions on the semantics of the application have been used to define the relations between the two schemas. For example, the above transformation specifies that the new class *marble* is defined as the union of the classes *interior* and *exterior*.

The applicability conditions of this transformation are obtained by applying the ACGA algorithm[5]:

---

[4] In this example, we make the assumption that the both the logical schema and the conceptual schema are given as DBS schemas. As outlined above, this not a too restrictive assumption since, in case other models are used, then these can be easily mapped in terms of the DBS model.

[5] *NewConstr* is the conjunction of all the initial schema constraints and of all those added by the composed transformation; *a* attribute-of C stands for the inherent constraint "*a* is an attribute of C".

1. $(NewConstr\text{-}\{i\_name \text{ attribute-of } interior\})\Rightarrow dom(name\triangleleft interior)\subseteq interior$
2. $(NewConstr\text{-}\{e\_name \text{ attribute-of } exterior\})\Rightarrow dom(name\triangleleft exterior)\subseteq exterior$
3. $NewConstr\Rightarrow name=e\_name\cup i\_name$
4. $(NewConstr\text{-}\{e\_tech\_char \text{ attribute-of } exterior\})\Rightarrow dom(tech\_char)\subseteq exterior$
5. $NewConstr\Rightarrow tech\_char=e\_tech\_char$
6. $NewConstr\Rightarrow marble=interior\cup for\_exterior\_m$
7. **pre** $n\in ran(name)\wedge t\in TECH\_CHAR$ **then**
   $tech\_char:=tech\_char\oplus\{(x,t)|name(x)=n\}$
   $\sqsubseteq$
   if $n\in ran(e\_name)$ **then** $e\_tech\_char:=e\_tech\_char\oplus\{(x,t)|e\_name(x)=n\}$

If we try to prove these conditions, we discover that the conditions 4 and 7 are false. The condition 4 is false since the domain of the attribute *tech_char* is greater than the set described by the class *exterior*. The condition 7 is false since the higher level operation specifies state transformations that are not implemented by the lower level one. In particular, the overriding set in the former operation can contain a pair whose first element is any marble object, whereas, in the latter operation, the first element of the same pair can only be an object of the class *exterior*. By reasoning on the failed proofs, we can try to repair the mistake originated by the reverse engineering process. In this case, for example, the two false conditions suggest to restrict the domain of the attribute *tech_char*. This can be done by introducing in the conceptual schema the constraint $dom(tech\_char) = exterior$.

As a consequence, the two applicability predicates that were false on the previous conceptual schema are now trivially verified.

6 Conclusions

This paper has presented a framework for supporting a correct database design. Differently form other proposals, this framework is not based on a fixed set of schema transformational operators stated at priori, but these operators can be built dynamically according the designer needs. This characteristic and the availability of a model that can be used to interpret several other database models, are the elements that mainly contribute to the flexibility of the framework. The paper has shown an example of how this framework can be exploited, not only for the design but also for supporting different stages of the database life-cycle. Other significant uses are possible [8,9]. We have, for example, experimented this framework for supporting the maintenance of the multimedia database for the MIAOW system [13]. This database, designed as part of the Marble Industry Advertising over the World ESPRIT Project (n. 3990), maintains information about stones and stone actors. The original design of this database consisted of a sequence of OMT-like schemas [15]. Each schema in the sequence is generated by ad-hoc transformations. The final schema can be directly mapped into an Illustra schema [11]. We first interpreted the original design of this database in terms of our framework. This permitted us to verify the correctness of the original design.

Then, by interpreting the changes to the conceptual schema, originated by the change of the requirements, in terms of particular schema transformations, we were able to predict, for each change, the minimal changes to be operated on the schemas that documented the design of the MIAOW database. This experience suggested us improvements to our framework and confirmed its versatility.

References

1. J.R. Abrial. *The B-Book*. Cambridge University Press, 1996.
2. P. Assenova and P. Johannssen. Improving Quality in Conceptual Modelling by the Use of Schema Transformation. *Lecture Notes in Computer Science*, n.1157, pp.277-291, Springer-Verlag, 1996.
3. C. Batini, G. Di Battista and G. Santucci. Structuring Primitives for a Dictionary of Entity Relationship Data Schemas. *IEEE Transactions on Software Engineering*, 19(4), April 1993.
4. P. Van Bommel. Database design by computer-aided schema transformations. *Software Engineering Journal*, pp.125-132, July 1995.
5. P. Mc. Brien and A. Poulovassilis. A Formal Framework for ER Schema Transformation. *Lecture Notes in Computer Science*, n.1331, pp.408-421, Springer-Verlag, 1997.
6. D. Castelli and E. Locuratolo. ASSO: A Formal Database Design Methodology. *Information Modelling and Knowledge Bases VI*, H. Jaakkaola et al.eds., IOS-Press, 1995.
7. D. Castelli and S. Pisani. *A Transformational Approach to Database Design*. IEI-CNR Technical Report, 1998.
8. D. Castelli and S. Pisani. Ensuring Correctness of personalised schema refinement transformations. *Proc. International Workshop on Verification, Validation and Integrity Issue in Expert and Database Systems*, 1998, to appear.
9. D. Castelli. A strategy for Reducing the Effort for Database Schema Maintenance. *Proc. Second Euromicro Conf. on Software Maintenance and Reengineering*, pp.29-35, Florence, 1998.
10. S. Ghannouchi, H. Ghezala and F. Kamoun. A Generic Approach for Data Reverse Engineering taking into Account Application Domain Knowledge. *Proc. Second Euromicro Conf. on Software Maintenance and Reengineering*, pp.21-28, Florence, 1998.
11. Illustra Server Release 3.2, 1995.
12. K.J. Lieberherr, W.L. Hürsch and C. Xiao. Object-Extending Class Transformations. *Formal Aspects of Computing*, 6, pp.391-416, 1994.
13. *MIAOW Multimedia Database: Revised Design and Implementation*. MIAOW-CNR-REP-001-007. 1996.
14. W. J. Premerlani and M. R. Blaha. An Approach for Reverse Engineering of Relational Databases. *Communication of the ACM*, 37(5), pp.42-49, 1994.
15. J. Rumbaugh, M. Blaha, W. Premerlani, F. Eddy and W. Lorensen. *Object-Oriented Modeling and Design*. Prentice Hall, Englewood Cliffs, New Jersey 07632, 1991.

Appendix: The Applicability Condition Generating Algorithm

The *Applicability Condition Generating Algorithm* (ACGA) takes as input a set of SRL transformations $\{t_1, t_2, ..., t_n\}$, their applicability conditions, the set *ver_appl*, specified below, and a DBS schema $<Cl,Attr,IsA,Constr,Op>$. It returns a set of applicability predicates. The description of the algorithm is given using an informal notation and makes use of the following abbreviations:

- *ACl/Attr/IsA*, *RCl/Attr/IsA*, *AConstr* and *RemSubst** are described in Definition 3;
- *Attr*(C), *AAttr*(C) and *RAttr*(C) indicate the set of attributes that are , respectively, defined on the class C in the initial schema, added to C and removed from C by the composed transformation;
- C_1 is-a C_2 stands for the inherent constraint "C_1 is a subclass of C_2";
- *ver_appl* is the set of applicability conditions that are proved to be verified when the composed transformation is defined.

The algorithm consists of four steps. For sake of brevity, only the step 4 is reported explicitly. The first step initialises the set $appl_o$ which maintains the applicability predicates returned by the algorithm. The second step generates a first group of applicability predicates. These require that the component transformations specify consistent modifications. The third step generates a temporary set *appl* of applicability predicates to be proved. This set is scanned in the fourth step. If a predicated of this set is found to be false, then $appl_o$ is set to "false" and the algorithm is terminated. Each predicate of the set that cannot be discharged by the checks operated by the algorithm it is inserted in the set $appl_o$.

Step 4 of the Applicability Condition Generating Algorithm

appl:=appl-*ver_appl*;
repeat
    p:=**extract**(appl); appl:=appl-p;
    case type(p) **of** $x \in Cl$ **then if not**($x \in (ACl \cup Cl)$) **then** $appl_o$:=**false**
% This predicate is false if x is not in the initial schema and there is no transformation in the composition that adds the class x. It is true otherwise.
    or $x \notin Cl$ **then if not**($x \notin Cl$) **then** $appl_o$:=**false**
% This predicate is false if the class x is in the initial schema. It is true otherwise.
    or $x \in Attr$(C) **then if not**($x \in Attr$(C)) **then** $appl_o$:=**false**
% This predicate is false if the x is not an attribute of C in the initial schema. It is true otherwise.
    or $x \notin Attr$ **then if not**($x \notin Attr$) **then** $appl_o$:=**false**
% This condition is false if the attribute x is in the initial schema. It is true otherwise.
    or $x \in IsA$ **then if not**($x \in IsA$) **then** $appl_o$:=**false**
% This predicate is false if the is-a relationship x is not in the initial schema. It is true otherwise.
    or $x \notin IsA$ **then if not**($x \notin IsA$) **then** $appl_o$:=**false**
% This predicate is false if the is-a relationship x is in the initial schema. It is true otherwise.
    or Free(E)$\subseteq (Cl \cup Attr)$

then if not(Free(E)-*(AC∪AAttr))⊆(C∪Attr)* then appl_o:=**false**
% The predicate is false if the free variables in E are not added variables or they do not belong to the initial schema. It is true otherwise.
or $x\notin$**Free(E) then if not(**$x\notin$**Free(E)) then** appl_o:=**false**
% The predicate is false if x is a free variable of E. It is true otherwise.
or $\neg\exists C\in Cl\cdot(C,C_1)\in IsA \lor (C_1,C)\in IsA$
    then if $C_1 \in (Cl\cap AC\cap RCl)$ **then do nothing**
        else if $(\exists C\in(C\cup ACl)\cdot((C_1,C)\in(AIsA\text{-}RIsA) \lor (C,C_1)\in(AIsA\text{-}RIsA))) \lor$
               $(\exists C\in Cl \cdot ((C,C_1)\in(IsA\text{-}RIsA) \lor (C_1,C)\in(IsA\text{-}RIsA))) \lor$
               $(\exists\ C\in Cl \cdot ((C,C_1)\in(IsA\cap AIsA\cap RIsA) \lor (C_1,C)\in(IsA\cap AIsA\cap RIsA)))$
        then appl_o:=**false**
% The predicate has not to be checked if the class C_1, that is removed, belongs to the initial schema and it is added by a transformation in the composition. It is false, if there are not removed is-a relationships that involve C_1.
or $\neg\exists a\in Attr(C_1)$ **then if** $C_1 \in (Cl\cap AC\cap RCl)$ **then do nothing**
    else if $(\exists a\in(AAttr(C_1)\text{-}RAttr(C_1))) \lor$
        $(\exists a\in(Attr(C_1)\cap AAttr(C_1)\cap RAttr(C_1))) \lor$
        $(\exists a\in(Attr(C_1)\text{-}RAttr(C_1)))$ **then** appl_o:=**false**
% The predicate has not to be checked if the class C_1, that is removed, belongs to the initial schema and it is added by a transformation in the composition. It is false if there are not removed attributes defined on C_1.
or $Constr\Rightarrow C_2 \subseteq C_1$
    then if $\exists C_3,\cdots,C_n \in (Cl\cup ACl)\cdot(C_1=C_2\cup C_3 \cup \cdots \cup C_n)\in AConstr$
    then do nothing
        else appl_o:=$\text{appl}_o\cup\{(Constr\land(AConstr\text{-}\{C_2$ is-a $C_1\}))\Rightarrow C_2 \subseteq C_1\}$;
% The predicate is true if there is a transformation in the composition that adds the class C_1 and defines it as the union C_2 and other classes.
or $Constr\Rightarrow \neg(C_1$ is-a-reach $C_2)$
    then appl_o:=$\text{appl}_o\cup\{(Constr\land AConstr)\Rightarrow \neg(C_1$ is-a-reach $C_2)\}$;
or $Constr\Rightarrow x=E$ **then if** $x=E\in AConstr$ **then do nothing**
               else appl_o:=$\text{appl}_o\cup\{(Constr\land AConstr)\Rightarrow x=E\}$;
or $Constr\Rightarrow \text{dom}(F)\subseteq C$
    then appl_o:=$\text{appl}_o\cup\{(Constr\land(AConstr\text{-}\{a$ attribute-of $C \mid \exists a\cdot$
    $a=F\in AConstr\}))\Rightarrow \text{dom}(F)\subseteq C\}$;
or $\text{body}_1 \sqsubseteq \text{body}_2$
    then appl_o:=$\text{appl}_o\cup\{[RemSubst^*]\text{body}_1 \sqsubseteq [RemSubst^*]\text{body}_2\}$
% The variable substitutions must be taken into account when evaluating the refinement relation.
until $\text{appl}=\emptyset \lor \text{appl}_o$=**false**;
return appl_o;

Human Resources Information Systems Improvement: Involving Financial Systems and Other Sources Data

Sergey Zykov

ITERA International Energy Corporation
15 Savvinskaya Nab., Moscow 119435 Russia
E-mail: szykov@itera.ru

Abstract. Human resources management systems are having a wide audience at present. However, no truly integrate solution has been proposed yet to improve the systems concerned. Possible approaches to extra data collection for decision-making are considered including psychological testing and fixed assets information as well as product sales data. Concept modeling is presented as a theoretical background for the systems in question. Current technologies in state-of-the-art HR management software are discussed. Design and implementation aspects of a Web-enabled integrate enterprise system with high security and scalability are described. Testing results for an improved enterprise-level HR system are given. Perspectives of the field in question are discussed.

1 Introduction

Human resources information and management systems (HRIMS) involve a collection of technologies that allow us to represent complex processes that center on personnel activities. An advanced HRIMS is based on the multimedia data management, workflow control with approval facilities, e-mail, scheduling and conferencing technologies. From an enterprise point of view, human resources management should include components for recruiting, planning, line management, employees training and testing, payrolls, and compensations and benefits administration. HRIMS help to remove layers of bureaucracy by optimizing HR forms storage, retrieval and exchange. New generation HRIMS should feature Web browsing and publishing facilities to allow resumes and vacancies processing.

2 Existing Approaches

Current approaches to HRIMS are based on hardware accents and software technologies dominating at present. *Conservative approach* originated from mainframe architecture, which is transferable to present-day LANs. Some of the systems payroll and leave data processing, multimedia personal data handling, and flexible form and report generation. In most cases, high security level is guaranteed by explicitly enabling/disabling rights for each entry form, report or query. Since systems of the kind are non-client/server ones, they lack flexibility of a distributed system and it is hard to develop and deploy applications and perform WWW data publishing. Though high security level together with relative flexibility make them a good choice for conservative companies and even some huge enterprises, in most cases systems of the kind use rather a primitive set of standard functions. Mainframe-based systems lack both front-end programming and development environment and export/import facilities.

More versatile approaches are existing both within proven *industrial systems* and end-user *open solutions*. Oracle Human Resources services are based on highly scalable and reliable relational database Oracle Server. The HRIMS features compact storage and effective retrieval of multimedia data, advanced form and reports generation, SQL-based procedure-oriented query language, cross-platform support and Web-wired applications development.

Personnel data can be compactly stored in a complex multimedia format including photos of the employees, their signature samples, interviews video records, certificate color copies, etc. Client/server support is guaranteed for most of the operating platforms. With Oracle Web Server, developed and deployed database-oriented applications become Web-enabled.

CASE-tools allow enhancing and optimizing HR-oriented applications using visual interface and an SQL-based PL\SQL language as a fundament and an object-oriented script language at lower level. Data interchange and database integration is possible within Oracle Financials modules which include general ledger, payable and receivable accounts management, manufacturing and purchasing control, fixed assets and project management facilities. Though there are certain integration points within Oracle Assets which can use personal data from HRIMS, Oracle Financials products on the whole are integrated loosely enough and much is still desired to build a real enterprise level solution out of them.

Understanding the field importance, Lotus Development Corporation also comes up with a concept of a HR system [6]. The system benefits non-structured data handling, advanced World Wide Web access facilities, mail routing and approval services, telephony solutions, scheduling for personnel training, cross-platform support, advanced replication, mobile users support and high security degree with encryption down to field level. The HRIMS provides a basis for the entire spectrum of HR activities including advertising, strategic recruiting, automated inquiry service, personnel activities testing and performance management. Workflow and e-mail services provide for fast and accurate negotiation approvals and let applicants immediately know the interview results. The system coordinates the entire organizational training process.

Though Lotus provides a really hi-tech groupware-oriented flexible solution for HRIMS, the database is too open (the concept is better for recruiting agencies than for enterprises), it has no specific features for testing and assessing personnel and no connection to financial data except through ODBC is available. There are, however, even more versatile approaches existing which are a combination of the above mentioned ones, e.g., Oracle InterOffice [6].

3 HRIMS Enhancement and Object Theories

Let us specify a set of basic HR operations: personnel movement, data archival, searching updating and publishing, appraisal, testing and training data maintenance. As soon as one moves from an *information* system to a *management* system one has to start controlling the information flows. To further enhance management, it is necessary to obtain critical approval points and then to start tracking approvals. Thus, we move from information processing to performance assessment. An intuitively transparent and mathematically rigorous way to implement access limitations is *access hierarchy* concept discussed in [3]. The approach concerned corresponds even better to HRIMS field since can be based on *personnel hierarchy*.

When it comes to management, various business processes like human resources, sales or tax management, etc. are similar in some aspects. People are generating documents and passing them along the personnel hierarchy to view, update or approve. That is why every information system producing reports becomes involved into enterprise document flow.

Let us assume an enterprise uses a HRIS and a financial system separately. Since the two information systems are not interconnected, information duplication and contradictions occur frequently, so it is really hard to provide corporate data integrity and problems occur with taxes, training and management.

Despite the fact that business processes concerned belong to different management systems, these processes have much in common. EMPLOYEES SEND REPORTs, each of which IS_A DOCUMENT, to other EMPLOYEES. This observation provides an idea of an object-based, groupware-centered integrated system for human, financial and possibly other kinds of resource management.

Let us illustrate the concept of access strategy dependent on personnel. Personnel hierarchy structure handles most of common access level granting cases, thus restricting basic *document routes* and general *approval routes* as well. Some routes are predetermined. However, it is a very hard task to explicitly define all the possible routes including OTHER PERSON and DOCUMENT exceptions handling. That is why *hybrid* approval routing is suggested. The candidates' approval is based on personnel hierarchy while at certain points exceptions are traced.

4 Implementation Suggestions and Interface Discussion

To implement a solution more effectively, it is necessary to decompose the general task down to subtasks and professionally implement the latter ones. In general, to perform such decomposition in a rapidly changing enterprise human resources environment, it is recommended to use advanced concept modeling technologies. Semantic networks technology mentioned in this paper in respect to HRIMS structure understanding and modeling suggests a CASE tool to be an adequate solution to represent an object-based system model in all its versatility. Possible tools to solve this task, implementing concept modeling ideas are practically approved by author LogicWorks ER-Win [3] and Oracle Designer/2000 [4].

Some huge enterprises have subsidiary variations in structure, so the task of personnel movements tracking under correct data integrity maintenance becomes a really hard one. Along with advanced CASE tool for modeling, we need a means to create applications in a fast way and to make "on the fly" code corrections. In other words, we need a RAD tool.

Lotus Notes is a really good toolkit for prototyping purposes (since it has a 4Gb limitation on database capacity it could work well only for relatively small enterprises with real systems). Another Notes drawback is that it is rather weak at highly structured data manipulation. High-end examples of RAD tools are PowerSoft PowerBuilder and Oracle Developer/2000.

For an enterprise HRIMS with a single data center, local servers and clients, central server reliability, scalability and advanced performance management are required.

Preferable solution is Oracle Universal Server that is the most scalable and reliable enterprise level server suitable for TPC-2 [5] transactions intensity level and equipped with a versatile set of fine performance tuning mechanisms [7].

Additional information sources to enhance the system quality and performance were intensively searched for. In an advanced HRIMS the accent should be shifted from *information* collecting, storage and processing towards personnel performance *management*.

Personnel assessment could give food for decision-makers' thought. Discovered additional information sources for performance management include psychology testing (e.g., position correspondence and "computer literacy" tests) as well as financials management system (such as payables, receivables, fixed assets and purchasing) data. Thus, a rigorous computer science based approach leads us to an advanced type of a highly integrated HRIMS with an emphasis on management.

An advanced HRIMS shares a large amount of personal data with financial (at least with its fixed assets, general ledger, project management and manufacturing modules) and psychology testing systems. That is why HRIMS should have a user-transparent, uniform, friendly interface with high export/import capabilities.

Forms and reports should be user-customizable since the environment (and, consequently, user requests) is changing rapidly. Operating system independence and Web-publishing capabilities are part and parcel of state-of-the-art enterprise systems. Possible advanced solutions are Oracle Forms and Oracle Reports. They both have an attractive, visual user-friendly interface and, according to FORS company, one of the leaders in the field of Oracle-based solutions implementation in Russia, they have a user-transparent interface extension that allows to visually customize queries, forms and reports using a semantically user-transparent language. Thus, users operate with meaningful native words instead of database field names. Oracle Reports has lately become integrated with Oracle Designer and it also has a procedural SQL-compatible PL\SQL query language equipped with powerful server tuning and query optimization facilities that include direct instructions to server, explicit data source pointing and other advanced features. Oracle Web Server provides a quick-and-easy World Wide Web data publishing. Data becomes accessible from any Web browser, which is an invaluable interface advantage for both recruiting agencies and applicants who use it for vacancies and resumes publishing.

5 System Examples

The system implementation process started from a mainframe-oriented DataDinamique UniQue HRIS. After involving additional information sources the following enhancements were made: integrated fixed assets, psychology testing assessment modules implemented, database structure optimized, query and report interface improved, multimedia data handling and higher security level added. The system is implemented at one of the branch offices. End users have been satisfied with its function set, interface features and performance.

An alternative HRIMS version has been implemented according to the above guidelines by a co-worker of mine using Lotus Approach DBMS [6]. In addition to the previously described system, it benefits WWW publishing ability, more efficient reaction time for semi-structured data queries and advanced approval strategy. Groupware-oriented and mainframe-based systems are good enough to be implemented as a prototype of an industrial integrated system. The next stage drawback is lack of state-of-the-art specific-oriented set of tools to create a mission-critical system. A toolkit reliable and scalable enough for a real enterprise system is Oracle set of products. However, even Oracle Human Resources system lacks the "glue" of information sources integration.

Industry-level system has not been implemented on the whole yet though some of local HR solutions and enhancement data sources are functioning already. The "heart" of the system is its data center installed on an IBM RS/6000 server. Software components of the data center are Oracle InterOffice [7], Oracle Financials, Oracle Human Resources, Oracle Web Server, Oracle Universal Server, Oracle Parallel Server, and IBM AIX.

Many of ITERA subsidiaries have a local branch office with clients communicating by Oracle Web Agent through IBM Global Network provided channel. It is also possible to use any Web browser to access common information such as vacancies and recruiting data. Additional benefits the system provides are: industrial level scalability and reliability, user-transparent interface, enhancements for multimedia data handling, Web access with publishing capability, application reports naturally transformable into groupware documents, multiple currency and tax collection standards and multi-language support.

6 Results, Conclusion and Perspectives

The paper presents an overview of existing approaches to HRIMS. Putting into service psychology testing data and financial system reports is suggested to enable a HRIS with certain features of a truly personnel performance management system of an enterprise level. A conservative mainframe-oriented HRIS improved with additional information sources data is now at personnel management decision-makers' disposal. Groupware-centering approach has been introduced as an effective way towards integrated enterprise system. To produce a really scalable and reliable industry-level system oriented on mission-critical tasks, it is advised to choose a uniform set of specific task-oriented tools like ones from Oracle.

Let us summarize possible trends in HRIMS industry: HR systems are getting mission-critical ready, groupware becomes a cementing link for enterprise-wide business processes information management facilities, toolkits are ready that allow end-users to create applications incorporating data from various enterprise systems. Uniform tools have been produced to customize forms, reports and server performance. Such tools are equally applicable for major types of enterprise-level systems including human resources, financials, goods and documents management.

The industry is moving from information processing towards business process management. Since various business processes are interrelated in an enterprise, such an integrate HRIMS should acquire additional information from its neighbor resource management systems. The author is going to continue efforts towards implementing a mission-critical industrial-level HRIMS as an integral part of a uniform groupware-centered business process management system.

References

1. Roussopulos N.D. A semantic network model of data bases, Toronto Univ., 1976
2. Wolfengagen V.E. Frame theory and computations. Computers and artificial intelligence. V.3. No.1, 1984, p.p. 1-31
3. Zykov S.V., Pogodayev G.G. Object-Based Groupware: Theory, Design and Implementation Issues. Proceedings of the First East-European Symposium on Advances in Databases and Information Systems. Vol.2. St.-Pb.: Nevsky Dialect, 1997, p.p. 10-17
4. Information on Oracle software available at WWW: http:// www.oracle.com
5. Sikolenko K.V. Oracle Server: current state. DBMS Magazine, No.1, 1997. p.p. 4-22.
6. Information on Lotus software available at WWW: http: // www.lotus.com
7. Biggs M. InterOffice: The Secret of Success. Network World Magazine, No.2, 1998. p.p. 104-105

Physical Structure Design for Relational Databases

Janusz Charczuk

Rodan-System
Jagielska 50c, 02-886 Warszawa, Poland
e-mail: Janusz.Charczuk@rodan.pl

Abstract. This paper contains a description of the optimisation method for large databases with heterogeneous applications. This method makes it possible to automatically define the physical structure of a relational database. The input to the optimisation algorithm are the SQL queries stored in text files which are executed on the database server in a real life applications. Our tool recognises the classes of SQL queries and their frequency, analyses semantics and as a result prepares suggestions for the following parameters of physical definition of the database: the key and physical structure of a table (from amongst Btree, Isam, Hash and Heap), set of optimal indexes (this means their key as well as physical structure). The principal information which the system uses within the database optimisation process are: frequency and classes of SQL queries in an application and the data value distributions. The selection of the optimal configuration of the database relies a Electre Method which is a multicriteria optimal choice method. The use of these techniques increases the efficiency of the system first of all because it reduces the number of pages which are read and written to disks as a result of the optimal choice of the physical structures of tables and indexes. The system supports Oracle, Informix, Sybase and CA-Ingres.

1 Introduction

Most of database systems need to tackle the efficiency problem in a concurrent multi-user environment. In this paper we present a method which helps to solve this problem. It is an alternative to the expensive upgrade of the computer system configuration. We propose the optimisation of the physical structure of the database, which in many cases produces satisfactory results. This optimisation is one of the basic responsibilities of the database administrator. However, nearly always the administrator does not have the principal information for tuning the database (e.g. what actual operations are executed on the server, which of these have the greatest impact on the efficiency of the whole system) and therefore he is unable to comprehend the number of design alternatives and dependencies between possible solutions. Every query determines the criterion for estimating the given structure of a table and its indexes. That is why the definition of the physical structure of the database can be treated as a multicriteria problem. The ideal tool, which solves the database optimisation problem, has the following characteristics:

- it does not immediately refer to the database which is optimised e.g. the changing of the system catalogue, the running of queries on real data because of security and the protection of confidential information, rules of access, etc.
- utilises real information about the application workload
- does not query the database server about costs of queries because such a result depends on many unpredictable factors e.g. the number of data pages actually stored in the buffer, etc.
- it finds an optimal (one or many) configuration of the database in acceptable time
- the result obtained are directly applicable in the database reorganisation process.

2 Loading of information

The first stage of optimisation process is the tracing of SQL queries, which are executed on the database server in the real life applications (we know real queries). Afterwards on the basis of text files (with queries) we recognise classes of SQL queries and their frequency (also called query-weights). The next step is loading of information about the logical schema of the database (list of tables, their attributes and other information). Finally we can „manually" change loaded data, for example add, delete or update queries, change of parameters describing tables (number and length of rows, number of unique values for attributes and remaining)

3 Generation of the physical structure of tables

The generation of the physical structure of individual tables of the database is a very important step. The number of possible combinations of the physical structures of tables and their indexes is enormous. Therefore it is essential to apply heuristics which will reject all nonfeasible configurations. The process of generating structures takes place in two steps. Firstly, we designate the table key and candidates for indexes A candidate for the table key or its index is a set of table attributes with a specified order of the attributes. The choice of candidates is governed by the following assumptions:

- during the execution of a single-table query the server makes use of not more than 3 indexes (table key and/or 2 external table indexes), during the execution of a multi-table query the server makes use of no more than 2 tables from indexes [6]
- the table and index key must be appropriately restrictive
- the key and the physical structure must match the operation involved in the query.
- the most frequently used candidates are best.
- the table key is the candidate which is most frequently utilised in queries

Important at this stage is the information on the distribution of real data. Secondly, we designate possible table configurations. In this stage we generate table configurations: firstly without any indexes (possible structures are B-tree, Isam, Hash and Heap), secondly with one the best index, afterwards with two best indexes, ... next with the n best indexes.

4 Selecting optimal database configurations

Terms. To solve the problem of multicriteria optimisation of a database we chose the Electre method which is described in detail in [3]. In the discussion of the multicriteria problem the following terms appear:

Terms / General meaning	Meaning in the context of database optimisation
Alternatives A. Possible variants, among which we wish to choose, preferably one optimal alternative A – the set of alternatives (solutions, variants, choices)	The set of parameter configurations of the physical definition of the database
Criteria. Criteria on the basis of which we will estimate alternatives	A query executed in the optimised system (the complete set of queries is denoted Q)
Weights criteria w_i - the weight of the i-th criterion	w_i - frequency of query execution in the system (probability)
Evaluations O. Functions of alternative evaluations for individual criteria. Assessments of alternatives will allow us to choose an optimal alternative $O_1, O_2, ..., O_m$ - functions of evaluation of alternative criteria. Let $O(a)$ denote a vector of an evaluation of the alternative a, $a \in A$: $O(a) = [O_1(a), O_2(a), ..., O_m(a)]$	$O_i(a)$ - functions which approximately estimate the number of pages read and or written during the execution of the query $q_i \in Q$. $O_q(a,b)$ - evaluation of a pair of physical structures (a, b) in table T on the basis of query q. This is the weight of query q (w_i) multiplied by a coefficient p, whose value belongs to the interval [0, 1] $O_q(a,b) = w \cdot p$
Congruence c(a,b). Congruence of alternatives a with alternative b is the sum of criterion weights, where on alternative a is no worse than an alternative b, divided by the sum weights of all criteria $c(a,b) = \dfrac{1}{W} \sum\limits_{j:o_j(a)\geq o_j(b)} w_j, \quad gdzie\ W = \sum\limits_{i=1}^{m} w_i$	The sum of the evaluation of a pair of physical structures (a, b) based on all queries in which table T is present, divided by the sum (W_T) of the weights of all the queries in which table T is present $c(a,b) = \dfrac{1}{W_T} \sum\limits_{q:\ in\ q\ occours\ T} O_q(a,b)$

Construction of overrunning relation S. The first stage of the Electre method depends on construction of the overrunning relation S between alternative pairs

a S b (alternative a is not worse than alternative b)

We determine the S relation on the basis of the coefficience of congruence and incongruence of pairs of alternatives. The S relation applies only when:

- on the one hand, congruence of alternative a with alternative b groups sufficiently many criteria or sufficiently important criteria, namely, those criteria which make the alternative a superior to b
- on the other hand, none of the incongruent criteria leads to too strong countervailing evaluation (the role of incongruence of coefficients is played by a generator of physical structures, which on the basis of queries rejects physical structures which are worse and selects better ones)

We use a simplified definition of the relation S (without the coefficient of incongruence):

$$a \, S \, b \equiv c(a,b) \geq C$$

The value of C is a threshold of congruence. The minimum acceptable value of C is 0.75. The maximum is 1. In the process of optimisation the threshold of congruence can be changed interactively (cf. next chap. point 5)

Determination of an optimal configuration of the database. The aim of this stage is to choose the optimal configuration of the database.

1. For each pair a, b $\in$ A we check whether the S relation between them is present.
2. On the basis of the relation S we create a directed graph $G = (Q,E)$, in which the alternatives present in the S relation are nodes Q. The set of edge E is defined as a $\leftarrow$ b, such that a S b. If the node (alternative) includes edges, this signifies that it is no worse than the alternatives from which those edges originate.
3. We identify the kernel of the graph N, which is the set of optimal alternatives. It is defined through a conjunction of the following two conditions:
   - for each b$\in$ Q-N there exists a$\in$ N, such that a S b (the essence of optimality)
   - for any pair a,b$\in$ N we do not have an S b (minimality of set N).
4. If the kernel of the graph N is empty, than optimal alternatives belong to so-called, optimal cycles defined by a conjunction of the following three conditions:
   - absence of the kernel of the graph
   - every alternative of the optimal cycle is no worse than the remaining cycle of alternatives
   - there does not exist an alternative worse than any freely chosen optimal cycle alternative
5. If the number of optimal alternatives (belonging to the kernel or the optimal cycles) is unsatisfactory, we change the incongruence threshold. If the kernel is empty, this means that we adopted too rigorous assumptions about C, thus we must reduce the value of C. If, on the other hand, the algorithm produced too many proposals and we cannot choose the best among them, this means that we accepted too relaxed assumptions about C, thus we must increase the value of C.
6. Steps 1-5 are repeated unlit we obtain a satisfactory solution.

5 Implementation

In practise, the optimisation of the physical structure of the database is carried out table after table according to the algorithm below:

1. for each table:
   - set S_i is generated (the set of possible configurations of the table T_i)
   - $B_i = \emptyset$ (the set of the optimal configurations of table T_i)
2. while there exist tables to be optimised
   - we select table T for optimisation. For optimisation we choose a table for which the value of P_i is the smallest.

   $$P_i = \sum_{q:\text{table } T_i \text{ exists in query } q} R_q$$

   where $R_q = U_1(q) \cdot U_2(q) \cdot \ldots \cdot U_n(q)$, n is the number of optimised tables,

   $$U_i(q) = \begin{cases} 1 & \text{where } T_i \text{ does not exist in } q \\ |S_i| & \text{in other cases} \end{cases}$$

   - we compare the configuration of the table T. As a result we obtain $B_i \subseteq S_i$.
   - $S_i := B_i$
3. optimal configurations the db are the Cartesian product of sets S_i: $S_1 \times \ldots \times S_n$.

The optimisation method described above was implemented with the use of the object-oriented programming environment CA-OpenROAD 3.5. The algorithm can be executed in parallel on an arbitrary number of PC computers. The program contains the application server and clients. The number of clients depends on the number of accessible PC computers. The application server manages tasks executed on clients in an automatic or manual mode. As a result of the above, the optimisation process (recognition of SQL queries classes, construction of the overrunning relation S) is working in parallel. The synchronisation takes place via the database. On the application server we can observe the state of optimisation process.

The complexity of this process is hard to determinate. The most complex part of it is the construction cost of the overrunning relation S. It depends directly on the number of generated table combinations. We significantly reduced the number of these combinations by using the appropriate method of indexes selection.

6 Conclusions

The choice of table structures and indexes is the basic aspect of the physical definition of a relational database. In this paper, we have outlined my work on the project and implementation of the tool, which automatically delineates the above parameters. We concentrated on optimising access to discs as, we believe, this is the most important factor of the efficiency of the whole system. It also lowers the number of locked data in a period of time, which results in reduction of the average time necessary to access data as well as the probability of deadlocks.

The utilisation of the Electre method of the multicriteria selection of the optimal alternatives suits this problem well. A very important characteristic of this methods is that it is „just". This means that, after changing alternatives, criteria or their weights, we achieve as a result an adequately modified set of solutions. This has a specific meaning in database systems because developing the database and creating new applications in the information system has a direct effect on the increase of the number of alternatives and criteria of their evaluations. By using the Electre method we have the ability to input new criteria, which are independent of the queries, for example, changing the discs and capacity configuration. The possibility of extending the above-described method exists with the new physical structures for data storage (join indexes, materialised views) or these which will appear in relational database management systems in future. It does not limit the problem of defining the database.

The tool we have created is destined for designers and administrators of relational databases and their applications. This version of the program makes it possible to set up the weight of queries „manually". This is especially useful for people extending their systems from the point of view of the possibility of checking definite situations. In this sense, the tool supports managers in undertaking decisions by presenting objective working factors of the information system, indicating problems which may appear in future. The program may also be used in the process of creating new systems before they are put into use. It is possible to simulate how individual queries will run in the system in the present physical structure of tables and to see the optimal query execution plan.

References

1. A.Albano, V. De Antonellis, A. Di Leva, Computer-Aided Database Design, North-Holland, 1985
2. B.Roy, Wielokryterialne wspomaganie decyzji, WNT Warszawa, 1990
3. B.Roy, Revue Française d'Informatique et de Recherche Opérationnalle 8, 1968, 57-75 Classesment et chiox en présence de points de vue multiple (La méthode ELECTRE)
4. S. Choenni, H. Blanken, T.Chang, On the Automation of Physical Database Design, Proc. of the ACM-SAC, 1993
5. S. Choenni, H. Blanken, T.Chang, Index Selection in Relational Databases, Proc. of the 5th IEEE ICCI, 1993
6. S.Chaudhuri, V.Narasayya, An Efficient, Cost-Driven Index Selection Tool for Microsoft SQL Server, Proc. of the 23th VLDB, 1997
7. Ch.Kilger, G.Moerkotte, Indexing Multiple Sets, Proc. of the 20th VLDB, 1994
8. W.Ogryczak, Wielokryterialna optymalizacja liniowa i dyskretna: modele preferencji i zastosowania do wspomagania decyzji, Wydawnictwa UW, Warszawa, 1997
9. H.Argenton, P.Becker, Efficient Retrieval of Labelled Binary Trees, Proc. of the ADTI, 1994
10. S.Ganguly, A.Goel, A.Silberschatz, Efficient and Accurate Cost Models for Parallel Query Optymalization, Proc. of the 15th PODS, 1996
11. INGRES Database Administrator's Guide for the UNIX Operating System, Ingres Corporation, 1991
12. M.Sysło, N.Deo, J.Kowalik, Algorytmy optymalizacji dyskretnej, Wydawnictwo Naukowe PWN, Warszawa 1993

Modeling of Census Data
in a Multidimensional Environment

Holger Günzel[1], Wolfgang Lehner[1], Stein Eriksen[2], Jon Folkedal[2]

[1]Department of Database Systems, University of Erlangen-Nuremberg,
Martensstr. 3, D-91058 Erlangen, Germany
{guenzel, lehner}@informatik.uni-erlangen.de
[2]Statistics Norway, KOSTRA Development Team,
Postbox 8131 Dep, N-0033 Oslo, Norway
{ser, jfo@ssb.no}

Abstract. The general aim of the KOSTRA project, initiated by Statistics Norway, is to set up a data reporting chain from the norwegian municipalities to a central database at Statistics Norway. In this paper, we present an innovative data model for supporting a data analysis process consisting of two sequential data production phases using two conceptional database schemes. A first data schema must provide a sound basis for an efficient analysis reflecting a multidimensional view on data. Another schema must cover all structural information, which is essential for supporting the generation of electronic forms as well as for performing consistency checks of the gathered in-formation. The resulting modeling approach provides a seamless solution for both proposed challenges. Based on the relational model, both schemes are powerful to cover the heterogeneity of the data source, handle complex structural information, and to provide a versioning mechanism for long term analysis.

Keywords: Data analysis, metadata, multidimensional model, census data

1   Introduction

In this paper we report the results and experience of an international cooperation between the data warehouse research group of the University of Erlangen-Nuremberg (Germany) and the KOSTRA development team of Statistics Norway (SN). The acronym KOSTRA (Kommune STat RApportering; [6]) stands for a project setting up a new statistical database, which is suitable for gathering, accumulation and analysis of census data of institutions of all norwegian municipalities.

1.1   The KOSTRA Reporting Chain

The currently existing reporting chain consists of a manual flow of data from widespread municipalities to SN. Data according to a specific topic are gathered by filling out forms, transported in a more or less heterogeneous way like sheets of papers, disks or modem to SN and fed into a database. The scenario causes problems in handling the immense number of reports, data inconsistencies, and missing data. In general, this errorprune process incorporating a lot of manual corrections should be replaced by an automated solution.

The KOSTRA project (figure 1) intends to simplify this reporting chain and increases the correctness of data by replacing paper sheets by an electronic one. As a consequence, the reporting will be standardized and automated from the point of data gathering, storage, and analysis. In a first step, data from several electronic sheets are gathered into a local database at each municipality. In a second step, data are encrypted and transmitted to SN. A Common Reception Service (CRS) at SN receives and stores the reported data for enabling an extraction process for analysis purposes. In a last step, the collected and cleansed data from the central database are analyzed at several places like internally within SN for public statistics or at different municipalities for their internal analysis providing a loop back analysis. Due to the analysis process, SN already uses an existing solution called Regional Database ([3]).

1.2   The Common Reception Service

As illustrated in figure 1, our design approach of the CRS consists of the Central Reception Server and two different kinds of structural information database. The Central Reception Server collects and physically stores the incoming data. Generally spoken, this server corresponds to a "Data Warehouse" ([4]). Structural information additionally covers data about the structure and the process correctly filling out an electronic sheet. Thus, we divide structural information into a dynamic part, used for the interaction with the user, and a static part, remaining stable during one gathering period. Metadata about transmission or the identification of different sources must be seen in a more general context and is beyond the scope of this paper ([8]).

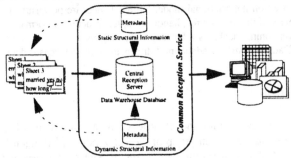

Fig. 1. The KOSTRA reporting chain

1.3   Difficulties in Modeling the Scenario

An automated reporting of census data causes several general problems and requirements. The data sources, the gathered data, and the structural information about the data cause an immense heterogeneity. To consider only the data perspective, there are forms with more than 100 questions. Two further requirements improving the current service concern the reporting process. On the one hand, every form or component may change during the reporting time, i.e. versioning approaches have to be considered. Moreover, SN requires a mechanism for generating and delivering forms to the different municipalities without an explicit intervention. On the other hand, monitoring of the reporting chain and checking against inconsistencies of the incoming data is extremly important. Altogether our innovative approach for an adequate data model contains exceedingly flexibility. A straightforward and traditional modeling approach would focus either on the data gathering and storage or on the perspective of an efficient analysis.

The structure of the paper is as follows: In section two we deal with the structural information of forms according to their usage and mapping to the relational model. The third section defines the requirements of an efficient analysis and proposes a conceptual database schema. The paper concludes with a summary and an outlook.

2 Metadata Schema Design for Structural Information

The structure of an electronic sheet or form represents the fundamental basis for gathering and analyzing of census data. This structural information controls the sheet generation process, supervises the fill out process, and determines the necessary consistency checks. As we will see in a consequence, it intensively affects the CRS.

2.1 Physical Structure of a Form

Census data can be divided in several topics, where each topic is related to a set of questions and represented by a specific sheet. Therefore the set of questions and the structure of the form are associated to a topic. Although the forms appear to be different and heterogeneous, a structural analysis of the existing forms shows that they all are based on the same skeleton. Each form is composed of an identification block consisting of information like the social number, the address, and one or more information blocks carrying data provided by the sender. In turn, each information block consists of a set of single questions. This combination of questions and information blocks belonging to the same topic is static during a reporting period.

In most cases the structure of electronic forms consists of more than one information block and more questions depending on each other. Therefore, a design model for a 'dynamic' structure is required. For example, an information block may be skipped, if a start-up question of one block links another block. Therefore, the structure at the instance level is highly dynamic caused by different ways of answering questions.

2.2 Static Structural Information

The knowledge of a form structure needs to be centrally stored for enabling a consistent data gathering process. During filling out a form, static structural information only influences the layout of the form and is independent of the data itself. Forms need to be designed very flexibly, because every form may be modified every reporting period resulting in a versioning of the single components of a form. Therefore the different structures of the sheets are stored within a static part of an information repository. The term 'static' emphasizes the fact that this kind of structural information keeps stable at least throughout one reporting period. To implement the physical structure, our proposal includes a metadata repository having an own conceptional schema and reflecting the relevant structure of the forms.

For the implementation of the scheme based on a traditional relational datamodel, we propose several tables for the electronic sheet itself, the information blocks and the questions as the basic items of the structural requirements. To fulfill the versioning, several time clauses denote the validity periods of the single components of the sheet.

2.3 Dynamic Structural Information

From a processing point of view, we demand that metadata monitors and guides each step of answering a sheet because some questions or other parts like information blocks depend on the answers of other components. To come up with a solution for this requirement, the semantic structure of the sheets need a dynamic part of an adequate representation within a metadata repository. In this way, a supervision of answering the question of a form and providing online as well as offline consistency checks are possible. However, the content of the dynamic part is influenced by the recorded information and directly effects the fill out process: On the one hand the dynamic structural information checks the plausibility of the values through rules or threshold values. On the other hand it monitors the correct input procedure of the sheet. If somebody answers that he is male, then all questions about pregnancy automatically should be skipped or should not be possible to answer.

Our proposal of modeling dynamic structural information is based on the ECA concept ([2]), considering the answer of a question as an event which is checked with a condition and followed by an action, if the condition evaluates to true. Since semantic checks are necessary before entering a sheet component and after answering a question, we require enter as well as exit conditions and actions. The enter condition always considers previous answers, whereas the exit condition always uses the answers of the current component. This proposal of ECA chains needs an intensive connection of user interaction and system-based semantic checks. It should mentioned here that the ECA principle may be also used for global off-line consistency at SN. Since these dynamic structures exist on all granularities of a sheet, relational tables are required for questions, information blocks and sheets.

3 Multidimensional Schema Design for Analysis Information

The promising profit of the discussed reporting chain emerges from the possibility of analyzing the gathered data. This yields in the requirements for an adequate conceptional schema to close the gap between integrating and storing the census data in a database system and efficient analyzing at the user level. This last requirement corresponds to what is generally known under 'OLAP' ([1]). Within the design phase, the multidimensional data model (cube) turned out to be an adequate model for the kind of sophisticated data analysis. In the multidimensional way of thinking, the data cube consists of several dimensions covering the structural information and cells storing the numeric (census) data. For a seamless implementation of this model, we fall back on existing relational technology. Our proposal uses a relational database engine with a relational data model generally known as star-schema ([4]). Within our star-schema approach, a fact table holds all census data. Dimension tables, organized around the fact table like a star, represent all structural information.

3.1 Multidimensionality

Typical analysis queries may be classified into time series analysis, sender analysis or a topic oriented analysis. Every analyst wants an uniform view on the data. In general not the individual object but a global view on a set of data is desired.

Therefore we need a data model which covers analysis perspectives and is tightly coupled with the application. In the following we propose a reasonable and simple multidimensional model to avoid sparsity and achieve a clear structure. Time and sender reflect two of four dimensions, since for each sender a form is filled out exactly once a reporting period. The other two dimensions follow the structure of a question, which can be divided into a header ('answer dimension') and a stub ('objective dimension'). All dimensions together determine the single facts, i.e. an answer of a single question. Figure 2 illustrates the multidimensional modeling idea and the connection between the time, sender and the 'question' array.

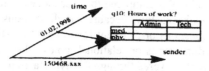

Fig. 2. The multidimensional approach

3.2   The Data Cube Model

Our proposal uses the dimensional modeling or star schema approach at the relational level. The central fact table within a star schema contains a composite primary key of the participating dimensions and the single numeric facts. The CRS fact table requires a composite key with the sender identification (SID), a reporting time interval and an ID of the objective and answer dimension. The fact attribute covers exactly one answer belonging to exactly one sender, in a time interval for one objective-answer relation.

FactTable (SID, ReportingInterval, ObjectiveID, AnswerID, Fact)

Since different questions have answers of different type, problems arise with that heterogeneous fact types of the fact attribute. The trouble is solved with our 'hyperfact' approach. A virtual hyperfact table consists of a union of several type specific fact tables with only one homogeneous fact type. The fact attribute of the 'hyperfact' table in turn holds the table names of the real fact tables (subordination, [7]). Therefore, an access of a specific fact requires two steps. In a first step the name of the real fact table is determined. In a second step, the answer is looked up type specific in the real fact table.

3.3   The Dimensional Tables

The dimensional tables cover all the structural information identified by the primary key attributes of the fact table. According to the four dimensions mentioned earlier, we require an answer, objective, time and source dimensional table to provide additional information and to enable OLAP analysis processes. The answer/ objective tables hold the structures for the header/ stub of a question. Since the time dimension orients at the gregorian calendar built in every database system, we do not require a specific time dimension table. The dimension table for reflecting the different senders differs to the answer or objective table. Problems arise, because a data source may be a person or a department, but the submitter, who is responsible for delivering these facts, may be always an institution. Therefore, there is a need for an explicit description of the source type and the submit type. Furthermore, additional attributes for the validity and attributes covering data for a personal identification like the social number or the department identifier.

3.4   Conclusion of the Modeling Approach

Using the proposed multidimensional data schema, the fact table grows fast, implying that no new techniques at the database-level are required, but for commonly used methods for improvements of access performance like bitwise indices or partitioning. The dimensional tables compared to other modeling techniques are very small. Altogether, the effort keeps low, because the dimensions and therefore the overhead is limited. New questions or different forms lead to a slightly larger cube, but do not result in more dimensions or relational tables. The heterogeneity of the electronic sheets are seamlessly covered through the hyperfact-approach.

4   Conclusion and Open Issues

Our modeling approach of the CRS for the new KOSTRA reporting chain is based on the structural information of the existing forms. In that way, the data model for the Central Reception Server is designed to handle incoming data and provide efficient analysis access to outgoing information. The fundamental basis is the multidimensional view on data. Instead of modeling each single answer and question within a straightforward approach, we divided the structural information from analysis information to achieve independency and performance. This implies, that the model is flexible enough to deal with extensions like new electronic sheets or data, versions and new data types. From a theoretical point of view, we handled versioning problems and immense heterogeneity within a multidimensional context. From the practical point of view the implementation is currently under development at SN. Our approach seems specific for this scenario, but could be simply modified and adopted to similar problems.

References

1. Codd, E.F.; Codd, S.B.; Salley, C.T.: Providing OLAP (On-line Analytical Processing) to User Analysts: An IT Mandate, White Paper, Arbor Software Corporation, 1993
2. Dayal U.; Hsu, M.; Ladin, R.: Organizing Long-Running Activities with Triggers and Transactions, SIGMOD Conference 1990, pp. 204 – 214
3. Eriksen, S.: Data Warehousing in Statistics Norway - The RD application, Statistics Norway, internal report, Oslo, 1997
4. Kimball, R.: The Data Warehouse Toolkit, John Wiley & Sons, Inc., New York, 1996
5. Smith, J.M.; Smith, D.C.P.: Database Abstractions: Aggregation and Generalization, ACM Transactions on Database Systems 2(1977)2, pp. 105-133
6. Titlestad, G.: KOSTRA - Model and solutions for a management for information ressources (in norwegian: KOSTRA - Modell og løsninger for informasjonsressurs-forvaltning), Statistics Norway, internal report, Oslo, 1996
7. Wedekind, H.: Database Systems I (in german: Datenbanksysteme I), Mannheim, BI Wissenschaftsverlag, 1981
8. Yang, J.J.: Overall user requirements to Metadata Management Systems, Statistics Norway, KITH, internal report, Trondheim, 1997

Author Index

Springer
and the
environment

At Springer we firmly believe that an
international science publisher has a
special obligation to the environment,
and our corporate policies consistently
reflect this conviction.
We also expect our business partners –
paper mills, printers, packaging
manufacturers, etc. – to commit
themselves to using materials and
production processes that do not harm
the environment. The paper in this
book is made from low- or no-chlorine
pulp and is acid free, in conformance
with international standards for paper
permanency.

 Springer

Lecture Notes in Computer Science

For information about Vols. 1–1397

please contact your bookseller or Springer-Verlag